JAMES JOYCE:
AN INTERNATIONAL PERSPECTIVE

IRISH LITERARY STUDIES

JAMES JOYCE:
AN INTERNATIONAL
PERSPECTIVE

Centenary Essays in Honour of the Late
Sir Desmond Cochrane

With a Message from Samuel Beckett
and
a Foreword by Richard Ellmann

edited by
Suheil Badi Bushrui and Bernard Benstock

Irish Literary Studies 10

1982
COLIN SMYTHE
Gerrards Cross, Bucks.

BARNES AND NOBLE BOOKS
Totowa, New Jersey

This collection first published on 16 June 1982
by Colin Smythe Limited, Gerrards Cross, Buckinghamshire

British Library Cataloguing in Publication Data

James Joyce: an international perspective.
– (Irish literary studies, ISSN 0140-895X; 10)
1. Joyce, James, *1882–1941* – Criticism and
interpretation – Addresses, essays, Lectures
2. Cochrane, *Sir* Desmond
I. Bushrui, Suheil Badi   II. Benstock, Bernard
III. Cochrane, *Sir* Desmond   IV. Series
823′.912   PR6019.09Z/

ISBN 0-86140-084-4

First published in the United States of America in 1982
by Barnes & Noble Books, 81 Adams Drive, Totowa, N.J.07512

Library of Congress Cataloging in Publication Data

James Joyce: an international perspective.
(Irish Literary Studies, ISSN 0140-895X; 10)
Includes index.
1. Joyce, James, 1882–1941 – Criticism and interpretation
– Addresses, essays, lectures.   2. Cochrane,
Desmond, Sir, 1918–1979.   I. Cochrane, Desmond, Sir,
1918–1979.   II. Bushrui, Suheil B.   III. Benstock,
Bernard.   IV. Series
PR6019.09Z6336   823′.912   82-6654
ISBN 0-389-20290-8 (Barnes and Noble) AACR2

Produced in Great Britain
Typeset by Inforum Ltd, Portsmouth
and printed and bound by Billing & Sons Ltd., London,
and Worcester

CONTENTS

SAMUEL BECKETT

I welcome this occasion
to bow once again, before
I go, deep down, before
his heroic work, heroic being.

Samuel Beckett

IN MEMORIAM
SIR DESMOND COCHRANE 1918–1979

The Arab world was greatly saddened by the sudden and unexpected death on 12 March 1979 of Sir Desmond Cochrane, late Honorary Consul General of the Republic of Ireland in Lebanon. The editors of this volume wish to register their profound appreciation for his outstanding services to Anglo-Irish studies in Lebanon and the Arab world, especially during the last decade of his rich and fruitful life.

Sir Desmond's contribution to the success of our work in the Arab world was extensive and of great importance. He sponsored almost every major activity of ours on both national and international levels. He gave generous moral and material support to a wide variety of projects: he sponsored exhibitions on Yeats, Synge and Joyce; encouraged translations of Irish literature into Arabic; and was the main driving force behind the publication of two first studies in Arabic on Yeats and Synge, and of several guides and handbooks on Ireland and her literary achievement. Without his whole-hearted and enthusiastic support our work would have been less known internationally and much slower in reaching the wide audience of those concerned with developments in this field.

As a diplomat he rendered invaluable service in strengthening Lebanese-Irish and Arab-Irish relations, and it is mainly owing to his efforts that Ireland today enjoys so much goodwill and respect in the Arab world. In all he did he demonstrated that unfailing gift of the Irish people, 'irrepressible gaiety and the saving grace of mother wit', enriched by an exceptional intellectual prowess. Above all he enjoyed a generous and magnanimous nature, which won him the love and warm friendship of all who came to know him or work with him here and abroad.

In honour of this distinguished Irish diplomat and patron of the arts, and in recognition of all that he has done for Ireland and Irish letters, we are dedicating this volume to the memory of Sir Desmond Cochrane. In addition, the series of centenary lecures given here in Beirut during the Joyce commemorations between 2 and 7 February 1982 were also named after Sir Desmond.

JOYCE AFTER A HUNDRED YEARS

RICHARD ELLMANN

A writer so immersed in legend as Joyce may appropriately be commemorated in the city of Beirut where St. George slew the dragon. For him there were many dragons: fear and cruelty, repression and prudery, hypocrisy and inertia. If he did not destroy them for all time – dragons never become extinct – he put them to rout. He was conscious that his was a heroic enterprise, though he despised 'heroics' and at first called his autobiographical novel *Stephen Hero* because of an ironic analogy with the ballad of the highwayman 'Turpin Hero'. As he announced when he was twenty-two, he wished 'to reunite the children of the spirit . . . against fraud and principality'. This centennial volume of essays about him confirms that his readers admire him for many reasons. Not the least is that he gave them a standard to carry into battle.

And yet he transcended the enemies he was opposing. His books present the possibilities of life so strongly as to leave behind those who would limit them. For the purpose he conscripted all that he observed and endured of life in Dublin and on the continent. But he also used all that he had read in literature. Homer and Shakespeare offered him most, but Dante, Goethe, Ibsen, and many others had their contributions to make too. He exploited his experience of music as well. The composers most important in *Ulysses* were Wagner and Mozart. For example, the *Circe* episode begins with a swancombed ice gondola which recalls *Lohengrin* and ends with a fire reminiscent of *Die Götterdämmerung*. In between Stephen raises his stick and strikes the lampshade in a way that is explicitly compared to Siegfried's raising his sword *Nothung*. Similarly, the stonebearded statue of the Recorder of Dublin recalls Mozart's Commendatore; the Commendatore's repeated yet unavailing cry to Don Giovanni, 'Pentiti', followed by the don's proud descent into the flames of hell, is echoed by Mrs Dedalus with her equally unavailing cry, 'Repent! O, the fire of hell!', to which Stephen responds with equally great despite. That the mind at its most fraught should be portrayable in terms of images from grand opera was appropriate.

Joyce exploited such material, as great artists did before him, by the right of the last comer. He saw them, as he saw himself, as joint participants in the affirmation of the human spirit. All his books in one way or another portray the artist, combative and triumphant. Not that romantic self-expression was his goal. He saw the artist as a model for the expansion of consciousness. In his early years Stephen Dedalus first lingers in debauchery, then in pietism, as if tempted first by body and then by soul, only to find at last his way towards their union. Similarly Bloom and Stephen in *Ulysses* plot a route past physical and mental perils to a more total existence.

While such adversary figures as Boylan and Mulligan, or Shaun in *Finnegans Wake,* epitomize in their different ways denial, neither is entirely put down. They too have their place in the 'universal history' which Joyce said his last book was to offer. As he says there of the gracehoper and the ondt, *'These twain are the twins that tick* Homo Vulgaris.' The real enemy in his work is not denial, for his no is encompassed by a much ampler yes, but sententiousness. Sententiousness would arrest the vitality of life by pigeonholing it. Fortunately, there are three forms of rescue: laughter, doubt, and the irresistible tendency of language to burst out of any enclosure. Saved by these, we can say with Goethe, *'Wie wahr! Wie seiend!'* This denseness of genuine being, doubting, laughing, and above all renewing itself in language, is the Ithaca to which all Joyce's literary wayfaring leads.

ACKNOWLEDGEMENTS

Colin Smythe Ltd. thanks the following for permission to quote extracts from the works of James Joyce:
to The Bodley Head for permission to quote from *Ulysses*; to Jonathan Cape Ltd. for permission to quote extracts from *A Portrait of the Artist as a Young Man*, *Dubliners*, *Exiles*, and *Chamber Music*; to the Society of Authors as literary representative of the Estate of James Joyce for permission to quote from *Finnegans Wake* and *Pomes Penyeach*.

Barnes & Noble Books thank Viking Penguin Inc. for permission to quote from *Exiles*, Copyright 1918 by B.W. Huebsch, renewed 1945 by Nora Joyce, Copyright © 1964 by the Estate of James Joyce; from *Dubliners*, originally published in 1916 by B.W. Huebsch, definitive text Copyright © 1967 by the Estate of James Joyce, from *Finnegans Wake*, Copyright 1939 by James Joyce, Copyright renewed 1967 by George Joyce and Lucia Joyce; from *A Portrait of the Artist as a Young Man*, Copyright 1916 by B.W. Huebsch, Copyright renewed 1944 by Nora Joyce, Copyright © 1964 by the estate of James Joyce; from *The Portable James Joyce*, edited by Harry Levin, Copyright 1946, 1947 by The Viking Press, Inc., Copyright renewed 1974, 1975 by The Viking Press, Inc.; and thak Random House Inc. for permission to publish excerpts from *Ulysses*.

Both publishers thank the Dolmen Press and John Montague for permission to reprint his poem 'James Joyce'.

INTRODUCTION

SUHEIL BUSHRUI AND BERNARD BENSTOCK

James Joyce was born in a suburb of Dublin on 2nd February, 1882. His father was a man of many talents with no aptitude for work; his mother was sensitive and pious. James was lucky to be the eldest child, for the family's fortunes gradually dwindled as he grew up. He received an excellent education at Roman Catholic schools, and for a while thought of training for the priesthood. Instead, however, he proceeded to the Royal University, Dublin, where he specialized in English, French and Italian.

Once he had decided to make his career as a writer, Joyce could see no future in remaining in Ireland, and from 1904 until his death in 1941 lived mainly in France, Italy and Switzerland, supporting his family by teaching languages. But though he severed his connections with his homeland in this sense, Irish life was to be the subject of all his prose writings.

Joyce's work has always been controversial, and will no doubt continue to be so, but it was unquestionably the product of extraordinary industry, dedication and intellect. He had two main gifts: a talent for words, including mimicry of the idiosyncratic speech of others, and a unique sensitivity to his environment, which enabled him to re-create the Dublin of his youth in astonishing detail. But his narrow and introverted personality, at best iconoclastic and at worst supremely egoistic, lost him much of the admiration and applause he felt his work deserved. As a young man, he told W.B. Yeats: 'It is too late: you are too old to be influenced by me.' Yeats commented that he had never met so much conceit with so little to show as justification.

Language is paramount in the work of Joyce. He was not an English writer; all his books are written in an Irish accent, and the last, *Finnegans Wake,* draws almost as much on French, Italian, German, Norwegian and Latin as it does on English. He used the English language as one who would have opted for another mother tongue given the choice; he felt it was alien to him, but realised he could not avoid it. This is eloquently expressed in *A Portrait of the Artist as a Young Man,* in the thoughts of the hero, Stephen Dedalus

1

–who represents Joyce himself. As the Jesuit Dean of Studies at the Catholic University, an Englishman, talks to him, Stephen reflects that:

> The language in which we are speaking is his before it is mine. How different are the words *home, Christ, ale, master*, on his lips and on mine! I cannot speak or write these words without unrest of spirit. His language, so familiar and foreign, will always be for me an acquired speech. I have not made or accepted its words. My voice holds them at bay. My soul frets in the shadow of his language.

The melancholy of this passage finds an echo in many different forms throughout his work.

Joyce's mind, too, was not English, but found more affinity with the ways and thoughts of the French, Germans and other European races not subject to English social conditions and ideas. After leaving Ireland he made his home in Trieste, then in Zürich, and finally in Paris. Moreover his work was hailed in France and America long before it was appreciated in England, and even today he is thought of more highly abroad than at home. It seems that for the Americans and the French at least he has expressed something about the modern world that is scarcely felt or acknowledged in England.

Joyce's first published work, some poems and stories, appeared in 1904, and a collection of youthful poems followed in 1907 under the title of *Chamber Music*. But his first significant publication, *Dubliners*, came out in 1914, although most of it had been completed a decade earlier. *Dubliners* consists of fifteen stories about life in the Irish capital, told with a vigorous realism. Everything is described in terms of objects or actions; reflections, except of the dramatic kind, are not allowed to the characters themselves. In some cases one character is the centre of the story, and everything that happens is part of a picture as seen by him, either to his benefit or to his disadvantage.

Many of the tales culminate in a moment of sudden unpleasant revelation, while others are unpleasant from beginning to end. The main purpose is to give an impression of the utter futility of Irish life – what Joyce called 'Irish paralysis'. A typical example is 'Counterparts', in which a clerk in a solicitor's office is bullied by his employers for carelessness, and then goes home and beats his little son unmercifully for letting the fire go out. In 'The Boarding House' a landlady entraps one of her lodgers into marrying her daughter by first allowing him to compromise her. And in 'Two Gallants', two seedy loafers conspire in the persuasion of a servant girl to steal from her employer.

The longest and perhaps the most powerful of the stories is 'The Dead', in which a young University lecturer's wife suddenly recalls an adolescent love affair with a youth who has since died. The lecturer, a picture of Joyce as he might have become had he stayed in Dublin, feels humiliated and as if he has never known her, and from this follows the realisation that all human beings are alone, isolated from each other.

If there is much of Joyce himself in *Dubliners,* there is even more in *A Portrait of the Artist as a Young Man,* which is tantamount to an autobiography. For Stephen Dedalus read James Joyce. Stephen is not always a very attractive hero, and this is one of the virtues of the book, which was published in 1916. It is, in its way, a guarantee of authenticity, and points up a trait that was to become increasingly characteristic of Joyce: ultimately *A Portrait* is about a university student from a family reduced to poverty deciding to sacrifice everything, including his parents, brothers and sisters, to devote himself to his art. Stephen's mother, who is devoutly Catholic, sees with distress that her most promising child is in revolt against his religion and his environment. He carries the hopes of the family, and is the only one equipped with the capacities to earn enough to save the family from complete squalor. But Stephen has a bitterness and loathing for all aspects of Irish life including the family, and in order to satisfy his pride and hatred he is prepared to become odious himself.

Perhaps Joyce conceived his hero originally as being an admirable romantic figure. The first draft of *A Portrait of the Artist as a Young Man,* published posthumously under the title *Stephen Hero,* seems to suggest this. But it is a tribute to Joyce's honesty as a writer that Stephen turns out otherwise, as a result of the fact that Joyce himself was not a very likeable person. Indeed, it is doubtful whether *A Portrait* would have achieved its popularity without the subsequent success of *Ulysses*, which gave rise to an interest in Joyce's life. But by the time *A Portrait* was published, the author's ideas about writing had changed considerably from those of the youth he describes. Stephen Dedalus is patently an adolescent who has not yet found his artistic bearings.

The next of Joyce's works to be published was his only play, *Exiles,* in which the main character, Richard Rowan, again represents Joyce himself. Richard does what Stephen only contemplates: exiles himself from the environment in which he was born and grew up. He then returns after nine years' absence, and his sentiments surely echo Joyce's own feelings about Dublin. The play was not a success, and only as recently as 1970, when it was first performed at a major London theatre, has it achieved the recognition it deserves.

By this time *Ulysses* had begun to appear in serialised form, though the full publication did not come out until 1922. It was very long (over 700 pages) for a novel, but it established Joyce's reputation as one of the foremost writers of his day. Stephen Dedalus reappears in it, and his encounter with the main character, Bloom, is the central incident. In a sense it is like a tale from *Dubliners* magnified to mammoth proportions, and indeed it was originally conceived as a short story for that book. All the events take place within a period of less than twenty-four hours, which is surely unique for a novel of such length; it almost certainly takes longer than twenty-four hours to read.

Throughout the day covered by the book we follow Bloom's every action and thought. He goes through a series of experiences which parallel those of Ulysses in the *Odyssey*, and there is a great deal of ironic contrast between sordid modern society and Homer. Bloom's marriage to Molly is unsatisfactory, and he uses Stephen as a means of re-asserting his dominance in the house. Molly's final reverie indicates that she has been considerably affected by his new stand. The point of the story for Bloom is therefore the necessity of readjustment in family relationships, a theme to be found elsewhere in Joyce. This readjustment applies on a much deeper level to the whole of mankind, with the strangely optimistic implication that there is redemption in reconciliation.

The way, for Joyce, is to accept all terms of the reality of human life as he sees it. Therefore his deepest experiences are portrayed against a grim background of life in Dublin, but this is infused with his poetic consciousness of the richness of life. What happens in *Ulysses* is of far less importance than what *is*: the thoughts and feelings of the characters, their awareness of things. The whole book is Joyce's vision of *their* consciousness; it is a state of mind.

If *Ulysses* is an attempt to represent one man's waking consciousness for the best part of a day, Joyce's final work, *Finnegans Wake*, could be said to represent one man's waking consciousness for a whole night. Like *Ulysses*, it began by appearing in fragments, and only achieved publication as a whole as late as 1939, on the eve of

4

the Second World War. Joyce is said to have been depressed by the unenthusiastic reception accorded his 'masterpiece', and his death followed soon afterwards in 1941. But in the prevailing political climate of the time no work of the nature of *Finnegans Wake* could seriously expect to be appreciated; its misfortune is that it has continued to elude the understanding of all but the most scholarly readers.

In order to represent the sleeping consciousness, or the dreaming mind, Joyce hit on the highly original idea of writing the book in a kind of nonsense language made up of portmanteau words and portmanteau sentences, enabling him to draw on his wide linguistic knowledge and introduce innumerable themes from history, geography and literature. The most easily discernible theme is that of resignation and reconciliation in the last section of the book; the rest is a tangle of guilty desires.

The basic situation is the dream of one man, H.C. Earwicker, an Irish publican, who lies asleep above his pub with his wife, daughter and twin sons. The children are adolescent, the parents in late middle age, and the family relationships are expanded through the medium of guilty erotic images. The children symbolise the young life which is growing up to replace the old, symbolised by the parents' decaying marriage. As in *Ulysses*, this picture of a human soul entangled in an earthly context is a vision of universal history.

But it seems probable that Joyce did not actually set out with an inspiration to present a vision of history or to reproduce the fantasies of the dreaming mind. These were only the means which, he discovered, enabled him to write as he wished, to develop his lyrical gift which reaches its zenith in the sensitive nonsense prose of *Finnegans Wake*. The real point of the book lies not in its meaning, but in its detachment from meaning; its function is to support the beautiful nonsense verse of which Joyce knew he was capable. The result is a form of pure song, charged with emotion and suggestion.

In some ways *Finnegans Wake* must be accounted a failure in that it is unreadable as a whole. Yet it is so delightful in parts that, as with Spenser's *Faerie Queene*, one is inclined to feel that the whole *must* be good. One also cannot but admire the extraordinary industry that must have gone into such a Gargantuan work. Even Spenser was not faced with such difficulties as those experienced by Joyce, many of which were due as much to his Irish birth as to the period in which he lived. Ireland had no modern literature except that created by a small group of Anglo-Irish. If Joyce had been born in England or France he might have been able to use the forms of 19th-century English or French fiction as a starting point. Having no such tradition to follow, he felt it necessary to create a unique individual path which required almost superhuman determination on his part – something that no creative artist should need in order to prove himself.

Now that a century has elapsed since Joyce's birth (and four decades since his death), his contribution to literature is being evaluated and appreciated to a greater extent than ever before, and on an international scale. There is a lively interest in his work, regardless of the tedious wrangling over whether or not he was a true genius. Aquarian minds are traditionally said to be ahead of their time, and perhaps Joyce was no exception. Unattractive man he may have been, except to his devoted friends, but his work has a quality of vision which no student of literature can dismiss, and a delight in language all its own. His centenary year, to be celebrated internationally, is surely a propitious time for the universal accolade, which has hitherto eluded him, to be accorded James Joyce.

James Joyce has always invited an international perspective for his work. An Irish phenomenon with broad European ramifications he became the focus of American academic scholarship, which has long since widened to include much of the modern world. His language systems alone make Joyce the singularly most cosmopolitan – in the best sense of the word – writer that the world has yet encountered, and as much as Dublin may be the epicentre of that world, Spanish serenos coexist with delicate Siamese, humpbacked Norwegian captains with African potentates, Transylvanians (Rakoczy) with Bagdadians (Haroun al Raschid) – all these in *Ulysses* alone. For Joyce the League of Nations did not reside in Geneva, but in any universal work of literature.

The rivers of the world will remember James Joyce for as long as they flow, in having his Anna Livia as their source. If, as Joyce once hoped, children in far distant lands find the name of their local tributary in *Finnegans Wake,* and monolingual Americans find snippets of their regional patois (by way of Huck Finn) there as well, semioticists and linguists can locate signs and signifiers in the *Wake* that are grist for their mills and more power to their elbows. Joyce drew from the languages and the religions of the known world, mountains and rivers, high-and-mighty and *hoi polloi*, all of us insects that crawl on the body of the buried giant.

Introduction

In the war of words, as in the war of worlds, Joyce was a pacifistic combatant, reconciling, coalescing, building bridges, breaking down barriers. It is appropriate that in a centennial celebration East and West should join hands in presenting not just an international perspective, but *international perspectives,* in which the only conflicts are academic, intellectual, interpretive, conceptual. Joyce never lost sight of the political difficulties that plagued his times, and he dreaded wars and hatred (the opposite of love) as incompatible with human life and the artistic spirit. It is in the Joycean spirit of a universal concept of peace and art that this volume of essays is conceived and dedicated.

JAMES JOYCE _____
(_____ nó Séamas Seoighe),

mo dhóigh dhe gurb uilíocht
a shaothar pinn faoin aon áit
's foinse 's fáth 's filíocht.

Faoin aon áit ghrean sé gréas
thug scéal Áth Cliath Duibhlinne
a h-aithle ealaín Cheannanais:
cheap an t-eagnaí an bith uile.

Ceannanas nó sealbh sinnsear
's ceilt 'Na Marbh' Bhruidhean toghla,
gí ghabh a n-iomlán i gcnuas
gruagach a dteanga ba dhrogall.

Má chnuas anraith bó thar lear
thar piseán Druimfhionn dúchais,
féile iasachta is spíosraí anoir
thug coire an Dagda bhrúchtaigh.

Spíosraí anoir ag fleadh Life,
eachtra athFhinn sin inscéalaí
Uiliséas iomraimh 's roiseadh
uige: athinsint fhinnscéalaí.

Roiseadh mná dílse istoíche
thug teaghlach uigingigh slán;
teanga dá roiseadh bheoigh choíche
Séamas Seoighe _____
(_____ nó James Joyce).

Gearóid Ó Clérigh

EXPLANATION BY WAY OF TRANSLATION

(1) Although James Joyce's writings deal with a single locality, they
have a universal quality which makes of them creative literature.

2) The pattern in which Joyce worked the story of this locality, Dublin (expressed in a composite of its Gaelic and Norse names), was modelled on the art of the (Book of) Kells (a 9th Century mss., whose intricacies Joyce is said to have spent long hours contemplating in Trinity College Library): the wise (or skillful) one captured (or invented) the whole world.

3) Kells or ancestral possession (i.e. heritage) and the hiding (a pun on 'Celt') of 'The Dead' in the Hostel of the Sacking (or v.v.) – reference: early Irish saga of the Sacking of Da Derga's Hostel, in which foreigners from across the Irish sea slay the High King of Ireland, while he is making a circuit of the country in a direction contrary to his taboo or 'geas', and the incorporation of this theme as Brown and 'gas' = death from English cultural influence, in Joyce's 'The Dead'; also the horse, Johnny, goes the wrong way round King Billy's statue in College Green, a monument to conquest. – Although Joyce incorporated these ancestral themes, he was loath (or shy) to grasp or master the wizard which was their language; 'shy' because 'I wish him no harm'.

4) Even if Joyce did prefer a mess of foreign pottage (i.e. of cows abroad; ref. proverb 'Cows abroad have long horns, what is foreign is more attractive') instead of a diet of the pea of the native Druimfhionn (= Ireland's 'split little pea'; Druimfhinn Donn Dilis, Faithful brown fair-backed 'Silk of the Kine': Ireland), nonetheless the cauldron of the Dagda (the Cornucopia of the Dag-da or 'good god' of the pagan celtic Irish) gave forth foreign (or on loan) generosity (or banqueting) and spices from the East.

5) Spices from the East at the feasting of the River (Anna) Liffey, such is the adventure (-story) of that secondary Fionn (Mac Cumhail, a hero of the Fianna sagas: Finn Again), the survivor, (= one who can tell a tale) Ulysses of the seafaring (a genre of early Irish imaginative adventure tale), and the unravelling of web: a retelling by a novelist (romancer: the words form a playback on corresponding words two lines previously).

6) The unravelling by a faithful woman at night preserved intact the home of the wanderer (= Viking, because Dublin is a Viking foundation); by unravelling a language James Joyce made it live for ever.

THE DUBLIN OF *DUBLINERS*

TERENCE BROWN

Thomas Flanagan, the critic and novelist, has pointed out that Joyce indulged in a certain understandable exaggeration when he proudly boasted that were the city of Dublin to be destroyed it could be rebuilt with *Ulysses* as a blueprint. 'It is', remarks Flanagan, 'one of the few claims made for that great novel that exceeds the mark, for in fact, only sections of the city are represented, and the characters are drawn from a narrow banding of the petty bourgeoisie.'[1] If Joyce had added that *Dubliners* would also help in any such reconstructive enterprise (which may well be necessary soon if the present 'redevelopment' of the city continues) his boast would interestingly have had greater substance, for it is one of the features of that book that a remarkably detailed impression of the city is made available to the careful reader. It is of course the great critical truism about the book that those aspects of Dublin that bear on the theme of the city's paralysis are those that Joyce includes in his text. Accordingly critics have tended to concentrate on the symbolic and thematic significance of the physical detail of the work, thereby somewhat neglecting the degree to which that detail in the book as a whole amounts to a considerable portrait of the city itself. Critics have been so intent to demonstrate in David Lodge's terms that '*Dubliners* is not a work of wholly traditional nineteenth century realism'[2] that they have to some degree obscured how much it provides one of the principal pleasures of realism – a richly detailed, exactly evoked physical milieu.

There is, firstly, the weather. If *Ulysses* allows us to learn of Dublin's weather on a peculiarly warm summer's day, punctuated by an unaccustomed clap of thunder, *Dubliners* informs us of climatic conditions in Dublin throughout the cycle of the year. Jackson I. Cope[3] has pointed out indeed that almost all the stories in the collection contain indications of the seasons in which they are set where they do not precisely refer to a month or period, or do not supply details of climate such as 'the short days of winter' ('Araby') or 'the grey warm evening of August' ('Two Gallants') or 'a bright Sunday morning of early summer, promising heat, but with a fresh

11

breeze blowing' ('The Boarding House') or 'a cold, fragrant air from out-of-doors' ('The Dead'). From all this a sense of the changing cycle of the Dublin weather emerges, almost surreptitiously, for the reader, and while his instinct may be, following Jackson Cope, to read this in thematic terms as an authorial strategy 'to prepare us to recognise the seasonal decline of the later stories as a dying fall rather than a cyclical renewal',[4] he cannot gainsay the fact that *Dubliners* is a book of the city's weathers.

The houses of Dublin are memorably realised throughout the book, almost, with their enclosed sombre demeanours, participating in the *dramatis personae*. Story after story presents oppressive pictures of Dublin's domestic architecture. The 'unassuming shop' in Great Britain Street in 'The Sisters' sets the note, and throughout the collection details of this kind create a composite portrait of a city whose architecture the reader begins to think he knows intimately. 'An Encounter' offers 'the squalid streets where the families of the fishermen live'; 'Araby' begins 'North Richmond Street, being blind, was a quiet street except at the hour when the Christian Brothers' School set the boys free. An uninhabited house of two storeys stood at the blind end, detached from its neighbours in a square ground. The other houses of the street, conscious of decent lives within them, gazed at one another with brown imperturbable faces,' and also tells us of the 'dark house' in which Mangan's sister lives, and the 'ruinous houses' by the railway track that takes the hero to Araby. 'Eveline' has 'little brown houses' and the 'bright brick houses with shining roofs' built by the developer from Belfast. In 'A Little Cloud' we see 'the gaunt spectral mansions in which the old nobility of Dublin had roistered', now the environment for a 'vermin-like life', and the 'poor stunted houses' on the lower quays that seemed to Little Chandler 'a band of tramps, huddled together along the river-banks, their old coats covered with dust and soot, stupefied by the panorama of sunset and waiting for the first chill of night to bid them arise, shake themselves and begone', while Mr. Duffy in 'A Painful Case' lived in 'an old sombre house'. And finally there is 'the dark, gaunt house on Usher's Island' in 'The Dead'. All the houses seem dark, self-absorbed, old and decaying, with the exception of those built by that brash Belfastman. Accordingly Dublin emerges as a city of declining houses, the brown streets and the brown bricks symbolic of their ancient decrepitude.

The rooms in the houses are evoked with no less detail and the pictures that Joyce draws of the living spaces of his Dubliners are equally dispiriting. They are invariably dark and mean in size. The 'darkened blind' that the hero of 'The Sisters' imagines at the beginning of the work strikes the key-note here, as does the 'narrow staircase' of the house of mourning in the same story with its 'little room' and 'empty fireplace'. Rooms are small and decrepit like the 'back drawing-room' in 'Araby' with its 'broken panes'; they are redolent as in 'Eveline' of 'the odour of dusty cretonne', furnished as in 'A Little Cloud' 'on the hire system' or sparsely to the point of niggardliness as in 'A Painful Case'. Rooms and houses are rented by the occupants; 'The Boarding House' with its complement of young men paying fifteen shillings a week for board and lodging seems emblematic in a city where only the Misses Morkan seem genuinely to approach the condition of decent bourgeois property owners, concerned to manage an ample domestic regime; and their hold on life, never mind on their rented property, is tenuous in the extreme.

The public buildings entered by Joyce's Dubliners are strikingly few in a book that purports to deal with the life of a city. The limited range of such buildings mentioned in the volume is of course a direct consequence of the limited class, the petty bourgeoisie, that consti-tutes its main social focus. However, the relationship between the buildings these Dubliners do enter and those they do not is worth noticing, for it suggests a feature of the city that was an important aspect of its life in the period Joyce set his fiction. The class to which Joyce is so attentive is clearly one of considerable cultural and social impoverishment. No galleries, museums, clubs, sports-centres, coffee-houses, great schools are mentioned as natural environments for his characters. When we have noted the hotel at which Ségouin stays and where Jimmy dines in 'After the Race', and the Royal University, at which Gabriel Conroy attended, in 'The Dead', we have climbed the social heights to which his characters attain. When we have listed the bazaar in a large hall of 'Araby', the King's Inns in 'A Little Cloud', the legal offices of 'Counterparts', a laundry in 'Clay', a private bank in 'A Painful Case', and concert halls in Earlsfort Terrace and the Rotunda in the same story, the Antient Concert Rooms and the Pro-Cathedral (by implication) and the General Post Office in 'A Mother', the Jesuit Church in Gardiner Street in 'Grace', the Academy (of Music), the Antient Concert Rooms, Adam and Eve's Church, a church on Haddington Road and the Theatre Royal in 'The Dead' we have exhausted the range of the public buildings entered by Joyce's characters in the book.

13

Apart that is from two cheap restaurants and a number of shops and stores (Pim's for example is referred to in 'Two Gallants', a card shop and second hand book stores get mentioned in 'The Dead'). In addition there are only the ubiquitous public houses referred to in the text, which suggest how central was the pub to the diminished social experience of the lower middle class Dubliner at the turn of the century.[5]

By contrast there is another Dublin from which Joyce's Dubliners appear remote, if not alienated. That is the Dublin of Anglo-Ireland manifested in a series of buildings and streets referred to in the story 'Two Gallants'. Nassau Street, the Kildare Street Club, Rutland Square (where the headquarters of the Orange Order was situated), Stephen's Green, Merrion Square, Hume Street, the Shelbourne Hotel, Trinity College, Duke's Lawn, Grafton Street, Baggot Street – the names toll with the inevitability of exclusion, suggesting a social milieu to which Lenehan in his peregrinations is an outsider, conscious only of his own galling irrelevance.

What this Dublin of public buildings suggests is a city of caste divisions and a city where the cultural and social implications of place and name are indelibly etched on the psyches of the various *personae*. No character is ever allowed more than the merest moment of freedom from a grid-plan of a Dublin he knows with an all too oppressive familiarity. And such moments are shown in 'Araby', for example, to be tawdry delusions. Indeed only in 'Eveline' is there the suggestion of any building development taking place (the Belfastman and his shining roofs again). The city is fixed in its paralysed physical condition, allowing its inhabitants no possibility of psychic freedom within its bounds, not even that common urban pleasure, the encountering of the new and unknown.

It is clearly a small city, though it boasts a tram system, trains and other modes of public transport (the car, presumably horse-drawn, that bears Mr Kernan away from the scene of his fall from grace in 'Grace', for example). Much of the centre of the city can be easily walked about as in 'Two Gallants', and train and tram journeys are short – 'From Ballsbridge to the Pillar, twenty minutes; from the Pillar to Drumcondra, twenty minutes' ('Clay') – the routes well-known. A sense of the city's enclosure upon itself is very strong in the book. There is almost no impression of the relationship it might bear to the countryside that surrounds it in fact. The characters are willing to contemplate a day trip to Howth ('Eveline'), a spin in a motor-car along the Naas Road ('After the Race'), or a few weeks' vacation in Skerries ('My good man is packing us off to Skerries for a few weeks' – 'A Mother'), but in general their magisterial indifference to the rural world that surrounds them is summed up in the classic Dublin phrase used of Harry in 'Eveline', who was nearly always 'down somewhere in the country'. Only when the Irish countryside can attain mythic dimensions as 'the West' can it begin to rival in the Dubliner's mind the romantic attractions of abroad, of London, the Argentine or Paris. Or when it's worth a moment's idle consideration in the Dubliner's terms – 'there were five or six working-men in the shop discussing the value of a gentleman's estate in County Kildare' ('A Painful Case').

Finally the reconstruction of Dublin in some dismal future when the city is no more, would, if it sought to be true to the Joycean blueprint, have to take account of the fact that Joyce's Dublin was a military city. There were soldiers (though the Dublin Metropolitan Police were an unarmed force) in its streets and pubs, and undoubtedly barracks were required to house them. In 'Eveline' we catch a glimpse of the soldiery: 'The station was full of soldiers with brown baggages'. In 'The Boarding House' Jack Mooney, the Madam's son, 'was fond of using soldiers' obscenities: usually he came home in the small hours' – perhaps after consorting with soldiers on the town, or in the kips; the hero's fathers in 'After the Race' had made good partly through securing 'some of the police contracts', and in 'Two Gallants' we infer the sinister presence of Dublin Castle with its complement of informers:

> Corley was the son of an inspector of police and he had inherited his father's frame and gait. He walked with his hands by his sides, holding himself erect and swaying his head from side to side. . . . He always stared straight before him as if he were on parade and, when he wished to gaze after some one in the street, it was necessary for him to move his body from the hips. . . . He was often to be seen walking with policemen in plain clothes, talking earnestly. He knew the inner side of all affairs and was fond of delivering final judgements.

The implication that Corley is himself a police informer, is a cog in the city's anti-subversion system, is clearly present here.

The fact that Joyce's Dublin was a city with military traditions is suggested throughout the book indeed in the frequency in which military metaphors are employed to heighten, one supposes, the

15

sense of futile conflict that is one of the book's themes. Ireland in 'After the Race' for example is merely involved in others' battles whatever the jejune hero might hope. Jack Mooney's soldierly braggadocio in 'The Boarding House' is only part of his mother's not so tender trap for the sexually unwary ('Jack kept shouting at him that if any fellow tried that sort of game with *his* sister he'd bloody well put his teeth down his throat, so he would'); the two gallants in the tale of that name are sad parodies of soldiers of fortune; Farrington's feelings in 'Counterparts' when he is 'savage and thirsty and revengeful' bear sour fruit in his failure in a feat of strength upon which depended 'the national honour'.

This metaphoric strand in the volume, to which I am directing attention, begins with 'The mimic warfare of the evening' in 'An Encounter', continues in 'Araby' when the children playing in the November evening 'ran the gauntlet of the rough tribes from the cottages'; it surfaces again in the opening sentence of 'After the Race' where 'The cars came scudding in towards Dublin, running evenly like pellets in the groove of the Naas Road', and recurs in 'Two Gallants' (where the tale as a whole is rooted in a martial parody), in 'A Little Cloud' ('richly dressed ladies, escorted by cavaliers'), in 'Clay' ('Maria thought he was a colonel-looking gentleman') and reaches a climax in two passages in 'Grace' and 'The Dead', where objects are arranged in parody of military tradition and the deployment of troops. Here is Mr. Kernan in 'Grace':

> He carried on the tradition of his Napoleon, the great Black-white, whose memory he evoked at times by legend and mimicry. Modern business methods had spared him only so far as to allow him a little office in Crowe Street. . . . On the mantelpiece of this little office a little leaden battalion of canisters was drawn up and on the table before the window stood four or five china bowls.

And in 'The Dead' the food and drink on the festive board are described in terms that seem to parody Dublin's and Ireland's military pretensions:

> A fat brown goose lay at one end of the table and at the other end, on a bed of creased paper strewn with sprigs of parsley, lay a great ham, stripped of its outer skin and peppered over with crust crumbs, a neat paper frill round its shin and beside this was a round of spiced beef. Between these rival ends ran parallel lines

of side-dishes: two little ministers of jelly, red and yellow; a shallow dish full of blocks of blancmange and red jam, a large green leaf-shaped dish with a stalk-shaped handle, on which lay bunches of purple raisins and peeled almonds, a companion dish on which lay a solid rectangle of Smyrna figs, a dish of custard topped with grated nutmeg, a small bowl full of chocolates and sweets wrapped in gold and silver papers and a glass vase in which stood some tall celery stalks. In the centre of the table there stood, as sentries to a fruit-stand which upheld a pyramid of oranges and American apples, two squat old-fashioned decanters of cut glass, one containing port and the other dark sherry. On the closed square piano a pudding in a huge yellow dish lay in waiting and behind it were three squads of bottles of stout and ale and minerals, drawn up according to the colours of their uniforms, the first two black, with brown and red labels, the third and smallest squad white, with transverse green sashes.

The scene is set for multi-national mock-heroic warfare, with Ireland the puniest assailant in the fray.

It is worth noting I think that this protracted military parody is included in a tale which by no means lacks military allusion. Military metaphors like those noticed in earlier stories recur in 'The Dead': 'An irregular musketry of applause escorted' Aunt Julia to the piano while Mr. Browne 'advancing from the door, gallantly escorted her'; Gabriel feels 'valorous' about his wife and he longs 'to defend her against something'. Later he feels some 'impalpable and vindicative being was coming against him, gathering forces against him in its vague world', and at the end the snow lies 'on the spears of the little gate'. There are also allusions to military tradition. The song discussed is 'Let me like a Soldier fall'; Michael Furey's song was 'the Lass of Aughrim'; and one of the dances danced is 'The Lancers'. We are also reminded of the Wellington and King William monuments with all their military associations, and told of grandfather Morkan going to a military review in the park.[6]

I take it that all this together with the parodic passage cited above serves as ironic counterpoint to the real *emotional* conflicts that confront Gabriel at the heart of the story, where traditions of martial aspiration, like those of hospitality he so sentimentally invokes and all the rest of Dublin's paralysed traditions that the book has laid bare, can serve him nothing at all. For Joyce, so

17

sedulously true to the city as he knew it, so intent to record its reality of detail and tradition, also wished for another kind of Dublin to exist, one where constrictions of all kinds, military, physical, economic, social, cultural *and emotional* would have no part. So perhaps it would not serve his memory so very well to rebuild a vanished Dublin after the model of *Dubliners* even though he has, through a precisely detailed art, made such possible.

NOTES

1 Thomas Flanagan, 'Introduction' to *The State of Ireland* by Benedict Kiely (Boston: David R. Godine, 1980), p. 4.
2 David Lodge, *The Modes of Modern Writing* (London: Edward Arnold), paperback ed. 1979, p. 125.
3 Jackson I. Cope, 'Joyce's Wasteland' in *The Genres of the Irish Literary Revival* (Norman: Pilgrim Books Inc., Dublin: Wolfhound Press, 1980), pp. 104–5.
4 *Ibid.*, p. 104.
5 F.S.L. Lyons notes that in an average year in the early years of the century the city boasted over 800 licensed premises. F.S.L. Lyons, 'James Joyce's Dublin', *20th Century Studies,* November, 1970, p. 10.
6 And of course John V. Kelleher in his famous paper 'Irish history and mythology in James Joyce's "The Dead" ' has suggested that Joyce may have in part modelled his story on a very martial source indeed, the saga 'The Destruction of Da Derga's Hostel'. See John V. Kelleher, 'Irish history and mythology in James Joyce's "The Dead" ' (Chicago: Reprints from the American Committee for Irish Studies), November, 1971.

THE READER'S ROLE IN *A PORTRAIT OF THE ARTIST AS A YOUNG MAN*

CHARLES ROSSMAN

For more than half a century, readers of *A Portrait of the Artist as a Young Man* have wrestled with the problem of Stephen Dedalus. Is Stephen a budding artist who survives the philistine pressures of family, church, and country to be poised, at book's end, for Daedalian flight? Or is he merely a self-infatuated aesthete whose flight will likely end, as Icarus's flight ended, in failure? Or is Stephen something else altogether, neither triumphant artist nor posturing adolescent?

Inseparable from such questions about Stephen are those about the effect of Joyce's irony. The reader seeks to understand both Stephen's character and what judgement of him the book, through its ironic tone, renders. The reader finally asks, then, not simply 'What is Stephen's nature?' but also 'How should we regard him?' For example, should one respond to Stephen's last diary entries with a tolerant smile of approval, with mocking laughter, or with troubled concern for his future? Critics who do not distinguish between Joyce and his narrator in *A Portrait* usually put these questions in different terms: 'To what extent does Joyce share, and to what extent does he criticize, the attitudes and behaviour of Stephen Dedalus?'[1]

For most critics writing before the impact of structuralist literary theory, such questions arose because of the density of Joyce's text. Several traits make *A Portrait* especially elusive of understanding: Joyce's relatively unmediated presentation of character; his reluctance to comment directly on character and action; his disjointed, paratactic narrative; his allusions to myth, legend, historical figures, and other artworks; and his complex, varying irony. The reader's task, from the traditional critical perspective, is to perceive and assimilate these traits. Some traditional critics confine their investigations to the details of the text itself, some search for corroborating details in earlier drafts of the novel, in other works by Joyce, in the facts of Joyce's biography, or in the cultural and historical background of the novel.

But however diverse their critical methods and interpretations, traditional critics share the commonsense assumption that they are investigating a literary object outside their own consciousnesses – *A Portrait of the Artist as a Young Man*, by James Joyce. Disputes might therefore be settled by re-examining that object, by exposing methodological flaws, or more rarely, by carefully assessing Joyce's intentions. The theoretical result would be reasonable consensus about the meaning of a determinate literary work.

In the wake of structuralism, however, both the work of literature and the act of reading have been radically re-conceived. The objective, determinate work of literature has become a 'text', a system of conventional signs having little to do either with the intention of the author or, for that matter, anything outside the text that such signs might be construed as referring to or representing. The text exists exclusively within language, and is just one conventional event in *écriture*, the vast intertextuality of history's anonymous linguistic events. Human purpose, referentiality, and objective meaning have all disappeared, either discarded as outworn conventions or exposed as illusions. Given this notion of the text, it follows that readers no longer *discover* the meanings inherent in literary objects, least of all meanings put there by authors. Rather, readers *produce* meanings. 'Meaning', if the word is used at all, now indicates the mental processes of the reader as his eye moves over the words: his expectations disappointments, pleasures, frustrations, and associations.

These developments are bound to be unsettling for a critic who has devoted much of his professional life to perceiving and understanding Joyce's achievement in *A Portrait of the Artist as a Young Man*, or any work by any artist. Such a critic must now either be on the defensive or confess his errors. If he does the first, he forfeits the gains made by several brilliant literary theorists over the past dozen years. If he does the second, he forfeits the humanistic purpose of literary study: the dialogue through time with other critics about the nature and meaning of specific works of literary art. It is an urgent dilemma confronting not only Joyce scholars but all reflective students of literature. Murray Krieger, for instance, has recently written that 'the major question I must answer' is how to reconcile the compelling developments in structuralist theory with a traditional theory of literature.[2] Surveying the much smaller terrain of critical commentary on the 'question of aesthetic distance' in *A Portrait of the Artist as a Young Man*, James Sosnowski poses an analogous question: 'How can the multiplicity of critical readings be *explained* without subverting the study of literature?'[3]

My purpose here is a modest attempt to resolve this dilemma. Toward that end, I first offer a brief polemical assessment of current thinking about authors, texts, and readers. Then, turning to Joyce's work, I touch on a few illustrative passages from *Stephen Hero* and *Dubliners*, before discussing *A Portrait of the Artist,* to illustrate how that work invites competent readers to discover it.

*   *   *

Recent literary theorists have corrected a number of excesses and biases of the old New Critics. By employing the double categories of diachronic and synchronic, for example, structuralists attack the New Critics' anti-historical bias. Similarly, the idea of intertextuality undermines one aspect of the 'genetic fallacy', opening for investigation the text's linguistic antecedents (without giving special privilege to the experience or intentions of the author), while the attention paid to the 'reader's response' repudiates the 'affective fallacy'. As a whole, the post-structuralist shift in emphasis from the object of perception (the 'text') to the mind of the perceiver (the 'reader') has exposed the New Critical reification of the isolated, autonomous work, of the poem-as-poem and the story-as-story. Even though New Criticism itself is a quarter century past its prime, its intellectual style of reifying the text had dominated criticism until a decade ago. We owe the post-structuralists gratitude for the liberating awareness of the 'problematics of the text'.

Yet that awareness is hardly a simple, unequivocal gain. Many 'reader response' critics, for example, flirt with reification of the *reader*, a hypostasis as simplistic and reductive as reification of the text. One such critic rather grandly proclaims that 'hypotheses generate evidence', another that 'facts do not cause interpretations; interpretations constitute facts'.[4] Norman Holland gives this view perhaps its purest expression. 'Meaning', Holland says, 'does not inhere in the words-on-the-page but, like beauty, in the eyes of the beholder.'[5] These statements, uttered with an air of fresh discovery that is almost touchingly innocent, posit an epistemological relativism that equates perception (the reader's response) with reality (the

21

text). From that extreme subjectivism, the collapse into solipsism occurs easily. It is a small step from asserting that 'hypotheses generate evidence' to concluding that all meaning is tautology, and a smaller step still from 'meaning is in the eyes of the beholder' to 'all readers read themselves'.

If we as critics wish to avoid solipsism, or if as human beings we wish to retain our engagement with the objective world as an explicable entity, we need to recall that the apprehension of a text is, in certain ways, no different from any other act of perception. The critics quoted in the previous paragraph forget what any good student of sophomore philosophy well knows: the perceiver exists, but so does the object of perception. To assert, for instance, that a perceiver helps to constitute reality (rather than the sweeping 'hypotheses generate evidence') is true. But such a truth necessitates neither that reality is indeterminate and unknowable nor that all knowledge is a product of the mind. It merely means, for example, that we know the function of a clock before we go to it to learn the hour; or conversely, that we do not read poems to learn the time of day. We must know that meanings are latent in a text before we can discover them. Indeed, this principle of the interpretation of language might well be extended, as Lukács suggests, to all human endeavours. In Lukács' words: 'Every human action is based on a presupposition of its inherent meaningfulness.'[6]

Of course consciousness is constitutive, purposive, even teleological. We know what a chair is before we sit on it, what a novel is before we read it. However, our knowledge is not *a priori*, but depends on recognition of the intentional and formal structure of the chair or novel, of the purposive relationship of parts to whole. 'Reality' is neither a reified external object nor a reified perceiver. Rather, it is a product of the interaction between the (never fully knowable) object-in-itself and the (fallible) mind of the perceiver, a synthesis which is open to infinite correction and revision.

All this suggests a rather paradoxical truth about literature – that the text is determinate *and* that the reader is constitutive of meaning. I have no intention of offering a full-blown theory of literary determinacy here, even if I were capable of doing so. But I should like to offer five 'working hypotheses' for an engagement with literature that is at once humanistic and responsive to recent theory:

1. *Literary works contain discoverable properties consciously given them by their authors, as well as discoverable properties*

22

unknown to their authors. It follows that it is an instructive pleasure for the reader to discover these properties.

2. *All language is open to multiple interpretation, dependent upon context and the competence of both speaker/writer and listener/reader.* Semantic ambiguity, however, implies neither that readers can learn nothing about the texts themselves, nor that readers read only themselves. The possibility of *multiple* meanings does not, *ipso facto*, legitimize *all* readings. Misreadings of a text are possible.

3. *Texts vary in the degree of their determinacy, usually according to the design of the author.* On the one hand, the address on an envelope, a recipe, and a scientific treatise offer relatively limited ranges of meaning. On the other hand, Dickens's *Great Expectations*, Joyce's *A Portrait of the Artist*, and Cortázar's *Hopscotch* open progressively wider ranges of meaning, inviting as well a distinction between intended meanings and meanings outside the author's consciousness. Some texts may be consciously designed as indeterminate, within limits imposed by the author. Thus, a reader of *Hopscotch* will find evidence supporting opposite conclusions as to whether Horacio Oliveira jumps from the window or not.

4. *Works of literature are in some way referential and make sense of human experience.* No matter how problematic the notion of referentiality, nor how determined by convention our notions of 'reality' or 'realism', words point to human experience and are uttered by experiencing humans. Therefore, even the most fragmented and subjective of modernist works refract an antecedent human 'reality', transposing it into a conventional literary reality, both of which have meaningful correspondences with the reader's own sense of reality.

5. *The author's intention deserves attention.* Intention is not the necessary and exclusive determinant of meaning. Nor is it a formulaic matter of an author transferring from his mind, via the text, a uniform and decipherable message to the mind of the reader. Rather, as Paul de Man has argued, intention is a blend of consciousness and desire on the author's part, and of apprehension limited by explicit perspectives on the reader's part.[7] Nevertheless, to strive to recover the author's intention, to give importance to the experience of the author and the process of creativity, is one way that readers affirm the humanism of literary study and enhance their own humanity. Even literary works manifestly designed as indeterminate embody significant intentions that demand contemplation.

Obviously, these five propositions attempt to reconcile naïve notions of the text (and world) as univocal and readily explicable with sophisticated notions of things-in-themselves as imperceptible and inexplicable. Pervading all five hypotheses is the Kantian argument that we fall into serious error if we conceive of the autonomous self as confronting an autonomous, previously existing object. The key word here is 'autonomous'. Selves and objects exist, but they become ordered, take the form that makes each 'experience', in an evolving relationship with each other. *All* perception and interpretation is fallible, because subject to the biases and preconceptions of the observer. Still, things exist in the world, and meaning resides in texts – correctible, consensual, more a matter of probabilities than of certainties, yet something to be discovered by, or disclosed to, minds. Words like 'understanding' and 'insight' refer to this relationship of perceiver to perceived.

My five hypotheses support a 'theory of literature' more than an account of 'texts', support an idea of literature as purposive and significant rather than as *écriture*. These hypotheses also have the advantage for a Joyce scholar of coinciding with Joyce's own beliefs, at least his apparent beliefs through the composition of *A Portrait of the Artist as a Young Man*. Having briefly expounded the theoretical basis from which, in my view, Joyce's 'ideal reader' would explicate *A Portrait*, the rest of this discussion will focus more practically on Joyce's own words.

*   *   *

Joyce's much discussed idea of the 'epiphany' is basically a theory of perception. Stephen Dedalus makes this clear when, near the end of *Stephen Hero*, he expounds the theory, in words too familiar to quote at length. A few excerpted phrases will make my point: 'By an epiphany he meant a sudden spiritual manifestation. . . . He told Cranly that the Ballast Office clock was capable of an epiphany. . . . All at once I see it and I know what it is: epiphany. . . . Imagine my glimpses at that clock as the gropings of a spiritual eye which seeks to adjust its vision to an exact focus. The moment the focus is reached the object is epiphanised' (*SH*, p. 211).[8] Stephen states the matter explicitly. The thing (the Ballast Office clock) is *out there*; the perceiver needs to adjust his focus carefully; under ideal conditions, an epiphany occurs: object and observer coincide to produce a pellucid 'reality'.

24

In an earlier, less familiar passage, Stephen corroborates this notion of perception as a delicate attunement of perceiver to object. He speaks of the artist's special faculty of perception as the ability to 'disentangle the subtle soul of the image from its mesh of defining circumstances' (*SH*, p. 78). In *A Portrait*, Stephen Dedalus advances a similar notion of perception. He explains to Lynch how, confronted by a basket, the 'mind first of all separates the basket from the rest of the visible universe which is not a basket', in order to 'apprehend it as *one* thing'. This phase of perception Stephen calls the discovery of the object's *integritas*. Two successive phases, the discovery of *consonantia* and of *claritas*, yield a radiant manifestation of 'the whatness of a thing'. That is, the mind discovers 'that thing which [the basket] is and no other thing' (*AP*, p. 213).

Joyce and Stephen agree, at least, on their theories of perception. Joyce's own youthful essays, notebooks, and letters frequently echo Stephen's belief that the mind can apprehend the objective world, that the observer can enter into and interpret phenomena. In 'James Clarence Mangan', for instance, Joyce scolds those of 'impatient temper' who disregard 'any method which bends upon these present things and so works upon them and fashions them that the quick intelligence may go beyond them to their meaning, which is still unuttered.'[9] Although Joyce here has in mind the way that an artist transmutes experience into art, his remark is also an early formulation of both Stephen's description of the 'artist's selective faculty' of 'disentangling the subtle soul of the image' and Stephen's more elaborately theoretical notions of the epiphany and of *integritas, consonantia,* and *claritas*.

What is most pertinent to this discussion is that Joyce's words in 'James Clarence Mangan' also describe the reader's experience of *Dubliners, A Portrait,* and much of *Ulysses*. Joyce has arranged the facts in these books so that the reader is led toward complex, epiphanic, narrative moments which reveal a situation, a circumstance, or a character but leave their 'meaning . . . still unuttered'. The reader must engage these books by attending closely to the literary facts, 'these present things,' in order to go beyond them to their meanings. In particular, the reader's task is to discover the potential meanings of the epiphanic moments. Wolfgang Iser has shown how *Ulysses* creates 'aesthetic blanks' that the reader fills, how Joyce prestructures potential meanings that are discovered and actualized through the process of reading.[10] What Iser has demonstrated about the design of *Ulysses* holds true for Joyce's earlier

25

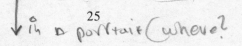

books, as well. They are also prestructured with 'blanks' or 'gaps' that the reader fills by discovering potential meanings. It is especially instructive for readers of *A Portrait*, seeking clues to that book, to examine how Joyce creates such 'aesthetic blanks' in *Dubliners*.

Repeatedly in *Dubliners* Joyce structures a story so that the reader is led to contemplate, at story's end, a character or situation that has been gradually disclosed. Sometimes we behold a character who is himself observing others, as with the boy in 'The Sisters', or Eveline, or Joe in 'Clay'. Perceiving more than the characters themselves, we judge both the circumstances and the silent witnesses. Our response fills the silence that the characters leave. In *A Portrait*, Joyce creates this sort of gap to powerful effect, perhaps most notably at the end of the Christmas dinner episode. During the entire dinner, Stephen remains a mute spectator of his family's emotional chaos and, especially, his father's tears. The aesthetic blank here is created by Stephen's absolute silence, by the fact that we are not permitted even to know his thoughts, as we are during the pandy-batting episode, even though we are certain that he is startled, bewildered, and suffering. The scene ends with this description: 'Stephen, raising his terror-stricken face, saw that his father's eyes were full of tears' (*AP*, p. 39). We see Stephen's terror as he watches his father, and we rush to assess the entire, complex struggle that has resulted in tears and terror, our reactions filling Joyce's carefully contrived, unbearably silent void.

Other stories in *Dubliners* lead the reader to observe a character who does not remain silent, who assesses himself or others, or a character whom the narrator assesses. Here the aesthetic blank arises from the incompleteness of such judgments. We take neither characters nor the narrator at face value, but stand instead at a distance from both, judging the judge. Such is the reader's taxing situation, in fact, at the end of most of the stories in *Dubliners*, with the most controversial example being Gabriel Conroy in 'The Dead'. To appreciate how Joyce prestructures meaning, or ambiguity, in *Dubliners*, however, another silent figure, also from 'The Dead', is more useful than the very accessible Gabriel: Gretta's ardent but delicate Galway admirer, Michael Furey, who died at age seventeen. Michael Furey illustrates many of the problems of perception and interpretation that Stephen Dedalus poses for readers of *A Portrait*.

What should a reader think of Michael Furey? After Gretta has told Gabriel the story of Furey's death and fallen asleep, Gabriel concludes that, although he has never felt like braving death for a woman by standing in the rain while seriously ill, 'such a feeling must be love'. Should a reader concur with Gabriel, or judge his judgment? Gabriel himself wonders whether Gretta told him 'all the story'. Should a reader share his doubts, or scorn them? Certainly, a reader must wonder what 'all the story' might suggest, since Gabriel appears to account himself a failure as a husband on the basis of Gretta's story, perhaps incomplete, of her passionate, adolescent lover. Put as extreme possible interpretations, the reader might ask whether Michael Furey is a silly, rather suicidal youth caught in the throes of puppy love, or whether he represents an ideal of love as selfless passion that Gabriel is capable neither of feeling nor, until Gretta's revelation, even of understanding?

It might be thought, as many recent theorists of 'reader response' criticism would likely argue, that the answer to the reader's question about how to evaluate Michael Furey simply depends on the reader's own point of view. After all, don't 'hypotheses generate evidence'? But in fact, whether a reader would, in 'real life', account Furey as an example of adolescent folly or of true and abiding love is simply irrelevant unless the reader has first apprehended Furey's significance for Gretta and Gabriel individually. These are the potential meanings that Joyce has created in the story, the aesthetic blanks that a reader fills.

Characteristically for Joyce, these meanings elude ready discovery. Gretta, for instance, reveals very little about the whole affair. In answer to Gabriel's direct question, 'O then, you were in love with him?', she responds only that 'I used to go out walking with him,' and later adds, 'I was great with him at the time.' In answer to Gabriel's query, 'what did he die of so young?', she replies 'I think he died for me.' Because the facts are scarce and uncertain ('at the time', 'I think'), and because Gretta recounts the story after having been annoyed and rebuffed at the party, both her motives and her reliability must be an issue for the reader. Gretta can hardly have invented a story that is so unsettling to Gabriel, but it may well be that she has exaggerated, over the years and because of a sentimental mood bred by a song heard at the party this night, Furey's romantic passion. On the other hand, it may also be, as Gabriel suspects, that there is more to the story than we have heard. Nor can the reader be sure as to whether Furey's memory has come back to Gretta for the first time in decades, or whether it has been silently haunting her all these years. Nor, finally, do we know what implications the recollection and telling have for Gretta's present life. Gabriel has been shaken to his core; will Gretta even remember it in the morning?

Given our programmed doubts about Gretta's memories of Furey, we necessarily experience Gabriel's reactions, however devastating they are for him, as problematical. Gabriel feels that he has played a poor part in Gretta's life, in contrast to a seventeen-year-old's suicidal devotion. And indeed, there is abundant evidence in the story to indicate that Gabriel's marriage has been less than perfect. Yet, there is also evidence that Gabriel exaggerates his failure with Gretta, just as he exaggerates his failure at the dinner party: 'He saw himself as a ludicrous figure . . . a nervous well-meaning sentimentalist . . . the pitiable fatuous fellow he had caught a glimpse of in the mirror' (*D* p. 220). Gabriel's 'riot of emotions', here and earlier at the party itself, depends less on the events that he responds to than on his own insecurities and pretensions. He wavers from extreme self-doubt to glib over-confidence all night, compensating for one emotional excess by plunging toward its opposite. The reader cannot, then, identify any one of Gabriel's emotional reactions to the story of Michael Furey as correct, 'true', or appropriate. Rather, we see Gabriel, as we see Gretta, contemplating the contingent and shadowy figure of a long-dead Galway youth, whose own motives and experiences are lost to time.

For the reader who wants to understand Michael Furey, the climactic episode of 'The Dead' and of *Dubliners* becomes something of a Chinese-box puzzle. We observe Gabriel, who listens to Gretta, who recalls a young man that she knew years before. As we attempt to draw closer to the situation, we discover that Gabriel's swelling emotions are perhaps inappropriate, that Gretta's report of the facts is thin and perhaps incomplete, that her memories themselves may be uncertain. The reader, of course, understands more of these contingencies and reciprocities than either Gretta or Gabriel. The reader's role, the aesthetic blank that the reader fills, is precisely that of ascertaining the scant facts and of perceiving that such facts have multiple possible meanings, depending on the perspective of the interpreter. We discover, too, that some meanings can never be known, that we must remain in doubt. For although we learn what Furey means to Gabriel, Furey's meaning to Gretta is only partially accessible. And of course, what Furey means to himself is never disclosed to Gretta, so far as we know, nor to Gabriel, nor to us.

Stephen Dedalus confronts readers with an enigma more baffling than the triangular gestalt of Michael Furey, Gabriel, and Gretta. Stephen exists in a fictional matrix that demands the reader's alert attention to the dynamics of facts, narrative tone, silence, distortion, perspective, and emotion. A special difficulty for readers of *A Portrait* is the discovery of an adequate interpretive context for a given epiphanic moment, scene, or episode. To cite a simple example, when Stephen anticipates going home for Christmas, early in chapter one, he imagines his arrival like this: 'All the people. Welcome home, Stephen! Noises of welcome. His mother kissed him. Was that right?' (*AP*, p. 20). Stephen's 'Was that right?' depends for its meaning on the reader's recollection that, six pages earlier, Stephen has been bullied by Wells about kissing his mother at bedtime. Stephen first admits that he kisses his mother before bed, then reverses himself and declares that he does not. Both answers provoke Wells's scorn. We must recall this moment of Stephen's pitiful eagerness to please Wells in order to understand the profound doubt that Wells has stirred in Stephen's mind: Is it right for a son to kiss his mother, *ever*, even upon returning home from school for Christmas?

In a sense, of course, everything else in *A Portrait* serves as the interpretive context for any single aspect. Yet in dozens of cases, Joyce prestructures the meaning so that a reader, to actualize it, must gather as the context *specific* moments elsewhere in the text. Sometimes the reader simply links two particular scenes, as with Stephen kissing his mother. Sometimes, however, the reader must make many connections to fill a specific, literal gap that Joyce has contrived in the text.

An example of such complex gap-filling occurs early in chapter two. Simon Dedalus comes home to dinner, flushed with his success at squeezing Stephen into a preferred Jesuit school, Belvedere College. Suddenly he says to Stephen, 'By the bye . . . the rector . . . was telling me that story about you and Father Dolan', and continues to relate a conversation in which the rector – Father Conmee, who had been rector when Stephen attended Clongowes Wood – described Stephen's protesting the pandy-batting given him by Father Dolan. Simon quotes the rector: 'Father Dolan and I, when I told them all at dinner about it, Father Dolan and I had a great laugh over it' (*AP*, p. 72). Joyce abruptly ends the episode, as he did the Christmas dinner scene, with a silent, blank space, giving us no overt indication of what Stephen, once again silently watching his father, thinks or feels. And as before, the reader fills the silence with his own inferences.

We remember Stephen's burning shame at his public humiliation by Father Dolan. We remember his sense of outraged justice at Dolan's brutality, his struggle to gather sufficient courage to lodge a protest with the rector, and his uplifting surge of triumph upon leaving Conmee's office – his proud discovery that the world of adults is, after all, just. Remembering – and remembering with a touch of pathos at Stephen's previous innocence – we imagine Stephen's shock at hearing what *he* experienced as heroic and noble reduced to 'that story', an anecdote about 'a manly little chap' told to amuse a group of feeding priests. Thirteen pages before, Father Conmee had seemed 'the decentest rector that was ever in Clongowes'. Now, he must seem a traitor to Stephen. He exposes Stephen's courage and triumph to popular laughter, rendering Stephen's earlier feeling of prideful accomplishment a farcical self-deception. His 'manly little chap' diminishes Stephen, who had compared himself to the heroes in *Peter Parley's Tales about Greece and Rome,* to something like a kewpie doll. Conmee's 'Ha! Ha! Ha!' twice quoted by Simon, must puncture Stephen like a chorus mocking his delusions. Stephen's father, of course, joins the chorus of mockers simply by telling the story with so little understanding of his son's perspective. Simon's hearty endorsement of the rector's betrayal – 'shows you the spirit in which they take the boys there' – is a dramatic irony that must be especially painful to Stephen, who had been looking forward to his father's return for dinner. As with Furey-Gabriel-Gretta, the reader embraces more in this episode than any single participant. Consequently, as we construct Stephen's probable reactions to his father's story, we also experience those reactions as an inevitable, however poignant, stage in the loss of childhood innocence. As we listen to Simon's unconscious affronts to Stephen, we also see the rift between father and son growing wider.

Episodes like this, where latent meaning is realized through the reader's linking of several previous scenes, usually expand and accrue as they themselves become the context for subsequent episodes. The matter of whether it is right or wrong to kiss one's mother, for example, develops into a partial context for later instances of kisses given, withheld, or merely discussed, most notably Stephen's observation that Pascal 'would not suffer his mother to kiss him as he feared the contact of her sex' (*AP*, p. 242). Such

30

evolving contexts often have a complex morphology. An idea, image, phrase, or situation may be carried forward as the necessary interpretive context for a later moment in the narrative, but may then dissolve into an associated idea, image, phrase, or situation which is itself carried forward to form a portion of the context of a still later narrative section, and so forth. The reader must keep every stage of the process simultaneously in mind in order to discern the potential meanings of any portion of the sequence. Wolfgang Iser's metaphor of a gap or aesthetic blank less aptly accounts for the reader's participation in this process than does the idea of a frame. The reader accumulates evolving contextual elements and brings them to bear, positions them like a frame around a painted scene, to reveal and apprehend the scene's purposive form.

For example, on the opening page of *A Portrait* the child Stephen registers two lines from a song: '*O, the wild rose blossoms/On the little green place.*' Stephen sings the song, claiming it as 'his song'. In so doing, he conjoins elements of different lines to form a new image: '*O, the green wothe botheth*', the green rose blossoms. Through his childish 'mistake', Stephen creates an ideal, aesthetic image, a beautiful, desirable, but entirely mental object. No attention is drawn to the image of the green rose, at this point, by either Stephen or the effaced narrator.

A few pages later, after Stephen has entered Clongowes Wood College, the image of the green rose recurs. Stephen and Jack Lawton, who compete for first place in the class of elements, are engaged in an arithmetic contest during class hour. At first Stephen tries earnestly to get the sum. But as he thinks himself falling behind Jack in the competition, his interest wanes. He begins to dwell on the beautiful colours of the badges each contestant wears, a white rose and a red rose. Then withdrawing further, he thinks about the beauty of colour in general, savouring even the words that name the colours. Abstracting himself further still from the competition of the classroom, Stephen recalls 'the song about the wild rose blossoms on the little green place'. He recalls the original song accurately, but he also remembers his creative mistake: 'But you could not have a green rose. But perhaps somewhere in the world you could' (*AP*, p. 12). The reader, by linking Stephen's sudden reference to the green rose with the song on the first page, perceives the formation of Stephen's consciousness. First, Stephen makes the previously unstated point that the green rose is, indeed, an ethereal and aestheticized ideal ('but you could not have a green rose'). Then he immediately makes the further point that perhaps such ideals are possible, after all, 'somewhere in the world'. Although Stephen has retreated from the painful competition of the existing world of Clongowes Wood College into his aesthetic imagination – from sums to colours to words to imagined images – his retreat is not mere escapism. He discovers in his imagination an ideal that might be implemented in the world. A reader should have this composite experience of withdrawal, imagined ideal, and return-to-world in mind when, some fifty pages later, we encounter Stephen's reveries about Mercedes from *The Count of Monte Cristo*. As with the classroom contest, Stephen has turned from an unpleasant external world to contemplate the contents of his own imagination, preferring the imagined figure of Mercedes to the 'silly voices' of the children around him. Even more than with the green rose, Mercedes functions less as a vehicle of flight from reality than as a model for an idealized alternative reality. Stephen longs 'to meet in the real world the unsubstantial image' of his ideal female (*AP*, p. 65). Moreover, that encounter with the ideal, Stephen believes, will transfigure him, too; like a wild rose become a green rose, he will be magically metamorphosed.

This sequence of transformations, from wild rose to green rose to imagined ideal to idealized woman to Stephen himself idealized, continues to evolve and to serve as an interpretive context for later scenes. Only the reader who has perceived the transformations and retains them in mind will realize the latent meaning of such scenes. I will cite only two brief examples. First, on the night of the Whitsuntide play in chapter two, Stephen protects himself from the humiliations of his environment and the assaults of Heron simply by ignoring them, by attending instead to the 'intangible phantoms' of his own mind, an internal 'adventure' that buoys him while he prepares his future. Similarly, in his diary entry for April 6, written at a time when the Dublin reality has been thoroughly rejected and Stephen has decided to implement his ideals elsewhere, he compares his own artistic intentions with those of Yeats's Michael Robartes: 'he presses in his arms the loveliness which has long faded from the world. . . . I desire to press in my arms the loveliness which has not yet come into the world' (*AP*, p. 251). From the green rose on the opening page of the novel to the 'loveliness which has not yet come into the world' on one of the last pages, from a child claiming 'his song' to a young artist crystallizing a statement of his artistic goals – such is the allotropic sequence that will frame, for the competent reader,

Stephen's final and grandest statement about flight to implement an imagined ideal: 'Welcome, O life! I go to encounter for the millionth time the reality of experience and to forge in the smithy of my soul the uncreated conscience of my race' (*AP*, pp. 252–53).

There are, of course, numerous other contexts, frequently of the accumulating sort that has just been demonstrated, that the alert reader will adduce for this passage from Stephen's penultimate diary entry. 'Welcome, O life!' may ring somewhat hollow in the ears of a reader who remembers, for example, that each of the two preceding chapters has similarly ended with high-flown rhetoric about 'life': 'How simple and beautiful life was after all! And life lay all before him' (*AP*, p. 146); 'On and on and on and on he strode . . . to greet the advent of the life that had cried to him. . . . To live, to err, to fall, to triumph, to recreate life out of life!' (*AP*, p. 172). 'Welcome, O life!' will sound more problematic still to a reader who has discovered that *A Portrait* moves through a series of gradually swelling moments of exultation, followed by sudden collapse – such as Stephen's aforementioned pride at the end of chapter one, upon 'successfully' protesting the pandy-batting, which is painfully deflated by his father during dinner. Another significant context is Stephen's aesthetics theory followed by his composition of the villanelle. How one evaluates the villanelle determines how seriously one takes Stephen's proclamations about his future in the last diary entries. Many relevant contexts extend beyond the book itself: the myth of Daedalus and Icarus, Joyce's *Ulysses*, and the history of the *Bildungsroman* form, to cite only three that competent readers will likely bring to bear.

I have stressed filling aesthetic blanks and adducing contexts because these entail a wide range of readerly activities. Two such activities demand further attention: getting the literary facts straight, and assessing perspectives properly, both those of the characters who offer and interpret facts and that of the narrator, whose selection and ordering of facts, and whose tone, finally lead us to the author's predetermined interpretations. The example of Michael Furey, Gretta, and Gabriel illustrates the elusiveness of fact and the ambiguity of meaning. In *A Portrait* even more than in 'The Dead', we are teased by elusive facts and ambiguous meanings. For instance, a reader cannot be certain why E. C. leaves without speaking to Stephen following the Whitsuntide play – or whether, for that matter, E.C. really attended the play in the first place. More crucially, readers continue to debate whether Stephen has a 'wet dream' prior to composing his villanelle – a matter of fact which may determine our evaluation of the villanelle and, consequently, our interpretation of Stephen's prospects at book's end.

As with Furey-Gretta-Gabriel, the facts in *A Portrait*, once clarified, have meanings that depend upon one's perspective. 'Manly little chap' is a compliment for Father Conmee, a source of pride for Simon Dedalus, and a stinging barb for Stephen himself. In the final scene before the diary, Cranly poses a series of searching questions to Stephen. Among them are: 'Do you love your mother?'; 'Have you never loved anybody?'; and 'Do you consider that poetry?' Like Gabriel Conroy's forlorn 'such a feeling must be love', the meaning of Cranly's questions depends more on Cranly's emotions and purpose than on any set of facts about Stephen (Does Stephen love God? E. C.? his mother?) that one might point to. For example, those readers who find Stephen a cold fish might easily endorse the implied 'no' of Cranly's rhetorical question, 'Have you never loved anybody?' What is essential for a reader to perceive is not whether Stephen has ever loved anyone, but the growing hostility on Cranly's part that the question reveals. Cranly is impatient at his friend's defensive cleverness, and perhaps offended at his free-thinking. A further meaning generated by Cranly's question is that Stephen, suddenly dropping his defensiveness, accepts the question at face value and answers it with surprising humility. A reader feels the disparity between Cranly's motives and Stephen's frankness, and fills yet another aesthetic blank with his own reactions.

The question of assessing the perspective engages readers most relentlessly, of course, during the last half-dozen pages of the book, Stephen's diary, where Stephen is presented to us in his own voice – straight, unmediated, without overt narrative context, and with no dramatic foil. Joyce has chosen to end his portrait of Stephen by giving us the budding artist raw, thus heightening amibiguity and increasing the reader's necessary involvement. We are ultimately left, once we become conscious of our own role as readers, not so much with the question 'What are we to think of Stephen?' as the more self-reflexive questions: 'How can we read alertly enough to get a sufficient perspective on Stephen?' or 'What context should we assess Stephen within?'

*   *   *

Caroline Gordon's startling judgment that *A Portrait* is about 'a soul choosing damnation' offers a provocative test case for my

34

contention that, although it may be true that 'hypotheses generate evidence', misreadings occur.[11] Indeed, it might be said of Gordon's judgment of Stephen that 'hypotheses generate misreadings'. This is not the place for an extended polemic; rather I will only demonstrate in brief how her argument works and why it may legitimately be called a misreading.

Gordon's mistake is not, of course, in having an opinion about the destiny of Stephen Dedalus, but in failing to distinguish between her own values and those dramatized by *A Portrait*. As I attempted to show concerning my hypothetical reader of 'The Dead' who asks 'what should I think of Michael Furey?', the reader's judgment of Furey is a private meaning, irrelevant to the text itself, that follows a preliminary assessment of what Furey means, within the text, to Gretta and Gabriel. Gordon confuses these categories of private and textual meanings. Put in terms of my earlier argument, she fails to discriminate among perspectives and to adduce an appropriate context. For example, she writes of the final conversation between Cranly and Stephen that in it 'the way he is to go is revealed to [Stephen]' (p. 390). She regards the conversation as exposing both Stephen's sin of intellectual pride and, consequently, his inevitable ruin. Cranly thus speaks *ex cathedra*, the agent of 'Truth', or at least of Joyce: 'Joyce is convinced that his hero is damned' (p. 393). To support these interpretations, Gordon would have to show, at least, that the religion presented in the book is true and universal, that abandonment of that religion leads to damnation, and that Cranly reflects the religious facts accurately. As a minimum, these propositions must be established to make an argument that the *textual* meaning, rather than the *ex post facto* private meaning, of *A Portrait* is that of a 'soul choosing damnation'.

Gordon does not convincingly argue any of these propositions. My point is not, of course, to repudiate her argument in order to offer alternative readings. I want to show that her judgment of Stephen is not, as many 'reader-response' critics would claim, simply one more, inevitably private, response to an indeterminate text, a response we can account for (rather than argue with) by examining her own hypotheses rather than *A Portrait*. To be sure, her hypotheses, like her evidence and her conclusions, invite scrutiny. But they also invite argument and renewed investigation of the text, to which we may appeal for evidence. Another reader might conclude, for instance, that the religion presented in *A Portrait* is a false, even noxious, parody of Christianity; that escape from it is

Stephen's personal salvation, and that Cranly tries to manipulate concepts like religion and mother-love to entrap Stephen out of resentment. That argument, like Gordon's, would require testing against the available evidence.

It should be clear that to classify Gordon's judgment of Stephen as a 'private meaning' is not to scorn private meanings. Indeed, as many people have observed, books read us as we read them. In entering the fictional world of Joyce's *A Portrait*, in order to perceive and understand as much of it as we may, we come to know and understand ourselves as well. That is the duality that makes literature valuable, the paradoxical double knowledge that we gain, of ourselves and of something external, through the aesthetic pleasure of scrutinizing a text.

NOTES

1 Two useful accounts of this controversy are: Chester G. Anderson, 'Controversy: The Question of Esthetic Distance', in James Joyce, *A Portrait of the Artist as a Young Man: Text, Criticism, and Notes*, ed. Chester G. Anderson (New York: Viking Press, 1968), pp. 446–54; and Thomas F. Staley, 'Strings in the Labyrinth: Sixty Years with Joyce's *Portrait*', in *Approaches to Joyce's PORTRAIT,* ed. Thomas F. Staley and Bernard Benstock (Pittsburgh, University of Pittsburgh Press, 1976), pp. 3–24.

2 Murray Krieger, 'Literature vs. *Écriture:* Constructions and Deconstructions in Recent Critical Theory', *Studies in the Literary Imagination*, 12 (Spring 1976), p. 6.

3 James J. Sosnowski, 'Reading Acts and Reading Warrants: Some Implications for Readers Responding to Joyce's Portrait of Stephen', *James Joyce Quarterly*, 16 (Fall 1978/Winter 1979), p. 53.

4 The first quotation is from Sosnowski, p. 43; the second from Steven Mailloux, 'Learning to Read: Interpretation and Reader-Response Criticism', *Studies in the Literary Imagination*, 12 (Spring 1979), p. 108.

5 Norman Holland, *Poems in Person: An Introduction to the Psychoanalysis of Literature* (New York: Norton, 1973), p. 98.

6 Georg Lukács, *Realism in our Time* (New York: Harper Torchbooks, 1971), p. 36.

7 Paul de Man, *Blindness and Insight* (New York: Oxford University Press, 1971), pp. 24 ff. See commentary by Charles Altieri, 'The Hermeneutics of Literary Indeterminacy: A Dissent from the New Orthodoxy', *New Literary History*, 10 (Autumn 1978), p. 73.

8 All references to Joyce's works are cited in my text to the following editions: *Stephen Hero* (cited as *SH*) (New York: New Directions, 1959); *Dubliners* (cited as *D*), ed. Robert Scholes and A. Walton Litz (New York: Viking Press, 1969); *A Portrait of the Artist as a Young Man* (cited as *AP*), ed. Chester G. Anderson (New York: Viking Press, 1968).

9 James Joyce, *The Critical Writings,* ed. Ellsworth Mason and Richard Ellmann (New York: Viking Press, 1959), p. 74.
10 Wolfgang Iser, *The Implied Reader* (Baltimore: Johns Hopkins University Press, 1974), pp. xii, 179–233.
11 Caroline Gordon, 'Some Readings and Misreadings', *The Sewance Review*, 56 (Summer 1953), 393. Subsequent references will be cited by page number in my text.

EXILES: A MORAL STATEMENT

DOMINIC DANIEL

A play so complicated as *Exiles*, constructed and woven with an intricate plot and very strong characterization, although it has not so far been found suitable for the stage, could perhaps be successfully adapted for radio. The play unweaves itself slowly and is fairly static, and Ezra Pound remarked when Joyce had finished writing the play that he did not think it would work on the stage.[1]

Exiles is, as Joyce himself commented, made up of 'three cat and mouse acts',[2] and is a largely autobiographical drama, written immediately after *A Portrait of the Artist as a Young Man* and before *Ulysses*. The main action takes place between four characters, Richard Rowan, his wife Bertha, their close friend Robert Hand – who is in love with Bertha – and Hand's cousin Beatrice Justice, who is in love with Richard. The supporting roles are filled by Brigid the maid and Archie, the Rowans' young son, both straightforward characters whose function is to provide a break in the main action of the drama. Brigid also supplies the audience with information about offstage and past action.

The title *Exiles* has several levels of meaning. Joyce himself, like Richard Rowan in the play, chose to leave Ireland and take up residence abroad. This was a form of self-imposed exile, as is the retreat of the intellectual mind into itself, which is also examined in *Exiles*. Richard Rowan is a writer, proud, independent and aloof, so much so that he exiles himself from society and cuts himself off from the other characters in the play, his wife and son included. This is his personal exile. During the play, through the force of his personality, he draws each of the other three main characters into a course of action which culminates in their individual exile or isolation.

The lead-up to the play is important for its understanding. Richard Rowan and Robert Hand, we learn, once shared a cottage in Ranelagh, where as young men they had many wild nights and parties. Both loved the same girl, Bertha, and it was Richard who eventually won her and then chose to exile himself with her to Italy. Robert Hand and his cousin Beatrice, both having lost Richard as an inspiring friend and companion, became engaged during his absence. Their liaison, however, has been unsuccessful, lacking the vital ingredient of the inspiration and powerful intellect of Richard. The latter has continued to write to Beatrice and to send her his work for comment; she, for her part, is in love with Richard and acts as his intellectual muse, but has fallen desperately ill in pining for him.

Immediately prior to the start of the play the Rowan family has arrived back from Italy to take up residence in Ireland again. Meeting them off the boat, Robert has gained the impression that Bertha is still attracted to him. Mindful of his defeat over her some years earlier, he takes up the challenge again and tries to win back her affection from Richard. Before long he is admitting his feelings to Bertha, which triggers off a series of confessions. 'We all confess to one another here', he tells Bertha.[3]

The play is based, at least partially, on Joyce's experiences with Nora Barnacle before their marriage, and there are four other people who influenced Joyce and on whom he was able to draw to form the plot of *Exiles*. Firstly there was Vincent Cosgrave, Joyce's most intimate friend, who did his utmost to take Joyce away from Nora during their courtship. He told Nora that Joyce's love would not last, and that 'the man was mad' anyway.[4] In *Exiles*, Bertha, thinking aloud, says that she thinks her husband, Richard, is a little mad,[5] and Robert Hand, Richard's best friend, tries to have an affair with her. Certainly, after the course of events of *Exiles*, Richard and Bertha can never resume their relationship quite as it was at the opening of the play. Cosgrave also tried to persuade Joyce that Nora had deceived him. This wounded Joyce deeply, because he was desperately in love with Nora, and his ensuing jealousy caused disruption in their relationship. The plot of *Exiles* is undoubtedly influenced by Joyce's memory of the heartache Cosgrave's deceit caused him.

Robert Hand's character seems also to be partly drawn from another of Joyce's close friends, Oliver St. John Gogarty, a well-known writer and poet of the time. Joyce's relationship with Gogarty was as much a rivalry as a friendship. They were both interested in medicine, and both ambitious writers and poets; but where their talents coincided, their personalities clashed. Gogarty taught Joyce to drink, perhaps wanting to bring him down from his pedestal of puritanical aloofness. Gogarty was obviously jealous of Joyce, and in a mocking way called him 'the Dante of Dublin',[6] because he had read and knew so much about Dante. Gogarty would have admired Joyce's poems, though whether the reverse

39

was true is less likely. Joyce, however, liked Gogarty's bawdy songs,[7] and used three of them in *Ulysses*. He saw Gogarty as one of Ireland's gay betrayers, and found him devoid of the deep feeling that makes loyalty possible; while Gogarty saw Joyce as an inverted Jesuit, whom he must 'rouse from Firbolg melancholy to Attic joy'.[8]

A third influence, Thomas Kettle, was one of Joyce's few friends at University College. Joyce appears to have taken some material from his friendship with Kettle and transposed it into the drama of *Exiles*. The article Robert Hand is said to have written on Richard Rowan in *Exiles* bears a certain resemblance to an article written by Thomas Kettle about Joyce for the *Freeman's Journal*.[9] Kettle's article mentions that writers flee the country for intellectual and economic reasons, and that 'if Ireland is to become a new Ireland, she must first become adjoined to Europe'.[10] This was also an idea of Joyce's, and he brings it into *Exiles*. Kettle also attempted to help Joyce with a teaching position, as in *Exiles* Robert tries to help Richard gain a position in the university.

A fourth friend, Roberto Prezioso, a Venetian journalist, could perhaps be said to be the greatest influence and the person on whom Joyce really modelled the character of Robert Hand. The name Robert(o) and the profession of journalist are two of the most obvious shared characteristics. Prezioso, who had been a pupil of Joyce's in Trieste, became a close friend not only to his former teacher but to Nora, and his admiration for her grew and grew.[11] Joyce watched with interest and even encouraged it, as in *Exiles* Richard Rowan watches Robert with his wife Bertha, and condones their behaviour in a detached way.

Richard is confident Bertha will return to him because, as he explains to his son Archie, a thing 'is yours then for ever when you have given it. It will be yours always. That is to give.'[12] Richard secretly knows that Bertha has never left him *emotionally*. Also part of the reason why Bertha acts out her emotional game with Robert is to try to make Richard jealous, so that he will come out of his intellectual exile, and once again draw near to her. In fact many times in the drama, after confessing what has happened between herself and Robert, Bertha asserts that Richard must be jealous, but he denies it over and over again, and so is ultimately the victor.

Joyce once reduced Prezioso to tears with an angry rebuke, but Richard has no need to get angry with Robert because he knows the latter's respect for him is so strong that he will always succumb to Richard rather than to Bertha. Robert's admiration – almost a hero-worship – for Richard is considerably stronger than his love for Bertha, with overtones of a homosexual relationship between the two men.

Roberto Prezioso was a great admirer of James Joyce's work, and of his musical and literary talent, which he tried to absorb, and this may well have had at least as much effect upon him as Nora's charms. During his affair with Nora, Prezioso told her that 'the sun shines for you'.[13] In *Exiles*, Brigid the maid says to Bertha of Richard: 'Sure he thinks the sun shines out of your face, ma'am.'[14]

Joyce has a tendency to use puns, and indeed many writers have employed the device of giving their characters names with double meanings. In the case of *Exiles* we may shorten the two main protagonists' names to Rich and Rob. Richard Rowan certainly sounds a superior name to Robert Hand, and the play is designed to make the former the one to be envied: 'every man . . . is Robert and would like to be Richard'[15] in the possession of Bertha. Joyce made Richard a writer of original, creative work, whereas Robert Hand wants to write original material but does not have the ability, and so is forced to pursue the less inspiring career of a journalist. Not only is he trying to 'rob' Richard of his wife, but as a journalist he is, in a sense, living off the drama in other people's lives.

Richard Rowan in fact towers above all the other characters in *Exiles* and most of the time controls them as if they were his puppets. Joyce took the surname Rowan from Hamilton Rowan, a patriot friend of Wolfe Tone.[16] The name and conduct of Rowan pleased Joyce so much that he gave it to his leading character, but was careful to make Richard deny any relationship with the patriot. Richard is at all times the master, the model whom Robert can look up to and envy, like a great man and one of his disciples. Robert desires most of what Richard possesses, including his wife. Robert is unmarried and a philanderer, and apart from his friendship with his cousin Beatrice he seems never to have had any deep feelings for a woman before Bertha. But the very strange relationship between Richard and Robert, with Bertha as a sort of uniting force between them, suggests they have some kind of homosexual feelings for each other. Joyce himself raises the point in his notes on the construction of the play:

The bodily possession of Bertha by Robert, repeated often, would certainly bring into almost carnal contact the two men. Do they desire this? To be united, that is carnally through the person

41

and body of Bertha as they cannot, without dissatisfaction and degradation – be united carnally man to man as man to woman?[17]

This is a possible deeper motive for Robert's pursuit of Bertha: because he loves Richard and is his great admirer; he wants all that Richard has, and so chooses to try and attract Bertha. In other words, the nearest he can come to a physical relationship with Richard is sexual union with the latter's wife. Richard himself seems to suggest it in telling Bertha:

> You may be his and mine. I will trust you, Bertha, and him too. I must. I cannot hate him since his arms have been around you. You have drawn us near together.[18]

Robert, for his part, tells Richard: 'She is yours, your work. . . . And that is why I, too, was drawn to her. You are so strong that you attract me even through her.'[19]

Robert Hand's approach to Bertha is simple and romantic. He even brings her roses, for which he later apologizes, and is generally placid and polite. The sadism Joyce mentions apropos of Robert, in his introduction to the play,[20] is scarcely in evidence. After Robert has kissed Bertha, he feels like committing suicide, knowing he will never get Bertha because his friend stands between them, and his conscience will not allow him to betray Richard. Giving way to this weakness and despair could be aimed at enlisting Bertha's sympathy, but this is rather too passive an approach to a woman, and might endorse the suggestion that his nature is homosexual. In front of Richard, Robert always appears meek and humble, and this shows the extraordinary respect he has for him.

Richard, on the other hand, is soemwhat masochistic in sacrificing the person he loves to what he interprets as his own destiny. Watching Robert and Bertha together is apparently a way of inflicting punishment on himself, and his underlying aggression emerges as the play progresses. It reaches a climax when he goes to the cottage where Bertha and Robert are to meet. Though Richard does not admit it to himself or to the others, he has reached a point where he cannot accept as a man what he has set in motion as a dispassionate writer. On the other hand Richard encourages adultery in Bertha as it seems it will give him the vicarious pleasure of possessing a bound woman through 'sharing' his friend's experience of intercourse with her.

Bertha not only never leaves Richard emotionally, but returns completely to him at the end of the play, when Robert becomes the one to exile himself by leaving for England after Richard's decisive action. Early on in the play, however, Bertha appears to some extent to relish the prospect of a change from Richard's endless nervous intellectual energy and curiosity, which leaves her fatigued and exhausted. Robert's placid politeness has quite a soothing effect, and Bertha is quite enchanted by it. But her attraction to Robert frightens her, and feeling the need to be reclaimed by Richard, she tries to make the latter jealous. But he denies the word to her face. 'I am not,' he says. 'Jealous of what?'[21] He is certainly not going to fall into that particular little snare.

Robert also tries to provoke Richard into taking action against him, into using the weapons which social convention and morality put into his hands as Bertha's husband, but again Richard will not be drawn. Instead he remains a detached observer, watching Robert bring about his own final defeat.

Bertha, as a normal woman and wife, needs Richard's husbandly affection. The apparent lack of love and attention from him, especially while she is clearly making up to Robert, turns Bertha's mind to disappointment and resentment. She has never known such coldness, such off-hand neglect, such self-exile. But her honesty forces her to tell her husband of her tryst with Robert at the latter's cottage. This finally provokes a response: Richard goes to the cottage and accuses Robert of betraying him. But when Bertha arrives, Richard tells her: 'Bertha, love him, be his, give yourself to him if you desire – or if you can',[22] and then withdraws, leaving a slightly bemused Robert and Bertha alone together. Richard once again has his hands on the strings.

When Bertha and Richard finally get back together at the end of the play, their relationship can never be the same; it will have been scarred by jealousy, and Bertha's soul marked by Robert's invasion. Richard, however, is even more battered and scarred than Bertha at the end, and she gives the appearance of being as strong and resilient as she was at the beginning.

Beatrice Justice's part in the drama is an ill-defined one. She and Robert are cousins, and they are both great admirers of Richard. The latter has for many years been sending drafts of his work to her from abroad for her comments, so it seems she is at least his equal in literary understanding. The relationship between Richard and Beatrice is therefore based on a meeting of minds. Even if Richard is unable to get involved emotionally with Beatrice, she fulfils an important function in his intellectual life. When he cross-examines her early in the play, she admits that her relationship with Robert is over and that it is only her affection for Richard which lingers on. But his union with Bertha represents an implacable barrier for her. When Bertha herself meets Beatrice, the feelings of fear and mistrust gradually give way to cordiality, making it possible for Richard to preserve his intellectual relationship with Beatrice. She, however, appears unable to form a fully satisfactory relationship with either man. Just as it would be impossible for Bertha and Robert to conduct their affair without the interest of Richard, so the attachment between Beatrice and Robert became sterile when Richard went away.

Although Richard wishes his wife would share in his freedom, he also secretly wishes to feel the thrill and horror of being cuckolded. By encouraging Bertha to become interested in Robert's advances, he leads her to disloyalty and all of them towards self-destruction, stretching the cord of fate to its utmost limit. Bertha, encouraged by her husband, does in fact leave herself open to the possibility of having an affair with Robert. There is no doubt she has a long-standing friendship with him, in spite of still being in love with Richard. But she does not appear to gain materially from her involvement with Robert. Having been manœuvred into it by various circumstances, she is too weak to break the net she is caught in. When it comes to the final question as to whether or not Bertha has remained faithful to Richard, Joyce provides no unequivocal answer, but draws a discreet curtain across the scene.

Although Bertha is propelled and influenced by Richard all the way through the play, she is not as passive as that implies. Love to Bertha does not mean the same as it does to Richard. She is too practical for idealism. Bertha's essential idea of love is a bond, which is barely possible with Robert. She starts her affair with him to use him as a pawn, so that she can get her own way with her husband. In fact by making Richard jealous she hopes to force him to put his work aside and pay attention to her needs.

Joyce himself was against all ritual, and even when his mother was dying he could not accept the church. She wanted him to go to confession, but he refused. He may have been proud in an artistic manner, but in a way he was also a scientist and an explorer, as we see in *Exiles*, where he tries to delve into the fundamental truths of his characters, stripping them practically to the bone.

Exiles: *A Moral Statement*

When Richard Rowan acts as a petty god in directing people's lives, he fails, and the result is confusion and retribution, since he has broken the laws of morality and social convention. This shows that *Exiles* is ultimately a moral statement.

NOTES

1 Richard Ellmann, *James Joyce* (London, O.U.P., 1966), p. 144.
2 James Joyce, *Exiles* (St. Albans, England; Granada Publishing, 1979), p. 155.
3 *Ibid.*, p. 104.
4 Ellmann, *op. cit.*, p. 166.
5 *Exiles*, p. 38.
6 Ellmann, *op. cit.*, p. 122.
7 *Ibid.*
8 *Ibid.*
9 *Ibid.*, p. 271.
10 *Ibid.*, p. 64.
11 *Ibid.*, p. 327.
12 *Exiles*, p. 55.
13 Ellmann, *op. cit.*, p. 327.
14 *Exiles*, p. 114.
15 *Ibid.*, p. 148.
16 Ellmann, *op. cit.*, p. 29.
17 *Exiles*, p. 156.
18 *Ibid.*, p. 94.
19 *Ibid.*, p. 77.
20 *Ibid.*, p. 157.
21 *Ibid.*, p. 60.
22 *Ibid.*, p. 94.

ON THE NATURE OF EVIDENCE IN ULYSSES

BERNARD BENSTOCK

'Is there any point to which you would wish to draw my attention?'
'To the curious incident of the dog in the night-time.'
'The dog did nothing in the night-time.'
'That was the curious incident,' remarked Sherlock Holmes.
  A. Conan-Doyle, 'Silver Blaze', *Memoirs of Sherlock Holmes*.

A casual glance at *Everyman's Dictionary of Fictional Characters*[1] should be enough to dismay any diligent reader of James Joyce's *Ulysses*: Leopold Bloom is listed as a journalist, Stephen Dedalus as a schoolmaster, and Philip Beaufoy has a wife named Mina. These three classifications alone indicate the range of possible blunders that a congenitally careless reader of *Ulysses* might make, but they also point in directions open to committed critics of *Ulysses* and – in an area where mistakes most often go unchallenged – teachers of *Ulysses*. Stephen might technically be considered a schoolmaster, but of the most minimal sort, and of so temporary a duration that it is safe to assume that he is no longer employed at Mr. Deasy's school by the 17th or 18th of June.[2] On the other hand, Bloom is not and never has been a member of the fourth estate; *Everyman's* compiler may have jumped to that conclusion by finding Bloom in the offices of the *Evening Telegraph* and assumed that anything in a pond is a fish. The Philip Beaufoy/Mina Purefoy conflation, of course, is an intentional mistake supplied by Joyce for Bloom's associative mind, and although corrected, recommitted and recorrected in Bloom's mind, it has retained its pristine innocence in the mind of the *Everyman* compiler. It is the sort of trap that Joyce, like Henry James, enjoyed setting for the unwary, but one that calls attention to itself so frequently as to become a running joke.

The traps in *Ulysses* are an integral aspect of the novel, where the subjectivity of individual characters provides a plane of evidence unsupported at times and as often unsupportable, and justifies the detective approach to literary criticism undertaken by various commentators, particularly Robert M. Adams in *Surface and Sym-*

bol: The Consistency of James Joyce's Ulysses.[3] But Adams and others often err by attributing the errors to the author himself. Joyce's fallibility was human enough, and the mathematical computations in Ithaca, for example, demonstrate the same hurried boredom and inexpert arithmetic found in our chequebook stubs month after month. Yet when it comes to crediting Mercadante with the composition of *Les Huguenots* and Meyerbeer with *The Seven Last Words on the Cross*, Joyce knew better and so did Leopold Bloom. C.H. Peake is accurate in noting the discrepancy,[4] but the error has an historic continuity in the novel that cannot be overlooked. Contemplating religious music while in All Hallow's, Bloom thinks of Rossini's *Stabat Mater* and then 'Mercadante: seven last words' (*U* 82). Passing the fabrics in the windows of Brown Thomas, Bloom remembers the Huguenots who brought dyeing skills to Ireland, and credits Meyerbeer with composing the opera (*U* 168). As he hears the singing in the Ormond and imagines Boylan approaching 7 Eccles Street, Bloom elides the *Stabat Mater* with the *Seven Last Words*: 'Molly in *qui est homo*: Mercadante' (*U* 282), and having left the Ormond he sees a picture of Robert Emmet, thinks of the statement from the dock, and concludes, 'Robert Emmet's last words. Seven last words. Of Meyerbeer that is' (*U* 290). At this point he senses an oncoming flatulence, blames the burgundy and cider he had drunk, but remembers the singers at the Ormond lifting their tankards – hence *Meyerbeer*. Mercadante: Meyerbeer – the confusion is so fixed in his mind by now that under extreme pressure, threatened by the anti-semitic Citizen, Bloom conjures up a pantheon of famous Jews: 'Mendelssohn was a jew and Karl Marx and Mercadante and Spinoza' (*U* 342). Sandwiched among the son of a Christian convert, a lapsed Jew and an excommunicated Jew, Catholic Mercadante is a strange inclusion – but Meyerbeer of course would have been reasonably accurate.[5] It is understandable, therefore, that when discussing music with Stephen and feeling somewhat out of his element, Bloom transposes Mercadante and Meyerbeer once again.

In tracking these events the reader is offered two possible assumptions: either that Bloom sometimes knows something which he at other times does not, or that on occasion Bloom trips over facts that he actually has at his disposal. The few remaining detractors of Leopold Bloom can still cling to the first choice, but most readers now realize the accuracy and logic of the second. At one time it was fashionable to conclude that Bloom was badly educated and is scatterbrained, and that he not only does not know that black absorbs heat or what parallax means (faults in his knowledge that he openly acknowledges), but that he invariably gets the law of falling bodies wrong. He knows it accurately, as is demonstrated when he first considers it: 'Thirtytwo feet per second, per second. Law of falling bodies: per second, per second' (*U* 72). In throwing the crumpled Elijah circular into the Liffey, he muses: 'Elijah thirtytwo feet per sec is com' (*U* 152). In this instance, as in the two reiterations in Circe hallucinations ('thirtytwo feet per second according to the law of falling bodies' and 'Thirtytwo head over heels per second. . . . Giddy Elijah' – *U* 528, 550), it is not an error but an abbreviation: Bloom no longer has to spell out for himself what he has already demonstrated that he knows.

Time not only heals but reveals, and the persistence of a misreading in *Ulysses* can almost make it gospel. To equate the Burton restaurant in Lestrygonians with the still-extant Bailey was a reasonable assumption several decades ago, so much so that a pamphlet recording the history of the Bailey actually credits that elegant eatery with being the disgusting pigsty described by Joyce. The street name is, after all, Duke Street, and since the Burton closed its doors quite a while ago, assuming an alliterated substitute seems logical enough – and even artistically skilful. Two pieces of evidence, however, correct the error: the Burton is listed in *Thom's Official Directory of Dublin* at 18 Duke Street (external evidence), and Bloom 'turned back towards Grafton street' (*U* 170) to get from the Burton to Davy Byrne's at No. 21 – the Bailey is directly across the street at No. 3 (internal evidence).[6] It did not take long for the error to be corrected, but it has taken forever for the correction to supersede it universally.

Of even longer duration is the validity of Molly's twenty-five extra-marital lovers, one (Mulvey) pre-marital and the remainder adulterous. A sexually promiscuous Molly Bloom has been a commonplace of *Ulysses* criticism, but within the past two decades the myth has been so totally discredited as to become an embarrassment to anyone who still has it in his possession. One by one critics have chipped away at the list fabricated from what must be taken as jealous suspicions of Bloom's invention (whether he actually believes in all or any of the items remains a subject for further inquiry): Stanley Sultan, Robert Adams, and Richard Ellmann challenged the roll-call, and David Hayman delivered the coup de grâce.[7] Except for the known Boylan, only Bartell d'Arcy has a claim to sexual intimacy with Molly, and a 'lover' not on the list, Lieut. Stanley Gardner, the best claim of all. Just as Western society has forced itself to accept the idea of an unhappily married woman racking up twenty-five affairs in almost nineteen years – well within the American national average – critics have had to accept a Molly Bloom almost as faithful as tried-and-true Penelope. Few commentators on *Ulysses* these days would deny Molly her durability, and even ex-neoFreudians are lining up to recant.

But if Molly has rarely if ever stepped outside the bounds of marital fidelity, what happens to the familiar chestnut that Bloom is a well-known cuckold in Dublin? Too many critics have blithely pointed to Bloom's horns to credit it as the individual mistake of any single critic, but in itself the error is compounded: Bloom's traditional role as familiar cuckold, and his present state as cuckold of the day on 16 June 1904. The first contention collapses with the dismissal of the list-of-lovers; prior evidence throughout the day renders it absurd. John Henry Menton and lowly Lenehan confess the extent of their involvement with Molly: Menton's is negligible ogling (ancient history) and Lenehan's a case of momentary light-fingerness when Bloom was pointing out constellations (all of us are in the gutter but Bloom is looking at the stars). No one in Dublin ever boasts of having seduced Molly Bloom, and no one is credited by anyone else with the accomplishment. Boylan of course has now succeeded where all others have defaulted, and is entitled to be considered 'the first term of his series' (*U* 731) – unless the series is really of those who have noticed, glanced at, admired, or desired Molly. And Boylan's discretion does him credit. There is no indication that the conqueror has told anyone of his intentions, disguising Molly as an 'invalid' when ordering fruit and port for her (*U* 227), and keeping the inquisitive Lenehan in the dark when hurrying out of the Ormond. Bloom is the only outsider with inside information and is sensitive to any possible leak when anyone asks about the organizer of Molly's tour ('Who's getting it up?' asks the nosey Nosey Flynn – *U* 172), nevertheless himself making the inadvertant slip about 'the wife's admirers' ('The wife's advisers, I mean' – *U* 313). Only the sharp barfly in Cyclops seems to intuit the possibility: 'That explains the milk in the cocoanut and absence of hair on the animal's chest. Blazes doing the tootle on the flute' (*U* 319). He cleverly puts the pieces together, yet as far as we can see he keeps his guesswork to himself, and *l'affair Boylan* remains a well-guarded secret on 16 June 1904, with only Bloom knowing enough about it to stay away from home at zero hour.[8]

In a recent article John Henry Raleigh manages to clear up a vast number of misconceptions, particularly about Leopold Bloom, although he does perpetuate the canard about Bloom as 'cuckold, and known to be such by others in his community'.[9] In almost every other case Raleigh is precise in adhering to the given materials of the text, summarizing Bloom as 'the only child of a bankrupt suicide; the sire of only one sickly male infant who died aged eleven days; a husband who has not had normal sexual relations with his wife for almost ten years', and so forth.[10] Three facts in this capsule are among those most frequently overlooked by *Ulysses* commentators: that Rudolph Bloom was bankrupt, that Rudy was born deformed, and that the Blooms have been having sex of sorts throughout the past ten years. Most prefer for reasons of their own to believe that Bloom's father pined away for love of his dead wife, and there is of course justification for the suspicion that he found life unhappy without her. But we have no specific date for her death (her son's most recent memory dates from High School days, circa 1880 at best – *U* 413), whereas we do know that her husband's suicide took place in 1887. Joyce's scheme in withholding certain 'facts' encourages speculation and allows variant readings: hints for the sentimental interpretation derive from Molly's thought, 'his father must have been a bit queer to go and poison himself after her' (*U* 767), and the fragmentary contents of the suicide note, '. . . with your dead mother . . . that is not more to stand . . . to her' (*U* 723). Molly is groping for paradigms of the devoted couple, and she may be making assumptions that suit her mood, while the note indicates that the old man anticipates being united with his wife, not that her death necessitates his own. More immediate is the opening phrase ('Tomorrow will be a week that I received'), which suggests a foreclosure notice. As is often the case in *Ulysses,* two possible interpretations evolve from the evidence, neither necessarily cancelling out the other.

There has long been a certain amount of wailing and sighing over the Bloom marriage. Those who describe Bloom as impotent (the single most common word in *Ulysses* commentary to classify him) apparently sidestep the physiological evidence of his ejaculations in masturbating and interrupted coitus. Those who allow him his biological virility concentrate on his psychological warps, and Bloom certainly has his peculiarities. But psychological manifestations suggest psychological causes, yet even the most committed members of the psychoanalytical school fail to relate the causes to Bloom, preferring to examine James Joyce instead. Whatever the author might have revealed on the couch that he so adamantly refused to occupy need not detract from the evidence he provided for Bloom's situation. Rudy born unhealthy (a fact for which *Ulysses* supplies an abundance of clues) managed to alter the sexual appetites of both parents, as both readily admit about themselves. Bloom was obviously the more seriously affected since he harboured the fallacy that the father was biologically responsible for a malformed male child: 'If it's healthy it's from the mother. If not the man' (*U* 96). And despite his yearning for a male heir, he practised the only kinds of sex with Molly that would preclude another pregnancy.

Wary of venereal disease Bloom usually avoids prostitutes; wary of social stigmas he generally avoids relations with other women. And aware of Molly's progressively depressed state he has stoically arranged her affair with Blazes Boylan, from the initial introduction to the assurance of a safe house on June 16th. He reveals his anxieties over the arrangements and his regrets, but basically he remains satisfied with the day's events. In many ways it was the best and safest compromise he could make under the circumstances, and as Raleigh implies, the Blooms have one of the best marriages in Dublin – at least as far as *Ulysses* is concerned. Which married couple could the Blooms envy – Charlie and Fanny M'Coy? Richie and Sara Goulding? Bob and Polly Doran? Mr. and Mrs. Tom Kernan? The MacDowells? Or before widowhood the Dedaluses, the Dignams? Or perhaps the Purefoys with their nine children? – certainly the sentimental favourite.

Despite his consistently clearheaded attention to the factual evidence in *Ulysses*, John Henry Raleigh does occasionally slip, as when he assumes that Joyce is disdainful of verisimilitude in making Bloom 'the behind-the-scenes philosopher or strategist for Arthur Griffith's Sinn Fein movement'.[11] It is not just that reason prevents us from accepting an historical movement founded by a fictional character, but that all the pieces in the puzzle conspire to show that no one is expected to believe this delightful absurdity. Bloom at no time credits himself with any such influence, nor does Griffith make any revealing statement to that effect. John Wyse Nolan's motivation in his magnanimous gesture is twofold: he is goodheartedly impressed by Bloom's generous donation to the Dignam orphan fund and he can show himself to be knowledgeable on inside secrets. Martin Cunningham asks Bloom to accompany them to the Dignam home not because of any strong feeling of friendship, but because of Bloom's expertise in insurance matters: he had been employed at David Drimmie's in that capacity. John Wyse Nolan is quite willing to make his elaborate claim. It gives him prestige as an inside source of information, and he takes full advantage of it. Two preferable sources are present to dispel any such silly idea: it is quite obvious from the thoughts on Griffith by both Leopold and Molly Bloom that our cautiously nonpolitical hero does not know Griffith well enough to advise him to tie his shoelace, much less found Sinn Fein.

The absence of a functioning narrator in *Ulysses*, the one voice in a conventional novel who can be relied on to give us the hard word on the subject, makes the going rough when unreliable information competes throughout with solid facts. That *Ulysses* has no omniscient narrator comes as a surprise to some and a disappointment to others, certainly to the author of a study that provides so much commentary on that fictional person. In *The Book as World* Marilyn French is on such intimate terms with this spectre that she comes close to providing name, rank, and serial number, but her glimpses of him are so contradictory as to refine him out of existence. He commences as a 'guide', is 'visible' in Wandering Rocks, but 'less intrusive than in Aeolus', is 'the author's surrogate, a malicious omniscient narrator' who 'knows that the reader is involved in the coming together of Stephen and Bloom, and he is mocking him for his interest'.[12] This particular reader not only isolates an actual narrator in *Ulysses* but declares war against him: 'I cannot think of anything in literature . . . that glories in the impairment of another and uses it as a weapon against him, but this is precisely what the narrator does to deaf Pat and the blind stripling.'[13] No one has ever accused Joyce of being callous toward the deaf and the blind, nor does Marilyn French apparently, and Bloom is certainly compassionate toward both, yet French senses overt hostility and attaches it to the 'narrator'. There is neither evidence for such animosity anywhere in Sirens, nor a palpable narrator present to belie Bloom's compassion, yet here is a reader who insists on the existence of both.

Tracing the French narrator through her analyses is in itself a mystifying odyssey: we are informed that 'in the first three chapters we are aware of no distance between the narrator and the character Stephen Dedalus' and that the 'character-narrator of the library scene adds derisive word play'.[14] The apparent confusion of Stephen with the narrative material of the Telemachia may be at the root of the dilemma, especially if we allow the tone of the portions outside the internalized thoughts to prejudice us toward Stephen's viewpoint – a not unacceptable interpretation, but nonetheless one fraught with pitfalls when taken too literally. The particular style of a chapter determines narrational tone, while the relevant context within the chapter establishes tonal variations. French's difficulty with narrative voice is that she reads the first half of *Ulysses* as written in a 'basic style', with stylistic changes occurring only in the later chapters. Even without Joyce's assertion of eighteen separate styles for the eighteen chapters,[15] it should be seen that no two chapters in *Ulysses* are quite the same (that the differences between Berg and Bach are enormous should not obviate the differences between Berg and Schönberg).

Ulysses distinguishes itself from conventional novels in more ways than are dreamed of in the conventional critic's philosophy. Even segments that are not internalized, dramatized, or given over to governing techniques distinct from 'ordinary' narration are nonetheless subject to stylistic determinants dictated by the specific context. Under traditional 'prosaic licence' the author allows a narrative voice to present the reader with certain givens to be taken as gospel, regardless of the degree of relevance: a character's date of birth may or may not pertain, but that Marion Tweedy Bloom was born on the eighth of September and shares a birthday with the Virgin Mary is hardly accidental. And in a book in which we know so many things about Leopold Paula Bloom, no birthday is specified – a tantalizing omission. Nothing presented by the narrative is either reliable or unreliable until tested by application to the context, just as information voiced by any of the characters requires testing. The same suspicions are applicable: why is M'Coy so quick to ask if Molly is well? Bloom suspects immediately, and reports that she is off on a tour so as to forestall requests for a borrowed valise. Bantam Lyons' equally innocuous greeting ('Hello, Bloom, what's the best news? – *U* 85) draws attention to Bloom's newspaper, and Bloom is so eager to rid himself of Lyons that he offers him the paper. Clive Hart for one is so suspicious of Lyons that he surmises that he purposely waylaid Bloom when he saw him enter the chemist's, that he might then be able to read the racing news without having to buy his own newspaper.[16]

When the Citizen reads out the English-sounding names from his newspaper, he is offering the truth, but not the whole truth: he conveniently deletes all Irish-sounding names that also appeared in the *Irish Independent* for 16 June 1904, since he has his own political axe to grind. No narrator makes this important distinction for the reader of *Ulysses*. Instead the narration remains above the battle, with no ulterior motive in the narrative process, taking on the protective colouring of the events narrated. Even the innocent words that open the novel describing Buck Mulligan as 'Stately, plump' (*U* 2) are not impartial, or necessarily consistent. Although ostensibly alone, Mulligan is posturing: 'stately' fits his view of himself, while 'plump' reveals what hides beneath the pose. Subjectivity and objectivity run parallel courses, and even the objective may not be literal. Bloom's mood of desolation is 'described' as 'Grey horror seared his flesh' (*U* 61), but we know enough to read this metaphorically, deriving from the character's sensibility rather than any narrator's opinion. The shape of Bloom's thoughts – though not the language of his thoughts – interferes, and interior monologue soon replaces narration. Yet when narrative resumes, it has been tinged by those thoughts: 'Quick warm sunlight came running from Berkeley Road, swiftly, in slim sandals'. The poeticization is Bloom's: he frequently associates sunlight with Milly (as he does warmth with Molly): 'Runs, she runs to meet me, a girl with gold hair on the wind' (*U* 61).

For those intent on corroborating Bloom's view of his daughter's ankles as slim, the omniscient narrator posited by Marilyn French and others is of no assistance, nor will he ever settle the controversy over Molly's proportions – pleasingly plump or overly fat? Sizing up Molly may ultimately prove to be an impossibility, since she exists for us as a fifteen-year-old girl in Gibraltar, an eighteen-year-old bride in Dublin, and a maturing woman apprehended at a series of instances through the years leading to 1904. And she has as many alternate existences in the prejudiced eyes of her various beholders. The closest that we come to an objective description (although highly personal) takes place when Bloom brings Molly her breakfast: 'He looked calmly down on her bulk and between her large soft bubs, sloping within her nightdress like a shegoat's udder' (*U* 63). The focus of this observation betrays the eyes of the observer; this is not a narrator describing for our benefit but Bloom describing for his own (*bulk* is as much his word as is *bubs*). The Mentons and the Lenehans are motivated by a mixture of lust and disdain, but even more acerbic is the Nameless One of Cyclops – 'The fat heap he married is a nice old phenomenon with a back on her like a ballalley' (*U* 305) – a fine touch of exaggeration in a chapter abounding in giganticism.

Although Molly may be the permanent victim of varying points of view, Milly's case may be solved by close attention to the nature of the conflicting evidence. Bloom can be forgiven for idealizing his daughter, but even Molly, who betrays her envy of her newly nubile rival, is maternally proud of Milly's comeliness. Yet Alec Bannon, apparently intent on wooing Milly, depicts her as a 'skittish heifer, big for her age and beef to the heels' (*U* 297). The implication of thick ankles contradicts Bloom's girl 'in slim sandals', but Bannon's phrase may not be intentional in its context. Milly had used the expression 'beef to the heels' (*U* 66) in her letter to her father to describe the peasant girls in Mullingar, and the two city dwellers, Milly Bloom and Alec Bannon, have adopted the phrase and delight in it – to the extent that Bannon flashes it before Mulligan once he has committed himself to mocking bovine-imagery with 'skittish heifer'. Feminine terminology makes it pejorative; masculine terminology may have it be flattering (just as Bloom's 'plump' for Molly is admiration, but Stephen's use of the same word for Mulligan is not). Bannon's careless connotation bends the case toward Bloom's slimmer Milly.

The absence of a functioning narrator robs us of a referee, and readers must depend on their own powers of observation, even in the face of inadequate and undefined evidence. Stylistic changes result in shifts in narrative tone (Bannon's reference to Milly is neither in his own words nor in those of an objective narrator, but are filtered through the style and vocabulary of Samuel Pepys, as manipulated by parodist Joyce). It is hardly surprising, therefore, that Marilyn French has trouble recognizing her imagined narrator whenever he changes his guise: 'The narrator here splits himself in two', she announces; 'The narrator splits himself into hundreds of different voices', she later adds; and finally, 'Penelope is a coda uttered by a different narrator',[17] Confabulations like these surely uncover the paucity of a quest for a licensed narrator in Joyce's *Ulysses*, compelling the reader to make individual decisions whenever discrepancies arise in the text.

When Joyce assigns narrative responsibilities for a preordained voice with its own distinctive tone, he does not necessarily invite unreliability. Samuel Pepys has no ulterior motive when it comes to the materials of *Ulysses*; *language itself* is the instrument of possible unreliability. And, on the basis of language fused through unsuspecting Charles Lamb, the paltry information concerning Bloom's adolescent affair with Bridie Kelly has led various critics down the garden path and around the bend. Some attest categorically that Bridie is a prostitute (*vide* French[18]) on the following evidence:

> He thinks of a drizzling night in Hatch street, hard by the bonded stores there, the first. Together (she is a poor waif, a child of shame, yours and mine and of all for a bare shilling and her luckpenny), together they hear the heavy tread of the watch as two raincaped shadows pass the new royal university. Bridie! Bridie Kelly! He will never forget the name, ever remember the night, first night, the bridenight. They were entwined in nethermost darkness, the willer and the willed, and in an instant (*fiat!*) light shall flood the world. Did heart leap to heart? Nay, fair reader. In a breath 'twas done but – hold! Back! It must not be! In terror the poor girl flees away through the murk. She is the bride of darkness, a daughter of night. She dare not bear the sunnygolden babe of day. No, Leopold! (*U* 413)

The subject here is seduction-leading-to-procreation, and what Lamb is impressed into providing is a record in his own manner of the private musings of Leopold Bloom as he remembers, conjectures, analyses, and editorializes. The attitudes are Bloom's, but they receive corroborative handling in what Joyce surmises would be Charles Lamb's appropriate mode of discourse under the circumstances. Any hope that Bloom harbours that the hurried contact engendered a longed-for son is quickly dashed by both the unlikeliness of the coincidental conception and the proscriptions of his own moral code. But what are the implications about Bridie Kelly? Whereas it is acknowledged that this had been Bloom's initiation into sex, is it also hers? Is it her 'bridenight', or does Bloom prefer to think so – and how could he know? Which one is the 'willer' and which the 'willed'? We may also speculate as to why the consummation takes place on Hatch street, although we notice that Gilbey's bonded stores are just around the corner from the High School. If Bridie is a prostitute, she unfortunately lacks the basic rudiments of the profession, a place of business. Plying her trade *al fresco* in the crannies of a well-policed street is hardly professional status.

Those who contend that Bloom pays for her services point to that 'bare shilling', but even if the shilling is literal, it could have been a gratuitous donation (Bloom sent Martha Clifford a money order on a far flimsier pretext) rather than a contract payment. And where does the 'luckpenny' pertain? It seems to be Bridie's already, and there is no reason to think that it changes hands at all. Nor are there any indications that the coins are coincidental with the night of the seduction. Even allowing for something more than merely metaphoric language, the moralistic designation of Bridie as a 'child of shame' may account for the reference to payment in exchange for sexual favours. When asked to share the universal responsibility for Bridie Kelly ('yours and mine and of all'), the reader may be understandably reluctant – but is it her sin or her sinful conception that is the issue advanced by the moralistic tone? Whatever prostitution invoked here may refer to an incident that engendered the 'poor waif' herself, not the one in which she may have created Bloom's hypothetical offspring. Such is the nature of moral imprecation, that it transcends the real aspects of a fictional text.

Bridie's 'reappearance' in Circe is usually cited as conclusive proof that she follows the world's oldest profession. Her spectre accosts Bloom in Nighttown, reminds him of their previous encounter (over two decades earlier), and re-solicits, although pursued and captured by a 'burly rough' before Bloom can respond (*U* 441). The setting is appropriate; the name is the same; she has presumably been hard at it all these years and still outdoors at night, but at least the rain has stopped, although she is still 'rainbedraggled'. Our sceptical minds easily disallow the Bawd's claim that Bridie is a virgin. Our ironic minds note that the price has gone up to 'ten shillings', with no assurance that the burly rough intends paying anything. The price is contingent on Bridie being a virgin, yet the Bawd continues to offer her at that price to Bloom even after the rough has had 'his pleasure' (*U* 442). And Gerty MacDowell, a latter-day Bridie with better claims to virginity, is next in line to solicit Bloom.

The Bridie enigma lies in the method of reading Circe, as different from all other chapters of *Ulysses*. The conventional approach accepts as functioning reality those events that could conceivably happen, and relegates to some form of psychological reality (the hallucination of a particular mind, sometimes of Bloom, sometimes of Stephen) those which violate verisimilitude. In Bloom's guilty mind Bridie was desecrated to the status of a whore in the Lamb passage, his own violation of her as the incident that branded her and sent her permanently into the streets. Under those conditions, the Bridie of Mabbot Street is as likely a figment of Bloom's mind, a spectre of the Bridie of Hatch Street and no more real than the

57

Gerty who succeeds her. Her attainment of professional standing becomes questionable, and only the evidence of the recollection transmuted through Charles Lamb remains applicable.

Bloom's apprehension that she became a prostitute certainly does not make her one, and there is little enough indication that that is actually his apprehension. His concern in Oxen of the Sun centres on the chance that he made her pregnant rather than that he made a whore of her (the setting in the red-light area does that). When disabused of the hope that she might have borne his child, Bloom's motive may have shifted. 'It must not be!' sounds suspiciously like religious imprecation, and the 'voice' that labels Bridie a 'bride of darkness, a daughter of night' may have as its concern her status as an abomination – a non-Jew. Bloom had just been thinking of his father ('with Jacob's pipe' – *U* 413) before conjuring up Bridie, and in Nighttown he had just been visited by Rudolph Bloom and accused of having 'left the house of his father and left the god of his fathers Abraham and Jacob' (*U* 437).

Circe is a deep, dark well into which so many things are dropped that never reach bottom and never make a sound. Simplistic attempts to separate finitely that which is reality from someone's presumed hallucination have been pitifully unsuccessful, and it becomes necessary to suspect anything taking place in Circe that cannot be retrospectively proven. At the end of Oxen Stephen and Lynch are heading for the kips, with Bloom tagging behind; at the beginning of Eumaeus Bloom is helping Stephen up and brushing him off, and he soon considerately fills in the exposition – what happened prior to the events in Nighttown:

> the very unpleasant scene at Westland Row terminus when it was perfectly evident that the other two, Mulligan, that is, and that English tourist friend of his, who eventually euchred their third companion, were patently trying, as if the whole bally station belonged to them, to give Stephen the slip in the confusion. (*U* 620)

Stephen is ill-disposed to think about, much less talk about, his Circean experiences, and consequently only bits and pieces bob up in Eumaeus and in Ithaca. What is verified in the first chapter of the Nostos is that Stpehen has somehow been knocked down (but no mention of the actual altercation with Private Carr), that he hurt his hand, presumably in that incident, that Lynch deserted him and is thus branded as Judas (compare Circe, *'Exit Judas'* (*U* 600) with Eumaeus, 'And that one was Judas' – U 615), and that Corny Kelleher was on hand to intercede with the police and prevent Stephen's arrest. In addition, Bloom remembers almost having been run down by a sandstrewer, ascertains that he has lost a trouser button, and reiterates his mishearing of Stephen's mention of Fergus as reference to a Miss Ferguson (*U* 609, 656).

Nor is Bloom particularly well disposed toward discussing his Circean adventures when he is reunited with his wife in the early hours of 17 June 1904; consequently the last chapter of the Nostos is totally devoid of any aftermath of Nighttown. In the central chapter, however, certain factors have their vestigial appearances, although some quantifiable evidence has been expunged: Bloom's double-entry bookkeeping ticks off the day in retrospect, but ignores the unsavoury visit to Bella Cohen's ten-shilling house completely. The appearance of the compilation of the day's expenditure is in itself legerdemain, and can hardly be credited with the product of an objective narrator (otherwise it would be complete and accurate). Given the imperative statement, 'Compile the budget for 16 June 1904' (*U* 711), two lists devolve from the context, with eighteen items under *Debit* and three under *Credit*. The nocturnal entries in the first column read as follows:

Tramfare	0.0.1
1 Pig's Foot	0.0.4
1 Sheep's Trotter	0.0.3
1 Cake Fry's plain chocolate	0.0.1
1 Square soda bread	0.0.4
1 Coffee and bun	0.0.4
Loan (Stephen Dedalus) refunded	1.7.0

The Coffee and bun can be discounted as having taken place at the cabman's shelter (after Circe), and the Tramfare brought Bloom back from Sandymount (before Circe), but how did he get from Holles Street to Nighttown? He was obviously present at the Westland Row terminus, but no train fare is recorded. If we trust Bloom's account in Circe, apparently mumbled to himself, he had a third class ticket that he must have bought: 'Nice mixup. Scene at Westland row. Then jump in first class with third ticket. Then too far' (*U* 452). But, along with the ten shillings paid for the privilege of visiting the brothel (*U* 558) and another shilling for the smashed lamp chimney (U 585), the train fare has mysteriously been expunged.

Ludicrously enough, what survives from the sojourn in Night-town is an account of Bloom's expenditure for food, almost none of which Bloom was witnessed to have actually eaten there. The pig's foot and the sheep's trotter were presumably purchased at Olhousen's just as the pork butcher was about to close up his shop (*U* 434), but the chocolate and bread only moments before. When Bloom first turns up on Talbot Street, he is *'cramming bread and chocolate into a side pocket'* (*U* 433), but only the chocolate is later apparent: he gives it to Zoe, who then in turn offers him some, which he eats (*U* 525–26). The unkosher meats are surreptitiously disposed of, and the soda bread remains a mystery.

Bloom's temporary role as Stephen's bank vault offers another mysterious element. Both the *Debit* and *Credit* columns record it as £1.7.0, so that receiving and returning the money create an even cancellation. Yet events in Circe belie the evenness of the amount, since Bloom actually took £1.6.11 into safe keeping ('That is one pound six and eleven. One pound seven, say' – *U* 559), and in Ithaca he repays Stephen the latter amount ('The former returned to the latter, without interest, a sum of money (£1.7s.0.), one pound seven shillings' – *U* 695). Stephen in actuality does receive one penny in interest, but that penny would have had to come out of Bloom's own money and should have shown up as a discrepancy in the balance between debit and credit. If the added penny had been Bloom's, and the Circe event was real, then another instance of juggled book-keeping has been practised to excise the brothel scene entirely from Bloom's account of his night. Determining which is the 'true account' can be risky, since the events in Circe could have taken place and still not show up on the bowdlerized ledgers. Two over-lapping texts exist, therefore, both quite plausible and each in its own way contributing to a facet of the narrative of *Ulysses*.

Stripping away all hallucinatory matter from the bare bones of the literal narrative of Circe, we have usually agreed on a skeletal plot that can be succinctly summarized as: Bloom follows Stephen and Lynch into Nighttown, locating them at Bella Cohen's, where drunken Stephen smashes a lamp, runs out into the street, is accosted by Private Carr, and knocked down, having been deserted by Lynch. Bloom rescues him and brings him out of Nighttown. Yet even these time-honoured 'facts' will not quite withstand precise scrutiny if we demand corroboration from their residue in the ensuing chapters. Omitted from Bloom's account of the day's events to Molly, and therefore solid negative evidence, is any mention of 'the visit to the disorderly house of Mrs Bella Cohen, 82 Tyrone street, lower, and subsequent brawl and chance medley in Beaver street' (*U* 729). What he does relate to Molly, and replete with the 'modifications' he makes in order to gloss over the unsavoury truths, concerns 'a temporary concussion caused by a falsely calculated movement in the course of postcenal gymnastic display, the victim (since completely recovered) being Stephen Dedalus' (*U* 735). From the doctored version advanced and the true account withheld we can verify that Stephen was hurt in connection with a brawl in Nighttown, although Private Carr's name is never mentioned after his appearance in Circe. We might be able to disentangle the 'brawl' (in Bella Cohen's establishment) and the 'chance medley' (with the British soldiers in Beaver Street), in which case Stephen's torn coat stems from the former event. In his kitchen Bloom had thought of repairing 'a fissure of the length of $1\frac{1}{4}$ inches in the right side of his guest's jacket' (*U* 677), which was presumably torn when he ran from Bella Cohen's, as a whore in the doorway so bluntly reported: 'He tore his coat' (*U* 586).

The 'chance medley', usually so vital to a reading of the narrative of the chapter, is nonetheless shrouded in mystification when the evidence from Ithaca is sifted. As they approach Eccles Street Stephen and Bloom are discussing, *inter alia*, 'prostitution' (*U* 666) – but this may merely be an extension of their talk in the cabman's shelter about the haggard streetwalker (*U* 633) – and 'Stephen's collapse' (*U* 666). Being knocked senseless by an irate Tommy is hardly the same as suffering a collapse, while a chance medley implies a mêlée (in its archaic meanings) and certainly a mingling of more than one (in any of its meanings). The fault once again is with the unreliability of language, which denotes more about the character of the person using it than the intention of his discourse. Stephen and Bloom have reached a point of euphemistic reference to whatever transpired on Beaver Street, and prefer to debate the causes of what they term Stephen's collapse. But their disputed causes are unrelated to Private Carr's fists:

> The collapse which Bloom ascribed to gastric inanition and certain chemical compounds of varying degree of adulteration and alcoholic strength, accelerated by mental exertion and the velocity of rapid circular motion in a relaxed atmosphere, Stephen

attributed to the reapparition of a matutinal cloud (perceived by both from two different points of observation, Sandycove and Dublin) at first no bigger than a woman's hand. (U 667)

Stephen's resilience may well have been marred by either his physical condition or the influence of a little cloud, while the First Cause of his collapse may still be attributable to the bellicose Harry Carr.

Far more significant for readers of Circe has been the symbolic victory won by Stephen Dedalus in his spirited attack on Bella Cohen's chandelier: the stage direction insists that '*He lifts his ashplant high with both hands and smashes the chandelier*', yet the Gasjet utters a rather pathetic 'Pwfungg!' (*U* 583). Bella of course maintains that 'The lamp's broken' and claims ten shillings damages, but Bloom relights the lamp, examines the '*crushed mauve purple shade*', and announces that 'Only the chimney's broken' (*U* 584), leaving only a shilling in payment. The grandiose gesture and its concomitant symbolic meaning, Stephen's exorcism of the shade of his dead mother, are deflated even within the context of the Circe chapter, yet the Stephen Dedalus who emerges from the experience seems soberer and calmer. Negative evidence (the curious incident of the dog in the night-time) carries weight, as we observe Stephen in Eumaeus and Ithaca, essentially relieved of the 'ghoul-and-corpse-chewer' rhetoric that had characterized him throughout the day.

Perhaps the clue to Stephen's sense of peace with his conscience can be found in one other carryover from closing moments of Circe to the closing moments of Eumaeus: sentimental Bloom, looking solicitously at the face of the comatose Stephen, muses, 'Face reminds me of his poor mother' (*U* 609), and then as they head toward Eccles Street, 'He looked sideways in a friendly fashion at the sideface of Stephen, image of his mother' (*U* 663). In the latter instance Stephen and Bloom are discussing music, and in the former Stephen is mumbling the words of 'Who Goes with Fergus', a song he remembers having sung to his dying mother (*U* 9). Mrs. Dedalus was undoubtedly a topic of discussion and thought as the two communed over cocoa in the Eccles Street kitchen. Stephen presents himself as 'eldest surviving male consubstantial heir of Simon Dedalus of Cork and Dublin and Mary, daughter of Richard and Christina Goulding' (*U* 682), and Bloom mentions his first having met Stephen 'in 1887, in the company of Stephen's mother, Stephen then being of the age of 5' (*U* 680). These reminiscences seem to evoke no strong reaction in Stephen, although the 'objectified' technique of the chapter may be responsible for masking emotional responses. Nonetheless, two significant items break through the restraints of the narrative method and reveal more than can be concealed: Bloom 'suppresses' any mention of the death of May Dedalus by considerately avoiding mentioning her funeral (*U* 695), and Stephen has a nostalgic memory of 'his mother Mary, wife of Simon Dedalus, in the kitchen of number twelve North Richmond street in the morning of the feast of Saint Francis Xavier 1898' (*U* 670), a milestone in Stephen's early life, when he could still feel the positive force of his religion in saving him from guilt and despair (see Chapter Three of *A Portrait of the Artist as a Young Man*).

A third significant incident caps the laying of the ghost of May Dedalus, but not without an equivocal aspect. Our last glimpse of Stephen in Bloom's back garden has him listening to the chimes tolling the hour from St. George's Church. Although to Bloom they once again echo the death knell for Paddy Dignam in a tone of gentle mockery. '*Heigho, heigho*' (*U* 70, 704), for Stephen they return the litany for the dead that caused him such anguish in the morning:

> *Liliata rutilantium. Turma circumdet.*
> *Iubilantium te virginum. Chorus excipiat.*
> (*U* 704, see also *U* 10)

But as Stephen fades from view, no invective follows that litany as did on the tower gunrest that morning ('Ghoul! Chewer of corpses! / No mother. Let me be and let me live' – *U* 10). If we read the intaglio for the cameo, and no dog has barked in the night-time, the post-Circean Stephen may have reached a point of stasis in the death-struggle with his mother's ghost, evidence of an event in Circe that has lasting reverberations throughout the closure of *Ulysses*.

NOTES

1   William Freeman, *Everyman's Dictionary of Fictional Characters,* revised by Fred Urquhart (London: J.M. Dent, 1963), pp. 1, 4, 12.
2   James Joyce, *Ulysses* (New York: Random House, 1961), p. 617. Subsequent references will appear in the text preceded by '*U*'.
3   (New York: Oxford University Press, 1962).

4   *James Joyce: The Citizen and the Artist* (Stanford, Cal.: Stanford University Press, 1977), p. 281.

5   Don Gifford, in *Notes for Joyce* (New York: E.P. Dutton, 1974), p. 309, speculates that the Mendelssohn in question may either be the composer or his illustrious Jewish grandfather, Moses Mendelssohn. The latter would destroy the comic juxtaposition. In another compilation of 'anapocryphal illustrious sons of the law and children of a selected or rejected race', Felix Mendelssohn is again coupled with Spinoza in an interesting quartette: 'Felix Bartholdy Mendelssohn (composer), Baruch Spinoza (philosopher), Mendoza (pugilist), Ferdinand Lassalle (reformer, duellist)' (*U* 687). Both references to Moses Mendelssohn in *Ulysses* include his potent given name (*U* 495, 687).

6   *Official Directory of Dublin* (Dublin: Alexander Thom's, 1904), pp. 2068, 2080. Where the habit of confusing the Burton with the Bailey started is difficult to determine. Richard M. Kain had it exact as far back as 1947 in *Fabulous Voyager* (Chicago: University of Chicago Press, 1947), p. 273, But William York Tindall in *A Reader's Guide to James Joyce* (New York: Farrar, Straus and Giroux, 1959), p. 172, has it wrong, as does the Bailey's own pamphlet: 'James Joyce refers to the Bailey in 'Ulysses' under the name Burtons. He used the Bailey as the locale for the Lestrygonian episode' – Ulick O'Connor, *The Bailey: The Story of a Famous Tavern* (Dublin: The Bailey Ltd., 1968), p. 8. A recent transmittal can be found in William Borders, 'In Praise of Ireland's Giants on a Literary Tour of Dublin,' *New York Times* Travel Section (Sunday, May 18, 1980), p. 22: 'the Bailey restaurant across the street ("Dirty eaters," Bloom thought).'

7   Richard Ellmann, *James Joyce* (New York: Oxford University Press, 1959), p. 386; Robert M. Adams, *op. cit.*, pp. 35–40; Stanley Sultan, *The Argument of Ulysses* (Columbus: Ohio State University Press, 1964), pp. 431–33; David Hayman, 'The Imperial Molly', *Approaches to Ulysses*, eds. Thomas F. Staley and Bernard Benstock (Pittsburgh: University of Pittsburgh Press, 1970), pp. 112–15.

8   See Shari Benstock, 'The Evasion Principle: A Search for Survivors in *Ulysses*', *Modern Fiction Studies,* 24 (Summer 1978), pp. 159–79.

9   'Bloom as a Modern Epic Hero', *Critical Inquiry*, 3 (Spring 1977), 596.

10 Raleigh, pp. 595–86.

11 Raleigh, pp. 592–93.

12 (Cambridge, Mass.: Harvard University Press, 1976), pp. 4, 9, 12, 19.

13 French, pp. 136–37.

14 French, pp. 55, 94.

15 A glance at Joyce's schema for *Ulysses* indicates immediately that he devised his chapters as discreetly separate entities.

16 *A Topographical Guide to James Joyce's Ulysses* (Colchester, England: A Wake Newslitter Press, 1975), p. 26.

17 French, pp. 16, 18, 21.

18 French, p. 180.

JOHN EGLINTON AS SOCRATES: A STUDY OF 'SCYLLA AND CHARYBDIS'

VIVIAN MERCIER

I

No doubt every devoted Joycean has a particular preference among the episodes of *Ulysses*; I certainly have. Non-Joyceans, on the other hand, presumably are left without a choice: all they know of *Ulysses* is 'Penelope', and they assume that the rest of the book closely resembles Molly Bloom's odorous monologue. My own particular favourite, for a great variety of reasons, is 'Scylla and Charybdis'. This essay will put forward a number of those reasons, but I suppose the overriding one has to do with Irish cultural chauvinism. I resent those critics who perform a kind of Caesarean section with Joyce, ripping him from the womb of Irish tradition generally and the Irish Literary Revival in particular. No passage in Joyce's work refutes them more effectively than 'Scylla and Charybdis'. The scene of this episode, according to Joyce's own schema, is 'The Library', but it is not just any library: we find ourselves in the Assistant Librarian's office in the National Library of Ireland. The art with which the episode is concerned is Literature. A number of the great figures in world literature are mentioned, and Shakespeare, of course, is examined in detail throughout: nevertheless, by far the largest national group of living authors referred to is Irish.

Let me call the roll briefly, beginning with those who in 1904 – the Abbey Theatre was to open in December of that year – were already making the English-speaking world aware of the resurgence of Irish literature. W.B. Yeats, J.M. Synge, Lady Gregory, George Moore (and his cousin and collaborator Edward Martyn), Douglas Hyde and Padraic Colum, besides being freely alluded to, are sometimes quoted and/or parodied as well. Lesser figures belonging to their movement are also named: James Sullivan Starkey ('Seumas O'Sullivan'), poet and bibliophile; A.E.'s co-worker Susan Mitchell; Fred Ryan, a journalist who wrote one play; George Roberts, better known as a publisher than as a poet; and the mysterious 'Piper'.[1] Participants in the informal symposium on Shakespeare, besides Joyce himself as Stephen and the poet Oliver Gogarty as Buck Mulligan, include the N.L.I. Librarian, T.W. Lyster; his Assistant Librarian, W.K. Magee; and the Keeper of Irish Manuscripts, R.I. Best. Magee was known as an essayist and poet under the pseudonym of 'John Eglinton'; his equally pseudonymous friend George Russell ('A.E.') – poet, playwright, editor, theosophist and organiser of agricultural co-operatives – also takes part. Among those engaged in the revival of the Irish language along with Hyde or in the preservation of its early texts along with Best, the following are mentioned: T. O'Neill Russell; Dr. George Sigerson, translator as well as eminent physician; and Father Patrick Dinneen (misspelt 'Dineen'), editor and lexicographer. Oscar Wilde was already dead in 1904, but Bernard Shaw, Frank Harris, and Professor Edward Dowden of Trinity College, Dublin, earn mention as Irishmen who, like Moore and Wilde, had already won fame in the international literary world before the new Irish movement began to draw attention. Thomas Caulfield Irwin, an Irish imitator of Tennyson, had died in 1892, and therefore seems too old to have been a *chela* or disciple of A.E. James Stephens, later to become an important figure in the Literary Revival, had not yet begun writing his 'clever sketches' (192), let alone works of more weight. His earliest publications, in *Sinn Féin*, date from 1907.* Louis H. Victory, whose name is as authentic as that of his fellow poet Lizzie Twigg in an earlier episode (165), seems to have been included only as an example of the poetasters who haunt the fringes of every new movement. Finally, Stephen MacKenna, at this time a foreign correspondent, would eventually win a different kind of fame as author of the modern translation of Plotinus' *Enneads* so much admired by Yeats. This list of Irish men and women of letters, nominated by a grudging contemporary, seems from the vantage point of 1982 entirely worthy of comparison with a team of two dozen writers similarly picked from any other country in the world *circa* 1904.

Though they may appear rambling enough at first, the thirty-five pages of 'Scylla and Charybdis' prove on closer examination to be among the most tightly packed with meaning in the whole of prose literature. They present several of the most persistent themes in

---

* The attribution of 'The Greatest Miracle', signed 'S' in the *United Irishman*, 16 Sept. 1905, to Stephens is a *canard*: Seumas O'Sullivan wrote it and republished it in *Essays and Recollections* (Dublin: Talbot Press, 1944), pp. 141–43.

Ulysses almost simultaneously, so closely woven together that the reader is not allowed to lose sight of any for more than a few moments at a time. The most important theme – so important that it might be called the key to *Ulysses* – is the relationship between art and life, more specifically between Shakespeare's art and Shakespeare's life. Stephen Dedalus argues that these were very intimately related indeed. What gives his exposition an intensity rarely to be found in academic discourse is his creator's secret purpose: *Joyce is giving himself away.* This man who was so reserved that he wished all his men friends to address him as 'Joyce' rather than 'Jim' or 'James', and who so rarely showed his feelings in private life except in those extraordinary love letters to Nora Barnacle, is pressing upon the readers of *Ulysses* clues to his own mystery. Those who accuse Richard Ellmann of the 'biographical fallacy' because he interprets Joyce's works in terms of his life deliberately ignore the obvious fact that Joyce makes Stephen joyfully embrace the alleged fallacy in his account of Shakespeare. It is true that when John Eglinton asks, 'Do you believe your own theory?' Stephen 'promptly' (*too* promptly, perhaps?) answers 'No' (213–14). But in any case Eglinton is referring specifically to what he calls 'a French triangle' (213), the theory that Shakespeare was cuckolded by one of his brothers. Nobody who takes part in the discussion, not even A.E. ('But this prying into the family life of a great man, Russell began impatiently' [189]), seriously questions the existence of a relationship between a writer's life and his work. The novelty of Stephen's analysis of *Hamlet* lies in his identification of Shakespeare not with Prince Hamlet but with Hamlet's father, the ghost.

> Is it possible that the player Shakespeare, a ghost by absence, and in the vesture of buried Denmark, a ghost by death, speaking his own words to his own son's name (had Hamnet Shakespeare lived he would have been prince Hamlet's twin), is it possible, I want to know, or probable that he did not draw or foresee the logical conclusion of those premises: you are the dispossessed son: I am the murdered father: your mother is the guilty queen, Ann Shakespeare, born Hathaway? (189)

My reading of this passage is that Joyce is pressing us to give up the facile identification of himself with Stephen Dedalus that he must have known most readers of *A Portrait* would make; instead, we are to see Bloom as a truer projection of the mature Joyce.

67

This awareness of Bloom's similarities to Joyce has become a commonplace of criticism since the publication of Ellmann's *James Joyce* in 1959 and subsequently of the second and third volumes of the *Letters,* which included most of the Joyce-Nora correspondence. What I am concerned to stress is that Joyce, using the Shakespeare analogy, had himself urged this view upon his readers, some of whom at least must have been able to take a hint. The earliest publication to link Joyce with Bloom that I know of is a 1948 article in French by Michel Butor,[2] but I remember startling a successor of Edward Dowden, the late Professor H.O. White, by expressing such a view as a graduate student in the early 1940s. I also remember expounding 'Scylla and Charybdis' along these lines in a City College of New York classroom before 1959. I don't claim any special clairvoyance: I was simply discovering what Joyce had put there for his readers to find.

I have run ahead of myself, skipping over a number of necessary steps in the argument: before identifying Joyce with Bloom, one ought first to present the reasons for identifying Joyce with Shakespeare. An untutored but intuitive reader might in fact snatch up the very first hint. On the second page of the episode Joyce makes John Eglinton say, 'Our young Irish bards . . . have yet to create a figure which the world will set beside Saxon Shakespeare's Hamlet' (185). It was the kind of remark Eglinton was likely to make, yet I think the words are entirely Joyce's own. Whereas his fellow Irishman Bernard Shaw constantly and openly invited comparison with Shakespeare, Joyce in his own secretive way is here issuing a similar challenge: eighteen years after 1904, he feels confident that *he* has created such a character – not Stephen Dedalus in his 'Hamlet hat' but Leopold Bloom. Once he has claimed equality with Shakespeare, it is but a short step to claiming identity.

Having repeated in *A Portrait of the Artist As a Young Man*, with Stephen as mouthpiece, Flaubert's axiom that the artist must not appear in his work any more than God does in his Creation, Joyce had come to realise that in the last analysis he had no subject matter other than his own consciousness. One may suspect also that his reticence was the obverse side of an unconscious or even conscious impulse toward exhibitionism. In a letter to his brother Stanislaus, he had reproached Oscar Wilde for revealing so little of himself in *The Picture of Dorian Gray*;[3] almost certainly he did not then know Wilde's *The Portrait of Mr. W.H.*, mentioned with such approval by Mr. Best in 'Scylla and Charybdis' (198). There, Wilde did reveal his homosexuality by attributing it to Shakespeare, just as Joyce reveals his own fear/desire of being made a cuckold by attributing it to Shakespeare and to Bloom.

In one of his references to Shakespeare's supposed obsession with wifely infidelity, Stephen casts a novel light on the difficulty of finding an author in his work: 'He [Shakespeare] goes back, weary of the creation he has piled up to hide him from himself, an old dog licking an old sore' (197). In other words, if the author does not appear in his work, if God is not found in his Creation, that does not mean that he is not there: he is not *absent from* but *hidden by* his work. Joyce is inviting his readers to an odd game of hide-and-seek, where we will search for him until he catches us.

Once we have accepted the analogy between Joyce and Shakespeare, we can hardly refuse to accept the analogy between Shakespeare and God; from this there follows logically the analogy between Joyce and God. John Eglingon reminds his hearers of Alexandre Dumas *père*'s remark: 'After God Shakespeare has created most' (212). Later, Stephen stands this idea on its head by comparing God unfavourably with Shakespeare, calling Him the playwright who wrote the folio of this world and wrote it badly (He gave us light first and the sun two days later)' (213). This witticism is a picturesque way of recapturing our attention for another major theme of 'Scylla and Charybdis' – the analogy between divine creation and artistic creation. The words 'create' and 'creation' figure frequently in the episode, though Joyce in his letters seems very sceptical about applying them to literary work and denies that he himself has any inventive powers at all. In the words of the Apostles' Creed, 'God the Father Almighty' is identified as 'Maker of Heaven and Earth': similarly, in 'Scylla and Charybdis' the creation theme is intertwined with that of the relationship between father and son – not merely God the Father and God the Son but all human fathers and sons.

We should pause here to consider why the nature of Jesus' relationship to God the Father is so frequently discussed throughout *Ulysses*. Is it because Joyce saw himself as a betrayed and suffering Christ figure? Stephen is certainly prone to identify himself with Christ, both in *Ulysses* and *A Portrait*, but I think the chief reason lies elsewhere: after all, the primary model for *Ulysses* is the *Odyssey*, not the Gospels. Now, Telemachus is unequivocally presented as Ulysses' son: to suggest any other paternity would have desecrated the image of the ever-faithful Penelope. But Stephen,

69

the Telemachus figure in *Ulysses*, is most emphatically not Bloom's physical son: an entire novel, already several years in print, stands there to prove it. Joyce could of course have abandoned the Stephen Dedalus of *A Portrait* and invented a new character – perhaps only Stephen under another name – to be Bloom's long-lost son in *Ulysses*. But his temperament, his need to reveal himself, did not allow this. Instead, he must look for a way to suggest that Stephen both was and was not Bloom's son: one must admit that, given his Catholic upbringing, he did not have to look very far. Jesus both was and was not Joseph's son, as in a sense he both was and was not the son of God. For Joseph, read Simon Dedalus, and for God the Father, read Bloom.

It is perhaps out of character that Stephen, who professes to have rejected the Church, should talk and meditate at such lengths in *Ulysses* about the Sonship of Jesus, but this habit of his helps the reader to keep in mind that there are sons and Sons:

> Fatherhood, in the sense of conscious begetting, is unknown to man. It is a mystical estate, an apostolic succession, from only begetter to only begotten. On that mystery . . . the church is founded and founded irremovably because founded, like the world . . . upon the void. Upon incertitude, upon unlikelihood. (207)

Stephen's obsession with the nature of Christ's Sonship has led him to examine the views of heretics on the subject. One of these, mentioned in 'Scylla and Charybdis', is 'Sabellius, the African, subtlest heresiarch of all the beasts of the field, [who] held that the Father was Himself His Own Son' (208). We must not ignore Sabellius – although Stephen tells us that Thomas Aquinas refuted him (208) – since his doctrine suggests the possibility that Bloom and Stephen are one and the same person. As indeed they are, for they are both aspects of Joyce.

Bloom resembles Stephen's portrait of Shakespeare much more closely than Stephen himself does, for he has a dead son, a beloved daughter, and an unfaithful wife. (Of these, Joyce in 1922 was only sure that he had a beloved daughter.) Also, Bloom is a Jew by race though not by religion; Stephen at one point tries to prove that Shakespeare was a Jew. Finally, Bloom is a ghost: at least, he haunts the episode like one, appearing first as a visiting card offered by an attendant, then as 'A patient silhouette . . . listening' to the 'voluble'

70

Lyster (200). A moment later, Buck Mulligan remembers having just seen him 'over in the museum when I went to hail the foamborn Aphrodite. . . . His pale Galilean eyes were upon her mesial groove. Venus Kallipyge. O, the thunder of those loins!' (201). He makes another silent appearance at the end of the episode.

After Stephen has presented his view of *Hamlet* at some length, and after the traditional view that Shakespeare is Prince Hamlet has been maintained against him, John Eglinton offers to resolve the conflict with a synthesis:

> Judge Eglinton summed up.
> – The truth is midway, he affirmed. He is the ghost and the prince. He is all in all.
> – He is, Stephen said. The boy of act one is the mature man of act five. All in all. In *Cymbeline*, in *Othello*, he is bawd and cuckold. (212)

Having pursued the analogical method thus far, I seem obliged to accept Stephen's change of front, which implies that Joyce is not only Bloom and Stephen, but everybody else in *Ulysses* as well, not excluding Pisser Burke. This position I find untenable, however, and in fact no one in his right mind would claim that Joyce's life experience or his personality exactly parallels that of Leopold Bloom. What we now know, from the letters and from Ellmann's biography, is that Joyce's paternal and conjugal feelings, not to mention his sexual temperament, were in many ways similar to Bloom's. In the later episodes of *Ulysses* he vicariously reveals that temperament, having given his readers, in 'Scylla and Charybdis', a strong hint about how to interpret them.

III

John Eglinton's affirmation that 'The Truth is midway' reminds us of the episode's original form in the *Odyssey*. Ulysses passed between Scylla and Charybdis, but he did not steer through the exact mid-point of the channel: instead, he went a little closer to Scylla's rock than to the whirlpool of Charybdis, preferring to lose six comrades rather than his entire ship and crew. Joyce offers three different correspondences for this episode in his schema: the rock is Stratford, Aristotle, Dogma, whereas the whirlpool is London, Plato, Mysticism. The respective equivalents for Ulysses are

71

Shakespeare, Socrates and Jesus. There is much about Jesus in the
episode, and plenty of dogma as well as heresy, but specifically
Christian mysticism is hard to find: perhaps theosophy, which is
ridiculed in more than one passage, stands for mysticism in general.
The idea that Christ represents a middle way between mysticism
and dogma seems not to occur elsewhere in Joyce: its place in the
history of ideas and in his work deserves to be investigated. Shakespeare's dilemma – having to choose between far-from-tranquil
domesticity in Stratford and the expense of spirit in London's waste
of shame – is made abundantly clear in the episode.

The Aristotle-Socrates-Plato analogy seems baffling, however,
until the key to it is found in Francis Bacon's *The Wisdom of the
Ancients*. Joyce actually owned *two* copies of a cheap reprint of this
English translation of a Latin work.[4] Bacon, like Joyce, sought and
found modern applications for classical myths: in his chapter on
Scylla and Charybdis, he interpreted them as 'the Rocks of Distinc-
tions and the Gulfs of Universalities; which two are famous for the
Wrack both of Wits and Arts'.[5] 'Distinctions' or definitions suggest
Aristotle at once, while 'Universalities' or universals suggest Plato.
Stephen mentally outlines his own Aristotelianism, in opposition to
the Neo-Platonism of A.E. and the theosophists, as follows:

> Unsheathe your [Stephen's] dagger definitions. Horseness is the
> whatness of allhorse. Streams of tendency and eons they wor-
> ship. God: noise in the street: very peripatetic. Space: what you
> damn well have to see. (186)

A.E. and his disciples are associated with images of the sea at
flood-tide and of whirling. At one point, while A.E. is speaking of
King Lear, Stephen mentally quotes, or rather misquotes,[6] from
A.E.'s *Deirdre*:

> *Flow over them with your waves and with your waters, Mananaan,
> Mananaan MacLir.* (189)

A little later, he thinks again of A.E.:

> Gulfer of souls, engulfer. Hesouls, shesouls, shoals of souls.
> Engulfed with wailing creecries, whirled, whirling, they bewail.
> (192)

If Stephen represents Aristotle, and A.E. Plato, who then stands for Socrates? I think we must conclude that John Eglinton does, although at one point he speaks up on Plato's behalf, scornfully calling Aristotle 'a model schoolboy'. It is Eglinton who consistently uses the Socratic method, addressing his most searching questions to Stephen, and it is he who best fits Joyce's conception of Socrates' position by proclaiming that the truth is midway.

Eglinton, in discussing Shakespeare's relationship with Ann Hathaway, draws a parallel between Shakespeare and Socrates:

> – A shrew, John Eglinton said shrewdly, is not a useful portal of discovery, one should imagine. What useful discovery did Socrates learn from Xanthippe?
> – Dialectic, Stephen answered. (190)

Joyce himself used the word 'dialectic' in his schema to describe the technique of the episode. If we omit those passages of 'Scylla and Charybdis' that take place in Stephen's mind, the rest becomes a recognisable twentieth-century imitation of a Platonic dialogue. Just in case we haven't noticed this fact for ourselves, Joyce gives our defective intelligences a pretty firm nudge:

> – Are you going to write it? Mr Best asked. You ought to make it a dialogue, don't you know, like the Platonic dialogues Wilde wrote. (214)

Best is speaking to Stephen about his theory, but Joyce is telling us what he himself has been up to, and at the same time, perhaps, issuing a challenge to Wilde, whose brilliant dialogues in *The Critic as Artist* and *The Decay of Lying* are hard to rival. I think we have to acknowledge that Joyce surpasses Wilde, if only because he introduces so many speakers, where Wilde limits himself to only two. Joyce refers, as far as I can see, to only one dialogue of Plato's, the *Phaedo,* which he mentions twice. First, disparagingly:

> – That model schoolboy [Aristotle], Stephen said, would find Hamlet's musings about the afterlife of his princely soul, the improbable, insignificant and undramatic monologue, as shallow as Plato's. (186)

Later, Stephen thinks of 'Phedo's toyable fair hair' (215), alluding

73

to a passage in which Phaedo describes how Socrates 'laid his hand on my head and gathered up the curls on my neck.'[7]

References to homosexuality occur frequently in the episode. Is Joyce suggesting that he himself, like Shakespeare and Socrates, has homosexual leanings? Perhaps, but when one is writing about Shakespeare and the *Sonnets* and using a format borrowed from Plato, mention of homosexuality hardly seems gratuitous. More arbitrary is Buck Mulligan's insistence that Bloom has a homosexual desire for Stephen:

> Did you see his eye? He looked upon you to lust after you. I fear thee, ancient mariner. O, Kinch, thou art in peril. Get thee a breechpad. (217)

Bloom, we may suppose, is looking at Stephen with a concern that, far from being lustful, is quasi-paternal.

If Joyce is consciously imitating a particular dialogue of Plato's, I think we can rule out the *Phaedo* at once. The conversation in the library office has little or nothing to do with survival after death. Mulligan's uproarious arrival and subsequent bawdy interruptions give us the correct clue, I believe: Joyce's model is the *Symposium*. Mulligan plays the role of Alcibiades, and to some extent that of Aristophanes as well. It cannot be denied that the nature of love, which is the overriding theme of Plato's dialogue, also has great importance in 'Scylla and Charybdis'. Almost every conceivable variety of love is mentioned in the episode, usually in connection with Shakespeare, beginning with his dilemma 'between conjugal love and its chaste delights and scortatory love and its foul pleasures' (201). Stephen mentally recalls some of his own foul pleasures with whores in Paris: '*Encore vingt sous. Nous ferons de petites cochonneries. Minette? Tu veux?*' (201) Shakespeare's supposed homosexuality is dealt with at length: 'As an Englishman, you mean, John sturdy Eglinton put in, he loved a lord' (202). Incest is described, in the words of St. Thomas Aquinas, as 'an avarice of the emotions' (205). This leads on quite logically to a more careful examination of the nature of love between parent and child:

> *Amor matris*, subjective and objective genitive, may be the only true thing in life. Paternity may be a legal fiction. Who is the father of any son that any son should love him or he any son? (207)

74

Amor matris means both the love of the child for the mother and that of the mother for the child. The one impossible perversion, according to Stephen, is incest between father and son:

> – They are sundered by a bodily shame so steadfast that the criminal annals of the world, stained with all other incests and bestialities, hardly record its breach. Sons with mothers, sires with daughters, lesbic sisters, loves that dare not speak their name, nephews with grandmothers, jailbirds with keyholes, queens with prize bulls. (207)

What a catalogue that is of the diversity of sexual self-expression! Despite all Shakespeare's amatory vicissitudes and his supposed fear of being cuckolded by his brothers, Stephen imagines a reconciliation between him and Ann Hathaway that is comfortingly normal and domestic: it takes place at the birth of 'his daughter's child' (195). Joyce's dialogue on love does not make as deep a philosophical penetration into the subject as Plato's, being more concerned with citing diverse examples of the passion than with analysing its nature. Nevertheless, both discussions end inconclusively, because of the disruptive influence of Mulligan in 'Scylla and Charybdis' and of Alcibiades in the *Symposium*.

IV

Having insisted that Joyce had the temerity to match himself against Shakespeare, I must assume that he was also measuring himself against his Irish contemporaries. The fact that neither Yeats, Synge nor Moore is a participant in the discussion in the National Library does not prove that they are above challenge, but only that they were not likely to have been present. The participants other than Stephen and Mulligan could be found in the Library most days of the week, three of them being employed there; the fourth, A.E., was a close friend of John Eglinton and apparently had a habit of dropping into his office. Lyster and Best, being scholars, are not regarded as rivals by Joyce, whereas he sets out to demolish A.E. by ridiculing and parodying what he knows of his work. He owned and had read at least part of *The Candle of Vision*, first published in 1918, because he draws on it in the paragraphs early in 'Scylla and Charybdis' which make fun of theosophy. A.E. had written, 'at the calling of the Ineffable Name the Holy Breath rises as a flame'.[8]

75

Joyce uses the phrases 'Holy Breath' and 'Name Ineffable' (185). In the 'Circe' episode A.E. appears as Mananaan Mac Lir, the Celtic sea god, uttering the mysterious syllables 'Hek! Wal! Ak! Lub! Mor! Ma!' (510). Joyce found these in the chapter 'Ancient Intuitions' of *The Candle of Vision:* A.E. claimed to have discovered intuitively that they were part of the universal primeval language of mankind.[9] When Stephen quotes A.E.'s poetry, one wonders if Joyce has deliberately chosen two very inept lines:

> *What of all the will to do?*
> *It has vanished long ago.* (206)

Weak as they are, they have more rhythm than those quoted from A.E.'s fellow theosophist, Louis H. Victory:

> *In quintessential triviality*
> *For years in this fleshcase a shesoul dwelt.* (192)[10]

When Lyster remarks that 'Mr Russell, rumour has it, is gathering together a sheaf of our younger poets' verses' (192), he – or rather Joyce – is guilty of an anachronism. *New Songs: A Lyric Selection Made by A.E. from Poems by Padraic Colum, Eva Gore-Booth, Thomas Keohler, Susan Mitchell, Seumas O'Sullivan, George Roberts, and Ella Young,* had been published in March 1904, three months before Bloomsday. Stephen listens with rapt attention to the chatter about this book, which mentions 'Young Colum and Starkey. George Roberts', and 'Miss Mitchell's joke about Moore and Martyn' (192). Was Joyce piqued at not being included in *New Songs*, although A.E. had accepted three of his short stories for the *Irish Homestead*? If so, why was he not equally hostile to John Eglinton, who had accepted a poem of his for *Dana* but rejected an essay entitled 'A Portrait of the Artist' as 'incomprehensible'.[11] Joyce's essay was in fact no more cryptic than Eglinton's maiden venture, *Two Essays on the Remnant*, and may have been modelled on it.

In order to understand the respect with which Stephen treats John Eglinton throughout the episode – a respect that Joyce appears to share, despite Mulligan's innuendoes – one has to look beyond 1904 to a book Eglinton published in 1917, *Anglo-Irish Essays.* Among the essays and reviews he then reprinted was 'Irish Books', first published in the *Irish Review,* 1911. Its chief burden was that there were *no* Irish books, that the Revival or Renaissance or whatever one liked to call it was all shadow and no substance. In 1917 he added an apologetic postscript to this outburst of spleen:

> This was of course a sorry account of the 'Irish Literary Renascence'; the collected poems of Mr. Yeats, AE, and others, Synge's plays, etc., will doubtless be called 'books' by generations of Irish readers. Mr. James Stephen's lively and delectable vein had in 1911 only begun to flow, and Mr. James Joyce had not yet published his highly instructive studies in the life of those young men who have chiefly to be reckoned with nowadays in arranging or forecasting the future of Ireland. The anticipation in the final paragraph might seem to have had a partial fulfilment in Mr. George Moore's *Hail and Farewell*.[12]

The shadows of the dead young men who had fought in the Easter Rising of 1916 fall across this paragraph, but it must have given great pleasure to Joyce, who was not accustomed to such praise from his countrymen, very few of whom had yet bothered to read *Dubliners* or *A Portrait*; Eglinton seems to have read both.

Many readers of *Ulysses* may feel that even though Eglinton is paid the compliment of being equated with Socrates and treated as a foeman worthy of Stephen's 'dagger definitions', he still receives pretty severe handling: the constant harping on his bachelorhood and Protestantism becomes especially tiresome. Nevertheless, Joyce has paid him a silent compliment that carries more weight than the overt ones: he has borrowed from him, as he did from A.E., but without making his creditor look ridiculous. Part of what Stephen overhears when the younger poets are being discussed can be traced back to the last paragraph of the 'Irish Books' essay and to the last sentence of its postscript:

> Did you hear Miss Mitchell's joke about Moore and Martyn? That Moore is Martyn's wild oats? Awfully clever, isn't it? They remind one of don Quixote and Sancho Panza. Our national epic has yet to be written, Dr Sigerson says. Moore is the man for it. A knight of the rueful countenance here in Dublin. With a saffron kilt? O'Neill Russell? O, yes, he must speak the grand old tongue. And his Dulcinea? (192)

John Eglinton had written:

we have a fancy that appearances in modern Ireland point to a writer of the type of Cervantes rather than to an idealising poet or romance writer. A hero as loveable as the great Knight of the Rueful Countenance might be conceived, who in some back street of Dublin had addled his brains with brooding over Ireland's wrongs. . . . We can conceive him issuing forth, fresh-hearted as a child at the age of fifty, with glib and saffron-coloured kilt, to realise and incidentally to expose the ideals of present-day Ireland. What scenes might not be devised at village inns arising out of his refusal to parley with landlords in any but his own few words of Gaelic speech. . . . His Dulcinea would be – who but Kathleen ni Houlihan herself, who really is no more like what she is taken for than the maiden of Toboso.[13]

It was only after the fact that Eglinton drew the parallel between Moore's *Hail and Farewell* (1911–14) and *Don Quixote*, but Joyce has him anticipate it in 1904.

Eglinton's mention of Moore draws our attention to an important sub-text of 'Scylla and Charybdis', and indeed of *Ulysses* as a whole. With judicious excisions the scene in the Library might be made to resemble many dialogue passages in *Hail and Farewell*, especially those where Moore has A.E. and/or John Eglinton as interlocutors. Does anybody imagine that *Ulysses* would have taken exactly the form it did had Moore never published *Hail and Farewell* or had he been hampered in doing so by libel actions? Joyce would at the very least have been much more circumspect in using the names of living people if Moore had not brought off his *tour de force*.

It is tempting to view *Ulysses* as an Irish version of *Don Quixote*, with Stephen as the Don and Bloom as Sancho, but one is left asking 'And his Dulcinea?' Besides, Bloom is really a mixture of Quixote and Panza – without any illusions about *his* Dulcinea. When Joyce wrote 'Our national epic has yet to be written', he undoubtedly added mentally 'and I am now writing it'. Eglinton's idea for a comic romance was a good one, but Joyce's for a comic epic was even better.

V

Every discussion of *Ulysses* must eventually come back to Bloom, and that is what 'Scylla and Charybdis' itself does. In the excited and eloquent peroration of his argument, Stephen says of Shakespeare:

He found in the world without as actual what was in his world within as possible. Maeterlinck says: *If Socrates leaves his house today he will find the sage seated on his doorstep. If Judas go forth tonight it is to Judas his steps will tend.* Every life is many days, day after day. We walk through ourselves, meeting robbers, ghosts, giants, old men, young men, wives, widows, brothers-in-love. But always meeting ourselves. (213)

Here, then, is what *Ulysses* in the last analysis is about: a man meeting himself. When Stephen and Bloom well and truly meet in the 'Eumaeus' and 'Ithaca' episodes, nothing very much happens. There is no great recognition scene like that in the *Odyssey* where Ulysses and Telemachus throw themselves into each other's arms and weep floods of tears. Nor is there any great change in Stephen or Bloom as a result of their hours together: they talk, but mostly at cross purposes; they part without any certainty that they will meet again. In the symbolism of 'Ithaca' they are comets whose paths cross at the bidding of forces beyond their control. Yet Stephen, unaware, has 'found in the world without as actual what was in his world within as possible'. He has had a glimpse of what he may be like at Bloom's age, but this means, as yet, nothing to him, because he has not so far found a woman in whose love he can trust as he could in his mother's. In 'Scylla and Charybdis', Stephen explicates *Venus and Adonis* in his own unique way:

> The greyeyed goddess who bends over the boy Adonis, stooping to conquer, as prologue to the swelling act, is a boldfaced Stratford wench who tumbles in a cornfield a lover younger than herself. (191)

Thus far he has been speaking aloud, but the next two lines record his private thoughts:

> And my turn? When?
> Come! (191)

We now know that on 16 June 1904 Joyce's own turn had come: that evening he 'went walking' for the first time with Nora Barnacle. In Ellmann's words,

> On June 16 he entered into relation with the world around him

79

and left behind him the loneliness he had felt since his mother's death. . . . June 16 was the sacred day that divided Stephen Dedalus, the insurgent youth, from Leopold Bloom, the complaisant husband.[14]

Thanks to *Ulysses*, however, that day does not divide them but unites them forever in the gallery of archetypes that great literature holds in trust for the world.

'Scylla and Charybdis' has a final felicity to offer us on its last page, the first reciprocal acknowledgement of each other's existence made by Bloom and Stephen on this day of days. They have already been in each other's vicinity three times – in 'Hades', 'Aeolus', and the present episode – though Stephen was not aware of Bloom in 'Hades'. Now, though without exchanging a word, they gesture to each other.

> About to pass through the doorway, feeling one behind, he [Stephen] stood aside.
> Part. The moment is now. Where then? If Socrates leave his house today, if Judas go forth tonight. Why? That lies in space which I in time must come to, ineluctably.
> My will: his [Mulligan's] will that fronts me. Seas between.
> A man passed out between them, bowing, greeting.
> – Good day again, Buck Mulligan said. (217)

Thus Stephen and Mulligan momentarily become Scylla and Charybdis, while Ulysses/Bloom passes safely between. The last word is left to Shakespeare, a quotation from *Cymberline* which may suggest Ulysses' gratitude – and Joyce's – at having negotiated a difficult passage:

> *Laud we the gods*
> *And let our crooked smokes climb to their nostrils*
> *From our bless'd altars*. (218)[15]

NOTES

1   *Ulysses* (New York: Random House, 1961), p. 191. All further references to this work appear in the text. 'Piper' is presumably W.J. Stanton Pyper, a friend of John Eglinton, who wrote some articles for Arthur Griffiths' *United Irishman* under the pseudonym 'Lugh'. See *Letters to W.B. Yeats*, ed. Richard J. Finne-

ran, George Mills Harper and William M. Murphy (London: Macmillan Press, 1977), I, 80–81.

2 'Petite croisière préliminaire à une reconnaissance de l'archipel Joyce' ['A Little Cruise Preliminary to a Reconnaissance of the Joyce Archipelago'] in *Répertoire: Études et conférences 1948–1959* (Paris: Les Éditions de Minuit, 1960), p. 205.

3 *Letters of James Joyce*, ed. Richard Ellmann (New York: Viking Press, 1966), II, 150. 'I can imagine the capital which Wilde's prosecuting counsel made out of certain parts of it. It is not very difficult to read between the lines. Wilde seems to have had some good intentions in writing it – some wish to put himself before the world – but the book is rather crowded with lies and epigrams. If he had had the courage to develop the allusions in the book it might have been better. I suspect he has done this in some privately-printed books.'

4 See Richard Ellmann, *The Consciousness of Joyce* (New York: Oxford Univ. Press, 1977), p. 99.

5 *The Essays . . . with the Wisdom of the Ancients,* ed. S.W. Singer (London: Bell and Daldy, 1857), p. 340.

6 Weldon Thornton, *Allusions in Ulysses* (Chapel Hill: Univ. of North Carolina Press, 1968), p. 164. This is an indispensable work for readers of *Ulysses* in general and 'Scylla and Charybdis' in particular, though there are errors and omissions. No doubt Professor Thornton is weary of being chided for his scepticism about the existence of O'Neill Russell: see *Allusions,* p. 172. There is a delightful sketch of the aging Celtic enthusiast by George Moore in *Hail and Farewell: Ave, Salve, Vale,* ed. Richard Allen Cave (Gerrards Cross, Bucks.: Colin Smythe, 1976), pp. 319–20.

7 Plato, *The Last Days of Socrates,* tr. Hugh Tredennick (Harmondsworth, Middlesex: Penguin Books, 1969), p. 143.

8 *The Candle of Vision* (1918; rpt. Wheaton, Illinois: Theosophical Publishing House, 1974), p. 133.

9 *The Candle of Vision,* pp. 129–30. 'Hek' is an error for 'Hel'.

10 Thornton identifies these two quotations, pp. 200 and 170.

11 Richard M. Kain and Robert E. Scholes, 'The First Version of Joyce's "Portrait" ', *Yale Review,* 49 (Spring 1960), 355.

12 *Anglo-Irish Essays* (Dublin: Talbot Press, 1917), p. 89.

13 *Anglo-Irish Essays,* pp. 87–88.

14 Richard Ellmann, *James Joyce* (New York: Oxford Univ. Press, 1959), p. 163.

15 At this distance in time, it is hard to remember how much I owe to William M. Schutte's brilliant *Joyce and Shakespeare* (New Haven: Yale Univ. Press, 1957). Certainly I learned a great deal from it about Bloom's resemblances to Shakespeare. Even at the time, though, I was disappointed – or perhaps relieved – that Schutte in his final chapter reached a conclusion quite different from mine. When I first read the passage just quoted in Ellmann, I could have said with Hamlet, 'O my prophetic soul!' Perhaps I ought to have published this article twenty years ago, but I have been using some of the material in teaching *Ulysses* for at least 25 years, besides giving three public lectures based on it during the past decade.

TWISTS OF THE TELLER'S TALE: *FINNEGANS WAKE*

JOHN PAUL RIQUELME

> ... the very being of writing
> (the meaning of the labor that constitutes
> it) is to keep the question *Who is speaking?*
> from ever being answered.
> – Roland Barthes, *S/Z*, section LIX

Although *Finnegans Wake* marks the end, both the conclusion and the teleology, of Joyce's writing, for a variety of reasons, critics have tended to treat the *Wake* as if it were relatively independent of his earlier works, even *Ulysses*. But this highly idiosyncratic narrative presents, at times in extravagantly extrapolated form, certain tendencies that are important in Joyce's early fiction, though not always as apparent there. The continuities involve Joyce's styles and his narrative structures, his representations of the artist and of consciousness, his metaphors of narration and of human experience, his linking of endings with origins. Joyce's concern with origins in the *Wake* and before it often takes the form of references to literary sources through allusion. Joyce's readers have long recognized him as a master of allusion. James S. Atherton's commentary, *The Books at the Wake: A Study of Literary Allusions in James Joyce's 'Finnegans Wake'*, published a quarter of a century ago, persuasively demonstrates Joyce's reliance on allusion in his final work.[1] With good reason, Atherton stresses Joyce's attempt to subsume the texts of other authors in our literary tradition within his own writing. Disturbed by this attempt, Atherton refers to it gingerly in various ways but typically as 'some odd idea'.[2] In my discussion of the *Wake*, I shall be exploring that odd idea's rationale, effects, and implications. Inevitably, the numerous allusions suggest Joyce's intense self-consciousness about the artifice of literature, a self-consciousness that has become a critical cliché. Rather than being explanatory, the cliché points to what needs explaining, not through the identifying of Joyce's sources but by interpreting the technique of allusion itself. To interpret that technique is to define Joyce's conception of the two activities most pertinent to the literary text as language: writing and reading.

Once we consider the *process* of alluding as well as the result of that process, the linking of writing with reading for Joyce becomes clear. No matter how often critics assert the symbolic nature of Joyce's works, his allusions are *not* symbolic in any easily defined way. Instead, they indicate the process of reading that was a crucial component of Joyce's acts of writing. We encounter implicitly again and again in Joyce's tales the image of the artist actively engaged in reading and re-using the literary tradition. Sometimes that image emerges in curious ways. Among the most curious is Joyce's propensity to allude to his own earlier writing in *Finnegans Wake*.³ The book is a veritable 'Aludin's Cove' (108.27), in which the thieving author plunders himself. Even the phrase 'Aludin's Cove', as Joyce uses it, reveals the tendency I have in mind. Here Joyce refers to *The Thousand and One Nights,* to Wyndham Lewis, and to *Ulysses*, since Lewis had said *Ulysses* was 'an Aladdin's cave of incredible bric-a-brac'.⁴ Joyce's transforming of the phrase makes Lewis' remark and, indirectly, Joyce's own earlier work, part of the narrative's bric-a-brac.⁵ In general, Joyce's allusions to *Ulysses* involve a similar layering of references. The superimposition is possible because *Ulysses* itself contains the network of allusions to Homer's *Odyssey* that critics have explored so thoroughly. By including *Ulysses* in *Finnegans Wake* through allusion, Joyce indicates the Homeric aspect of his late writing and the connection to his own earlier work. To begin investigating the Homeric nature of aesthetic creation in Joyce's fiction, it will be helpful to look first at the artist as character in the *Wake*.

Numerous passages of *Finnegans Wake* focus, though often not exclusively, on the process of artistic creation. Many of these passages concern either Shem the Penman or one of the letters that appear repeatedly during the narrative. In the *Wake*, Joyce adopts a protean narrating persona. This labile teller describes a character, Shem the Penman, who writes books that are the fictional equivalents of the author's books. As several passages suggest, these texts are self-representations of Shem. Through this curious, pseudonymous, fictional presentation of the author as Shem and of Shem as an author in *Finnegans Wake*, Joyce's narrator manipulates the complicated relationships among author, teller, and tale with comic intensity. He does so by focusing on the doubling of self that accompanies every act of narration, every adoption by an author of some persona as teller. We perceive the manipulation and doubling in the *Wake* in part because Joyce incongruously assigns his own works to Shem. By implication, Joyce's texts, like Shem's, including the *Wake* itself, are self-representations of the character who is an author *and* of the real author. As autobiographical fiction, then, the *Wake* extends and distinguishes itself from Joyce's other autobiographical narratives by invoking them and their writer. We shall want to probe the nature of the connections between the *Wake* and the earlier fiction as we explore Joyce's presentation of the artist. For Joyce to assign his own published works openly to a character is a new departure. In *A Portrait* and in *Ulysses*, Stephen Dedalus writes a villanelle, keeps a journal, composes some verse on the strand, and tells stories, but Joyce never published any of those works separately under his own name. He did, however, occasionally use the pseudonym 'Stephen Daedalus'. As we shall see, allusions to Joyce's published works in passages dealing with Shem the Penman are unmistakable. More specifically, Shem's writing, like at least one version of the recurring letter, resembles *Ulysses* in striking ways. Joyce emphasizes his connection to the Penman through the name he assigns him. Joyce's persona as writer becomes linked to his character by the shared comparison with Jim the Penman, the notorious forger.

While the tale presents character, in this case as an author, it also constitutes a representation of the teller as the real author's narrating persona. Because the artist's self-representation frames the character as artist, the reader can gauge the teller's own activities by comparison with the actions of the character. The interlocking configurations of teller with characters resemble the complicated framing and linking frequently presented by the narrating voice in the *Wake* in passages reminiscent of 'The House that Jack Built'.[6] With respect to Shem the Penman, we can conclude the following about the relationship of author to teller and to character in *Finnegans Wake:* Joyce wrote the book whose teller describes a writer who reads a book that resembles a book that Joyce wrote and who lives in a house that looks both like a book and like the 'jas jos' inside the house whose interior resembles the end of a book that Joyce wrote. The warrant and the details for describing the relationship in this convoluted way are to be found in I.7, the chapter of the *Wake* that dwells at the greatest length on Shem, his life, and his works.

To complicate the situation, the reader can become enmeshed in something like these configurations. We tend to lose our distance from them, if only temporarily, for at least two reasons. On the one hand, the language of the *Wake* forces us to collaborate with Joyce by rewriting his text as we read it through our actively recreative response. But more to the point about the specific presentation of Shem in I.7, *he* is described as *both* reader and author. The text he reads and writes appears to be *Ulysses*: 'It would have diverted, if ever seen, the shuddersome spectacle of this semidemented zany amid the inspissated grime of his glaucous den making believe to read his usylessly unreadable Blue Book of Eccles, *édition de ténèbres*' (179.24–27). As the writer of *Ulysses* or a book like it, for Shem to read that book would be for him to read '*the book of himself*' (*U* 187), to adopt a prominent phrase from 'Scylla and Charybdis' that alludes to Mallarmé. The colours of both Shem's places of habitation, his den and the book he reads and writes, are *shades of blue*. The den is glaucous, and the Book of Eccles is blue, as was the first Paris edition of *Ulysses*, an *édition de luxe*, transmogrified here to an *édition de ténèbres*. Shem's book is also blue because of its supposed obscenity.

According to Shem's brother Shaun, whose attitudes permeate much of the narration in I.7, Shem has martyred himself: 'O, you were excruciated, in honour bound to the cross of your own cruelfiction!' (192.17–19). Some of the details of Shem's existence reiterate the self-destructive aspects of writing. More generally, repeatedly in the *Wake,* self-destruction characterizes the activity of aesthetic creation. It does so in part because artistic making, as a central element in the presentation of HCE and his family, becomes a metaphor embracing birth, sexuality, and death. For Joyce, writing is the copula as copulation linking birth and death. Specifically, it is a *felix culpa*, a fortunate fall that results in a creation like birth and in an expenditure of energies leading to death. The death and the birth are inseparable. Joyce indicates that inseparable quality in some of his many puns on *felix culpa*: 'finixed coulpure' (311.26), 'phaymix cupplerts' (331.2–3), 'Colporal Phailinx' (346.36). The culpable, happy coupling of aesthetic creation as metaphor for life is corporeal, or nearly so. And it is a finish that is also a phoenix, an ending that marks a new beginning.

Shem's text, the site of his 'cruelfiction', is 'unreadable' because of its difficulty. As Anna Livia comments about her spouse, Shem's father, in the extended postscript to the long letter of IV, every text, 'Every letter[,] is a hard but yours sure is the hardest crux ever' (623.33–34). Here, in the typical fashion of the *Wake*, frame and tale, narration and narrative, are superimposed. Both of the fathers of the character-as-artist who writes difficult texts, the father of the narration and the father of the narrative, create difficult texts. All these works spell in their sibylline leaves the name of the father, here HCE in '*h*ardest *c*rux *e*ver'. Shem, the fictional author of *Ulysses*, is 'bound' within the binding of the book itself. He *is* that book. In his act of creation Shem has made ink from his own urine and excrement in order to write on his body:[7] '[he] made synthetic ink and sensitive paper for his own end out of his wit's waste' (185.6–8). For Shem, the act of writing is the remaking and the annihilation of the artist, both of which form the subject of the tale the artist writes. The dual process reveals itself in various ways in the language of the *Wake*. It resembles '*The abnihilisation of the etym*' (353.22) referred to in one of the bracketed interludes that occur during the skit by Butt and Taff in II.3, the Tavern chapter. The apparent destruction of the word and of truth (Greek, *etymos*: true; *etymon*: true sense of a word) is also the creation of them, seemingly *ex nihilo*.[8] In a passage I shall come back to later since it alludes to the printing of the text, we find that the process of making attempts to sustain 'the sameold gamebold adomic structure of our Finnius the old One' (615.6–7) in spite of decomposition, perhaps partly as a result of it. The atom, whether 'etym' or Adam, maintains a recognizable integrity amid the detritus of experience. Shem's aesthetic creations, like Joyce's books, emerge from detritus, from waste, from the leftovers of earlier acts of creation. This is Joyce's law of the conservation of literary matter. The scraps include the unused portions of the author's previous attempts to create, parts of the earlier creations, and portions of works left behind by other writers. We know for instance that early in the writing of *Finnegans Wake* Joyce began collecting material in a notebook divided according to his own earlier writings. This is the notebook that has been published as *Scribbledehobble*.[9] We cannot be certain, of course, how much of the material included in this notebook was originally intended for the earlier works, how much was simply triggered by Joyce's retrospective reaction to those works, and how much was entered for other reasons unknown to us. But one rationale for the notebook is clear. Joyce was consciously attempting to connect the new work to the earlier ones at the start of his process of writing. More important for readers of the *Wake*, whether or not they read the notebook, in the self-conscious activity of making art from waste, Joyce inscribes that activity within the tale he tells.

The following passage from I.7 describing Shem's excremental acts of creation presents the author's relation to his writings at length:

> He shall produce nichthemerically from his unheavenly body a no uncertain quantity of obscene matter not protected by cop-riright in the United Stars of Ourania . . . with this double dye, brought to blood heat, gallic acid on iron ore, through the bowels of his misery . . . the first till last alshemist wrote over every square inch of the only foolscap available, his own body, till by its corrosive sublimation one continuous present tense integument slowly unfolded all marryvoising moodmoulded cyclewheeling history (thereby, he said, reflecting from his own individual person life unlivable, transaccidentated through the slow fires of consciousness into a dividual chaos, perilous, potent, common to all flesh, human only, mortal) but with each word that would not pass away the squidself which he had squirtscreened from the crystalline world waned chagreenold and doriangrayer in its dudhud. (185.28–186.8)[10]

The *édition de ténèbres* is a 'nichthemeric', that is a night-Homeric and a non-Homeric production simultaneously continuous with and different from its creator. The Greek word from which Joyce derived 'nichthemerically' also means the duration of a night and a day, the span of time to which *Ulysses* is devoted. The 'usylessly unreadable' book reflects an 'unlivable' life, a life that is fiction, a construction of words. It transforms the author's individual person into a 'dividual', that is, both a divided-dual and a more than *in*dividual, but still human form. The slow fires of consciousness effect the transformation. These are the fires of imagination that burn with sufficient intensity to temper and strengthen but not to weaken or destroy the metal being produced. They are the long-lasting, self-perpetuating, phoenix-like fires of the printed word. These endure longer than the quickly burning, self-consuming fire that is the process of doubling by which the author's empirical self creates his aesthetic self. The references to acid and ore underscore the suggestion of a tempering and refining, such as that involved in the production of metal. The product refined by division of its elements is rid of impurities, free of anything not 'common to all flesh'.

The result of the transforming, creative act is at least dual. Both a text and the writer's persona as teller are engendered, the writer passing through a series of protean, allotropic states defined by each work he writes. The text is a continuous present tense integument, either literally, as in the case of the 'Circe' and 'Penelope' episodes of *Ulysses*, or more generally in the sense that every aesthetic object occupies something like an eternal present. Every fiction exists in a different relation to time from that of the author, who grows old in the squidlike, reproductive activity of producing words that will not pass away. In the presentation of the squidself waning 'chagreenold and doriangrayer in its dudhud' as it creates, the word 'dudhud' indicates the activity (deed-hood), its creative nature (dadhood), and its failure (dudhood) to preserve absolutely the self of the creator, except as language. As the writer becomes more wholly part of the past by expending energies in the act of creation, the text created becomes more completely and permanently present, as it preserves the author but fails to keep him from passing away. Like Wilde's Dorian Gray, the artist destroys himself in the act of creating a persona, or mask.[11] The writer contributes to his own demise by producing passages of language that defeat the passage of time.

The confrontation between the Gracehoper and the Ondt in III.1 suggests the contrast between writer and reader by focusing on their different relations to time. The Gracehoper, like Shem, is a 'capsizer' (418.5), someone who rocks the boat and perhaps is mad as a hatter. After the Gracehoper 'sekketh rede' (418.6) from the Ondt, the parable concludes with a poem in which the Gracehoper poses a crucial question: *'why can't you beat time?'* (419.8). The question implies that the Gracehoper's ability to make melodies, which involves both keeping time to music and defeating time, distinguishes him as an artist from his brother creature who only reads. While extreme, the contrast is not absolute, especially given the ambiguities of the Gracehoper's statement and his manner of living. In order to beat time by making music, he must expend himself to limits that threaten his annihilation. Consequently, he needs the Ondt as his helper, listener, reader, whatever the differences between them. As Shem's act of reading his own work indicates, the roles of writer and reader are not necessarily radically distinct. Rather, they coalesce into a composite, 'dividual' form. The combination occurs because of the complementary nature of writing and reading. Several other details of the parable suggest that the two figures are not entirely distinct. By the end, the Ondt has begun to cavort in the way the Gracehoper did previously (417.24–32; cp.

414.22–35). In the poem, the Gracehoper emphasizes the possible reversal by suggesting the Ondt exchange roles with him by playing Jacob to his Esau (418.35). And he seems to be addressing himself as well as the Ondt in the final question about beating time, since he too suffers from 'chronic's despair' (417.35–36). The alignment of the two figures in the parable is only one instance of the repeated coalescence of opposites in the *Wake*. Here the merger is rendered as the Ondt's metaphorically coming to live in the Gracehoper's house when the Gracehoper actually comes to visit the Ondt's house. At the beginning of the parable, the Gracehoper lives in a house 'cald fourmillierly Tingsomingenting' (414.34), while the Ondt lives in a house 'cold antitopically Nixnixundinix' (415.29). But by the end, the Ondt is acting 'like thingsumanything in formicolation' (417.26–27). Through various linguistic plays and repetitions, Joyce links each character with the house of his antagonist. I mention these details about the houses because Shem and his later incarnation Glugg live in dwellings that merge the two abodes of the parable. And in Joyce's earlier fiction, home, especially the act of leaving or returning home, is central. Shem's house is not only 'the Haunted Inkbottle' but 'Niggs, niggs and niggs . . . stinksome inkenstink' (183.5–6). Glugg's 'shome' (213.4) is 'a hovel not a havel . . . with a tingtumtingling and a next, next and next' (231.1–2). The houses are their inhabitants' books, in which characters like Butt and Taff can apparently become '*now one and the same person*' (354.8), as they do in the *Wake*.

In 1.5, the chapter concerning the 'untitled mamafesta' (104.4), reading as textual inspection provides the means for coalescing to occur:

> Closer inspection of the *bordereau* would reveal a multiplicity of personalities inflicted on the documents or document. . . . In fact, under the closed eyes of the inspectors the traits featuring the *chiaroscuro* coalesce, their contrarieties eliminated, in one stable somebody similarly as by the providential warring . . . our social something bowls along bumpily, experiencing a jolting series of prearranged dissapointments, down the long lane of (it's as semper as oxhousehumper!) generations, more generations and still more generations. (107.23–36)

The emergence of one somebody, which takes place because of reading as investigation, happens in the readers' processes of mind during a state of consciousness like dreaming, not in any scene accessible to the waking senses. The 'multiplicity of personalities' refers not only to the numerous characters of the text. It includes the author's changing personae and the multitude of readers, whose minds may be as multiple and divisible as the author's seems to be. Because the social process of communication accomplished through writing and reading the book always fails in some way, more generations are required in order to compensate for the disappointments inherent in using language. The generations include the further creations of the author and of other authors. And they are the later generations of readers, some of whom will be authors, who will inspect the text anew. The coalescing process and the generations never reach an absolute end. They are always with us and always only partially successful, like the perpetual ('semper') nature of language, which is indicated by the reference to the beginning of the Hebrew alphabet in 'oxhousehumper'.[12] The shifting quality of language helps generate the multiplicity of protean characters in the *Wake* that may be inspected and fused. Because the fusion involves the processes as well as the products of aesthetic making, reader fuses with writer and listener with teller as the acts of generating approach a universal state. The story of the profligate Gracehoper together with the comment about the inspection of the manifesto implies that writing is the self-consuming generating of texts. But the self-consumption as a kind of burial gives rise to generations of readings that are resurrections. Tome is tomb to be opened. The book is simultaneously the writer's epitaph and progeny, his end and his continuance. In I.5 the teller announces himself to be 'a worker, a tombstone mason' (113.34) in a passage that then indicates he is a weaver of Oriental carpets. The pattern in the carpet is the track of the teller as 'proteiform graph' (107.8), 'tracing of a purely deliquescent recidivist' (107.10). The deliquescence of this habitual criminal is dual: both his melting away or dissolving in the book as river and his repeated acts of division to create networks, as in the veins of a leaf. His *Wake* is both the River Liffey speaking and the 'leafy speafing' (619.20).

The author's activity is at once defensive and self-revelatory. Shem seems to have devised a squirtscreen between his squidself and the world as a shield behind which he withdraws. But one of the passages quoted above also suggests that the squidself is itself the squirtscreen which the author has produced spider-like using the materials of the world to write what the narrator calls 'the mystery of himsel in furniture' (184.9–10). This mystery, analogous to a religious mystery concerning the status of the divine creator, involves the simultaneous continuity and discontinuity between self and world, between teller and tale, and between reader and tale. The furniture mentioned is part of a pervasive group of references in the *Wake* to printing, the mechanical process that intervenes between author and book but also makes the book and the communication of reader and writer possible. In printing, furniture consists of wooden or metal pieces used to create both the blank spaces between type and the blank margins of the pages.[13] In both I.7 and at the conclusion of the *Wake*'s final monologue, the ambiguous use of the preposition 'from' captures the paradoxical mysteries of writing and reading. *From* the materials of the world Shem makes himself as he screens himself from the world: 'the squidself . . . he had squirtscreened from the crystalline world' (186.7–8). Anna Livia addresses both her husband *and* the reader when she claims that 'you're changing from me' (626.36). On the final page of the *Wake*, she informs those who are changing because of her and away from her that 'My leaves have drifted from me' (628.6). The leaves of the book emanating from the artist must eventually be separated from the writer at the 'phoenish' (4.17) of the text. To reach that point of separation is the end for reader, writer, and character. The reader who is 'phoenished' (130.11) has changed from, both because of and away from, the experience of reading a text whose leaves and leavings are still in the reader's possession and in possession of the reader.

The statement about Shem's self-revelation in the furniture of printing occurs at the end of a long paragraph describing his house, 'The House O'Shea or O'Shame . . . known as the Haunted Inkbottle' (182.30–31) or the 'inkbattle house' (176.31). The description reiterates the intimate connection between teller and tale. As Stephen Dedalus suggests in his analysis of Shakespeare's relation to *Hamlet*, the author's text is haunted, because it contains the writer's ghostly voice (*U* 197). The exterior of the House O'Shame (Shame's House or James's House) resembles both the real author's eye-patched physiognomy and the cover of a book with the fictitious author's assumed name imprinted, 'with his penname SHUT sepiascraped on the doorplate and a blind of black sailcloth over its wan phwinshogue' (182.32–34). The penname SHUT names Shame's Hut while indicating again the excremental nature of the writing.[14] When the book as house is opened, the contents, presented as an epic catalogue of miscellaneous litter, are the inky, personal, perhaps poisonous, puzzle of the writer: 'For this was a stinksome inkenstink, quite puzzonal to the wrottel' (183.6–7). The word 'inkenstink' fuses ink and instinct, and it continues the scatological references. The writer's inky end-stink is the result of his ink-instinct to represent himself in language. The smell may owe something to the manner of storing the leather appliances for inking type in printing shops during the period in which hand-presses were used. The leather pelts were kept soft by soaking them in urine. The practice is said to have given something more than a faintly scented aroma to the printing house.[15]

A prominent allusion to Molly Bloom's monologue occurs at the end of the catalogue of the house's contents. This allusion emphasizes the identity of Shame's house and Shem's book with Joyce's *Ulysses*. The catalogue contains a string of monosyllabic equivalents for the English word 'yes' (184.1–2). Two of the syllables that are juxtaposed, 'jas jos', are the abbreviated name of the real author, whose identity is always implicit in the text. According to the narrator of this chapter, in the house as book 'one stands, given a grain of good will, a fair chance of actually seeing the whirling dervish . . . writing the mystery of himsel in furniture' (184.4–10). By entering the author's book as house, the reader can inspect the house that Jack built in order to discover the Jack who built the house.

The document that Shem, or one of his avatars, reportedly writes together with his mother ALP is a letter, various versions of which are quoted from time to time.[16] In III.1 the collaboration of mom and Shem, 'mem and hem' (422.33), is mentioned specifically. One of the most enigmatic representations of the letter helps explain the author's abbreviated signature in the litter of Shem's house and the relation of signature and letter to the *Wake*'s overall structure. This version, only two lines long, is reported towards the end of the trial in I.4, between the conclusion of testimony ('And so it all ended' [93.22]) and the meandering deliberations of the four justices:

What was it?

A . . . . !

? . . . . O ! (94.20–22)

These two elliptical lines evoke alpha and omega, which mark the letter's limits and its context. This is the letter in its barest possible form. In the beginning was the letter, then letters, then an epistle as simple as a, b, c.

Twists of the Teller's Tale

"The letter! The litter!" (93.24)

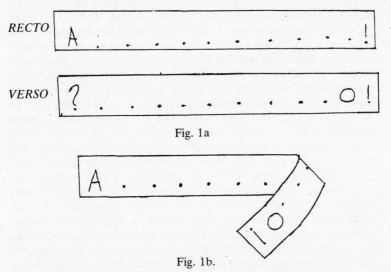

RECTO

VERSO

Fig. 1a

Fig. 1b.

"furrowards, bagawards, like yoxen at the turnpaht" (18.32)

"by writing thithaways end to end and turning, turning and end to end hithaways writing" (114.16–17)

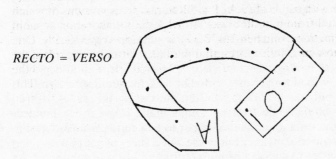

RECTO = VERSO

Fig. 1c.

"an all forabit" (19.1–2)

"Doublends Jined" (20.16)

"thorough readable to int from and . . . and this applies to its whole wholume" (48.17–18)

The paragraph preceding the question emphasizes the connection of the lines with sea and river. 'The letter! The litter!' (93.24) is
echoed a few pages further on in 'The latter! The latter!' (100.2), an
even closer approximation to the Greek word for sea, *thalatta*. In
III.1, immediately after the Gracehoper's poem, 'the latter' is mentioned as part of the parable's closing: 'In the name of the former
and of the latter and of their holocaust. Allmen' (419.9–10).
Aesthetic creation as *Finnegans Wake* presents it may be described
using the terms of this conclusion. The image of the former, that is,
of the maker, whether divine or aesthetic, appears in the maker's
creation, no matter if that creation be the divine son or an aesthetic
letter composed of alphabetic letters. For Joyce, in the literary text
'maker mates with made' (261.8), like dancer with dance in Yeats's
'Among School Children'. The mystery of the former's production
of the letter and his continuity with it is indicated by the ghostly
presence in 'the latter'. Although the aesthetic former is temporally
prior to his creation, the letter eventually displaces the former
because of the work of art's peculiar temporal status. The forming
spirit originally behind the letter finally takes up a position within it.
Anna Livia as river, whose presence the motif immediately preceding the letter in I.4 announces, is apparently both behind and within
her epistle: 'Now tell me, tell me, tell me then!' (94.19). Because
she is the writer *and* the subject of the letter, what the letter tells is
'me'. It always tells *now* of the writer's 'me' that existed *then*. The
river motif together with the question followed by an 'A' indicating
an answer connects the letter with the multitude of questions and
answers that occur in the *Wake* and especially with the dialogue of
the two washerwomen in I.8. Born by wave and retrieved by hen,
the letter is told by the 'elm that whimpers at the top . . . [to] the
stone that moans when stricken' (94.4–5): 'It was folded with
cunning, sealed with crime, uptied by a harlot, undone by a child. It
was life but was it fair? It was free but was it art?' (94.8–10).
    Some of these descriptive details make sense if the letter is
written out on a long sheet of paper to be cunningly folded, not in
the conventional manner but in the way a sheet of paper is doubled
over on itself to create a Möbius strip. The Möbean version of the
letter mirrors the shape of the book that is its context (see Figure 1).
The letter so conceived is the winding sheet or twisted tale that
defines the recirculation of the narration in *Finnegans Wake*. It is
told by whimpering elm to stricken, moaning stone because the
book containing the letter that stands for the book is a printed

94

document, an inked impression like that made by pressing wood on stone in some kinds of printing. As the narrator says with reference to the river in the last paragraph of this chapter, 'we have taken our sheet upon her stones' (103.9). The sheets here are the laundry, but they are also the sheets of paper pressed on stone to print what will eventually be the leaves of a book.

As Clive Hart, among others, has noted, in general the letter in *Finnegans Wake* is the image of the book.[17] That this particularly enigmatic letter can stand for the whole text is indicated in several ways. The notion of synecdoche, part standing for whole and whole for part, is introduced early on in the *Wake* in the assertion that 'When a part so ptee does duty for the holos we soon grow to use of an allforabit' (18.36–19.2). While suggesting the possible relationship of the petit, or small part, to the whole, of bit to all, this sentence presents the alphabet, or 'allforabit', as that relationship itself. The alphabet implicit in the letter of I.4 defines one possible relation of part to whole, letter to text. *Finnegans Wake* as 'farced epistol to the hibruws' (228.33–34) contains letters that contain letters. By alluding to alpha and omega, first and last letters of the Greek alphabet, and to the connotations of those letters, especially their traditional connection with the all-pervasive presence of the divine creator, the letter reinforces some of the passages about Shem. Both small and large, contained and containing texts resemble sacred books in which the image of a creator is inscribed. Consequently, we stand 'a fair chance of actually seeing' the aesthetic creator whose mystery is contained in the mechanically printed book.

The implications of the two-line version, including the connections of letter with book, with sacred books, and with writing and printing, are not all immediately evident from the letter in isolation, even though some of them are evoked by the letter's context in I.4. They emerge more clearly when the letter is placed in the network of passages dealing with Shem, the *Odyssey*, Joyce's texts, and the art of printing. In II.2, the passages following the failure of Glugg, one of Shem's incarnations, to guess 'heliotrope' the first time in the guessing game illustrates the kind of repetition with variation that creates the network I have in mind. Many of the details of Shem's life are mentioned again but assigned to Glugg. When he leaves home, he writes 'his farced epistol to the hibruws' (228.33–34). Either the exile or that epistle, probably both, is like *Ulysses*, the twelve middle episodes of which are alluded to in order

(229.13–16). Glugg writes at his mother's dictation for auditors who include 'Caxton' (229.31), the famous printer of Malory. The question the narrator puts about Glugg's activities, 'Was liffe worth leaving', conflates several of the elements associated with writing in this and other sections of the *Wake*. Was it worth leaving Ireland, as the accused seems to do after the trial in I.4 and as the wandering writer inevitably does in Joyce's fiction? That leaving is also the turning of the river Liffey into printed leaves. And the production of leaves is death, our leaving this life. By reinforcing through repetition some of the perspectives presented in other parts of the narrative, this kind of reprise clarifies the basic aspects of the character-as-writer's life and brings a modicum of order to individual sections and finally to the work at large.

In the first and last chapters of the *Wake*, in its alpha and omega, some sense of the book's overarching order emerges, though briefly. If we take the elliptical letter as a paradigm for the whole work, we expect to find connections between the beginning and the end that amount to more than the continuation of the final words on the first page. As we shall see, similar passages near the book's beginning and its ending echo and complement one another. Their placement and implications help explain the letter of I.4, just as *it* creates a structure in which their placement and implications make sense. Together with the elliptical letter, the early and late, former and latter sections tell us some important things about the small and large structures of the *Wake*, about its parts as separate but linked and as very nearly interchangeable.

BEGINNINGS AND ENDINGS / COMPOSITION AND DECOMPOSITION (I.1 and IV)

Although the beginning and the ending of the *Wake* do not repeat one another in any slavish way, there are some evident similarities. We find the connecting links mostly between the ten pages or so (10–20) following the tour of the 'museyroom' and those preceding ALP's final monologue (609–19). The *Wake*, then, has a postlude and a prelude consisting of its last and first few pages (619–28; 3–10). And the pages immediately preceding the postlude bear comparison with the section immediately following the prelude. These comparable sections contain the first and last full statements of the sentence Joyce borrowed from Edgar Quinet and transformed,[18] the first and last lengthy references to the letter, and the first and last dialogues between invader and native. For the most part, the order of presentation in I.1 reverses that of IV. If we treat the narrative as a continuous loop with ends joined, the repetition in reversed order forms a chiasmus, like the sequence of dates announced in I.1: '1132 A.D. . . . 566 A.D. . . . (Silent.) 566 A.D. . . . 1132 A.D.' (13.33–14.11). The two passages I want to look at closely occur just after the dialogues. The earlier one (18.17–21.4) is placed between the dialogue of Mutt and Jute and the story of the prankquean. The later one (613.8–615.11) follows the dialogues of Muta and Juva and of Patrick with the druid but precedes the final letter and monologue of ALP.

The passage in I.1 begins by inviting the reader to stop, 'please stoop' (18.17), to experience the words of the printed text that the teller offers, and to recognize the complex implications that make those words a world.[19] The reader who is 'abcedminded' may be able to 'rede' the world of 'this claybook', with its 'allaphbed' (18.18–19). The 'abcedminded' can learn the book's 'allforabit', the constituent elements of its language and the manner in which part and whole stand for one another. Often in the *Wake* the word 'clay', as in 'claybook', suggests the French word *clef* and its English equivalent 'key'. *Finnegans Wake* is like a *roman à clef*, since at least one character, Shem the Penman, can be associated with a real person, the author. The writer's inspiration, like that of the god of creation, provides the 'human only, mortal' (186.4–5) clay-like book with life. And the word 'clay' connects the book with the four commentators, called 'Mamalujo' after the names of the four gospellers, Matthew, Mark, Luke, and John. These four, who frequently appear with their ass, the apparent narrator at times in Book III, are referred to as 'claymen' (475.18). Shem is also a 'keyman' (185.15). Especially in the context of other references to the art of printing, the words clay and ass, like furniture, sheet, and leaf, indicate the making of the book. Since 'clayman' mixes clay, water, and dispersing agents for use in papermaking, the book that employs the paper so made and that inscribes within itself the process of making could be called a claybook.[20] This reading is confirmed when we learn that Shem the 'keyman' did in fact make his own 'sensitive paper for his own end out of his wit's waste' (185.7–8). But as we have already seen, that paper is Shem's own skin. The 'only foolscap available' is 'his own body' (185.35–36). Consequently, the artist makes *himself* from his own mortal clay when he writes the book of himself as the mystery in furniture. His book, like the narratives about Earwicker's naming, will inevitably be 'andrewpaulmurphyc' (31.35), or anthropomorphic; they reveal the shape of a man and of mankind. It seems entirely likely that Joyce would have known the tradition of calling the compositor in a printing shop the 'ass'.[21] In this early passage the history of writing is explicitly linked to the making of books and to this book. According to the narrator, even in an age in which there was 'as yet no lumpend papeer' (19.31), 'the world . . . was and will be writing its own wrunes for ever' (19.35–36), just as it is now. While the world writes simultaneously its runes, or songs, and its ruins, we are asked to 'rede' the world of the claybook produced by the writing, the book of clay that is both the shape of man made from earth and the printed book made of sheets manufactured by claymen and composed by the compositor as ass.

Both within this printed book and in this history of man's development, the fact of printing announces itself as one aspect of the world 'writing its own wrunes for ever':

> . . . and Gutenmorg with his cromagnom charter, tintingfast and great primer must once for omniboss step rubrickredd out of the wordpress else is there no virtue more in alcohoran. For that (the rapt one warns) is what papyr is meed of, make of, hides and hints and misses in prints. Till ye finally (though not yet endlike) meet with the acquaintance of Mister Typus, Mistress Tope and all the little typtopies. Fillstup. So you need hardly spell me how every word will be bound over to carry three score and ten toptypsical readings throughout the book of |Doublends Jined (may his forehead be darkened with mud who would sunder!) till Daleth, mahomahouma, who oped it closeth|thereof|the. Dor. (20.7–18)

Gutenberg, the inventor of printing with movable type, appears as the morning 'with his cromagnom charter . . . great primer' that is both the Magna Carta and a Cromagnon letter. Great primer is a size of printing type. The letter presumably resembles the earlier 'meanderthalltale' (19.25), or Neanderthal story, that is the 'meandertale' (18.22) of wanderings we are asked to 'rede'. The printer as maker of the document is himself the 'omniboss', hero and author of the story being told, who emerges from the press, like a newborn child, 'rubrickredd'. A book may be embossed for decoration, but this 'omniboss' is the context of the whole. (Our English word 'boss' derives from the French *bosse*, meaning hump or hunch, the mark of

HCE.) The printer is compositor and reader as well as hero and writer since the act of printing involves the composing and then the reading of the rubrics composed. The printing of rubrics, that is, passages in red, indicates the sacred nature of what emerges from the press: the religious books that Gutenberg actually printed; the book itself, like *Finnegans Wake*, as 'wordpress', or storing place for words, from which Gutenberg emerges (in *A Portrait* Dante stores her brushes in a press); and Gutenberg himself as a book-like entity, the maker who has achieved some measure of identity with the books he produced. Gutenberg and the author who speaks here are 'rapt', wrapped in the winding sheets of their own creations. The book of Gutenmorg seems to be Homeric since, like the Homeric mornings, this one is red, if not rosy-fingered (German, *Morgen-röte:* dawn). One version of a recurring event in the *Wake*, the encounter of the General with Buckley, occurs 'on that redletter morning' (50.31–32), which among other times is the morning on which the letter is read. And the ballad at the end of I.2 written by Hosty about Earwicker is 'privately printed at the rimepress of Delville' with a 'red woodcut' (43.25–26). Gutenberg's stepping forth is associated with the power of 'alcohoran'.[22] Whatever else that word refers to, it includes the vowels A and O in a chiastic sequence, a-o-o-a, indicating the presence of something like the divine alpha and omega in sacred books. Through the letters of language, that presence becomes disseminated into the human world generally but specifically into this text. In alphabetical arrangements that are 'allforabit', spelling creates chiastic sequences suggesting a presence in the words whose virtue allows Gutenmorg to step forth.

Chiasmus is illustrated two pages earlier in the first paragraph following the dialogue of Mutt and Jute: 'furrowards, bagawards, like yoxen at the turnpaht. Here say figurines billycoose arming and mounting. Mounting and arming bellicose figurines see here' (18.32–34). The reader is to say and see what the teller sees and says the figurines say and see. The story is both chiastic and, like Martha Clifford's encoded address in 'Ithaca' (*U* 706), boustrophedontic. When ending and beginning are one, progress becomes a winding movement of the bag of words backwards down the furrow just made. The various plays on 'backwards' in the *Wake* sometimes indicate the looking-glass perceptions of the compositor, who must reverse through 'backwords' (100.28), 'tantrist spellings' (571.7) the shapes and sequences of characters in the act of setting type. If the printer provides one analogue for the writer in *Finnegans Wake* because the work of printing involves letters and ink, then so does the actor in a theatrical troupe when the troupe is the 'players of Inkermann the mime' (48.10). The saga which they perform is 'readable to int from and', as would be a chiastic, continuous integument that could be started in the middle and read toward the introduction. In fact, when we read ALP's letter in IV, after 'Dear', we begin *in medias res* with 'And', and then proceed toward the book's end and introduction. Of the persons in the saga, both characters and actors, as in a story whose double ends are joined, 'no one end is known' (48.24).

Through the virtuoso and protean power of imaginative enactment and making associated with acting, writing, and printing, in *Finnegans Wake*, *homo ludens* as *homo faber* mimes, in comic Promethean fashion, the status traditionally associated with the godhead. Since human creations are full of the misprints, hints, and concealments (such as Shem's concealment behind his squirtscreen), for which paper is one medium, the words of 'the book of Doublends Jined' (20.15–16) will be bound, as are all words in books, to require multiple readings. These readings include the repeated perusals of the printer's proofs needed for making corrections and revisions. And they are the multiple meanings that proliferate until the person who opened the book 'closeth thereof the' (20.17–18). The closing of the *Wake*, its final word, is, of course, 'the'. The distinction made between 'finally' and 'endlike' (20.11–12) in the passage about Gutenmorg indicates that 'the' is not likely to be entirely final. Eventually, that is, finally but not absolutely finally, reader and author reach a state of repletion that is more a filling up ('fillstup' [20.13]) than a full stop. The book's last 'the' lacks the punctuation of the full stop, since the end is the 'int'. Reader and author reach a provisionally final state when they 'meet with the acquaintance of Mister Typus, Mistress Tope and all the little typtopies' (20.12–13) in such a way that the words can be bound over for closure though not for ending in any categorical sense. When such closure takes place, the general, the myth, type, or archetype becomes incarnated in a specific place and at a specific occasion (in two senses of *topos*). Type as *model* then proliferates as 'typtopies', both further incarnations of the myth and multiple copies in the typeface of printed books. In the making of the book, the typed copies of MSS are set in printing type to make passages (*topoi* again). In their complementary experiences with the text, reader and author meet with the acquaintance and make the acquaintance of type and *topos* as they become familiars of the text. The author meets with the printer, the person acquainted with types who is indispensable for publishing. And the author as teller meets with the reader, who must already be acquainted with printing type in order to experience the text. At the same time, the author makes the reader into a new acquaintance by creating the reader's persona. If the author chooses, as Joyce did, he can develop strategies for letting the reader perceive the continuity and overlap of reading, writing, and printing in the bookmaking process. Through the allusions to printing in the *Wake*, the reader can realize the experience of meeting author and printer, the acquaintances of type and *typos*. The writer, his text as epistle, and his printer concerned with letters, all together 'once for omniboss step rubrickredd out of the word-press', when the rubrics are read.

*   *   *

At this point it is worth pausing briefly to consider why Joyce decided to include printing terms in his text. Hugh Kenner has recently commented that *Ulysses* 'was set in type the Gutenberg way, by hand': 'There had been typesetting machines for 30-odd years, but "Ulysses" was surely the biggest book of any importance to be set by hand since William Morris had set the Kelmscott Chaucer in 1893–96. . . . Moreover, the "Ulysses" typesetters, of whom there were at least 26, lived in Dijon and knew no English whatsoever, which means they held strings of meaningless letters in their heads while swivelling back and forth between typescript and typecase.'[23] This situation surely contributed to the statement in the *Wake* that the letter has 'a multiplicity of personalities inflicted on' it (107.24–25). Given the problems Joyce had with publishers prior to *Ulysses* and the nature of the printing of that book's first edition, by the time Joyce came to write *Finnegans Wake*, he must have largely integrated the giving of instructions to printers into his notions of writing and reading. Since his printers were his readers and, inevitably, he was theirs when he received proofs, Joyce must have considered the printer to be his collaborator and, frequently, his antagonist. In consequence, printing terms become primary metaphors as well as literal descriptions for the making of his books.

The printing terms have an advantage over other metaphors for literary creation. They can be rendered more immediately in the reader's experience of the book than other language describing writing since we have before us printed matter. There is always a large disparity inherent in any narration that tries to present the physical and imaginative acts of writing something down. In *A Portrait*, for example, we do not see Stephen's handwritten stanzas when he writes the villanelle on the rough surface of the cigarette packet. We cannot. Instead, we perceive the stanzas neatly printed in italic type. In the *Wake*, Joyce can create more immediate effects using printing terms and typography. In II.2, the Schoolroom chapter, one of Shem's avatars, Dolph, gives his brother Kev instructions for constructing a geometrical figure that represents ALP's genitals.[24] The procedure consists of first marking a point 'A', or alpha, on the left, then a point 'L', or lambda, on the right. These are the centres for drawing two intersecting circles of radius AL, one of whose intersections determines the point 'P', which is marked last at the bottom of the diagram. On the page in which Dolph directs the connecting of the letters into a triangle, or delta, the left-hand margin contains the following comment in italics: *'Zweispaltung as Fundemaintalish of Wiederherstellung'* (296.L1). Next to that comment Dolph is instructing Kev 'to mack a capital Pee for Pride down there on the batom'' (296.5–6). The marginal comment, which means 'division into two is fundamental to restoration', resembles the statements in *Ulysses* that without sundering is no reconciliation. But *zweispaltig* also happens to be a German typographical term that refers to printing in double columns. The marginal comment, then, resembles the author's direction to the printer to set a page with double columns. And that is how the pages of this chapter are set, with double columns of marginal comments flanking the central passages. While Kev is directed to make a capital P at the bottom of the diagram, we are told by the superscript indicating a footnote to look at the bottom of the page. There we find that the first word of the note begins with a capital P. Dolph's instruction is like the typical instruction a proof reader gives to a printer to make a letter a capital. Through his use of typography and a typographical term Joyce is able to align Dolph's instructions for constructing the diagram with the author's instructions to his printer for making the page and with his directions to his readers. All are involved in analogous activities. The literal directions of movement involved are from the left to the right and then down. And those are the directions along which writing and reading proceed.

*   *   *

Once the book has been opened, once it has become rubrics for reading, it can only be closed 'finally (though not yet endlike)' in the middle. The reader of this text whose ends are joined is always in the midst of its language because of the invitation to participate actively in the uttering of the tale. To 'rede . . . its world' (18.18–19) is both to read the story and to utter it since *Rede* in German means speech. As the final paragraph of the section about Gutenberg in I.1 reports, this text is busily in motion for us. The narrator advises us to 'look what you have in your handself': 'The movibles are scrawling in motions, marching, all of them ago, in pitpat and zingzang for every busy eerie whig's a bit of a torytale to tell' (20.21–23). The movable type of Gutenberg is alive and in motion in the hand of the person holding the book. This sentence, itself set in movable type, contains the alphabetical, synecdochic tale that it says movable type contains. That story, implicit in the letter, concerns the container that contains itself, in which the teller as 'eerie' whig has and is a story to tell: 'the movibles are scrawling . . . *all* . . . *for* . . . *a bit* . . . to tell' (my emphasis). And it concerns the past continuing into the present, where 'ago' is still a-going.

The teller's vision of aesthetic processes, both creation and response, makes the realistic aspects of fiction, including his own, laughable. He suggests that 'You can ask your ass if he believes' (20.26) this 'One's upon a thyme' story that proliferates to 'two's behind', then 'three's among' (20.23–24), and so on, to an infinite number of possible stories. However unbelievable the tale, the sustaining reality that involves teller with reader is written into it by the movables. This reality of the coalescing 'multiplicity of personalities inflicted on the documents' (107.24–25) emerges in the use of pronouns in I.1 just before the story of the prankquean. After enjoining the reader to listen, 'Lissom! lissom!' (21.2), the teller says ambiguously, 'I am doing it' (21.3).[25] Here the teller speaks for himself, for the reader, and for ALP, who is confirming the teller's claim that 'it's sure it was her not we' (20.36). Reader, teller, and character are doing 'it' together. The specific nature of 'it' matters much less than the parallel acts of 'doing'.

In *Finnegans Wake,* truth in art does not require verisimilitude, or it does so only incidentally. The wish the teller expresses at the end of I.2 concerning 'the rann that Hosty made' (44.7–8) about Earwicker, a rann spoken by many, applies to this book to be 'rede' by many: 'may the treeth we tale of live in stoney' (44.9). When the wood of the engraving block meets the impressing stone, printed matter emerges as truth, having achieved a stone-like character. The stoney permanence resembles an epitaph carved by the 'tombstone mason' (113.34): 'Here line the refrains of' (44.10). This suspended sentence, truncated like the entire text, raises the question of exactly whose refrains and whose remains the lines of the ballad contain. The teller lists numerous possible names for the rann's subject, including an alphabetical sequence, but finally decides to 'parse him Persse O'Reilly else he's called no name at all' (44.14). But the ballad is also the remains and the refrains of its writer, whose song shares the honour with its author of being 'the king of all ranns' (44.16–17). Maker, again, mates with made. Hosty's composing the ballad matches the two acts that start and end I.2, the speaking of 'Humphrey Chimpden's occupational agnomen' by the 'sailor king' (31.11) at the beginning of the chapter and the teller's similar act of naming the subject of the ballad at the end. The speakers' actions and their subjects become intertwined when narration and narrative, speaking and utterance are parallel. The earwigger becomes Earwicker. And the parser names a Persse. *Finnegans Wake*, the ballad, and the various versions of Earwicker's naming are 'andrewpaulmurphyc' (31.35) not just because they are shaped in the image of humankind, but because multiple voices speak them. The anthropomorphic form is that of 'Mister Typus, Mistress Tope and all the little typtopies', the members of the human family transformed into type and into acquaintances of mythic types. All the contributing voices tell the story that includes them. In the welter of reading the 'movibles' of the 'meandertale' (18.22), the reader 'finds the nameform ... that entails the ensuance of existentiality' (18.25–28), the form of the name that tells the story of life's continuity and in so telling sustains the name in the form of the tale that names teller and character.

*   *   *

The counterpart in Book IV for the passages in I.1 inviting us to 'rede' and to 'lissom' completes the earlier passages by revealing one goal of the tale and of its ending: 'that the heroticisms, catastrophes and eccentricities transmitted by the ancient legacy of the past, type by tope, letter from litter, word at ward ... may be there for you' (614.35–615.8). As the teller says earlier in IV, 'what we have received, that we have transmitted' (604.30). When the past is transformed into a tale, the legacy may survive in the future as part

104

of a continuous present tense integument reflecting the 'ensuance of existentiality'. That ensuance involves the implied appearance of Gutenmorg at the end of *Finnegans Wake* in the arrival of the morning laundry, 'mournenslaund' (614.8) in morning's land. Here, the laundry, as elsewhere in the *Wake*, is linked with ALP and with the washing of the sheets to be laid on the river's stones: 'Mopsus or Gracchus, all your horodities will incessantlament be coming back from the Annone Wishwashwhose, Ormepierre Lodge, Doone of the Drumes, blanches bountifully and nightsend made up, every article lathering leaving several rinsings' (614.1–5). The penultimate title for the 'mamafesta' given in I.5 contains the phrase '*So is My Washing Done by Night*' (107.1). Now, just before we read the letter, which begins with mention of dirt, the night's laundry arrives, 'Delivered as . . . Clean . . . Close' (614.10–13). The laundry consists of 'horodities,' ditties about heroes and whores as well as ancient histories such as those of Herodotus reporting heroic and erotic action ['heroticisms' (614.35)]. But the 'blanches' that have undergone 'rinsings' are also the clean sheets that in handpress printing were always wetted and allowed to stand overnight.[26] These provide the 'vergin page' (553.1) on which the hen can scrawl her 'scribings' (615.10). Only clean sheets, still damp from rinsing would take ink evenly. Without them, the work of printing could not proceed in the morning.

The 'Close' of 'the' that clothes the end is an 'endnessnessessity' (613.27) setting 'a marge [shore and margin] to the merge of unnotions' (614.17). Because it starts again the soiling and laundering, the marge of closing transforms rather than truncates. Mookse and Gripes become 'Mopsus or Gracchus' under the aspect of 'Gudstruce' (613.12), a truth and truce in which the 'crisscouple be so crosscomplimentary, little eggons, youlk and meelk, in a farbiger pancosmos' (613.10–12). The agon of you and me results in complementarity. The 'laud of laurens' (613.15), the lord who tells the story that begins with a reference to 'Laurens County's gorgios' (3.8), 'now orielising benedictively when saint and sage have said their say' (613.15–16), along with all the other battling opposites of the book, announces the nature of the merging that includes reader and teller as well as the various pairs of dialoguists: 'Yet is no body present here which was not there before. Only is order othered. Nough is nulled. *Fuitfiat!*' (613.13–14). The eggs cooked in the text as pan recall the ones Shem habitually prepares (184). And they are the completed book as 'a homelet not a hothel' (586.18) for teller, characters, and readers, produced when the author 'pits hen to paper and there's scribings scrawled on eggs' (615.10). The creation is not *ex nihilo*. Rather it is an affirmative act nullifying nought, that is, not nullifying anything and negating the concept of nothing. The order authored makes the old order into another order. *'Fuitfiat'* ('It was; let it be') places the dialogues of IV in relation to the initial one between Mutt and Jute by reversing the 'Fiatfuit' (17.32) which occurs during that earlier colloquy. The aesthetic reordering takes the shape of chiasmus through reversal and repetition. The 'pancosmos', the world we have 'rede', is a 'chaosmos' (118.21), or cosmos as chiasmus, described at length in I.5 as a world in which 'every person, place and thing . . . was moving and changing every part of the time' (118.21–23) through the 'continually more and less intermisunderstanding minds of anticollaborators' (118.24–26); that is, reader and writer.

The paragraph of IV immediately preceding the question that introduces the final version of the letter links the book to its printing, to the alphabetic structure of its types and myths, to the river, and to the readers:

> Our wholemole millwheeling vicociclometer, a tetradomational gazebocroticon (the 'Mamma Lujah' known to every schoolboy scandaller, be he Matty, Marky, Lukey or John-a-Donk), autokinatonetically preprovided with a clappercoupling smeltingworks exprogressive process, (for the farmer, his son and their homely codes, known as eggburst, eggblend, eggburial and hatch-as-hatch can) receives through a portal vein the dialytically separated elements of precedent decomposition for the verypetpurpose of subsequent recombination so that the heroticisms, catastrophes and eccentricities transmitted by the ancient legacy of the past, type by tope, letter from litter, word at ward, with sendence of sundance . . . in our mutter nation, all, anastomosically assimilated and preteridentified paraidiotically, in fact, the sameold gamebold adomic structure of our Finnius the old One, as highly charged with electrons as hophazards can effective it, may be there for you, Cockalooralooraloomenos, when cup, platter and pot come piping hot, as sure as herself pits hen to paper and there's scribings scrawled on eggs. (614.27–615.10)

Now known as 'Mamma Lujah' (614.28), the 'millwheeling vicocic-

lometer' (614.27), presumably a mill on a river, has become identified with its own characters become readers: 'every schoolboy
scandaller, be he Matty, Marky, Lukey or John-a-Donk'
(614.28–30). The book is self-moving, self-perpetuating, and self-
consuming, 'autokinatonetically preprovided with a clappercoup-
ling smeltingworks exprogressive process' (614.30–31) that pro-
duces both fusion and purification by smelting. The 'smeltingworks
exprogressive process' is the end of the making of *Work in Progress*
(the original, provisional title of the *Wake*) through a reversal
identical with the first step in the production of new books. The
'decomposition' mentioned in the paragraph includes the taking
apart of composed type. This 'endnessnessessity' (613.27) anticipates the process of composing and decomposing again. In order for
'heroticisms' to 'be there for you', there must be available 'the
dialytically separated elements of precedent decomposition for the
verypetpurpose of subsequent recombination' (614.33–35). The
recombination occurs 'anastomosically' (615.5) by the fitting
together of pre-existing parts, both of type and of 'the ancient legacy
of the' past recycled in each new work. Through anastomoses, the
new text emerges 'type by tope, letter from litter', out of the
leavings of the literary tradition to express 'the sameold gamebold
adomic structure of our Finnius the old One' (615.6–7). At this
finish of the text, the reader 'finally (though not yet endlike)' makes
the acquaintance of 'Mister Typus, Mistress Tope and all the little
typtopies' (20.12–13) announced in the first chapter. That acquaintance accompanies our perception of the book's 'adomic structure'.
In that structure, the atom is an Adam within a 'Finnius', a beginning within an end.

*   *   *

The reintroduction of the letter at the book's ending evokes the
earlier representations of the letter but especially the enigmatic one
of I.4. By the time of its close the text has defined a perspective for
recomposing the earlier version and fitting it into the pattern that
version itself defines. If no other way, the final, fullest letter is
related to the earlier, shortest one because they begin and end
similarly. The body of the longer letter begins with the A of 'And'
(615.12), and the P.S., if it does not continue beyond one paragraph, concludes with the O of 'too' (619.19). We might be able to
discount the similarity except that this beginning and ending recur

elsewhere in the text. For example, II.2 begins with the A of 'As' (260.1) and ends with the 'o' of 'too' (308.25). *That* final 'o' is also the last letter of a letter. Two other passages in II.2 provide further confirmation. The eighteen words of the first paragraph as prelude begin with A and end with 'oo' (260.1–3), as does the following sequence of seven syllables in a paragraph devoted to letters: 'ah eh oh let me sigh too' (278.10–11). The numbers eighteen and seven will come up again.

One of the ostensible differences between the two letters concerns the passages following them. After the final letter, ALP's monologue leads into the beginning of the text, actually is the beginning, except that the nature of this narrative does not allow for the illusion of an originating beginning. There is an obvious parallel here between the two letters, especially if ALP's monologue is read as continuing the P.S. Since the letter begins with 'And', then merges with the introduction of the book, like the saga mimed by Inkermann's players, it becomes 'readable to int from and . . . and this applies to its whole wholume' (48.17–18). The seemingly unusual Möbean configuration of the letter in I.4 and the transforming of the whole volume into an analogous narrative sequence through the final letter direct the reader's attention to the *Nachtrag* as a model for narration in *Finnegans Wake*. The shape of the telling in the *Wake* seems unusual not because it is unique but because most writers devise a conventional screen to disguise the aspects of narrative that all Joyce's texts exhibit, the later ones more explicitly. The continuity and mutual framing of elements in the Möbean letter provide a model for the narration according to the principle voiced by one of the washerwomen in I.8: 'Never stop! Continuarration!' (205.14). Telling that is informed by this principle, as Joyce's narration generally is, insures the 'ensuance of existentiality' through an entailing that makes each text a serpent biting its own tail.

The letter of I.4 is followed not by a monologue but by the wandering deliberations of the four justices, the escape of the accused, and the story of his later life and demise. Eventually, however, the chapter ends with references to the babbling river, upon whose stones we have taken our sheet. Before that ending, the network of implications associated with the letter, including the defining presence of alpha and omega in the text, the allusions to printing, and the doubling back caused by joined ends, all appear in the story of the escapee. Because the a's and o's are presented especially prominently in the passage concerning the judges' deliberations, the reader may become sensitized to the proliferation of these vowels. Within a few lines of the letter appear the words 'Somany Solans' (94.27), 'a'duna o'darnel' (94.31), and the 'Ah ho' (94.33) that becomes a refrain elsewhere in *Finnegans Wake*.[27] The repeated appearances of these vowels in conjunction evoke the letter's form and its shapes as the text's form and as the pervasive signs of aesthetic creation within the narration. Of course, we need to be careful not to interpret the appearance of a's and o's in a monomaniacal or indiscriminate way. Since there are only five vowels in English, and since punning often depends on the substitution of one for another, the narration of the *Wake* abounds with instances of these two vowels used in curious ways. But, the placement and clustering of the a's and o's can lend them some special significance. In the passages I have selected, though by no means everywhere in the *Wake*, they indicate the omnipresence of the book's creator. Rather than a divinity, he is simply the ordering force of a work which, like Shem's creations, represents the author. Within this frame of self-portrayal, the syllables 'jas jos' in Shem's inkbottle house say more than just yes twice. The author signs his texts not only by affixing a name to a title page but by the mere act of writing. Like Gutenberg as 'Gutenmorg', the maker emerges from the book as wordpress by merging with it. Squirting out from the pressings comes the screen that is the author's image. If 'jas jos' abbreviates the real author's name, the combinations of vowels here and in some other parts of the *Wake* abbreviate the abbreviation. Letter and house, with their similar alphabetical contents, bear analogous relationships to the whole tale. Not only do we find ourselves in the house that Jack built, but Jack turns out to have been an architect who kept models of all the houses he built. The author's name as signature is contained within book, house, and letter, composed of each in its entirety, and imprinted on the cover that forms the 'marge' between the book and its environs.

* * *

Clearly, the simple Möbius strip works well as a paradigm for the macrostructure of the *Wake*, the book of 'Doublends Jined'. But it does not help describe the microstructural aspects of the book, particularly the complicated network of repetitions with variations that, like the elliptical letter itself, often stand in some synecdochic relation to the book's larger structure. We need a more complicated

model for visualizing geometrically the *Wake*'s interlocking complexities. Such a model can be generated out of the Möbius strip.

The totality of the book's segments are like a Möbius strip from
which many other strips have been propagated. If a paper model of
a Möbius strip is cut down its middle, not across its edges, the
resulting geometrical entity is not two independent strips but one
strip twice as long as the first, though narrower, containing two
twists rather than one. While this second strip is related to the
original one geometrically, the properties are not identical. The
surfaces of both original and doubled strips are finite but in part
unbounded, like the surface of a sphere. That is, we can draw a line
on each strip that will be continuous with itself, like the equator on
the globe. By following this line, it is possible to traverse an entire
side of the strip and return to the starting point. The line so
traversed constitutes a nonbounding cycle, since it does not form
the boundary of a two-dimensional figure on the strip's surface,
although such two-dimensional figures could be drawn on the strips.
The original strip and its immediate offspring created by cutting
differ in the relation of verso to recto. As the earlier drawings (Fig.
1a, b, c) indicate, in the original Möbius strip, verso and recto are
one and will both be traversed by any line drawn on the surface that
is a nonbounding cycle. Consequently, the original strip has only
one side. For the doubled strip and for any later strips made by
cuttings, recto and verso are not one. The new strips have two sides.
When cut in the manner described, the narrower lengths of joined
recto and verso from the original form a new recto and new verso
narrower than the first strip. The length of each new recto and each
new verso is identical to that of the entire first strip. Although each
side contains elements of the entire length of the parent strip, one
side is not continuous with the other. Repeated cuttings create a
convoluted mass of interlocking strips, not wholly independent of
one another, since they are coupled like twisted links of a chain. All
the strips are geometrically related because their lengths are all
equal and because some of their edges fit together like the pieces of
a jigsaw puzzle. Varying the widths and angles of cutting will produce a different shape for each strip. (See Figures 2a, b, c.) The mass
of connected strips that can be generated gives us the closest
geometric equivalent to the doublings, repetitions, and transformations in the narration of *Finnegans Wake*. The interlocking strips
originating from the one Möbius strip all tell versions of the same
story contained in the source that they replicate with variations.

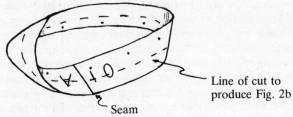

Line of cut to
produce Fig. 2b

Seam

Fig. 2a
The strip to be cut.

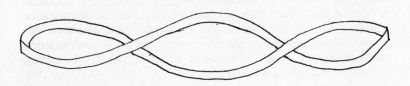

Fig. 2b
The strip after one cut, now twice as long with two twists

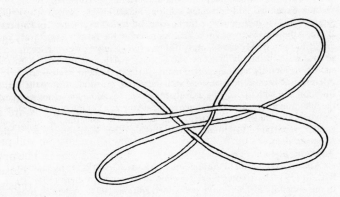

Fig. 2c
The strip after two cuts.
Each bisected strip contains two twists.

Each new space of paper, though only part of the first strip, tells its own rendition of the whole story. We have here something like the production of clones, the original entity being divided and doubled into simulacra of itself possessing related genetic structures. Like the parts of Humpty Dumpty, it seems hardly possible to put the fragments back together again into an original shape.

The cutting involved in transforming the single Möbius strip into its multifoliate offspring may remind us that the process of printing and binding books traditionally involves cutting and sewing cunningly folded papers. The importance of cutting and sewing in bookmaking probably has something to do with the recurring appearance of the tailor in the *Wake*. It also helps explain why ALP as Finnegan's widow is 'the tailor's daughter' (28.7). This '*figlia del tuo figlio,*' child of the tailor and progeny of the author as teller, mother of Shem the writer and draper (421.25), is 'sewing a dream together' (28.7). The result is the memorializing 'mamafesta' that stands for and within that other memorial, the book sewn together that we may unstitch and resew it. Penelope, we recall, was an unraveller as well as a weaver.

NOTES

1   In the criticism of Joyce's writing Atherton's book (New York: Viking Press, 1959; reprinted Carbondale, Illinois: Southern Illinois University Press, 1974; second, expanded and corrected edition, Mamaroneck, New York: Paul P. Appel, 1974) is indispensable for anyone interested in allusions in *Finnegans Wake*. Atherton discusses Joyce's allusions under the rubrics 'structural', 'literary', and 'sacred'. My commentary differs from his more extensive treatment in several ways, primarily in scope and emphasis. Atherton attempts with good success to identify and categorize many of the prominent sources for Joyce's references. My essay deals instead with the author's attitude toward the literary tradition and with the way he uses that tradition to define his stance as teller of the tale. Inevitably, my discussion overlaps Atherton's commentary in places. I wish to acknowledge my debt to his fine study and to point out that I gave much greater importance to Homer and to Joyce's other works in the *Wake* than Atherton does.

2   Atherton, p. 45.

3   As Atherton points out in the appendix, 'All Joyce's works are mentioned in the *Wake*' (259). He devotes a brief section of his study to them (106–10).

4   In the appendix of *The Books* (expanded edition, 1974), Atherton provides a long list of allusions to Wyndham Lewis, including this one. See his entry for references to critical discussions of Joyce and Lewis by Hugh Kenner and Adaline Glasheen (265–66).

5 Margot Norris discusses the bric-à-brac of the *Wake* as the material for *bricolage* in *The Decentered Universe of 'Finnegans Wake'* (Baltimore and London: The Johns Hopkins University Press, 1976), pp. 130–40.

6 Various passages in the *Wake* allude to 'the hoax that joke bilked' (511.34), including 271.25–29, 274.22, 369.13–15, 375.4, and 580.26–36.

7 Leonard Barkan discusses the tradition of such uses of the body in *Nature's Work of Art: The Human Body as Image of the World* (New Haven: Yale University Press, 1975). He does not include Joyce in his study.

8 Brendan O Hehir and John Dillon, *A Classical Lexicon for 'Finnegans Wake': A Glossary of the Greek and Latin in the Major Works of Joyce* (Berkeley, California: University of California Press, 1977), p. 326. Unless otherwise noted, all glosses involving Joyce's use of Latin and Greek are from this volume.

9 James Joyce, *Scribbledehobble: The Ur-workbook for 'Finnegans Wake'*, ed. Thomas E. Connolly (Evanston, Illinois: Northwestern University Press, 1961).

10 Robert Boyle has discussed this passage in his essay 'Portrait of the Artist as Balzacian Wilde Ass' in *A Conceptual Guide to 'Finnegans Wake'*, ed. Michael H. Bengal and Fritz Senn (University Park and London: The Pennsylvania State University Press, 1974), pp. 71–82.

11 Robert Boyle has suggested a similar interpretation for 'chagreenold' as an allusion to Balzac's story *Peau de Chagrin (Conceptual Guide*, pp. 76 ff.).

12 William York Tindall, *A Reader's Guide to 'Finnegans Wake'* (New York: Farrar, Straus and Giroux, 1969), p. 109.

13 William Savage, *A Dictionary of The Art of Printing* (London: Longman, Brown, Green, and Longmans, 1841; rpt. London: Gregg Press Ltd, 1966), p. 248. The information about printing employed in this essay is drawn primarily from Savage and from Philip Gaskell, *A New Introduction to Bibliography* (Oxford: Oxford University Press, 1972). Gaskell provides a history of book production through the middle of this century. Savage's dictionary includes a great many details concerning the practice and the traditions of letterpress printing.

14 In her *Third Census of 'Finnegans Wake': An Index of the Characters and Their Roles* (Berkeley, California: University of California Press, 1977), Adaline Glasheen suggests that as a verb 'pen' means to shut up (p. 229).

15 Gaskell, p. 126.

16 In the indispensable first appendix, 'An Index of Motifs in *Finnegans Wake*', to *Structure and Motif in 'Finnegans Wake'* (Northwestern University Press, 1962), Clive Hart lists the 'Major Statements' (232) of the letter. He does not mention the elliptical version of I.4.

17 Hart, p. 200.

18 Clive Hart discusses the longer allusions to Quinet's sentence in Chapter VII of *Structure and Motif* (pp. 182–200).

19 In his first appendix to *Structure and Motif*, Hart notes a dozen occurrences of the enjoinder to 'stop. Please stop', which he identifies as one of the letter's motifs (p. 233).

20 For this definition of 'clayman', see Philip Babcock Gove, ed., *Webster's Third New International Dictionary* (Springfield, Mass.: G. and C. Merriam Co., 1963), p. 418.

21 Savage, p. 24.

22 Adaline Glasheen links 'alcohoran' with Paul Horan (49.15), probably on the

basis of orthography (*Third Census,* p. 129).

23 Hugh Kenner, 'An Insane Assault on Chaos' (a review of *The James Joyce Archive* and *James Joyce's Manuscripts: An Index), The New York Times Book Review* (June 22, 1980), pp. 7 and 26–27.

24 Louis O. Mink mentions several interpretations of the diagram while explaining his geographical view in the 'Introduction' to *A 'Finnegans Wake' Gazetteer* (Bloomington and London: Indiana University Press, 1978), xxv–xxvi.

25 Cp. 'Listen, Listen! I am doing it' (571.24). This statement also concludes a paragraph containing references to printing.

26 Gaskell, p. 125.

27 Hart lists 'ah ho' and 'ah dear oh dear' as the characteristic sighs, respectively, of Mark Lyons and Luke Tarpey, two of the four annalists associated with the four provinces of Ireland. Whatever the specific ascriptions to characters, the proliferating a's and o's often suggest a creating presence of some sort as both end and beginning. For instance, in I.6, the fourth question (140.8–141.7), whose answer seems to be 'Dublin', includes several repetitions of a's and o's. Allusions to the four provinces do suggest the presence of the four annalists, but the a's and o's are linked as well to the 'd' and the 'n' of Dublin as 'origin' and 'end' (140.9).

THE POETRY OF JAMES JOYCE

FRANCIS WARNER

The wonderful measure and smack of Joyce's prose is not to be found in his poems; nevertheless, they make a fascinating study. Echoing his artificer, Stephen Dedalus explains to Cranly that

> The lyrical form is in fact the simplest verbal vesture of an instant of emotion

a 'cry or a cadence or a mood'.

> He who utters it is more conscious of the instant of emotion than of himself as feeling emotion.

When Joyce comes to write prose,

> The narrative is no longer purely personal. The personality of the artist passes into the narration itself, flowing round and round the persons and the action like a vital sea.[1]

It also fills them out from inside, as Keats knew, and could certainly operate through narrative verse. Consider John Donne's growing mandrake root:

> His right arme he thrust out towards the East
> Westward his left; th'ends did themselves digest
> Into ten lesser strings, these fingers were:
> And as a slumberer stretching on his bed,
> This way he this, and that way scattered
> His other legge, which feet with toes upbeare.
> Grew on his middle parts, the first day, haire,
> To show, that in love's business hee should still
> A dealer bee . . .[2]

One scarcely goes to Joyce for verse of this kind. However, a glance at 'A Memory of the Players in a Mirror at Midnight' shows something of the same gritty delight. The difference is that in Donne's poem we are aware above all of the feelings of the mandrake; in Joyce's of the poet:

> They mouth love's language. Gnash
> The thirteen teeth
> Your lean jaws grin with. Lash
> Your itch and quailing, nude greed of the flesh.
> Love's breath in you is stale, worded or sung,
> As sour as cat's breath,
> Harsh of tongue.
>
> This grey that stares
> Lies not, stark skin and bone.
> Leave greasy lips their kissing. None
> Will choose her what you see to mouth upon.
> Dire hunger holds his hour.
> Pluck forth your heart, saltblood, a fruit of tears.
> Pluck and devour![3]

Joyce peers at Donne 'despoyl'd of fallacies' through Yeats's spectacles. We remember Yeats's letter to Donne's editor, Sir Herbert Grierson, in 1912:

> [I] find that at last I can understand Donne . . . I notice that the more precise and learned the thought, the greater the beauty, the passion.

and letters to Lady Gregory from Yeats about Pound:

> Ezra never shrinks from work . . . A learned companion, and a pleasant one . . . He . . . helps me get back to the definite and the concrete, away from modern abstractions.[4]

By which, presumably, he means the Celtic Twilight. The result was the Yeatsean style already foreshadowed in 'The fascination of what's difficult'.

> There's something ails our colt
> That must, as if it had not holy blood
> Nor on Olympus leaped from cloud to cloud,

Shiver under the lash, strain, sweat and jolt
As though it dragged road metal.

The same 'verbigracious bigtimer', having left behind modern abstractions, can now write a marvellous, jaw-breaking line such as

Where we wrought that shall break the teeth of Time

in that finest of all his poems of friendship, 'The New Faces'.
Joyce is aware of all this happening between *Chamber Music* (1907) and *Pomes Penyeach* (1927). Hence the difference in style between 'Lean out of the window / Goldenhair' and 'They mouth love's language. Gnash'. During this period Joyce learns to plump out, Hopkinslike but in prose, the human mouth from inside, instead of describing it as in the first three lines of 'A Memory of the Players' like an irritated dentist. The words now tongue the cheeks, and touch inside the teeth:

Wine soaked and softened rolled pith of bread mustard a moment mawkish cheese.[5]

In Joyce's poem above (from *Pomes Penyeach*) we know the poet feels betrayed (hence the Judas number thirteen); prefers, like Caesar, a 'warm human plumpness' near him, such as Molly's ('Your lean jaws'); and has Lear's lashing beadle (or is it the flagellating God of Francis Thompson's 'Hound of Heaven'? 'Naked I wait Thy love's uplifted stroke!') on literary mind. Oddly, the rare side of Donne, and more particularly the familiar side of Donne's Elizabethan fellow-singers, whispers from the wings through the second verse; not least of the anonymous author of 'I saw my lady weep'.

Leave off in time to grieve

becomes

Leave greasy lips their kissing

bringing greasy Joan from her pot in *Love's Labour's Lost*. After Yeats, he can now risk a jaw-breaker:

Will choose her what you see to mouth upon and with a nod to Swinburne ('a fruit of tears'), end with a flourish playing Prometheus with Dedalus:

Pluck and devour!

It is not the Donne of the *Satires* that fathers most of Joyce's poems: rather is it Donne and Dowland's

> Stay, O sweet, and do not rise,
> The light that shines comes from thine eyes;
> The day breaks not, it is my heart,
> Because that you and I must part.
> Stay, or else my joys will die,
> And perish in their infancie.   (Grierson, p. 432)

> Of that so sweet imprisonment
>   My soul, dearest, is fain –
> Soft arms that woo me to relent
>   And woo me to detain.
> Ah, could they ever hold me there,
> Gladly were I a prisoner!

Chamber Music XXII

and we must return to the earlier book of poems. Many critics have drawn attention to the links with 'the asphodel fields of Fulke Greville and Sir Philip Sidney' (Horace Reynolds),[6] Rochester (Arthur Symons)[7] Waller and Herrick (*Manchester Guardian*)[8] and noted 'a deliberate archaism and a kind of fawning studiousness' (Morton D. Zabel).[9] What strikes us though today in the nineteen-eighties, surely, is the splendidly jarring technique Joyce cultivates of placing an askew word exactly where one might have expected the traditional lyric resolution.

> What counsel has the hooded moon
>   Put in thy heart, my shyly sweet,
> Of Love in ancient *plenilune*,
>   Glory and stars beneath his feet –
> A sage that is but kith and kin
> With the comedian *capuchin*?

Chamber Music XII

Why should the critic italicize? Let the words speak for themselves, and not only those from *Chamber Music*.

> The sly reeds whisper to the night
> A name – her name –
> And all my soul is a delight
> A swoon of shame.
>
> "Alone" (1916)

Back to the earlier volume:

> How sweet to lie there,
>   Sweet to kiss,
> Where the great pine forest
>   Enaisled is!
>
> *Chamber Music* XX

Many of the words that provide this effect are indeed 'antique' but the effect of their use in this way is most modern.

> Happy Love is come to woo
>   Thee and woo thy girlish ways –
> The zone that doth become thee fair,
> The snood upon thy yellow hair.   XI

> Go seek her out all courteously
>   And say I come,
> Wind of spices whose song is ever
>   Epithalamium.   XIII

and better still, remembering 'the more precise and learned the thought, the greater the beauty, the passion',

> That mood of thine, O timorous,
>   Is his, if thou but scan it well,
> Who a mad tale bequeaths to us
>   At ghosting hour conjurable –
> And all for some strange name he read
> In Purchas or in Holinshed.   XXVI

Now this is splendid. Far from ruining the delicate lyrics, this is what makes them worth re-reading. We soon forget that the lady's mood was timorous, but happily remember unexpectedly meeting once more the inspirers of Shakespeare and Coleridge. We are astonished to find cherubs like boy scouts using their bugles as loud-speakers:

> When thou hast heard his name upon
> The bugles of the cherubim
> Begin thou softly to unzone
> Thy girlish bosom . . .   XI

still more to find this a summons to nuptials. But nuptials they are. For this consummation nothing less than the greatest, the *Song of Songs,* must be versified (XIV). He can crack Yeats's Celtic bells with a grammarian's googly (no, he does not write 'innumerable' and follow Keats):

> While sweetly, gently, secretly,
> The flowery bells of morn are stirred
> And the wise choirs of faery
> Begin (innumerous!) to be heard.   XV

He can call up Greensleeves from the grave:

> Dear heart, why will you use me so?
> Dear eyes that gently me upbraid
> Still are you beautiful – but O,
> How is your beauty raimented!   XXIX

He can even disturb "The Blessed Damozel" once more:

> His hand is under
> Her smooth round breast.   XVIII

But by the last poem in the book he is doing something different. For Pound, 'I hear an army charging' was one of 'the few beautiful poems that still ring in my head' – and how well Pound writes on *Chamber Music*![10] Horace Reynolds listens for Yeats's "Hosting of the Sidhe" as he reads this poem. We should do better to remember Yeats's "Valley of the Black Pig":

. . . the clash of fallen horsemen and the cries
Of unknown perishing armies beat about my ears.

when we read

> I hear an army charging upon the land
> And the thunder of horses plunging, foam about their knees.

Morton D. Zabel welcomes 'Suckling and the Cavaliers' and 'the minor work of Crashaw' to aid our appreciation of the early poems; but the pressure of sensuous thinking in Crashaw is unlike anything in the poems of Joyce, and Joyce is best when he is furthest from the only Suckling he resembles, the coy one.

Joyce may indeed be, in *Chamber Music*, as he confesses, a 'sweet sentimentalist (XII), but the sentimentality is redeemed not only by the overall theme and shape of the book, to which we shall come in a moment, but also by many incidental felicities over and above those mentioned, not least Joyce's ability to capture 'a gesture and a pose' or (to exchange Eliot for Pound) a medallion:

> Firmness,
> Not the full smile,
> His art, but an art
> In profile.

If medallion is too strong a word, then Joyce's still moments are at least clear-cut snapshots.

> All softly playing
>   With head to music bent,
> And fingers straying
>   Upon an instrument.   I

We hear much about his musicality, but should also note how visual many of the songs are.

> The old piano plays an air,
>   Sedate and slow and gay;
> She bends upon the yellow keys,
>   Her head inclines this way.   II

My love goes slowly, bending to
   Her shadow on the grass   VII

(We are in the world of Bonnard rather than the Pre-Raphaelites.)

The sun is in the willow leaves
   And on the dappled grass
And still she's combing her long hair
   Before the lookingglass.   XXIV

This is not to deny his ear. He can fill a line with every open vowel.

For lo! the trees are full of sighs

'the verse with its black vowels and its opening sound, rich and lutelike', as Dedalus says, misquoting Nashe; and indeed Joyce wrote to Gogarty as early as 1900:

> my idea for July and August is this – to get Dolmetsch to make a lute and to coast the south of England from Falmouth to Margate, singing old English songs.

The musicality, and the visual awareness, the ability to evoke mood with 'the cross run of the beat and the word, as of a stiff wind cutting the ripple-tops of bright water' as Pound notes,[11] all draw us back to these poems, but there is a deeper music, of the intellect beyond the senses, that lifts *Chamber Music* above slightness, and to bring this into focus we must go back to Joyce's own words on the book.

On 19th July, 1909, he wrote to G. Molyneux Palmer from Trieste:

> I hope you may set all of *Chamber Music* in time. This was indeed partly my idea in writing it. The book is in fact a suite of songs and if I were a musician I suppose I should have set them to music myself. The central song is XIV after which the movement is all downwards until XXXIV which is vitally the end of the book. XXXV and XXXVI are tailpieces just as I and II are preludes.

We are now in a position to see the work whole. The central climax of the suite is the *Song of Songs,* greatest of all love-poems and neatly versified by Joyce. At the centre of this (thirty-five words before it in a poem of seventy words) is the upstanding and timeless cedar of Lebanon. The poem immediately preceding this one urges

> Go seek her out all courteously
>   And say I come,
> Wind of spices whose song is ever
>   Epithalamium.

In other words, as was hinted earlier in this note and in later words of this poem, a 'bridal wind is blowing'. *Chamber Music* is a book that presupposes marriage at its centre. The poem following XIV (the climax) begins

> From dewy dreams, my soul, arise,
>   From love's deep slumber and from death,
> For lo! the trees are full of sighs
>   Whose leaves the morn admonisheth.

We can now see that those poems leading up to the *Song of Songs* are all of hopeful expectancy. But by XXX

> We were grave lovers. Love is past . . .

'the movement is all downwards' after the cedared celebration, and XXXIV 'which is vitally the end of the book' lays a gentle tombstone on the memory of the romance:

> Sleep now, O sleep now,
>   O you unquiet heart!
> A voice crying 'Sleep now'
>   Is heard in my heart.

The tailpiece, the final line of the book, simply reads

> My love, my love, my love, why have you left me alone?

So the whole process, from wooing, proposal, eager anticipation of marriage, fulfilment (either real or imagined), betrayal and desertion by the woman is complete, and the poet is left alone, rueful, in despair, exchanging

> those treasures I possessed
> Ere that mine eyes had learned to weep   XXIII

for a new outward emblem of an inner state, the whirling laughter of a charging army of horsemen, clanging upon his heart as upon an anvil, fighting bitterness with an anguished rhetorical question.

The book survives because, over and above the individual qualities of single poems, the sequence is not only (as many critics have implied) more than the sum of its parts, but that sum is the archetypal theme of the depth and intensity of male devotion measured against the playfulness and 'slydynge corage' of a female who is unable to sustain a love involving those highest stakes we call marriage. Joyce may at times be sentimental in this book, but we do not feel he is insincere; and in the end we grieve with him (or his poet in the verse-narrative) and remember the woman as beautiful, sweet-bosomed, musical, goldenhaired, but girlish and spiritually inadequate to cope with the poet's intensity and the integrity of a serious relationship.

Pomes Penyeach does not make this claim on us. 'You don't think they're worth printing at any time?' asked Joyce? 'No, I don't.' replied Pound. 'Read Ralph Cheever Dunning. They belong in the Bible or the family album with the portraits.'[12] Not so. We have already enjoyed 'A Memory of the Players in a Mirror at Midnight', and the last poem in the book brings back Hopkin's (and Thompson's)

> I did say yes
> O at lightning and lashed rod

with a vengeance:

> *Come*! I yield. Bend deeper upon me! I am here.
> Subduer, do not leave me! Only joy, only anguish,
> Take me, save me, soothe me, O spare me!

The childhood carol 'Star of wonder' is briskly turned insideout in 'Bahnhofstrasse':

> Ah star of evil! star of pain

(Swinburne's to blame, not Baudelaire), and he can both bring on the earlier techniques:

> Uplift and sway, O golden vine,
> Your clustered fruits to love's full flood,

Lambent and vast and ruthless as is thine
Incertitude!

'Flood'

and send them up with a straight face in 'Simples':

Be mine, I pray, a waxen ear
To shield me from her childish croon.

'Simples', opines Morton D. Zabel, 'must rank as one of the purest lyrics of our time.'[13]

Joyce has changed since the earlier volume. We have word-coinage that looks forward beyond *Ulysses*:

And long and loud,
To night's nave upsoaring,
A starknell tolls
As the bleak incense surges, cloud on cloud,
Voidward from the adoring
Waste of souls.   'Nightpiece' (1915)

The puns on 'tonight' and '(k)nave' scarcely succeed; 'voidward' passes; 'starknell' is good and the pun on 'Waste' excellent. In the first verse of this same poem Francis Thompson's 'I fled him down the arches of the years' reappears (perhaps) in

Ghostfires from heaven's far verges faint illume,
Arches on soaring arches,
Night's sindark nave.

but we read this today with added relish recalling Joyce's later pliant girls and knavish priests after dark in Phoenix Park: 'bidimetoloves sinduced by what tegotetabsolvers'.[14] Richard Ellmann has skilfully unfolded the biographical mystery within 'She weeps over Rahoon':

Still trying to penetrate (Nora's) soul, he wrote a poem to express what he felt to be her thoughts about her dead lover and her living one. He shifted Bodkin's grave from Oughterard, seventeen miles from Galway, to the Galway cemetery at Rahoon with its more sonorous name . . . The dead sweetheart was brought into a mortuary triangle with the two living lovers. With a sense of sacred coincidence Joyce found a headstone at Rahoon with the name J. Joyce upon it.[15]

Ellmann also explains why the first poem in the book is called 'Tilly':

> The word 'tilly' means the thirteenth in a baker's dozen; Joyce had thirteen (instead of twelve) poems in *Pomes Penyeach*, which sold for a·shilling [16]

and points out that it was written as early as 1904, some months after his mother had died, and James had found and read a packet of love-letters from his father to his mother.

> Boor, bond of the herd,
> Tonight stretch full by the fire!
> I bleed by the black stream
> For my torn bough!

None of them are in the same league as that perfect poem "*Ecce Puer*", written after Helen Joyce's difficult pregnancy and on the day of the birth of Stephen James Joyce, his grandson. The deep joy is set in perspective by the recollection in the last verse that Joyce's own father had died only forty-nine days before. It is superb. As in a different context Samuel Beckett wrote of Jack Yeats's achievement, so here: we will not criticize; 'simply bow in wonder'.[17]

> Of the dark past
> A child is born;
> With joy and grief
> My heart is torn
>
> Calm in his cradle
> The living lies.
> May love and mercy
> Unclose his eyes!
>
> Young life is breathed
> On the glass;
> The world that was not
> Comes to pass.

126

A child is sleeping:
An old man gone.
O, father forsaken,
Forgive your son!

NOTES

1   The three quotations are from *A Portrait of the Artist as a Young Man*, p. 194, Triad Panther/Granada edition.
2   Donne, *The Progress of the Soule*, verse XV.
3   *Pomes Penyeach*, p. 23, Faber and Faber edition of 1966.
4   The letters are dated 1 January 1915, and 3 January 1913.
5   *Ulysses*, p. 222, Bodley Head edition, 1960.
6   See *James Joyce: The Critical Heritage*, edited by Robert H. Deming, vol. II, p. 649.
7   Ibid., vol. I, p. 38.
8   Ibid., vol. I, p. 41.
9   Ibid., vol. I, p. 46.
10   *The Future*, May, 1918 (also infra, p. 413).
11   *Literary Essays of Ezra Pound*, Faber & Faber, 1954, p. 14.
12   See Richard Ellmann's *James Joyce*, p. 603, for the full anecdote.
13   Deming, vol. one, p. 48.
14   *Finnegans Wake*, Faber & Faber, p. 4.
15   Ellmann, pp. 335–6.
16   Ibid, p. 142.
17   'Hommage à Jack B. Yeats', Les Lettres Nouvelles, 2e année (Avril 1954).

JAMES JOYCE

Under the dented hat
with high black band;

that long face, sloping
like a gable down
to the jutting jaw;
sallow skin, scant
moustache, swallowed

by dark sudden-
ly glinting glasses

those slender fingers
cramped around a
walking stick or
white wine glass;
it could be my

father or yours;
any worn, life

tempered man if
the caption lacked
the detail – bright as
heresiarch or fallen
angel – of his name.

John Montague

A TURNIP FOR THE BOOKS – AN ESSAY IN CELEBRATION OF JAMES JOYCE ON HIS CENTENARY, BY A FELLOW DUBLINER

DAVID NORRIS

> He [Joyce] made clear to Beckett his dislike of literary talk.
> Once when they had listened silently to a group of intellectuals at
> a party, he commented, 'If only they'd talk about turnips'.[1]

There is a particular zest and flavour to my celebration of one
hundred years of James Joyce born not merely of the fact that I am
in a modest way a scholar of his works, but of the natural pride one
takes in a child of the neighbourhood. For the Joyce of eighty, a
hundred, years ago is still in essence my neighbour here in Dublin. I
open my own hall door in the morning, and glancing up the street
catch sight of the heavy hall door of Belvedere College, from which
the young Stephen Dedalus emerged into the secular world. From
my study window I can look across into rooms graced by the shades
of Sir John Mahaffy, Lady Maxwell and Professor Maginni. My
evening promenade around Mountjoy Square is accomplished in
the spectral company of the superior, the very reverend John Conmee S.J., while on my way to the local chip shop I can play a tune on
Leopold Bloom's front railings. Passing in the other direction I can
collect my newspaper from the shop of Mr. Lucky Duffy in Great
Britain (now Parnell) Street, to whom the cases, painful or pleasur-
able of so many characters fictionalized by Joyce are but the factual
if fading memories of a Dublin childhood.

Joyce's interest in these streets and their inhabitants, however,
was never merely local or antiquarian, and although it was about
them that he wrote uniquely and exclusively, his was no mood of
simplistic celebration. Indeed his brother Stanislaus even suggested
ironically that so generally applicable was Joyce's scathing analysis
of urban life that there were many continental cities which should
consider erecting a statue of the writer in their central square in
gratitude to a kindly fate for ensuring 'that that uncompromising

129

realist was not born within their boundaries'.² Stanislaus gives a pronounced and, I believe, proper emphasis to James' role as an *interpreter* of city life, a notion that carries a special resonance for the sharp eyed student of Joycean prose.

> My brother's major work came at the close of an epoch of Irish, perhaps one may say, of European history, to give a comprehensive picture of it in the daily life of a large city. He always held that he was lucky to have been born in a city that is old and historic enough to be considered a representative European capital, and small enough to be viewed as a whole; and he believed that circumstances of birth talent and character had made him its interpreter. To that duty of interpretation he devoted himself with a singleness of purpose that made even the upheaval of world wars seem to him meaningless disturbances.³

Interestingly Joyce himself leaves several clues for us even in his early writings that suggest both his concurrence with this view of his work and possible guidelines that may illuminate the way for his readers. In *Dubliners* for example the process undertaken by the author is apparently a species of literary scatoscopy. As the medical scientist scrutinizes bodily eliminations under the microscope as an aid to diagnosis, so Joyce, who in youth fancied himself as medical student, set to a minute analysis of the eliminations of an entire culture as the excretion of an exhausted language system by the semi-paralysed citizens of his native city is revealed through the lens of a style of 'scrupulous meanness'.⁴

The motivating principle for this unusual approach, so disturbing to his contemporaries, can be found in the circumstances that shaped his life in Dublin. By birth and education he belonged to the Catholic upper middle class, yet his father's profligacy ensured that by early adolescence his actual experience was not materially different from that of most of his neighbours in the north city slums to which the family had by then moved. To the sensitive child the discrepancy between the pious precepts of his Jesuit education and his father's constant exhortation 'always to be a gentleman' and 'never to peach on a fellow',⁵ on the one hand, and the squalid reality of the life around him on the other, must have been at first confusing and then revelatory. Some measure of the astonishing, even heroic degree to which these wounds of his formative years were cauterized by the comic genius can be obtained if one consults the record of contemporary actuality provided as a gloss by Stanislaus Joyce's *Dublin Diary:*

> Food is good and warmth is good. This is a good house to learn to appreciate both in. We do weeks on one chance insufficient meal, and a collation in the days I have been stripped of my garments, even of my heavy boots, willingly stripped to pawn them and feed on them.[6]

Remarkably this extract describes the real state of affairs in the Joyce household within a few weeks of the day Joyce chose to celebrate in the pages of *Ulysses* – 16th June 1904.

In *Ulysses* this shipwreck of the family fortunes and the resulting treacherous undertow is imaged in Stephen's reflection on the fate of his sister Dilly and its implications:

> She is drowning. Agenbite. Save her. Agenbite. All against us. She will drown me with her, eyes and hair. Lank coils of seaweed hair around me, my heart, my soul. Salt green death.[7]

Such hazardous water could be safely navigated only with the compass of a central spiritual certainty.

The problem, and it must have seemed at times an insoluble one, was to locate some such pivotal reality in the prevailing ambivalence of late 19th century Ireland. In the politics of the time, an historical watershed had been provided by the destruction of Parnell, a man deemed unfit to lead on the grounds of his adultery with Mrs. O'Shea by a nation whose capital city sported the largest brothel area in Europe. The once brilliant social life of Dublin had gradually dwindled to a level of comfortable suburbanism after the extinction of the independent parliament with the Act of Union in 1800. Culturally the appetite of the majority of solid burghers was satisfied with the sonorities of 'Lawn Tennyson' or the melodic sentimentality of Thomas Moore in poetry, the theatricality of Dion Boucicault in drama and the wistful cadences of Balfe, Benedict and Sullivan in the music of opera and ballad. If finally the young Joyce looked to the church as the place most appropriate for spiritual renewal, he seemed to find there increasingly not religion but religiosity, a husk from which the vital source of energy had shrivelled and withdrawn.

In 'Stephen Hero',[8] with its description of the clergy as vermin,

131

locusts and lice feeding on a corrupt host, the vehemence of his denunciation testifies both to the intensity of the believer's disappointment at the unmasking of a charade and to the economy and integrity with which the method of later work brought such excess under artistic control. Thus it became ever more urgent for Joyce, placed as he was by his own social circumstances at a critical angle to his environment, to discover a method by which focus could be restored, the blurring and distorting effects of spiritual hemiplegia eliminated, and a process evolved which could express accurately the universal values encountered in his own experience.

The key to the creation of an authentic value-system it seemed clear was language, that main vehicle of the intellectual and cultural life of a people, and Joyce set out in his writing to resolve a complex of personal aesthetic and spiritual problems by synchronising language and the reality it sought to reflect. Thus the miracle performed in his daily office by the 'priest of eternal imagination'[9] concerned not in summoning the real presence of Christ to the elements of the Eucharist, but rather recharging the texture of words, of language itself with the presence of real meaning, restoring it to full power as an instrument of human communion.

In *A Portrait of the Artist* Joyce uses the technique of an embryonic development pattern in language to illustrate a correlation between psychological and linguistic growth. The concern with language and its manipulation shared by Stephen and his creator is, however, evidently more than just a structural or stylistic device; it is also for both part of a process of personal validation. Stephen's mastery of language enables him to cling to a sense of personal worth despite the growing squalor of his home life by regularly winning first place in the class each Tuesday with his weekly essay. Then, when the inevitable disaster occurs, the scene is given a special poignancy in the minutely observed detail of the imagery through which it is presented:

On a certain Tuesday the course of his triumphs was rudely broken. Mr Tate, the English master, pointed his finger at him and said bluntly:

This fellow has heresy in his essay.

A hush fell on the class. Mr Tate did not break it but dug with his hand between his crossed thighs while his heavily starched linen creaked about his neck and wrists. Stephen did not look up. It was a raw spring morning and his eyes were still smarting and weak. He was conscious of failure and of detection, of the squalor of his own mind and home, and felt against his neck the raw edge of his turned and jagged collar.'[10]

Joyce creates a kind of chiming effect by reiteration of the word neck and the images of collar and cuffs, while the trailing off of this reverberation into discord with the opposition of the master's beautifully laundered linen as against the pitiful indication of the scholarship boy's poverty in his turned and jagged collar discloses the genuine pathos of the situation. It is significant that what is exposed here is the raw nerve of social rather than intellectual vulnerability. That a memory of this desolate feeling of exposure survived even the full adoption of a mandarin style in life and art can be seen in the repetition of a closely similar image at the opening of *Ulysses*, where the 'wellfed voice' of plump Buck Mulligan grates on Stephen's consciousness as he gazes at 'the fraying edge of his shiny black coat-sleeves'.[11] Silence, exile and cunning, the induration of the shield, only gradually allowed superiority of intellect to become a defence against the shafts of the mercenary and the mediocre. Throughout his life attempts were made to denigrate Joyce by reference to the sordid aspects of his childhood experience, but by the 1920s, when George Moore, 'a genuine gent / That lives on his property's ten per cent',[12] thought fit to cavil at his background – 'Joyce, Joyce, why he's nobody, from the Dublin docks; no family, no breeding',[13] he was safe from such taunts. He knew by then that if he were no 'gentleman' according to the tests applied by his own father, George Moore or even Virginia Woolf, he was more rarely an aristocrat of the mind.

There is indeed a splendid irony in the way in which this great artist was able to send a whole epoch of literary 'gentlemen' scouring the trivia of his life for clues to the meaning of his work. Moreover the security finally achieved in the midst of this flux meant that Joyce could, in his role of priest, physician and prophet, turn outwards from the contemplation of his own soul to confront the complexities of humanity at large. For despite the acknowledged ironies of the fictional portrait, what was being forged in the smithy of his soul was not alone the identity of an artist but also in a real sense 'the uncreated conscience' of his 'race'.[14] The corollary of this is that Joyce intended his meaning to be generally accessible to the sane and careful reader, not merely the province of the academician or aesthete, and it is worth remembering that even his

133

celebrated remark about *Ulysses* that 'I've put in so many enigmas and puzzles that it will keep the professors busy for centuries arguing over what I meant, and that's the only way of insuring one's immortality'[15] implies a considerably less flattering estimate of the intelligence of his critics than of the ultimate intelligibility of his creation. He knew intuitively and by experience that the average academic mind, while it can happily analyse pattern, is often delicate and hesitant before the risk-ridden responsibility of pronouncing upon significance. In the most fantastic confidence trick of all, the master forger used the world of scholarship to ensure the survival of his work and the celebration of his personality, and moreover, as in the case of many of the more discreet and subtle forms of viral life, the function of the carrier was utilitarian, the real target lay elsewhere. Why else would this apparently most hermetic of artists write to his brother that Wordsworth (that 'man speaking to men'[16]) 'of all English men of letters most deserves your word "genius" '?[17]

That Joyce saw himself also as a man speaking to men and his art as a speaking picture, a mirror held up to nature, is evident both from his fictional works and his letters. He knew well himself that his art not only reflected nature but provided sections of his audience with a fairly traumatizing glimpse of themselves in his 'nicely polished looking-glass'.[18] Indeed the problematic reception of his early writing was frequently occasioned not so much by the obscurity as by the clarity and directness of his meaning. Joyce's forthrightness, for example, in the early broadsides 'Gas from a Burner' and 'The Holy Office' make equivocation an impractical method of evading the reality he portrayed. These two energetic squibs show him blowing the whistle on the conspiracy of silence, hypocrisy and spurious delicacy that traditionally enervated Irish life. In 'Gas from a Burner' the speaker represents this conventional habit of mind, and Joyce exposes through the many discrepancies of his speech the underlying inadequacy of such platitudinous assumptions about life and art. The 'Ladies and Gents' apostrophized in the poem have sensibilities too delicate to survive an encounter in print with the vulgar realities of the Wellington Monument or the Sandymount tram,[19] yet their susceptibilities are apparently not greatly jarred by the colloquial ejaculation 'Shite and onions' that accompanies the high-minded rejection of such humble artistic materials. This metaphysical conceit* greatly favoured by John Stanislaus Joyce in

---

* According to the Johnsonian definition whereby a metaphysical conceit consists of

conversation nevertheless roused him to gentlemanly fury when his son actually wrote it down.[21] This is one minor instance among many of Joyce practising the virtue of 'connection' preached about by the Timid Spirit of E.M. Forster in more conventional form. In fact one might say that Joyce's proven ability to 'connect the passion and the prose',[22] as opposed to Forster's limp sermonizing on the topic, suggests the difference between the properly ordained priest who has sacramental powers and the lay preacher who has not.

To Joyce the vocation of the artist, 'to try slowly and humbly and constantly to express, to press out again, from the gross earth or what it brings forth . . . an image of the beauty we have come to understand',[23] was paradoxically one that required almost saintly qualities of integrity and dedication. Moreover, fascinated as he was by the imagery of religious observance, he plundered theological terminology for phrases to describe the artistic process – epiphany, epicleti, eucharist, even admitting vicariously that his complex aesthetic theories were no more than 'applied Aquinas'.[24] It is natural, therefore, that we should find ourselves returning repeatedly to the image of the artist as priest, and not surprisingly we discover that, when we do, Joyce like any good pastor has embedded in his works the substance of a parable for the guidance of his flock. If we begin genesis-like at the beginning with Joyce's first published work of fiction, a story entitled 'The Sisters', the essential material of the parable can be assembled.

At the centre of this story is the impact of the death of an old priest, his former instructor, on the imagination of a small boy. The scene opens with the child speculating on the priest's imminent demise, and as he does so, three words are allowed by Joyce to resonate in his mind – paralysis, simony and gnomon. Now of course it is naturalistically appropriate for the narrator to roll round in his head and on his tongue a strange, scarcely understood word in the company of other similarly difficult and puzzling terms. As with the young Stephen in similar circumstances incantation seems to him almost capable of bringing about comprehension by osmosis –

> Words which he did not understand he said over and over to himself till he had learned them by heart: and through them he had glimpses of the real world about him.[25]

'heterogeneous ideas yoked by violence together'.[20] Few ideas would appear so naturally heterogeneous as shite and onions until welded together in the expostulatory heat of one of John Stanislaus' diatribes.

However, it is clear that Joyce as an artist has not been random in his selection of this apparently casual collection of words. Paralysis has long been understood as not only the immediate physical circumstance of the priest, but also symptomatic of that wider hemiplegia of the will – the condition Joyce saw as characteristic of his fellow citizens and which he set out to examine in *Dubliners*.

Simony is also a fairly accessible word which derives from the New Testament figure of Simon Magus who attempted to acquire by barter the magical properties of the Holy Spirit, which he saw as a kind of superior conjuring trick. In Joyce, the notion of simony expands beyond the circumstantial mercenary exchanges duly recorded in each of the *Dubliners* stories to cover any attempt to project a specific material equivalence for things of the spirit. The notion of simony is used by Joyce particularly in *Dubliners* and *A Portrait* to expose the hucksterish calculations and self-protecting shrewdness of the characters. It is also the central accusation contained in these books against the institutions of religion which are portrayed as devices more intent on appropriating and restraining the energies of the Holy Spirit than on liberating those of the Human Spirit. From this view derives a whole series of images representing the theological and dogmatic traditions of Christendom as a rigid, stifling encrustation on the living word of Christ – chalices, confessionals, monstrances, even exploding into the baroque with a Ken Russell style cash register that rings up the lobotomized 'paterings' of adolescents as 'frail columns of incense or as a slender flower'.[26]

To complete the triad what shall we say of gnomon? In my guise as 'plain reader' (and don't let us forget that this story first appeared in the 'Pigs' Paper' as the result of an invitation from George Russell to write something 'simple'[27]) I am a little disheartened at the amount of pointed geometrical paraphernalia and debris through which I am expected by some of my academic colleagues to pick a nimble way to the path to understanding. If *Dubliners* is, as I have heard whispered, about a series of psychological parallelograms wandering wistfully round Dublin as they plaitively search for their missing bits and pieces, then the 'pigs' to whom it was originally addressed must be still scratching their wings with their trotters in puzzled wonderment, and Joyce must stand convicted of a major literary flaw – the total inability to communicate a primary level of meaning to his readers for over half a century. However, I believe that this is more related to that process of mystification by which critics enhance their own reputation for cleverness at the expense of the integrity of their subject's work. Indeed, as Hemingway, who made both a virtue and a literary style of crystalline clarity, says, 'there are many mysteries, but incompetence is not one of them'.[28] So may I, dear plain reader, attempt in my perhaps brash way something of a spring cleaning, and clearing out an accumulation of exegetical intricacies that I believe have obscured the text, ask what is the 'simple' meaning of 'gnomon'? The answer quite straightforwardly is that it is a Greek word meaning 'interpreter', which brings us back by a commodius vicus of recirculation to the word underlined by Stanislaus as representing Joyce's chief function in relation to his native city. Moreover, lest we miss the point Joyce goes to the unusual trouble of translating the term for us two stories later on in 'Araby', where the child narrator constructs his own explanation for some typical Joycean 'noises off' and announces that he 'could interpret these signs'.[29] The interpretation offered is not a particularly rarefied one but aptly enough an acknowledgement of the drab Dublin reality that his uncle has, like Freddy Malins 'turned up screwed' again.[30]

If we apply the suggestions gleaned from our examination of these three key words to an analysis of 'The Sisters', the concealed form of this elliptical, enigmatic story emerges from the page as in that child's game wherein a picture is gradually formed from the joining up of a series of printed dots. 'The Sisters' itself, as we recall, evaporates irritatingly into just such a cloud of dots, in the manner of those mysterious North American rivers which disappear suddenly and tantalisingly into the desert sands. However, throughout the narrative we watch as the boy, acting as 'gnomon' himself, puzzles his head over old Cotter's unfinished sentences, and then in a dream reaches into his subconcious mind for images to assist in the interpretation of the riddle of the priest's paralysis and death. In the surreal world of sleep the child applies the third word from his treasury of hieroglyphics to the priest and labels him *Simoniac*. In what does his simony consist? It is time for us too, Joyce seems to suggest, to become interpreters.

The old priest we learn was 'too scrupulous always';

It was that chalice he broke. . . . That was the beginning of it. Of course, they say it was all right, that it contained nothing, I mean. But still. . . .[31]

137

To Father Flynn, a crude and pedantic literalist in the performance of his religious duties, the chalice, however his sisters may dissimulate in his defence, is a sacred vessel containing the real substance of the Godhead. Yet when the catastrophe struck and he suffered it to crash to the sanctuary floor, the veil of the temple was not rent, there was no thunderflash at his blasphemous carelessness, no sign was manifested of the presence of a vengeful and insulted God save that most sinister of all, the awful hollowness of silence. In a split second the mists of superstition part, his imaginative certainties are challenged and in a moment of existential truth the universe turns to him its bland unfeatured countenance; but he cannot measure up to the tragic intensity of the experience and the instant of revelation passes. Unlike Kurtz in Conrad's 'Heart of Darkness', he does not return from his encounter with emptiness satanically ennobled. He has seen the Horror, but in his panic denies it. Instead, he retreats into the hollow forms of religiosity. Malignantly he erects a barricade of sterile legalisms, 'books as thick as the *Post Office Directory* and as closely printed as the law notices in the newspaper',[32] against the innocence of the child, persuading him that aspects of the church's life that he 'had always regarded as the simplest acts' were in fact 'complex and mysterious'.[33] Herein lies the fundamental hemiplegia of the will, more debilitating than any merely physical paralysis, a classical example of the simoniacal inversion at work. Measure against the strictures of the old Pharisee the words of Christ himself –

> except ye be converted, and become as little children, ye shall not enter into the kingdom of Heaven[34]

or again

> Suffer little children to come unto me, and forbid them not; for of such is the kingdom of God.'[35]

No wonder then that Fr. Flynn's emblem is the empty chalice. At last we know in the deepest sense what went 'wrong with him. . .'.

It is possible, in other words, to comprehend the story at its most significant level of meaning without recourse to that process of mystification to which we can all as critics tend at the expense of the integrity of the artist's work. I believe that Joyce warns us deliberately in at least two other places in *Dubliners* alone against too rigidly symbolic an interpretation of his work as being a form of critical simony. We have, for example, the pathetic pseudo-poet, Little Chandler with his Mittyesque melancholy, weighing his soul to see if it was a poet's soul, composing complacent reviews of poems he is incapable of actually creating, and sprinkling his hypothetical verses with 'allusions' in case the English critics failed to register *the Celtic note*.[36] Even more telling in 'The Dead', Gabriel's unwitting violation of his wife's human reality by sentimentally enshrining her in the prison-frame of his symbolic dream picture, 'Distant Music',[37] is both a mark of his imaginative incompetence and his failure to interpret her emotional experience accurately. Once again the symbolic structure applied, ornate, arrogant and spiky, like the simoniacal image of the monstrance in *A Portrait* – 'the flashing gold thing into which God was put on the altar'[38] – is discovered to be empty. The bird has flown from its gilded cage and of its former presence all that remains is a hardening crust to comfort the credulous.

However, my real point, positive rather than negative, is that there is much in Joyce for us all, academics and amateurs alike, to profit by and enjoy if only we listen carefully and not too solemnly to his words. For it's all, as Bloom acknowledges in *Ulysses*, 'on account of the sounds it is'.[39] Take the two stories we have looked at in greatest detail. 'The Sisters' is about paralysis; Joyce therefore ensures, as any sensitive reader will confirm, that the very texture of the prose itself is crippled and halting in its movements. Proof? Well, I suggest that sceptics attempt a simple practical test. The compilation of separate lists of the parts of speech used by Joyce as linguistic ingredients, particularly modifiers such as adjectives and adverbs (a parsimoniacal exercise of which I have been guilty myself), discloses a constant rhythmic pattern in which the overall negative implications of the language absorb and submerge any sporadic intrusion of positive values among the adjectives, while through the adverbs the very motion of the prose itself assumes something of the sluggish and imperfect movement of the paralytic. In 'The Dead' Joyce's 'Musemathematics' is at its most subtle as he employs a verbal effect comparable to that of sympathetic resonance in keyboard music, in which the strings of a chord that is depressed without being actually played resonate harmonically with notes struck by the melody. In terms of the language structure of 'The Dead', Joyce depresses a minor chord creating the subtle accompaniment of a sinister resonance which runs counter to the apparently positive values of the prose at a propositional level. Thus the phrase, for example, describing the Miss Morkans' party, 'Never once had it fallen flat',[40] gives the information on a factual level that the party was always successful, but actually creates quite a different impression in the mind of the reader by virtue of its tortuously negative suggestion. Instances could be multiplied almost endlessly. The pictures which decorate the apartment deal on the surface with positive subjects – a scene of two lovers, but they are Romeo and Juliet and a sticky end to romance is implied; two sweet little Fauntleroys turn out on closer inspection to be the Princes in the Tower and they, as we know, wound up under the stone slab of a staircase; a group of young men attracted to the door of the drawing room by that tinkling of a piano melt away again when they realise that it is only Mary Jane playing her 'Academy piece, full of runs and difficult passages'.[41]

What is true of *Dubliners* holds also for *A Portrait of the Artist*. A central crucial moment is Stephen's decision to opt for the priesthood of Art in preference to that of Rome. Joyce gives us this information delicately obliquely and by suggestion through subtle changes in the quality of the language. Stephen emerges after his interview with the director of vocations from the portals of Belvedere College to the accompaniment of long drawn out vowel sounds which are suddenly interrupted by the lilting, syncopated rhythms of a group of young men 'striding along with linked arms, swaying their heads and stepping to the agile melody of their leader's concertina'.[42] Joyce characterises the group as a quartet, a word that rises optimistically in the stress of its second syllable, while six pages further on a similar group of Christian Brothers becomes a 'squad'. The emotional reality of Stephen's choice is reflected beautifully and economically in the contrasting sound of the two words selected.

In *Ulysses* itself Stephen's concentrated intellectual soliloquy on the protean dilemma of the artist attempting to fix a moment of reality amid the flux, to 'snatch out of time the passionate transitory',[43] is vividly and immediately communicated to any reader who can hear in his mind the 'fourworded wavespeech: seesoo, hrss, rsseeiss, ooos'.[44] Even in *Finnegans Wake* where Joyce claimed he would 'wipe alley English spooker, multaphoniasically spuking, off the face of the erse', he was careful, as Ellmann records, to leave at least some handles for the universal average reader, telling the initially hostile Max Eastman that he was glad that he had at least appreciated the book's humour for

It would be terrible to think that I had done all that work and not given you any pleasure at all. . . . For certainly the motive of an artist – of all artists, whether they are conscious of it or not – is to give pleasure to others,

and remarking on the proliferation of river names in Anna Livia Plurabelle,

said he liked to think how some day, way off in Tibet or Somaliland, some boy or girl in reading that little book would be pleased to come upon the name of his or her home river.[45]

In *Finnegans Wake* a voice asks pertinently, 'Do you hear what I'm seeing, hammet?'[46] Just so does the Spirit of Joyce whisper subliminally, not only to the intellectual, but to all who have ears to hear, so that with his aid we can indeed fly to knowledge,

Through the hole in reason's ceiling
without ever going to College.[47]

And where now is that spirit of Joyce? Is it economically housed in the shiny gold monstrance of modern scholarship waiting to be doled out to the meek tongues of the faithful, or is it rather as I like to think wide awake and laughing softly to itself, not at us from its last confessional box in the Fluntern Cemetery, but with us from the warm and human pages of his work into which each new reader breathes an imaginative life partly his own, and partly the author's? Ah well, howandever, in any case, Adieu Joyce, À Dieu.

NOTES

1 Richard Ellman, *James Joyce* (New York London Toronto: Oxford University Press, 1959), p. 715.
2 Stanislaus Joyce, notice of Patricia Hutchins, *Joyce's Dublin, Partisan Review*, p. 104.
3 Stanislaus Joyce, *My Brother's Keeper* (London: Faber, 1958), p. 42.
4 James Joyce, Letter to Grant Richards, 5th May 1906. *Letters of James Joyce,* vol. II, edited Richard Ellmann (London: Faber, 1966), p. 134.
5 James Joyce, *A Portrait of the Artist as a Young Man* (London: Penguin, 1960), p. 9.

6 Stanislaus Joyce, *The Complete Dublin Diary of Stanislaus Joyce,* ed. George E. Healey (Ithaca and London: Cornell University Press, 1971), p. 77.
7 James Joyce, *Ulysses* (London: The Bodley Head, 1966), p. 313.
8 James Joyce, *Stephen Hero* (London: Jonathan Cape, 1975), pp. 198–9.
9 James Joyce, *A Portrait . . .* , p. 21.
10 James Joyce, *A Portrait . . .* , p. 79.
11 James Joyce, *Ulysses,* p. 4.
12 James Joyce, 'Gas from a Burner', in *The Essential James Joyce*, ed. Harry Levin (London: Penguin), pp. 349–50.
13 Richard Ellmann, op. cit., p. 543.
14 James Joyce, *A Portrait . . .* , p. 253.
15 Ellmann, op. cit., p. 535.
16 William Wordsworth, Preface to the *Lyrical Ballads* in *The Poetical Works of Wordsworth* (London: Oxford University Press).
17 James Joyce, *Letters*, ed. Richard Ellmann, (London: Faber, 1966), vol. II, p. 91.
18 James Joyce, *Letters,* ed. Stuart Gilbert, (London: Faber, 1957), vol. I, p. 64.
19 James Joyce, 'Gas from a Burner'.
20 Samuel Johnson, Life of Abraham Cowley in *Lives of the English Poets* (London: Dent, Everyman's Library, 1975), p. 11.
21 Ellmann, op. cit., p. 348.
22 E.M. Forster, *Howards End* (London: Penguin, 1965), epigraph.
23 James Joyce, *A Portrait . . .* , p. 209.
24 Ibid., p. 62.
25 James Joyce, *A Portrait . . .* , p. 62.
26 Ibid., p. 148.
27 James Joyce, *Letters,* vol. II, p. 43.
28 Ernest Hemingway, *Death in the Afternoon* (London: Penguin, 1966), p. 54.
29 James Joyce, *Dubliners,* p. 31.
31 Ibid., p. 174.
31 Ibid., p. 15.
32 Ibid., p. 11.
33 Ibid., p. 10.
34 St. Matthew, ch. 18 v. 3.
35 St. Luke, ch. 18 v. 16.
36 James Joyce, *Dubliners,* p. 71.
37 Ibid., p. 207.
38 James Joyce, *A Portrait . . .* , p. 46.
39 James Joyce, *Ulysses,* p. 359.
40 James Joyce, *Dubliners,* p. 173.
41 Ibid., p. 183.
42 James Joyce, *A Portrait . . .* , p. 160.
43 Patrick Kavanagh, 'The Hospital', *Collected Poems* (London: McGibbon and Kee, 1964), p. 153.
44 James Joyce, *Ulysses,* p. 62.
45 Ellmann, op. cit., p. 610.
46 James Joyce, *Finnegans Wake,* p. 193.
47 Kavanagh, 'To Hell with Common Sense', op. cit., p. 155.

SIN AND SECRECY IN JOYCE'S FICTION

AUGUSTINE MARTIN

When invited to reflect on my reactions as an Irish Catholic to the fiction of James Joyce I found my mind swooping back to a number of dramatic moments in my reading experience, moments when a shock or shudder of recognition registered a strange accord between personal experience and artistic revelation. These moments cannot be unique to me, or even to those who share my upbringing, but I suspect that those brought up in another tradition may not feel them with such force. Further, I feel reasonably certain that the power of Joyce's writing derives in part from the urgency and pain with which these moments are suffused. They involve religious taboo, the Catholic sense of purity defilement and repentence, a dramatic distinction between the inner and the outer self, the confessional impulse and the concept of secrecy. I was brought up in a world similar in its theology and religious practice to that of Joyce. It is a world that was virtually overthrown by the Second Vatican Council in mid 1960s, so that I think it unlikely that more recent generations of Irish readers or Catholic readers anywhere will have read Joyce quite as I did. But as my reaction to the books on first reading is somehow bound up with their narrative strategy, the response may be worth recording, insofar as it can be honestly and accurately recalled.

The issue was vividly recalled for me when I was asked to review Richard Ellmann's edition of the *Selected Letters*[1] some years ago, with their notorious Fontenoy Street letters to Nora in the year 1909. These letters brought back the passages that had shocked me in *A Portrait of the Artist as a Young Man* when I read it as a first year undergraduate. These passages were not the hell fire sermon – which I took in my stride, nothing new there, Thomas Merton notwithstanding – but those passages where Stephen reviews his sins of the flesh and braces himself for Confession:

> Could it be that he, Stephen Dedalus, had done those things? His conscience sighed in answer. Yes, he had done them, secretly, filthily, time after time, and, hardened in sinful impenitence, he

143

had dared to wear the mask of holiness before the tabernacle itself while his soul within was a living mass of corruption.[2]

Confess! He had to confess every sin. How could he utter in words to the priest what he had done? Must, must. Or how could he explain without dying of shame? . . . . Confess! O he would indeed be free and sinless again![3]

The antiphon between secrecy and confession, the sense of an occluded and furtive inner life and a composed and fraudulent exterior dominates the three central chapters of *Portrait* from that mysterious, jolting epiphany the hero undergoes in the Cork anatomy theatre where he confronts the word *Foetus* carved on the desk while his father's extrovert chatter continues in the background. He is forced to hide his flushed face:

> But the word and the vision capered before his eyes as he walked back across the quadrangle and towards the college gate. It shocked him to find in the outer world a trace of what he had deemed till then a brutish and individual malady of his own mind. His recent monstrous reveries came thronging into his memory. . . .
> – Ay, bedad! And there's the Groceries sure enough! cried Mr Dedalus.[4]

The recurrent imagery of filth, slime and bestiality – the goat connotations of 'capered' may be intended – within, and the mask of urbanity, even of sanctity, without, unfolds itself as a powerful resource of rhetoric as the novel develops. The narrative structure of *Stephen Hero* employs no such sophisticated antinomy. Between writing the two books Joyce seems to have felt the weight of this confessional desire in his personal life before, perhaps, he determined upon it as a device of narrative. Indeed the publication of the Fontenoy Street letters makes it clear that his marriage to Nora Barnacle had provided the confessional which allowed him to release the pressure of this inner guilt, to heal the wound of his shame and loneliness, and clear the way for the remarkable experiments of his prose in delivering to fiction those secret processes of the unconscious that had never previously been dramatised in respectable fiction.

The letters in question were written from 44 Fontenoy Street, Dublin, in 1909, and were occasioned by the false assertion of

Cosgrave – Lynch in *Portrait* – that Nora had been unfaithful to him in those crucial days in summer 1904 when they had fallen in love. The sense of betrayal released in Joyce an outpouring of erotic longing, tender, obscene and poetic at turns, which he embodied in a series of the most remarkable love letters ever published, to Nora in Trieste. It is probable that this uncensored display of hitherto occulted desire in prose, however private, may have awoken him to the possibility of similar revelations in fiction. For the present purpose it is sufficient to note the different registers of eros canvassed in the letters and its consistency with the theme and tone of Stephen's inner reveries and outer gestures.

The letters range passionately from masochism and self abasement, through fetishism, coprophilia, auto-eroticism, bestiality and joyful carnality to raptures of exquisite spiritual tenderness. In short, the one thing that can be absolutely predicated of these letters is that they are emphatically love letters, that they seem to have been received and answered with a commensurate frankness, and that the relationship between the Joyces was one of exceptional sexual spontaneity and candour. Thus within their discourse James could conclude a letter in terms like these:

> Nora, my faithful darling, my sweet-eyed blackguard schoolgirl, be my whore, my mistress, as much as you like (my little frigging mistress! my little fucking whore!) you are always my beautiful wild flower of the hedges, my dark-blue rain-drenched flower.[5]

But more frequently is the imagery of bestiality and ordure deliberately and zealously indulged: 'the act itself, brief, brutal, irresistible and devilish'. 'My love for you allows me to pray to the spirit of eternal beauty and tenderness mirrored in your eyes or to fling you down . . . like a hog riding a sow, glorying in the very stink and sweat.' There is nothing of Lawrence's 'sense of health' in Joyce's sexual reveries. On the contrary it exults in the drama of its privacy: 'O, I wish that you keep all those things *secret, secret, secret*. As you know, dearest, I never use obscene phrases in speaking. . . . When men tell in my presence here filthy or lecherous stories I hardly smile. Yet you seem to turn me into a beast.' In confirmation of this last point, Italo Svevo wittily recalls that 'Joyce one day called me to task because I allowed myself to make a rather free joke. "I never say that kind of thing," said he, "though I write it." So it seems that his own books cannot be read in his presence.'[6]

When I read these letters for the first time, though I was mildly shocked, I was not surprised. I was meeting face to face what I had already perceived through the prism of the fiction, through the refractions of Stephen, Leopold, Molly. There the sudden and the more gradual shifts between public and private, conscious and unconscious, the willed and the involuntary act of the imagination, had engendered a large measure of the narrative excitement. These tensions and transitions had in fact supplied for the traditional resources of suspense and reversal, replacing them with a new sense of drama as vivid, to adopt Henry James's phrase, 'as the surprise of a caravan or the identification of a pirate'.

As he crossed the square, walking homeward, the light laughter of a girl reached his burning ear. The frail gay sound smote his heart more strongly than a trumpet blast, and, not daring to lift his eyes, he turned aside and gazed, as he walked into the shadow of the tangled shrubs. Shame rose from his smitten heart and flooded his whole being. The image of Emma appeared before him and, under her eyes, the flood of shame rushed forth anew from his heart. If she knew to what his mind had subjected her or how his brutelike lust had torn and trampled upon her innocence! Was that boyish love? Was that chivalry? Was that poetry? The sordid details of his orgies stank under his very nostrils: the sootcoated packet of pictures which he had hidden in the flue of the fireplace and in the presence of whose shameless or bashful wantonness he lay for hours sinning in thought or deed; his monstrous dreams, peopled by apelike creatures and by harlots with gleaming jewel eyes; the foul long letters he had written in the joy of guilty confession and carried secretly for days and days only to throw them under cover of night among the grass in the corner of a field or beneath some hingeless door or in some niche in the hedges where a girl might come upon them as she walked by and read them secretly. Mad! Mad! Was it possible he had done such things?[7]

The counterpoint of images is now familiar: light laughter, frail gay sound, smitten heart, boyish love, innocence, chivalry, poetry, all the sanctioned values and aspirations; then the familiar bestiary – brutelike lust, monstrous dreams, apelike creatures, the furtiveness of sootcovered packets and hingeless doors. But more significant, perhaps, for our understanding of Joyce's art is 'the joy of guilty confession' in which the young hero wallows. The secrecy in which he clutches his moral enormity must find vent in this sort of perverse revelation, and in the hope that a kindred spirit, 'a girl', might be ambushed by and share in that defilement. It is hardly fanciful to suggest that Stephen's surreptitious confessions in *Portrait* have an affinity with their author's epistolary confessions in the Fontenoy Street letters. Or that the release afforded by the latter may well have shown their author the way in dramatising the crisis of conscience in his teenage hero.

What is certain is that the crisis of conscience is Irish and Catholic in its terror, its ardour and its intensity. It is closely related to the extravagant reverence for the Blessed Virgin which has characterised Irish Catholic education for at least a century. Her cult is surrounded with liturgy and theology of very great beauty, and there is every evidence that Joyce responded with remarkable fervour and veneration to that devotion in his early years. It was inevitable that it coloured his earliest apprehensions of women, the beloved mother figure in the early pages of *Portrait* and his friend Eileen Vance, whom he consciously identifies with the imagery of the Litany of Our Lady: 'Eileen had long thin cool white hands too because she was a girl. They were like ivory; only soft. That was the meaning of *Tower of Ivory*. . . . Her fair hair had streamed out behind her like gold in the sun. *Tower of Ivory. House of Gold.* By thinking of things you could understand them.'[8] The association persists with the years. As he wrestles with his conscience during the Retreat and tries to raise his soul from its 'abject powerlessness' he reflects:

> God and the Blessed Virgin were too far from him: God was too great and stern and the Blessed Virgin too pure and holy. But he imagined that he stood near Emma in a wide land and, humbly and in tears, bent and kissed the elbow of her sleeve.[9]

Then, in a plangent phrase from Newman, Joyce enacts the Virgin's forgiveness: 'it had not offended her whose beauty *is not like earthly beauty, dangerous to look upon, but like the morning star which is its emblem, bright and musical.*' Victorian schoolboys everywhere had, I'm sure, to deal with agonies of sexual suppression and guilt, but only Irish Catholics had to cope with such piercing symbols of purity and virtue. The very poet in Joyce made his case the more traumatic. Consequently the transgressions of coarser natures, like those of

Lynch and Temple, are mere routine by comparison with those of the young Stephen Dedalus. Therefore, when Stephen makes the final break, dramatised in the fourth chapter of *Portrait,* there is nothing temperate or gradual about it. It is a radical rejection of the world of grace, a deliberate fall into 'the swoon of sin' which he had welcomed at the close of Chapter Two on his return from Cork.

There are three critical phases in Chapter Four. Dorothy Van Ghent has argued convincingly that Stephen's consciousness is always circling outwards in time and space: her model is the inscription on his textbook which begins with 'Stephen Dedalus/Class of Elements' and spirals outwards to end with 'The World/The Universe'. But there is also a circling inwards, towards secrecy, silence and cunning. The third chapter had opened with Stephen circling furtively inwards on the brothel area of Dublin and proceeded to reveal the manner of his hypocrisy at the college Sodality. Chapter Four begins with an account of his amended life with its secret and elaborate mortifications of the flesh:

> To mortify his smell was more difficult as he found in himself no instinctive repugnance to bad odours, whether they were the odours of the outdoor world such as those of dung and tar or the odours of his own person among which he had made many curious comparisons and experiments.[10]

Then abruptly he is talking to the director of vocations in the parlour at Belvedere. Here Stephen's carefully cultivated mask of propriety manages the conversation with the Jesuit, while his secret self acts as an occult chorus to the dialogue. When the director tries to draw him into a manly Jesuit conspiracy at the expense of the Capuchins with his reference to their cassocks as 'les jupes' Stephen smiles assent, but his thoughts are at a tangent to the suggestion: 'The names of articles of dress worn by women or of certain soft and delicate stuffs used in their making brought always to his mind a delicate and sinful perfume.'[11]

The counterpoint between his words and thoughts continues through the interview. The director dwells on Stephen's exemplary conduct as prefect of the Sodality of Our Lady and asks him to consider the priestly vocation:

> He listened in reverent silence now to the priest's appeal and through the words he heard even more distinctly a voice bidding

him approach, offering him secret knowledge and secret power. He would know then what was the sin of Simon Magus and what the sin against the Holy Ghost for which there was no forgiveness. . . . He would know the sins, the sinful longings and sinful thoughts and sinful acts, of others, hearing them murmured into his ears in the confessional under the shame of a darkened chapel by the lips of women and of girls.'[12]

The obsession with 'soft stuffs', 'sinful perfume', 'secret knowledge', a subverted priesthood – Simon Magus is a cult figure in Hermetism and Rosicrucianism – remind us that the novel is set in the Nineties, the shag-end of the Decadence. The pathos of Stephen's fantasies derives in part from the fact that he is a sort of Herod without a Salome, Des Esseintes without the enabling income. More significantly, however, he has determined upon his own strategy of man and mask, silence and cunning – exile is yet to come.

As he leaves Belvedere he has decided against the priesthood. He now resolves that he will wander in 'the ways of sin', that he will fall because 'Not to fall was too hard'. As he crosses the Tolka a disenchanted image of the Blessed Virgin standing 'fowlwise' in a 'faded blue shrine' marks the end of his affair with grace. The secular beauty of the girl on the beach and the outburst of 'profane joy' with which he greets it sets him on his way to becoming what he terms in the final chapter 'a priest of eternal imagination, transmuting the daily bread of experience into the radiant body of everliving life'.[13] It must be noted, however, that this proud formulation does not wholly compensate him for the fact that Emma will not resort to his priesthood but to that of the 'priested peasant', Father Moran, when she comes to 'unveil her soul's shy nakedness' in confession. The husband of Nora Barnacle does much better.

There used to be an old preacher's trick of rhetoric in which a churchful of youngsters on 'retreat' would be assured on a rising note of menace: 'And when you commit that sin, my dear boys, I may not see you, your parents may not see you, but God sees you!' It is not often remarked that more of the action in *Ulysses* is solitary, the thoughts and deeds of private individuals, than of any major novel before or since, with the exception, perhaps, of *Robinson Crusoe*. And often when the action is not entirely solitary – as in Nausicaa – it is frequently surreptitious or furtive. Joyce, in the role of an unaccusing and unretributive god, sees it all. The reader becomes a sort of artful voyeur, spying benignly on the sins and secrecies of other voyeurs:

> Mr Bloom, alone, looked at the titles. *Fair Tyrants* by James Lovebirch. Know the kind that is. Had it? Yes. . . .
> He read the other title: *Sweets of Sin*. More her line. Let us see.
> He read where his finger opened.
> – *All the dollarbills her husband gave her were spent in the stores on wondrous gowns and costliest frillies. For him! For Raoul!* . . .
> Warmth showered gently over him, cowing his flesh. Flesh yielded amid rumpled clothes. Whites of eyes swooning up. His nostrils arched themselves for prey. Melting breast ointments (*for him! For Raoul!*) Armpits' oniony sweat. Fishgluey slime (*her heaving embonpoint!*). Feel! Press! Crushed! Sulphur dung of lions![14]

The transition from titillation to disgust, from erotic romance to physiological realism, is typical of Bloom's sensibility. Yet he carries his novelette, his dark secret, through all the vicissitudes of his day: 'by Moulang's pipes, bearing in his breast the sweets of sin, by Wine's antiques in memory bearing sweet sinful words, by Carroll's dusky battered plate, for Raoul'.[15]

Stephen, artist, whose role it is to 'wrest old images from the burial earth', indulges his typically more strenuous and structured reverie outside the window of Russell's jewelry:

> dull coils of bronze and silver, lozenges of cinnabar, on rubies, leprous and winedark stones.
> Born all in the dark wormy earth, cold specks of fire, evil lights shining in the darkness. Where fallen archangels flung the stars of their brows. Muddy swinesnouts, hands, root and root, gripe and wrest them.
> She dances in a foul gloom where gum burns with garlic. A sailorman, rustbearded, sips from a beaker rum and eyes her. A long and seafed silent rut. She dances, capers, wagging her sowish haunches and her hips, on her gross belly flapping a ruby egg.[16]

No other fictional form or method could accommodate a reverie so private, so thorough – in which the implications of precious stones as wealth, idolatry, slavery, beauty, evil, sexual adornment are tracked back to their aboriginal essence – so seemingly gratuitous.

That thrust of secret exploration, that challenge of the forbidden regions of the psyche, which were begun in the first stories of *Dubliners* and pursued in the apostasies of Stephen in *Portrait*, have here developed into the radical fictional adventure of which this passage is one of the supreme achievements. They are, of course, to develop in turn to the phantasmagory of Bella Cohen's den and the nightmares of Earwicker in *Finnegans Wake*.

It is a commonplace that before Joyce – if we except the limited experiments of Dujardin which Joyce generously acknowledged – novelists confined themselves largely to narrative, paraphrase, action, dialogue, and in certain rare cases such as *Moby Dick*, interior monologue; and that their plots, comic, tragic, satiric or romantic, were mostly taken over from the drama. Characters revealed themselves to each other, or less frequently to the reader, through the mediation of the authorial voice – as in *Portrait of a Lady*, Chapter XLII. Like theatre, fiction was a public art where the inner workings of the mind found resolution and expression through social forms – conversations, letters, confessions, actions, hints, explanations. Joyce frequently remarked to Bugden and others that literature had still left too much unsaid, that even Shakespeare had been forced, by the formal restraints, to leave unsaid so much that matters deeply to mankind. Joyce's 'stream of consciousness' – we cannot avoid the term – was his means of getting to that unexpressed world, of catching movements of mind, fancy and reverie, often before these movements had achieved the finality of thought. It was a colossal undertaking, like trying to turn up the light fast enough to see the darkness. The uniqueness of *Ulysses* resides in the marvellous variety of tone, mood and rhythm achieved within its pages. Therefore the term should at least be changed to 'streams of consciousness'. Because while the method may have been primarily useful in exploring the murkier regions of the private conscience which I've been discussing – and for which its inventor paid the bitterest price – it afforded him opportunities in comic freedom and intellectual elaboration unknown to the novel as he had found it.

Bloom is in Westland Row watching for a flash of ankle as a lady prepares to ascend a carriage across the street. M'Coy stands insensitively before him with the tedious story of how he had come to learn of Paddy Dignam's death from Hoppy Holohan:

– Why? I said. *What's wrong with him?* I said.

151

Proud: rich: silk stockings.

– Yes, Mr Bloom said.

He moved a little to the side of M'Coy's talking head. Getting up in a minute.

– *What's wrong with him?* he said. *He's dead,* he said. And, faith, he filled up. *Is it Paddy Dignam?* I said. I couldn't believe it when I heard it. I was with him no later than Friday last or Thursday was it in the Arch. *Yes,* he said. *He's gone. He died on Monday, poor fellow.*

Watch! Watch! Silk flash rich stockings white. Watch!

A heavy tramcar honking its gong slewed between.

Lost it. Curse your noisy pugnose. Feels locked out of it. Paradise and the peri. Always happening like that. The very moment. Girl in Eustace street hallway. Monday was it settling her garter. Her friend covering the display of. *Esprit de corps.* Well, what are you gaping at?

– Yes, yes, Mr Bloom said after a dull sigh. Another gone.

– One of the best, M'Coy said.[17]

It is hard to decide which of our heroes may feel his sense of loss the keener as life and death, paradise and Hades are caught on the same hook of dialogue. The drama is hardly less lively when Bloom is alone with his curious visions of bliss:

Do ptake some ptarmigan. Wouldn't mind being a waiter in a swell hotel. Tips, evening dress, halfnaked ladies. May I tempt you to a little more filleted lemon sole, miss Dubedat? Yes, do bedad. And she did bedad.

This sprightly prelude leads into the charged erotic passage in which he recalls his lovemaking with Molly on Howth Head, which leads in turn to his cool curiosities about goddesses, their diet, the perforations of statuary in the National Museum.

The Nausicaa scene where Bloom and Gerty MacDowell hold their wordless, distant intercourse – 'A long seafed silent rut'? – on Sandymount Strand takes the language of secrecy to a new pitch of elaboration, a more nuanced sense of the human comedy. One side of Gerty's mind knows exactly what is going on, the other side screens this knowledge, insists on translating it into the gush and rapture of the novelette:

O! then the Roman candle burst and it was like a sigh of O! and everone cried O! O! in raptures and it gushed out of it a stream of rain gold hair threads and they shed and ah! they were all greeny dewy stars falling with golden, O so lively! O so soft, sweet, soft!

. . . She glanced at him as she bent forward quickly, a pathetic little glance of piteous protest, of shy reproach under which he coloured like a girl. He was leaning back against the rock behind. Leopold Bloom (for it is he) stands silent, with bowed head before those young guileless eyes. What a brute he had been! At it again? A fair unsullied soul had called to him and, wretch that he was, how had he answered? An utter cad he had been.[18]

As Bloom moves on from his telepathetic conquest his mood brightens to a sort of jaunty self-gratulation: 'Anyhow I got the best of that . . . *Lingerie* does it.' The guilt is transitory, if not actually enjoyable. We have travelled a long way from the trapped mortification of the sixteen year old Stephen. In the case of the wily Ulyssean Dublin Jew the outer and the inner man have a more genial working relation, at least during the hours of daylight. With the fall of night the moods and techniques change so often and so radically as to put these later episodes beyond the general scope of the present inquiry.

Similarly the Stephen we meet in Proteus is a livelier, wiser man than the hero of *Portrait*. Walking along Sandymount Strand he can mock the solemnity of his secret lusts: 'Cousin Stephen, you will never be a saint. . . . You prayed to the devil in Serpentine avenue that the fubsy widow in front might lift her clothes still more from the wet street. *O si, certo!* Sell your soul for that, do, dyed rags pinned round a squaw.' But his jauntiness cannot slide round his guilt with the ease of a Leopold Bloom. Steeled in the school of old Aquinas and drilled in the moral disciplines of Loyola, he can never escape the need for analysis and self-accusation, however jocular the tone. He is seldom more engaging than in this episode where he discloses his artistic vanities, assuring us in passing that he did not have to travel far for the comic fantasies of that potential poet, Little Chandler:

Reading two pages apiece of seven books every night, eh? I was young. You bowed to yourself in the mirror, stepping forward to applause earnestly, striking face. Hurray for the Goddamned idiot! Hray! No-one saw: tell no-one. Books you were going to write with letters for titles. Have you read his F? O yes, but I prefer Q. Yes, but W is wonderful. O yes. W. Remember your epiphanies on green oval leaves, deeply deep, copies to be sent if you died to all the great libraries of the world, including Alexandria? Someone was to read them there after a few thousand years, a mahamanvantara. Pico della Mirandola like.[20]

It is clear that Joyce is enjoying the double-take: no-one saw; no-one need ever know. But he insists on telling. He is the great betrayer of secrets. His art is a monstrous and sustained breach of confidence. He gives us all away. That is why he has been treated for so long with such distrust. Our rage has been that of Caliban on seeing his reflection in a two-way mirror, Joyce's 'nicely polished looking-glass'. He may even feel a little guilty himself at what he has been doing, and this may account for the strangled solemnity of parts of *Portrait*. But in the passage just quoted that mood has been replaced by a sort of erudite glee, epitomised in that last sentence.

The green oval leaves echo the 'Emerald Tablet' of Hermes, god of writers, whose cult was from Alexandria, and who gave the Egyptians laws and letters. He has been invoked as Thoth in the last chapter of *Portrait* where he is imaged as 'writing with a reed upon a tablet'. Pico had been a devotee of Hermes's secret cult. So much for learned allusion. On the demotic level Italians still regard Pico as the epitome of learned omniscience. If asked a difficult question an average Roman or Triestine might well reply: 'Chi son' io? Pico della Mirandola?' (Who do you think I am? Pico della Mirandola?) Dubliners, on the other hand, have a trick of language by which they append 'like' as a detached suffix to nouns, adjectives and adverbs to achieve a sort of conspiratorial intimacy: 'He came up to me sort of quiet like, you know?' It was kinda Sunday like, you know what I mean?' Stephen is walking; the whole passage is pedestrian in the rhythm of its phrasing: ambulatory, self-mocking, idiomatic, secret, erudite like – in short Pico della Mira*n*dola like.

All fiction involves a conspiracy of understanding between writer and reader, a tonal accord by means of which the fictive message can pass reliably back and forth between the reader and the text. In one sense or another there is always a shared secret. The first sentence of *Pride and Prejudice* draws one immediately into such a conspiracy, and to the end of the story that pact never falters. But the arcana of Merryton or Netherfield could be spoken of without blushes, certainly without that 'flame' that so often burns on Stephen Dedalus's cheek. His milieu and his upbringing presented him with a vivid and dangerous challenge to which his artistic nature responded with extraordinary subtlety and courage. To meet that challenge, to explore those regions of the psyche that beckoned to him, he was forced to invent a range of technical and linguistic resources unequalled in power and range through the length and breadth of modern literature. The sound barrier of his enterprise was that of social reticence, the wall – at least the façade – between the public and private self that Victoria's reign had so consolidated, and which the Catholic Church in Ireland had so reinforced. Breaking through to those secret chambers was a heroic undertaking. Bringing generations of readers into sympathy and accord with that occluded world inside, getting the fictive current running both ways, was the supreme achievement of his literary genius. At least so it seems to one Irish reader.

NOTES

1   *Selected Letters of James Joyce*, ed. Richard Ellmann (London: Faber, 1975).
2   *A Portrait of the Artist as a Young Man* by James Joyce (New York: Viking Critical Library, 1968), p. 137.
3   Ibid., p. 140.
4   Ibid., p. 90.
5   *Selected Letters*, p. 181.
6   *James Joyce* by Italo Svevo, translated by Stanislaus Joyce, Monograph (New York: *City Lights Books,* 1950), unpaginated.
7   *Portrait* . . . , p. 115–16.
8   Ibid., pp. 42–43.
9   Ibid., p. 116.
10   Ibid., p. 151.
11   Ibid., p. 155.
12   Ibid., p. 159.
13   Ibid., p. 221.
14   *Ulysses* by James Joyce (London: Penguin, 1960), p. 235.
15   Ibid., p. 256.
16   Ibid., pp. 240–241.
17   Ibid., pp. 75–76.
18   Ibid., p. 175.
19   Ibid., p. 364.
20   Ibid., p. 46.

THE VULGARITY OF HEROICS: JOYCE'S *ULYSSES*

DECLAN KIBERD

It is no accident that the last lines of *Ulysses* reads 'Trieste-Zürich-Paris, 1914–1921'. Joyce had to scurry with his family from city to city in his attempt to avoid the war and to create a beautiful book in a Europe bent on self-destruction. He seems from the outset to have anticipated Tom Stoppard's brilliant joke in *Travesties*:

> What did you do in the great war, Mr Joyce?
> I wrote *Ulysses*. What did you do?

In later years, when asked how he felt about the war, Joyce would remark absent-mindedly 'O, that – I hardly noticed it', but it is clear through every chapter of *Ulysses* that it touched him to the quick. The heroic abstractions for which young soldiers died seemed to have an increasingly hollow sound to the writers of his generation. Ernest Hemingway wrote later of his experience on the Italian front in *A Farewell to Arms*:

> Abstract words such as glory, honour, courage, or hallow, were obscene beside the concrete names of villages, the numbers of roads, the names of rivers, the numbers of regiments and dates. . . . I was always embarrassed by the words sacred, glorious and sacrifice.

The point is made even more tersely by Stephen Dedalus, who says in *Ulysses* that he fears the big words which make us so unhappy. If history is a nightmare, it is a heroic deception from which all Europe – and not just Ireland – is trying to awake. As he sits at the head of his class teaching Roman History, Stephen contemplates the futility of war with a mind which reflects not only the costs of victory to Pyrrhus, but also Joyce's personal experience of the bombardment of buildings in 1917:

> I hear the ruin of all space, shattered glass and toppling masonry, and time one livid final flame.

156

It is at once a vision of Mr Deasy's Last Day and of contemporary Europe – even more poignantly, it is a protest against both. So is the entire book.

Men had gone to war and maimed their bodies, so Joyce fled the war-zones and penned no celebration of abstract virtue but a minute account of the body and its attendant frustrations. Soldiers were dying in defence of the outmoded heroic values which permeate the *Odyssey*, so Joyce set out to prove that if Ulysses was a god, he was certainly a god with a limp. The very humility of Bloom becomes a reproach to the myth of ancient heroism and, finally, man's little-ness is seen to be the inevitable precondition of his greatness. Quietly but firmly, Joyce insists that the Greeks were human and flawed like anybody else. He had said so in a letter to his brother Stanislaus as early as 1905:

> Do you not think the search for heroics damn vulgar? . . . I am sure however that the whole structure of heroism is, and always was, a damned lie and that there cannot be any substitute for the individual passion as the motive power of everything.

Ulysses is the logical outcome of that letter, for it is a protest against the vulgar heroics of militarism, but also against the sad machismo of sexual conquest.

In those early years of the century, Joyce was reacting against the cult of Cuchulain, purveyed by writers such as Pearse, Yeats and Lady Gregory. As a youth of twenty-one, he had written a pamphlet attacking the Irish Literary Theatre for its surrender to the vulgarity of nationalism. Remarking that the Irish had never got beyond a miracle play, he ended, 'The Irish Literary Theatre must now be the property of the most belated race in Europe'. When this swaggering failed to evoke a response, the young rebel made his celebrated and misunderstood visit, which terminated with the observation that Yeats (all of thirty-seven at the time) was too old to be helped. Behind the mockery and the pride, Joyce was making a subtle point – that the two men came from different ages and worlds. Yeats, though only seventeen years older than Joyce, believed in ancient heroism and the big words that made the next generation so unhappy. Joyce was more modern. He believed that the ordinary was the domain of the artist – sensationalism and heroics could safely be left to the journalists. He felt a deep aversion to Lady

Gregory's *Cuchulain of Muirthemne*, the epic tale of a man who defended the gap of the North against all comers even unto death. The central theme of the book was the skill of Cuchulain in glamorised combat, his capacity to make violence seem heroic. Joyce repudiated it at once, with the conviction that such stories did not truly express the character of the Irish people. To the end of his days Joyce bitterly resented the common view of the Irish as inveterate quarrellers. When Wyndham Lewis spoke of the fighting Irish in a conversation, Joyce replied thoughtfully, 'That's not been my experience . . . a very gentle race.' His objection to the Cuchulain cult was that it perpetuated the ancient libel of the pugnacious Irish abroad, while flattering the vanity of susceptible Irishmen at home by giving them an inflated sense of their heroic destiny. Like Synge, he believed that a writer's first duty was to insult rather than flatter his countrymen, to shock them into an even deeper awareness of their own duplicity. He had written *Dubliners* as a chapter of the moral history of his country and had ended *A Portrait of the Artist as a Young Man* with the promise to forge the conscience of his race. 'Moral history' and 'conscience' are not words used of a satanic dissident in Dublin, but they show that Joyce saw himself as a patriot, with something more valuable than the heroics of Yeats and Pearse to teach his fellow-countrymen. That something was very simple. Joyce exploded for ever the myth of the fighting Irish and, through his hero Bloom, he depicted them as a passive and intelligent race. Honest to a fault, he was quick to point out how this wise passiveness could very easily become something else, downright laziness. So he finally revealed an even more distressing truth than the myth of the bellicose Paddy – the fact that all too often the besetting vice of the Irishman was not pugnacity but paralysis.

In considerations such as these lies the answer to the question asked so often by readers of *Ulysses* – if Joyce wished to base his massive book on an ancient legend, why did he turn to Greek rather than Gaelic mythology? Cuchulain had already been appropriated by the militant nationalists in Dublin, whereas Joyce was a pacifist and an internationalist. So his review of Lady Gregory's work was anything but flattering – he denounced her stories as setting forth the folk mind 'in the fullness of its senility', and compounded the offence by publishing the review in the Dublin *Daily Express*. He had already got financial help from her in return for the assurance that he had found no man in the country with a faith like his own. This was a strange way to repay her kindness, and stranger still was

the exchange between Mulligan and Stephen about the matter in
Ulysses:

> – Longworth is awfully sick . . . after what you wrote about that
> old hake Gregory. O you inquisitional drunken jew jesuit! She
> gets you a job on the paper and then you go and slate her drivel to
> Jaysus. Couldn't you do the Yeats touch?
> He went on and down, mopping, chanting with waving grace-
> ful arms:
> – The most beautiful book that has come out of our country in
> my time. One thinks of Homer.

Yeats had written those words in *his* review of the Cuchulain book
and had been rewarded for his fidelity with a remittance through the
post and, later custard and hot-water bottles at Coole. To the young
Joyce that review seemed insincere, its praise too high-flown to be
credible. Yeats's words rankled so much that he remembered them
over fifteen years later and put them into a book on which they
would have constituted the perfect comment. It is almost as if Yeats
has made the right statement but applied it to the wrong book. If the
praise is ludicrous as an account of Lady Gregory's senile folk-lore,
then Joyce will write an urban folktale of which the same words
provide a laconic summary. This is just one of the many jocular clues
to his method which Joyce inserted into *Ulysses*, and he was disappointed that so few of his early readers seemed to understand the
real meaning of that parallel with the *Odyssey*.

To us today that meaning is clear, not only because of the guidance of many masterful critics but also because the intervening
decades have have taught us to endorse Joyce's critique of military
heroics. The draft-dodger Ulysses did not wish to go to Troy, said
Joyce, because he knew that the official reason for the war, the
dissemination of the culture of Hellas, was only a pretext for the
Greek merchants who were seeking new markets. The analogy with
a contemporary Europe plunged into war in order to provide markets for the barons of the steel industry was not lost on Joyce. His
hero was a nobody who had no desire to be a somebody, a pacifist
and family-man unique in his very ordinariness. The all-round man
is neither a Faust nor a Jesus, for he eschews the vulgarity of sexual
conquest and the heroic self-conquest of celibacy. Despite his admiration for the gentleness of Jesus, Joyce rejected him as an incomplete man, remarking to Frank Budgen: Jesus 'was a bachelor, and

never lived with a woman. Surely living with a woman is one of the most difficult things a man has to do, and he never did it.' Jesus forgave his enemies but Leopold Bloom submits to an even more arduous discipline and forgives his faithless wife.

There can be no more moving moment in modern literature than that in which Bloom ponders his new status as cuckold. The self-confident strut of Boylan to Molly's lair is superbly captured in the *martellato* cadence: 'did he knock Paul de Kock?' Against this jaunty imperiousness, Bloom's sad lines of submission seem jagged with painful hesitations:

> Too late. She longed to go. That's why. Woman. As east stop the sea. Yes: all is lost.

Yet it is at this moment that he becomes a true hero with the courage to see Molly's infidelity as part of the larger process of nature. His sentences may be jagged, his cadences irregular, but they look forward to Molly's own soliloquy. That 'yes' will be taken up as the key word of her monologue, as will his comparison of the currents of sexual attraction to the inexorable waves of the sea. So already, even in the hesitant line which records their sundering, Bloom and Molly stay married after all, sharing the same unspoken words and images. All through the book they act in an unconscious harmony and yet they never seem to share their lives in any conscious way. Bloom forgives his wife in his own mind, almost before the evil deed is done, but he never manages to put his tired arms around her at the end of the day and forgive her in person. The tragedy of their wedded love, as Yeats would say, is the perpetual virginity of their souls which have so much in common but never commingle. For theirs is a classic 'silent' marriage, the Irish version of divorce, where what is stated is far less poignant than what is implied or simply suppressed. The use of interior monologue in depicting Bloom and Molly leaves the reader with the eerie feeling that he knows both parties better than they care to know one another – and that they have a great deal more in common than external circumstances reveal. Indeed, the tragedy of the interior monologue is the cruel contrast it offers between the immense richness of the individual mind and the poverty of its social occasions. The final effect of all the interior monologues in the book is to show just how many unspoken thoughts men share and how seldom these are successfully expressed.

The clearest example of this is the frustratingly limited rapport achieved by Bloom and Stephen when finally they meet towards the end of the book. Having invested many hours and much labour in decoding the narrative up to this point, the reader is entitled to expect some return for his pains in the shape of a satisfactory climax. Moreover, there is much in the foregoing narrative to suggest that this will indeed be a meeting of souls and minds. Throughout the day both men have acted in an unconcious harmony, whether they were rejecting militarism or simply regretting their own loneliness. By the shore on Sandymount Strand the same thought strikes Stephen that will strike Bloom in the same location hours later – that death by drowning is not the worst way to go. But this affinity between the two men goes deeper than their conscious musings and may be detected also in their private fantasies and dreams. From his broken sleep of the previous night Stephen recalls a dream in which an Oriental appeared, presaging Bloom:

Open hallway. Street of harlots. Remember. Haroun al Raschid. I am almosting it. That man led me, spoke. I was not afraid. The melon he had he held against my face. Smiled: creamfruit smell. That was the rule, said. In. Come. Red carpet spread. You will see who.

That passage tersely predicts the events to come – the street of harlots where Bloom will offer fatherly aid and his later invitation that Stephen spend the night in his home. Even the bizarre detail of melons held against the face seems to intersect with Bloom's own erotic fantasies, one of which causes him to compare his wife's buttocks to melons and to hold them to his face, cheek caressing cheek. Already the dreams of Stephen and Bloom are overlapping, as if to suggest a genuine affinity in their aspirations.

How disappointing, then, to read through 'Eumaeus' and to find that the meeting between the two is scarcely as momentous as we had hoped. Joyce celebrates the opening of the lines of communication between both men with an illustration of his growing pessimism about the power of language to communicate anything. Bloom is exhausted and cannot keep up with the more intellectual Stephen. He marvels at the melodious sounds of some nearby strangers speaking in Italian, only to be told by Stephen that they were haggling over money. As so often in *Ulysses*, the foreignness of language is stressed along with its treachery of withheld meanings.

161

Many of Bloom's sentences peter out because he is so tired and the narrator of the entire section employs tired clichés which conceal far more than they reveal. He fails utterly to describe the Bloom and Stephen whom we feel we have come to know so intimately over hundreds of pages. He shows his disregard for truth by mimicking the newspaper misprint 'L. Boom'. Even for Stephen at this moment of moments Bloom seems to have no fixed identity, and he drunkenly identifies the saviour who has just offered him bread '*Christus* or Bloom his name is, or, after all, any other'. All of these details, filtered through the undependable mind of a less than gifted narrator, emphasise the limits of linguistic communication. Because the reader is frustrated in his desire for a meaning at the climactic moment of the book, he is forced finally to consider not the meeting of the two men, but rather the language which fails to describe it. Once again Joyce has shown more interest in a way of seeing than in the event seen. Once again the rich potential of the individual mind is betrayed by the impoverished idiom of social intercourse.

The ultimate tragedy of non-communication in *Ulysses* is the sexual arrest in the marriage of Leopold and Molly Bloom. The language of the body proves no more expressive than the language of the mind, yet both idioms point to the same truth – that people have more in common than they will ever allow themselves to know. Bloom, the womanly man, should be the ideal mate for Molly, the manly woman.[2] But this she can seldom admit, preferring to condemn him for his passivity, his desire to be dominated, his effeminacy. One of Bloom's earliest acts in the book is to straighten the bedspread before he leaves Molly's room. No sooner does he walk along the footpath outside the house than he begins to imitate the walk of a passing girl. By the time he reaches Nighttown in 'Circe', he is enjoying fantasies of himself as a woman enduring domination and degradation. Such instances would seem to confirm Molly's view of all that was wrong with him. Yet, the paradox is that it was this 'feminine' element in Bloom which attracted her to him in the first place. The very refinement in Bloom which made the relationship possible now seems to be preventing its development. Nevertheless, it is to that refinement that Molly returns in her closing moments, after she has rejected the loutishness and *machismo* of Boylan who slapped her bottom and cared little for her pleasure. She turns her thoughts to Bloom and remembers why she chose him for a husband: 'yes that was why I liked him because I saw he understood or felt what a woman was'. That lazy acceptance is not untinged with irony, for she recalls thinking to herself 'as well him as another', a moment curiously parallel to Stephen's hazy acceptance of '*Christus* or Bloom his name is, or, after all, any other'. Such parallels reinforce the conviction that Molly's soliloquy is no mere appendix tacked onto the end of the book but rather the complex resolution of the work's manifold themes. Her monologue proves that it was the man in her who first fell in love with the woman in Bloom. On the other hand, her aggressiveness, her love of coarse language, her healthy virility have all been necessarily repressed in her unsatisfactory encounter with Boylan, the boringly traditional roué. These elements in her personality which so delighted Bloom (and, one feels, could excite him once again) would merely frighten Boylan. Indeed, so perverse and strange is the sexuality of Molly Bloom that it has even unhinged some feminist critics, who have accused Joyce of creating a sexual object of male fantasy rather than a credible flesh-and-blood woman. Such an interpretation fails to take account of Molly's complex psychology, of the fact that she is as often a sexual object to herself as to the men in her world. Again and again, she contemplates her own body with all the clinical detachment of a rake appraising his latest conquest:

> I bet he never saw a better pair of thighs than that look how white
> they are the smoothest place is right there between this bit here
> how soft like a peach easy God I wouldnt mind being a man and
> get up on a lovely woman O Lord

It is clear from such a passage that the passive and womanly Bloom is not just her lawful but her ideal mate. Yet she continues to fly in face of the evidence and dream of an old-fashioned and vulgar hero. In her appalling lack of taste she can still see Boylan as a 'catch' and admire his fine taste in clothes, although the shopgirl in Thornton's silently despised the spiv who stared uncouthly at her legs, 'got up regardless, with his tie a bit crooked'. The shopgirl's assessment is simply Joyce's quiet reminder to the reader that the search for heroics is always 'damn vulgar'.

In offering *Ulysses* as an antidote to the warlike Cuchulain, and in offering Bloom as an ironic countertruth to the ancient Greek, Joyce never quite forgot that his object in *Ulysses* was to write the first urban folktale. This was to be a conscious rejoinder to the senile rural lore collected by Lady Gregory in *Cuchulain of Muirthemne*, and for a while Joyce toyed with the possibility of mimicking her title by calling his book *Ulysses in Dublin*. In comments to friends on his work, Joyce repeatedly stressed that his real inspiration was not the literary but the oral tradition and he recalled that Homer's *Odyssey* and Lady Gregory's *Cuchulain* were simply written versions of a tale that passed from mouth to mouth long before reaching the written page. Of *Ulysses* he remarked 'I have put the great talkers in my book, they and the things they forgot' and 'if anyone doesn't understand a passage of mine, all he need do is to read it aloud'. T.S. Eliot was right in sensing that the fourteenth chapter of *Ulysses* exposed the futility of all literary styles, but he did not point to the corollary – that this was done the better to clear the way for the consummation of the oral tradition in Molly Bloom.

If the book poses a difficulty for the reader, the problem arises out of the tension between its status in the library as a written book and its irretrievably oral contents. There were times when that tension seemed to become too much for Joyce himself, times when he began to question the capacity of a printed book to carry all the meanings he intended. In the heart of a paragraph in *Ulysses* is written the unanswered question: 'Who ever will read these written words?' That may well be the one line in the book which the author wrote with a straight face in his capacity as James Joyce. It was the fact that the words had to be *written* that worried him, what they lost in the transition from speech to paper. Molly Bloom was wiser, perhaps, for despite her belief that you could fill a book with Poldy's sayings, she was never foolish enough to write them down. But Joyce was daring enough to write Nora Barnacle's words into Molly's monologue and he must have realised the awful distance between speech and writing when, far from rebuking her husband for stealing her most private ideas, she failed utterly to recognise them as her own on the printed page.

A simple example from Molly's soliloquy will make that gap between the literary and the oral *Ulysses* clear. Her passage opens and closes and re-echoes with the word 'yes', and on this point the critics are in splendid agreement that this is Joyce's closing affirmation of the human spirit. But it is only the written 'yes' which means what it seems. In Dublin, more often than not, the oral 'yes' means 'no'. It is the omnipurpose 'yes' of negation, the suppressing 'yes' which a compulsive talker will use to suppress a comment from the lips of another – a way of acknowledging the presence of another without permitting him to speak. It can even be used to interrupt the flow of another's conversation ('Yes and . . .'), in order to assert oneself rather than suffer the indignities of further listening. In a city of compulsive talkers it is a useful weapon, but it is not necessarily the affirmation which the critics, with their fondness for a happy ending, seem to think. Oscar Wilde once said, 'The good ended happily, the bad unhappily, that is what Fiction means', but that is not what Molly Bloom means. There is monomania as well as affirmation in her repeated 'yes', just as there is a basic subversion of the Victorian principle by which all mothers taught their daughters to say 'No' endlessly, until a suitably middle-aged suitor with an adequate income merited the magic word 'yes', after which the luckless girl was advised to lie back and think of England. Molly lies back and thinks mostly of herself, sometimes of Bloom, but her affirmation is at least as ambiguous as her 'yes'. She affirms her own sexuality but she also indicates her grave disappointment with her body, after the failure to find physical gratification either with Boylan or Bloom. Those who find such positive meanings in her monologue would do well to consider the tragic implications of a soliloquy uttered by a party to a 'silent' marriage alongside a snoring and indifferent partner. This woman has nobody to talk to but herself.

In an earlier scene, Bloom had come to a similarly negative conclusion about the human body, when he had fantasised in the sight of Gerty MacDowell on Sandymount Strand: Gerty, too, achieves an emotional climax as the Roman candles and fireworks burst in the sky. The technique of the section is Tumescence-Detumescence, which is to say that the section opens quietly, builds slowly to a crescendo, explodes and falls:

> And then a rocket sprang and bang shot blind and O! then the Roman candle burst and it was like a sigh of O! and everyone cried O! O! in raptures and it gushed out of it a stream of rain gold hair threads and they shed and ah! they were all greeny dewy stars falling with golden, O so lively, O so soft, sweet, soft!

But after the ecstasy of climax, Gerty rearranges her skirt over her legs, which Bloom had so admired, and begins to walk away:

> She walked with a certain quiet dignity characteristic of her but with care and very slowly because Gerty MacDowell was . . .
> Tight boots? No. She's lame! O!

165

The endlessly repeated sound O! O! O! O! which had marked the moment of ecstasy is now a curt echo, as if in hollow mockery of Bloom's earlier excitement. We have come a long way from the *martello* strut of 'Did he knock Paul de Kock?' So it is fitting that the very line which describes Bloom's recognition of her lameness should itself limp along, with full stops and starts after each word or two, as if to reenact the difficulty of Gerty's movement: 'Tight boots? No. She's lame! O!' (Here the cryptic Bloom needs only half a line to utter four sentences, in contrast with his wife who will later consume an entire chapter with eight.) And two pages later, the innocent open-sounded O! is again repeated just once in mockery to describe Boylan's gasp of pleasure with Bloom's wife, when indeed the wide-eyed ecstasy of O! is usurped by the more knowing self-satisfied grunt of Ah!:

> O, he did. Into her. She did. Done.
> Ah!

– or is that Ah! the wistful sigh of a defeated man? Joyce was a keen musician and this deliberate patterning of sounds right through the chapter will be fully appreciated only by someone who reads the passage aloud. Its meaning is the way in which our wasted bodies deny our fondest aspirations – the blushing beauty is lame, the fallen woman is left unsatisfied, the frustrated Bloom is still frustrated, unable even to finish the sentence he writes in the sand 'I AM A . . .'. Yet the paradox is that, in his pained recognition of Gerty's defect, he has created within his own mind a line of pure poetry, which tells us more about her inner state than the coy innuendoes which filled her own monologues.

So, yet again, Joyce has given us an essay in ways of seeing, in two contrasting literary styles, rather than in the thing seen. If this adds to the multidimensional view of Bloom, then it adds also to the lustre of Molly's performance in the closing chapter. There is a sense in which Gerty's language is itself rather lame, a little too magaziny and contrived, and therefore not an honest account of her real enough emotion. This contrasts with the blunt homeliness of Molly Bloom with her endless requests to 'tell us in plain words'. Through these two women, Joyce describes two very different ways of looking at Bloom and at their own bodies. In either case, the difference is between the woman who uses the language to confront experience and the woman who abuses language to avoid the irreducibly actual female posterior (so beloved of Bloom). As if already in training for her role as prim aunt, Gerty and her friends can only speak of it with ladylike daintiness as the 'beetoteetom', but, hundreds of pages later, Molly counters such Victorian coyness in a priest: 'Lord couldnt he say bottom right out and have done with it?'

Yet Molly is finally no more happy with the human body than Gerty and both ladies share with Bloom and Stephen an acute awareness of bodily frustration. Bloom is roused to sympathy by Gerty's limp, which serves to remind him of all kinds of bodily disorder, his own and others':

> Poor girl! That's why she's left on the shelf and the others did a sprint. . . . A defect is ten times worse in a woman. But makes them polite. Glad I didn't know it when she was on show. Hot little devil all the same. Wouldn't mind. Curiosity like a nun or a negress or a girl with glasses. That squinty one is delicate. Near her monthlies, I expect, makes them feel ticklish. I have such a bad headache today. Where did I put the letter?

So, in a few sentences, he has thought of lame-legged women, girls with glasses, girls with a squint, menstruation and the feminine headache. And even before this medical dissertation, Gerty's thoughts had been turning towards her own anaemia and the respective merits of iron jelloids or the Widow Welch's female pills. It need hardly be added that the youthful Stephen Dedalus is no more blessed in his earthly body – he spends most of the book groping his short-sighted way through Dublin; and an object as innocent as a shell on a beach is sufficient to evoke a hypochondria which is positively metaphysical in its juxtapositions: 'My teeth are very bad. Shells.'

In saying that *Ulysses* was the epic of the human body, Joyce was only telling half the truth. Being that, it is also, more crucially, an epic of bodily frustration. This is only to be expected in a book which is an assault on the vulgarity of bodily and sexual heroism and a plea for an intelligent tolerance of all our imperfections. Joyce's attitude to the body was anything but romantic. We know how he replied to the disciple who asked to kiss the hand that wrote *Ulysses*, just as we admire the common sense of the man who questioned the promptings of the romantic heart with the remark that 'the seat of the affections is lower down'. The 'epic-of-the-human-body' theory was just one of the many critical smokescreens with which Joyce, through the good offices of Stuart Gilbert, managed to shroud his book. The common-sensical reader who traces what actually happens to the characters in *Ulysses* will not be fooled by such hopeful over-statements, for he will concentrate on how the characters experience their own bodies rather than on how the critics interpret the symbols.

NOTE

1 Most biographical details in this article are taken from Richard Ellmann's authoritative *James Joyce* (1959). I am deeply indebted not only to the book but also to its author.
2 Although Richard Ellman was the first critic to tackle this theme, the most satisfactory analysis of the androgyny of the Blooms was made by David Hayman, 'The Empirical Molly', in *Approaches to Ulysses*, eds. Staley and Benstock (Pittsburgh, 1970), pp. 108–135.

NIGHT FOX
(for James Joyce)

In a forest of dark
town houses, she watches in a silence
deeper than the wild. Harbinger
of death, padding delicately,
daintily, beautiful in herself.

Her velvet eyes watching the
tall stalks of night-flowering
lights, she pads along the ground
cover of post boxes and bins.

Her mouth has changed its shape
to take the city's foods. Her ears
quiver but do not hear our voices
as people shelter indoors,
the final exclusion.

So a poet goes through the city
streets, though he passes into
the houses. His mouth adapts
to the ironies of city words
but his heart remembers something
wilder, different, and he laughs
to see the last strange creatures
to romp under the moon.

Suzanne Brown

JOYCE AND RIMBAUD:
AN INTRODUCTORY ESSAY

PHILLIP HERRING

Of the major literary influences on James Joyce, perhaps the most underestimated one today is that of the revolutionary French poet Arthur Rimbaud. It is common knowledge that Joyce could recite Verlaine and Baudelaire by the hour, that he derived much from the Symbolist aesthetic, and that the mind of Stephen Dedalus in *Ulysses* is steeped in French culture, but as yet no sustained effort to connect Joyce and Stephen specifically with Rimbaud has appeared in print. What has been written is sometimes contradictory or confusing. While Hugh Kenner calls Stephen a 'Dublin Rimbaud',[1] David Weir disputes this notion, calling the resemblance 'external and general', and choosing Baudelaire over Rimbaud as the major Symbolist influence on Joyce.[2]

At least two of Joyce's Dublin friends would have agreed with Kenner: C.P. Curran wrote a few paragraphs about Joyce's interest in Rimbaud during their University College days, specifically about the French poet's theories of linguistic experimentation, and his mysteriously enigmatic manner. He also mentioned Joyce's ability to recite Rimbaud's 'Voyelles' from memory.[3] Oliver St. John Gogarty, on the other hand, wrote venomously of how reading Rimbaud changed Joyce for the worse, making him an anti-social ingrate who rejected all that was conventional and decent. Eventually, he suggests, this led to a loss of mental balance and the hopelessly obscure *Finnegans Wake:*

> From Flushing I received a postcard with a photograph of Joyce dressed to resemble Arthur Rimbaud. Rimbaud's revolution against established canons made him a god to Joyce. We must not leave Rimbaud out of the reckoning; if we do, we fail to understand the influence that fashioned Joyce. Rimbaud, disgusted with mankind, had withdrawn from the world. The logical end was for him to withdraw from all authorship because his kind of private writing would lead only to talking to himself. Joyce did not withdraw, so he ended by listening to himself talking in his sleep – 'Finnegans Wake'.[4]

170

Gogarty was, of course, woefully biased in his analysis of the important processes that shaped Joyce's literary development. His biographer, Ulick O'Connor, naïvely echoes the half-truths gleaned from his subject: 'When Joyce started to adopt Rimbaud's custom of deliberately reviling those who helped him, Gogarty found himself unable any longer to stomach his friend's Latin posturing.'[5] In this comment there may even be an unintentional inference that if Joyce was Rimbaud, then Gogarty was Verlaine. The waters have been considerably muddied.

Baudelaire, Rimbaud and the Romantic Tradition

Joyce would have rebelled against the conventional order had he never read Arthur Rimbaud, but it is hard to imagine any avid reader of literature at the end of the nineteenth century not being fascinated with Rimbaud's life and work, especially one who so valued originality and the dramatic gesture of defiance. Rimbaud lived what was probably the most adventurous life of any poet of the modern age. Although Joyce was by nature unadventuresome, he certainly sensed a strong affinity in other ways, and we know that affinity was a matter of great importance to him. Ibsen, for instance, who was an early model, fought against provincialism in a former colony on Europe's edge; John Sullivan was the Irish tenor Joyce might have become; Rimbaud loathed all that was French and provincial – especially his native Charleville. He was a stunningly authentic genius while still in his teens, a quintessential artist-rebel whose proto-Surrealist poems, daring life-style, and striking aesthetic theories dazzled a generation of writers. At University College, Joyce would have been about the age when Rimbaud gave up poetry to become a wanderer and student of languages. After a stint in Paris, Rimbaud's favourite city, Joyce would give up medical school and the prospect of a conventional career to elope with a chambermaid for Pola and Trieste, a school of languages and a life of uncertainty and penury.

Although Joyce knew about Rimbaud long before, the only two letters in which he mentions him are from September 1905 and October 1906, not long after his flight to the continent with Nora; in the earlier letter he clearly sees Rimbaud as a kindred spirit:

It is possible that the delusion I have with regard to my power to write will be killed by adverse circumstances. But the delusion which will never leave me is that I am an artist by temperament.

171

Newman and Renan, for example, are excellent writers but they seem to have very little of the temperament I mean. Whereas Rimbaud, who is hardly a writer at all, has it.[6]

The second letter, from Joyce to his brother Stanislaus, Richard Ellmann cites as proof that Joyce read Arthur Symons' *The Symbolist Movement in Literature* (London, 1899), a book dedicated to W.B. Yeats.[7] C.P. Curran (p. 31) says that Joyce read Symons in 1900 or 1901, and that his copy of Verlaine's *Les Poètes Maudits* (Paris, 1884), which also has a section on Rimbaud, is dated 1902. Although Joyce may have read Verlaine first, Symons' book had the greater impact on him, as it did on writers and students of literature in the English-speaking world generally. Curran (p. 29) describes the effect on his fellow Dublin students:

Huysmans' symbolism of colours fitted in, too, with the Rimbaud sonnet, *Voyelles*, which Joyce would repeat to me. Imitating Rimbaud and *À Rebours*, we would push these *fin-de-siècle* fancies, as I imagine students were doing in every university town, to the correspondence of colours with the sounds of musical instruments and with the sense of taste, compiling, for example, monochrome meals, tables d'hôte in black puddings and caviare, black sole with Guinness and black coffee.

Although Symons' book was hailed as the first real introduction of the French Symbolists in English, the first mention of Rimbaud in print probably came in a newspaper article by George Moore, where he was lumped together with LaForgue. Moore had it reprinted in 1891 in a volume of essays entitled *Impressions and Opinions*. Since Joyce knew of Moore quite early, either his article or *Les Poètes Maudits* was perhaps his first source of information on Rimbaud. If the source was Moore, the introduction could hardly have been more misleading. The impression it gives is of a frail, etherial boy dragged across Europe by a lecherous old Verlaine, who supposedly stabbed the boy in a drunken frenzy. Rimbaud is said to have lain 'hovering between life and death' for several weeks in a Brussels hospital.

In addition to the Moore article, Verlaine and Symons, Joyce probably read Paterne Berrichon's biography of Rimbaud, published in 1897 under the title *La Vie de Rimbaud*, which Symons mentions. Berrichon, who married Rimbaud's sister, published a second book entitled *Jean-Arthur Rimbaud, le poète* (Paris, 1912). Joyce's interest in the French poet can be documented as late as the publication of Edgell Rickword's *Rimbaud, the Boy and the Poet* (London, 1924), which was in his library.[8] Into Buffalo notebook VIII.B, which Hans Walter Gabler dates 1919–1920, Joyce copied 'Voyelles'.[9] That Rimbaud was a model for Shem the Penman is a matter of speculation, since there is some blurring of distinction with Baudelaire and other artist-pariah figures.

Arthur Symons' *The Symbolist Movement in Literature* remains the single most important source for the young Joyce's understanding of the 'enfant terrible' of French poetry, because it contains the essential Rimbaud to which he responded. It recounts his life, emphasizes the rebellion, his visionary nature, the originality, and it quotes only one poem – 'Voyelles', the one poem which we know Joyce could recite from memory. Later he must have read the *'lettres du voyant'* on sense disorientation. The following brief sketch of Rimbaud's life is distilled mostly from Symons.

Jean Nicolas Arthur Rimbaud, born in 1854 in Charleville in the Ardennes, was a brilliant, though reluctant student. He was graduated from the Collège de Charleville in 1870 at the age of sixteen; between 1870 and 1873 lie his years as a poet. After graduation he ran away to Paris by train, but lacked the necessary fare. He was caught, confined for fifteen days and sent back home. Soon thereafter Rimbaud returned to Paris on funds received for selling his watch, and begged to be taken in by André Gill, a painter-poet whose address he had come across. He was not welcomed, and after several days was obliged to return home on foot. After one more try at door-knocking in Paris, Rimbaud sent an assortment of his poems to Paul Verlaine, who had already made his mark in the literary world. Verlaine was so enthusiastic that he invited the boy to Paris, where Rimbaud stayed for nine months as his guest.

The two poets learned much from each other during these formative years. The seventeen-year old boy astonished the Parisian literary world with his rudeness and paganism, but above all with his originality. The weak-willed Verlaine fell completely under Rimbaud's spell and deserted his pregnant wife to follow him through Belgium and England. In August 1873, Verlaine shot his friend in the wrist and was sent to jail for eighteen months. Symons neglects to mention either the shooting or Rimbaud's unmerciful beating of Verlaine with a club when next they met in Stuttgart, an act that understandably ended their relationship. Rimbaud returned to Charleville to write *Une Saison en Enfer*, which he published in the same year. *Les Illuminations*, a collection of prose poems, appears to have been started in 1871, and finished in 1873, but remaining unpublished until 1886.

In November 1873, Rimbaud renounced literature in favour of life. He began a life of wandering that finally led him to a position as gun-runner and trader in Abyssinia, where he was based in Harar. There he experienced high adventure and extreme danger, but in 1891 he contracted a cancer in one leg that continued to worsen. He went to Aden, then to Marseilles, and on to Charleville, but he was determined to get back to Africa; after much difficulty, he had himself sent to Marseilles again. His leg had, in the meantime, been amputated too late, and the spreading cancer caused his death on November 10, 1891, at the age of thirty-seven.

Rimbaud was a visionary poet in the French Romantic tradition of Hugo, Banville, Verlaine, and, above all, Baudelaire. Through Baudelaire he was influenced by Boehme, Swedenborg, Poe, Blake, and De Quincey. Two famous letters of May, 1871, contain his discourse on the history of poetry from the aspiring visionary poet's viewpoint, and, more importantly, reveal his theory of sense disorientation:

Now, I am degrading myself as much as possible, Why? I want to be a poet, and I am working to make myself a *seer*: you will not understand this, and I don't know how to explain it to you. It is a question of reaching the unknown by the derangement of *all the senses*. The sufferings are enormous, but one has to be strong, one has to be born a poet, and I know I am a poet. This is not at all my fault.[10]

I say one must be a *seer*, make oneself a *seer*.
The poet makes himself a *seer* by a long, gigantic and rational *derangement* of *all the senses*. All forms of love, suffering, and madness. He searches himself. He exhausts all poisons in himself and keeps only their quintessences. Unspeakable torture where he needs all his faith, all his superhuman strength where he becomes among all men the great patient, the great criminal, the one accursed – and the supreme Scholar! – Because he reaches the *unknown*! Since he cultivated his soul, rich already, more than any man! He reaches the unknown, and when, bewildered, he ends by losing the intelligence of his visions, he has seen them.

Let him die as he leaps through unheard of and unnamable things: other horrible workers will come; they will begin from the horizons where the other one collapsed! (Fowlie, p. 307)

In the second letter the Romantics are judged according to their success as visionaries. 'Lamartine is at times a seer. Hugo . . . in his last volumes. Musset is . . . loathsome . . . [But] the second Romantics are very much seers: Théophile Gautier, Leconte de Lisle, Théodore de Banville. But, since inspecting the invisible and hearing the unheard is different from recovering the spirit of dead things, Baudelaire is the first seer, king of poets, a *real God*! . . . The new school, called Parnassian, has two seers, Albert Mérat and Paul Verlaine, a real poet' (Fowlie, p. 309).

'*Voyant*', or 'seer', needs some definition if we are to understand the word as Rimbaud used it. An appropriate context is given in M.H. Abrams' *Natural Supernaturalism*, Chapters 7 and 8, on visionary experience. Abrams emphasizes that the constant themes of Wordsworth and other English Romantics contain this imperative: that the poet must learn to experience freshness of sensation while viewing the common, everyday scenes in nature. Rimbaud shared this aim in part, but preferred to achieve originality through artificially induced sensations, or visionary distortions of perception. Romantics wish to see afresh as a child might see in order 'to make the old world new not by distorting it, but by defamiliarizing the familiar'.[11] Wordsworth wished 'to liberate the vision of his readers from bondage to the physical eye, habitual categories, social custom, and caste prejudice, so that they may see the world that he has come to see.'[12] Rimbaud goes the Romantics one better and shows us sights unseen before or since by his readers; freshness of sensation, defamiliarization, originality of vision has become the final goal rather than a means of liberating readers, the result being poems calculated to startle and amaze.

Abrams (p. 414) places Baudelaire in the visionary tradition by citing his advocacy of freshness of sensation and child-like seeing – 'the child sees everything *new*; he is always *intoxicated*' – but the emphasis has shifted to the agony of vision, the *voyant* poet's fixation, possession, and obsession in the act of contemplation. Vision has become a malady. From here it is but a step to Rimbaud's 'artist as sickman' who feeds on the distilled poisons of his own system. Martin Bock has recently discussed Baudelaire's indebtedness to Thomas De Quincey, part of whose *Confessions of an*

175

English Opium-Eater Baudelaire translated as *Un mangeur d'opium* (Paris, 1860), in his linking of intoxication with vision.[13] A member of the *Club des hachichins* who had experimented with drugs, Baudelaire praised wine over other drugs and warned against the dangers of addiction in his essay *Du vin et du haschisch* (1851) and 'Le poème du haschisch' (1860). His *Les Paradis artificiels* (1860) and *Helvétius* (see Rickword, pp. 95–96) are the most likely sources of Rimbaud's ideas of sense disorientation.

Where Rimbaud parted ways with Baudelaire was on the subject of addiction, which, for a poet willing to risk insanity in his quest for freshness of sensation, was a rather small matter. Edgell Rickword, whom Beck quotes, says that while in Paris, Rimbaud 'moved among . . . men of letters like a drunkard or a visionary. He intoxicated himself, systematically, with alcohol, hashish, and tobacco. He relished the impressions of insomnia, and lived like a somnambulist.'[14] The result of this *voyant* regimen was the sort of violent, surrealistic, sensational vision of corruption seen in the following stanzas from 'Le Bateau ivre':

> I have seen enormous swamps ferment, fish-traps
> Where a whole Leviathan rots in the rushes!
> Avalanches of water in the midst of a calm,
> And the distances cataracting toward the abyss!
>
> Glaciers, suns of silver, nacreous waves, skies of embers!
> Hideous strands at the end of brown gulfs
> Where giant serpents devoured by bedbugs
> Fall down from gnarled trees with black scent!
>
> (Fowlie, p. 117)

Here we see the *voyant* posing as a madman journeying through a strange, beautiful, and rather horrifying land of the imagination totally different from the Charleville he detested.

The technique in some ways anticipates Imagism; and, as Mark Schorer reminds us, the visionary quality of Rimbaud's poetry is generally reminiscent of Blake. In Rimbaud and Blake, as distinct from Wordsworth, the emphasis is on imagination rather than nature, vision rather than observation. Of course Blake would never have written 'down with God' on public benches, as Rimbaud did; for him the visionary moment was holy. It is hell on Earth that Rimbaud sees, and it is to Satan that he lends his voice.[15] He often reflects the Symbolist interest in suggestion, evocation, synaesthesia, but it is the beauty of *delirium tremens* that he prefers to evoke in his visionary poetry. The terrible price Rimbaud says he paid for freshness of sensation was, however, willingly paid.

From Rimbaud's *dérèglement de tous les sens* to synaesthesia, or the reverse, is but another step; for Stephen Dedalus, as for Rimbaud, Huysmans, and other writers, the step was an important one. Synaesthetic experience promised uniqueness of sensation which could lead to originality of expression – perhaps even the new language to which many poets aspire. Here the line of descent is principally from Poe to Baudelaire (especially 'Correspondances') to Rimbaud's 'Voyelles' to Joyce's epiphanies, the 'Proteus' episode and beyond in *Ulysses*.[16]

'Correspondences', from *Les Fleurs du Mal*, speaks of nature as a temple, of man reaching it 'through symbols dense as trees that watch him with a gaze familiar'. 'Some perfumes are, like children, innocent, / As sweet as oboes, green as meadow sward / – And others, complex, rich and jubilant, / The vastness of infinity afford, / Like musk and amber, incense, bergamot, / Which sing the senses' and the soul's delight.'[17] Odours, sounds, feelings mingle – not quite synaesthetically perhaps – but close; here the similes are unmixed; there is the conventional 'green as meadow sward' and the stranger, more evocative similes ('perfumes innocent as children'; 'as sweet as oboes'). But the overall effect, of suggestion, of sensual evocation, is one many poets of the nineteenth and twentieth centuries, from Mallarmé to Wallace Stevens (cf. 'Peter Quince at the Clavier'), sought to emulate.

'Voyelles' is a direct descendant of 'Correspondances'; like Baudelaire, Rimbaud compiles images for telling effect, but here the strange metaphor has become monstrous, the etherial suggestion a violent assault on the sensibililty. The Fowlie translation (p. 121):

Vowels

A black, E white, I red, U green, O blue: vowels,
One day I will tell your latent birth:
A, black hairy corset of shining flies
Which buzz around cruel stench,

Gulfs of darkness; E, whiteness of vapors and tents,
Lances of proud glaciers, white kings, quivering of flowers;
I, purples, spit blood, laughter of beautiful lips

In anger or penitent drunkenness;

U, cycles, divine vibrations of green seas,
Peace of pastures scattered with animals, peace of the wrinkles
Which alchemy prints on heavy studious brows;

O, supreme Clarion full of strange stridor,
Silences crossed by worlds and angels:
– O, the Omega, violet beam from His Eyes![18]

Mallarmé meditated on the shapes and sounds of letters, but Rimbaud seems to be the first to associate them with colours. The logic of this particular linking still escapes us, and, though critics have used considerable violence in yoking the sonnet's vowels and colours together, the logic is surely a private one. Are the vowels Greek because of the omega, or French with 'O' transposed to suggest the ultimate letter in the Greek alphabet? Or does it matter? And was the poem inspired by a child's colouring book that Rimbaud had read? One can do little more than speculate about these matters, or even the seriousness with which this synaesthetic linking is to be taken, but the point is that an entirely new dimension seems to have been brought to poetry. If a reader could assimilate the system, a virtual kaleidoscope of flashing colours would strike the mind's eye as the words are read. The visual arts would seem to have merged with the literary, so that in addition to rhythm, sound, sense, allusion, and the other common properties of poetry, there would be colour. Obviously the idea turned out to be more a matter for aesthetic speculation than for reader response, but 'Voyelles' certainly stimulated the imaginations of Joyce and his generation.

'Voyelles' remains Rimbaud's most influential poem, though hardly his best. Part of its importance lies in the fact that writers took Rimbaud at his word that he had invented a new language of correspondence. He seemed to succeed where others had failed. Edmund Wilson wrote, 'all the exponents of Symbolism have insisted that they were attempting to meet a need for a new language. "To find a tongue!" Rimbaud had cried. "One has to be an academician – deader than a fossil – to make a dictionary of any language at all." '[19] Rimbaud went on to say, 'This language will be of the soul for the soul, containing everything, smells, sounds, colours, thought holding on to thought and pulling' (Fowlie, p. 309). In more direct reference to 'Voyelles', Rimbaud said in 'Alchimie du verbe': 'I invented the colour of the vowels! –*A* black,

178

E white, *I* red, *O* blue, *U* green. – I regulated the form and movement of each consonant, and, with instinctive rhythms, I prided
myself on inventing a poetic language accessible some day to all the
senses. I reserved translation rights' (Fowlie, p. 193). These lines
were written partly with tongue in cheek. Still, he set other writers
to imagining the same thing; it is in this that his influence is most
deeply felt.

Rimbaud, Joyce, Dedalus

Though Blake is a model for the young Stephen Dedalus in his
budding visionary stage, Rimbaud embodied more of the particular
kind of revolutionary qualities that Joyce admired. He was an
apostate, a vagabond, a pariah who rejected religion, family, country, and every kind of convention. He struck the Luciferian pose,
inspired the Decadents, and in all things seemed to surpass others in
rebellion. In this even Baudelaire seemed to take second place.
Rimbaud's exile, his experiments in synaesthesia, his search for a
new language, the violence of his imagery, surpassed only by the
violence of his disgust – all this would have been enormously appeal-
ing to a writer like Joyce. Thus, in *Stephen Hero*, we find some
justification for Kenner's christening Stephen the 'Dublin Rimbaud'. We read that Stephen

> sought in his verses to fix the most elusive of his moods and he put
> his lines together not word by word but letter by letter. He read
> Blake and Rimbaud on the values of letters and even permuted
> and combined the five vowels to construct cries for primitive
> emotions. To none of his former fervours had he given himself
> with such a whole heart as to this fervour.[20]

In Joyce's *A Portrait of the Artist as a Young Man,* it is through
words, language, that Stephen Dedalus comes to know the world
around him, his reality being continually shaped by vocabulary
acquisition.[21] 'Words which he did not understand he said over and
over to himself till he had learned them by heart: and through them
he had glimpses of the real world about him' (*AP*, 62). As a young
boy he speculates about the onomatopoeic implications of 'kiss' and
'suck' (*AP*, 11; 15), and once he encounters a euphemism he takes
literally, when Dante belches and calls it 'heartburn' (*AP*, 11).
Instinctively, he grasps the mystical power of words, a sure sign of
the artistic temperament. In this he resembles the boy in 'The

Sisters', who has embroidered 'paralysis', 'gnomon', and 'simony' with private meanings. Stephen seems destined to follow in the footsteps of writers who have sought a new language for poetic expression; in *A Portrait* the language he comes to use is obviously derivative of Newman, Pater, and the *fin-de-siècle* writers, especially in his villanelle, but like Rimbaud, who echoed Baudelaire until he found his own voice, he is gradually moving closer to originality of expression. The discovery of new literary languages and forms, a feature of *fin-de-siècle* writing generally, was a major concern of Joyce as well, from the evolutionary prose of *A Portrait* to the linguistic experimentalism of *Finnegans Wake*.

From *Stephen Hero* through *Ulysses*, synaesthesia is often the subject of Stephen's thoughts when he is alone, evaluating his perceptions, honing his verbal skills, exploring the freshness of his sensations. In a climactic scene of Chapter Two of *A Portrait*, the disgusted Stephen leaves the school play to walk rapidly down the hill. 'Pride and hope and desire like crushed herbs in his heart sent up vapours of maddening incense before the eyes of his mind' (*AP*, 86). His agony of despair is calmed by the odour of horse piss and rotted straw. Herbs in the heart, eyes of the mind, the reassuring smell of corruption, these are the terms of a kind of metaphorical thinking highly unusual in a schoolboy – unless, of course, he or the narrator has been reading Symbolist poetry. In Chapter Four, having just rejected with finality the priestly vocation, sure now that he was meant to be an artist, Stephen turns for guidance in his thinking to 'Voyelles', 'Correspondances', and Symbolist theory, which will now shape his development:

He drew forth a phrase from his treasure and spoke it softly to himself:
– A day of dappled seaborne clouds.
The phrase and the day and the scene harmonized in a chord. Words. Was it their colours? He allowed them to glow and fade, hue after hue: sunrise gold, the russet and green of apple orchards, azure of waves, the greyfringed fleece of clouds. No, it was not their colours: it was the poise and balance of the period itself. Did he then love the rhythmic rise and fall of words better than their associations of legend and colour? Or was it that, being as weak of sight as he was shy of mind, he drew less pleasure from the reflection of the glowing sensible world through the prism of a language manycoloured and richly storied than from the con-

templation of an inner world of individual emotions mirrored perfectly in a lucid supple periodic prose? (*AP*, 166–167)

Later Stephen listens to the cries of circling birds: 'like the squeak of mice behind the wainscot: a shrill twofold note. But the notes were long and shrill and clear and fine and falling like threads of silken light unwound from whirring spools' (*AP*, 224). Still later, Stephen thinks: 'A trembling joy, lambent as a faint light, played like a fairy host around him. But why? Her passage through the darkening air or the verse with its black vowels [A = *noir*] and its opening sound, rich and lutelike?' (*AP*, 232–233). In such moments of intense aesthetic reflection, Stephen is to Rimbaud as Rimbaud was to Baudelaire; the apprentice stage was a necessary stop on the road to a new language of poetic expression. The vehicle was synaesthetic thinking.

In the Martello Tower, where, Oliver Gogarty said, Joyce talked of little but Rimbaud, Buck Mulligan stands on the parapet, wipes his razor clean of shaving soap with Stephen's handkerchief, and says: '– The bard's noserag. A new art colour for our Irish poets: snotgreen. You can almost taste it, can't you?' A few lines later he also calls the sea 'snotgreen' (*U*, 5).[22] The handkerchief is obviously the main point of reference, but there are other allusive ones. Mulligan's quip comes after a decade in which there appeared seemingly countless slim, green volumes of Irish Revival poetry such as Chandler of Joyce's story 'A Little Cloud' envisions publishing. Green is Ireland's colour, and 'snotgreen' is an appropriate, if disgusting, colour for decadent art (if it must have one). But what makes the colour still more apt is that both Mulligan and Dedalus know that 'morves d'azur' (snotgreen) comes from Rimbaud's 'Le Bateau ivre' (line 76). Later Stephen will lay 'the dry snot picked from his nostril on the ledge of a rock, carefully', in a parody of creative activity (*U*, 51). In a comical way, Mulligan is signalling his disgust with Stephen and Rimbaud, who, Gogarty said, taught Joyce ingratitude. The Francophile standing before Mulligan, possibly Ireland's first decadent poet, will not soon forget his biting wit.

It is hardly an accident that 'Proteus', the art of which Joyce said was philology, is also the most colourful episode of *Ulysses*, or that Rimbaud's colour 'Snotgreen' appears in the episode's fourth line (*U*, 37). In *Ulysses*, as in *A Portrait*, the French poet is most in Stephen's thoughts when walking alone, reading the book of himself, measuring his progress as an artist against the certain loss of vocation (priest in *A Portrait*, teacher in 'Nestor'). The difficult opening of 'Proteus' is most often interpreted in terms of its internal references to Aristotle's *De Anima* (Books II and III) and Jacob Boehme's *Signatura Rerum*, but while Stephen is in a sense learning to read God's signature in nature, as Wordsworth did, he is more precisely learning to be a seer in the visionary sense. He closes his eyes to perceive, an act his aesthetic principles and his theory of epiphany, as discussed in *Stephen Hero* and *A Portrait*, show to be essential to his growth as an artist. Stephen, like his French predecessor, has assimilated a literary tradition he can use. Thus, in continual flux in the opening of 'Proteus' are nature, thought, literary and philosophical references, and language, the entire effect being quite definitely synaesthetic:

> Ineluctable modality of the visible: at least that if no more, thought through my eyes. Signatures of all things I am here to read, seaspawn and seawrack, the nearing tide, that rusty boot. Snotgreen, bluesilver, rust: coloured signs. Limits of the diaphane. But he adds: in bodies. Then he was aware of them bodies before of them coloured. . . . Shut your eyes and see.
>
> Stephen closed his eyes to hear his boots crush crackling wrack and shells. . . . I am getting on nicely in the dark. My ash sword hangs at my side. Tap with it: they do. . . .
>
> Rhythm begins, you see. I hear. . . .
>
> Open your eyes now. I will. One moment. Has all vanished since? If I open and am for ever in the black adiaphane. *Basta*! I will see if I can see.
>
> See now. There all the time without you: and ever shall be, world without end. (*U*, 37)

Stephen reads nature, shuts his eyes to see, says 'rhythm begins, you see, I hear', and finally opens his eyes to see if he can see. Having seen so much already, he then sees time. The perceptual exercises are complete, the command by Rimbaud that the artist make himself a seer has been obeyed. Once the mood has become set, Stephen is more prepared to see, think, evaluate, and experiment with words that will express his vision.

Like Wordsworth, he will see and describe the commonest things and occurrences in nature, but unlike him this will give him no pleasure, for he is deeply embittered by life, haunted by the past and fearful of the future. In 'Telemachus' he scorns the usurper; in

'Nestor' the oppressor; in 'Proteus' he scorns himself. His self-hatred derives from his sense of failure as a writer – that he is still honing the tools of his art, and as yet has produced only a few derivative poems. Like Yeats and Rimbaud, Stephen knows that artistic skill is cultivated, that artists make themselves artists; being born with artistic temperament is hardly enough. Though he concentrates on these matters in 'Proteus', dumps file cabinets of relevant material into his consciousness as he walks on the beach, Stephen is still the artist as a young man, impatient that he is still apprenticed to the singing masters of his soul. Readers see his metempsychotic affinities with Icarus, Daedalus, Telemachus, Hamlet, and Christ and accept them, but Stephen seems to share Mulligan's view that he is nothing but a *poseur*, an imposter (one meaning of the word 'artist' in Ireland), freshly returned from Paris in his 'Latin quarter hat' and flaunting the newly acquired veneer of French culture: 'God, we simply must dress the character' (*U*, 41). Gogarty spoke of receiving a photo of Joyce wearing the complete Rimbaud costume; in *Ulysses* Stephen wears Mulligan's boots, hand-me-down trousers, and distinctly foreign head gear, a sign that he is not yet his own man.

Though Stephen might not agree, apprenticeship is, of course, a commonly accepted means of attaining mastery. In 'Proteus', Stephen is apprenticed to no writer more consciously than Rimbaud. The idea there is to forge out of his personality a new being who will see anew, express anew. Rimbaud was thinking along these lines when he wrote: 'I is someone else. It is too bad for the wood that finds itself a violin. . . . For I is someone else. If brass wakes up a trumpet, it is not its fault' (Fowlie, p. 305). The phrase *'Je est un autre'* has struck a chord in Stephen's mind during this hour on the beach, where he feels his identity as much in flux as language, tide, and sea. 'Yes, used to carry punched tickets [in Paris] to prove an alibi if they arrested you for murder somewhere. . . . Other fellow did it: other me. Hat, tie, overcoat, nose. *Lui, c'est moi* (*U*, 41). Later, he thinks 'My soul walks with me, form of forms' (*U*, 44). He imagines himself among his Viking ancestors 'on the frozen Liffey, that I, a changeling' (*U*, 45). Still later he thinks, 'Me sits there with his augur's rod of ash, in borrowed sandals' (*U*, 48). Remembering a borrowed pound, while in the library, he will use a theory of molecular change to release himself from the debt: 'Wait. Five months. Molecules all change. I am other I now. Other I got pound' (*U*, 189). Stephen walks, thinks almost continually about Paris, listens to the 'fourworded wavespeech: seesoo, hrss, rsseeiss, ooos' (*U*, 49), and feels thoroughly uncomfortable with himselves. Wherever he walks, Rimbaud's footprints seem already imprinted on the sand.

Feeling unfortunate, perhaps, not to have written 'Voyelles', and perhaps remembering the theory of the children's book as the poem's source, Stephen ridicules himself: 'Books you were going to write with letters for titles. Have you read his F? O yes, but I prefer Q. Yes, but W is wonderful. O yes, W' (*U*, 40). 'The virgin at Hodges Figgis' window on Monday looking in for one of the alphabet books you were going to write' (*U*, 48).

Joyce himself overshadows all of Stephen's models, but the biographical parallels with Rimbaud are striking. They reject country, family, religion for a revolutionary aestheticism and see exile as their inevitable destiny. The young poets are fervently religious as boys, brilliant, though erratic students who become caught up in social rebellion. Enid Starkie says that Rimbaud 'was a religious nature looking for spiritual certainty'.[23] Henry Miller affirms that, at the age of twelve, 'Rimbaud's piety was so exalted that he longed for martyrdom'.[24] Stephen's faith is a major theme of the works in which he appears. The rebellious Rimbaud cried, 'death to God', while cunning Stephen refuses to kneel at his dying mother's bedside. Their revolt became an all-out battle against matriarchy. The son of an absent father (cf. Simon Dedalus in *Ulysses*), Rimbaud's battles for freedom of movement, conduct and expression were frantically waged against a domineering mother. Attempting to coerce him into a return to the fold in 'Circe', the ghost of Stephen's mother '*raises her blackened, withered right arm slowly towards Stephen's breast with outstretched fingers*' (*U*, 582).

If mothers are anathema to artists, father figures (as opposed to real fathers) are consciously sought; in this Rimbaud's name must be added to those of Telemachus, Icarus and Hamlet as an archetypal figure whose most memorable acts are determined by the authority of present or absent fathers. Stephen's discussion of paternity indicates that the subject is of some importance to him (*U* 207–208), and *Ulysses*' Homeric structure is a promise that father-son relations will be crucial. Rimbaud's father, an army captain, abandoned the family; in Georges Izambard, Rimbaud's teacher, and later in Verlaine, the poet sought a father figure intelligent enough to direct his development as a poet, while, at the same time, having the capacity for the love and understanding he had lacked at home. One result of this search was homosexuality.

The disgust that Stephen and Rimbaud feel at the national coalition of Church and bourgeoisie becomes a revolutionary philosophy. Since Ireland suffered from British domination, and France from its recent defeat in the Prussian war, each artist (like Baudelaire) felt a sense of racial inferiority. This is the subject of 'Mauvais Sang', in *Une Saison en Enfer* (Fowlie, pp. 174–183), and of several of Stephen's comments in *A Portrait* and *Ulysses* (cf. *AP* 203; *U* 645).

In *Finnegans Wake*, the character of Shem, especially in 'Shem, the Penman' (*FW*, 169 ff.), is a caricature of the artistic temperament (so offensive to Gogarty), which Joyce associated with Rimbaud and himself in his letter of September 1905 (*vide supra*).[25] There is little need to catalogue the anti-social traits of Shem, or his persona Glugg 'the bold bad bleak boy of the storybooks' (*FW*, 219), Although he is Irish, not French, he is the quintessential artist as *voyant*, poet, outcast, rebel, and threat to all decent people; he is a 'stinksome inkenstink' (*FW*, 183), the 'first till last alshemist [who] wrote over every square inch of the only foolscap available, his own body' (*FW*, 185). Rimbaud, of course, wrote 'Alchimie du verbe' (which contains Shem's name), where he discussed 'Voyelles' (Fowlie, pp. 192–195).

In *A Portrait*, Stephen's body is liceridden, even his 'mind bred vermin' (*AP*, 174; 234), but this was hardly a subject for literature until Rimbaud wrote 'Les Chercheuses de poux' (Fowlie, pp. 92–93); Shem, as seen by Shaun, is disgusting beyond anything they can imagine – a 'condemned fool, anarch, egoarch, hiresiarch, [who has] reared [his] disunited kingdom on the vacuum of [his] own intensely doubtful soul' (*FW*, 188), a 'seeker of the nest of evil in the bosom of a good word' (*FW*, 189) – a *voyant*, the son of a *voyeur* – in short a madman.

Though by implication Rimbaud seems present in Shem's character, he is there as part of a visionary tradition extending back to the biblical prophets and forward through Boehme, Swedenborg, Blake, Baudelaire, de Nerval and others who lived lives of the imagination, who risked persecution for heresy, and whose cultivated eccentricity seemed a sign of their incontrovertible dedication to truth. In using himself as the chief model for Shem, Joyce showed that he felt he belonged in that visionary company; it was with a sense of pride that he scrupulously exposed his vices and faults, imaginary or real, in a manner parodic of Rousseau, cataloguing them with a satirist's pen to make of his own hide, so to speak, a tapestry.

For once Gogarty was right. The influence is there, from *Stephen Hero* to *A Portrait* to *Ulysses*, on the mind of Stephen Dedalus as it must have been on that of the young Joyce, being most apparent in reveries where aesthetics is the subject. When Stephen tries to push on toward truly original theories of experimentation, his thoughts weave synaesthetic patterns in colours and vowels that remind us that Rimbaud represented for Stephen a classical case of anxiety of influence. The French poet had either to be vanquished or assimilated in the mind, but in any case gone beyond for Stephen to be able to write. Since Stephen must overcome self doubts, gaining mastery over his masters in order to blossom in his vocation (and his story is essentially about this struggle), he shares with Rimbaud a dimension of intercourse that sheds a greater light on his character than do the shadowy forebears most often evoked by critics – Telemachus, Hamlet, Icarus, Daedalus – none of whom was known for his experiments with language or literary form.

By *Finnegans Wake*, Rimbaud had about served Joyce's purpose; although his interest doubtless remained, his use of the French poet, as with so many other writers, had become more ornamental than essential.[26] The experimentalism of Rimbaud and 'Voyelles' was a stage – perhaps even a blockage – through which Stephen had to pass to attain mastery; *Ulysses* reflects this process in plot and form. *Finnegans Wake* proclaims on every page the virtuosity to which Stephen aspires, one surpassing anything of which Rimbaud could have dreamed. Hence he is little celebrated in Joyce's final work. Stephen's struggle for mastery was no longer the subject, which had now become literary virtuosity itself. Still, those with unusual perceptual abilities may occasionally catch a glimpse of the young French master on the Wakean Parnassus, in rather reduced circumstances, detached from the work itself, paring his fingernails as if he bore no responsibility for the babulous funferall below.

NOTES

1   Hugh Kenner, *Dublin's Joyce* (London: Chatto and Windus, 1955), p. 24.
2   David Weir, 'Stephen Dedalus: Rimbaud or Baudelaire?', *James Joyce Quarterly*, XVIII (Fall 1980), p. 87. Two articles on Joyce's debt to Baudelaire and the French Symbolists fail to mention Rimbaud. These are J. Mitchell Morse, 'Baudelaire, Stephen Dedalus, and Shem the Penman', *Bucknell Review,* VII (March 1958), 187–198; and M.E. Kronegger, 'Joyce's Debt to Poe and the French Symbolists', *Revue de Littérature Comparée*, XXXIX (1965), 243–254.

3   C.P. Curran, *James Joyce Remembered* (New York and London: Oxford University Press, 1968), pp. 30–32. Cited in text as 'Curran'.

4   Oliver St. John Gogarty, 'They Think They Know Joyce', *The Saturday Review of Literature,* XXXIII (March 18, 1950), p. 9.

5   Ulick O'Connor, *The Times I've Seen: Oliver St. John Gogarty, A Biography* (New York: Ivan Obolensky, Inc., 1963), p. 86.

6   *The Letters of James Joyce*, 3 vols., eds. Richard Ellmann and Stuart Gilbert (New York: The Viking Press, 1966), II, 110; 173.

7   Richard Ellmann, *James Joyce* (New York: Oxford University Press, 1959), p. 244. Joyce says of Gerhart Hauptmann that 'His temperament has a little of Rimbaud in it. Like him, too, I suppose somebody else will be his future', referring to Symons' often misunderstood statement of Rimbaud that 'Even in literature he had his future; but his future was Verlaine' (*Letters,* II, 173); Arthur Symons, *The Symbolist Movement in Literature* (New York: E.P. Dutton & Co., 1919), p. 295. The most important work on Joyce, Symons, Verlaine and the Symbolists has been done by David Hayman in *Joyce et Mallarmé*, Paris, Les Lettres Modernes, 1956 (2 vols.).

8   Thomas E. Connolly, ed., *The Personal Library of James Joyce: A Descriptive Bibliography, The University of Buffalo Studies,* XXII (April 1955), item 252.

9   A facsimile copy of VIII.B appears in *The James Joyce Archive,* eds. Michael Groden *et al.* (New York: The Garland Publishing Co., 1978), in the volume entitled *Notes, Criticism, Translations and Miscellaneous Writings,* vol. II, p. 381. Also in Joyce's hand appear poems by Albert Samain, Stéphane Mallarmé, Léon Bloy, and prose selections from Walter Pater.

10 *Rimbaud: Complete Works, Selected Letters,* trans. & ed. by Wallace Fowlie (Chicago and London: University of Chicago Press, 1966), p. 303. Hereafter cited in text as 'Fowlie'. This work contains both the original French and an English translation. Some readers might prefer the *Œuvres Complètes d'Arthur Rimbaud*, Paris, Éditions Gallimard, 1963.

11 M.H. Abrams, *Natural Supernaturalism: Tradition and Revolution in Romantic Literature* (New York: W.W. Norton & Co., Inc., 1971), p. 379.

12 *Ibid.,* pp. 406–407.

13 Martin Bock, 'The Disoriented Voyager: Theories of Sense Perception and the Visionary Moment in Modern Literature', Ph.D. Dissertation, University of Wisconsin-Madison, 1981, pp. 52–55.

14 Edgell Rickword, *Rimbaud: The Boy and the Poet* (Castle Hedingham, Essex: The Daimon Press, Ltd., 1963), p. 47 (first pub. 1924).

15 Mark Schorer, *William Blake: The Politics of Vision* (New York: Vintage Books, 1959), p. 385 (first pub. 1946).

16 See articles by Kronegger, Weir, and Archie K. Loss, 'Presences and Visions in *Exiles, A Portrait of the Artist* and *Ulysses*', *James Joyce Quarterly,* XIII (Winter 1976), pp. 152–154.

17 The complete works of Charles Baudelaire in French are to be found in *Œuvres Complètes*, ed. Marcel Ruff, Paris, Editions du Seuil, 1968. A good English translation, and one I have used here, is *Baudelaire: Selected Poems*, trans. Joanna Richardson (Harmondsworth, England: Penguin Books, 1975), pp. 42–43. Here is the original poem:

'Correspondances'

La Nature est un temple où de vivants piliers
Laissent parfois sortir de confuses paroles;
L'homme y passe à travers des forêts de symboles
Qui l'observent avec des regards familiers.

Comme de longs échos qui de loin se confondent
Dans une ténébreuse et profonde unité,
Vaste comme la nuit et comme la clarté,
Les parfums, les couleurs et les sons se répondent.

Il est des parfums frais comme des chairs d'enfants,
Doux comme les hautbois, verts comme les prairies,
– Et d'autres, corrompus, riches et triomphants,

Ayant l'expansion des choses infinies,
Comme l'ambre, le musc, le benjoin, et l'encens,
Qui chantent les transports de l'esprit et des sens.

18 Here is the original poem:

'Voyelles'

A noir, E blanc, I rouge, U vert, O bleu: voyelles,
Je dirai quelque jour vos naissances latentes:
A, noir corset velu des mouches éclatantes
Qui bombinent autour des puanteurs cruelles,

Golfe d'ombre; E, candeurs des vapeurs et des tentes,
Lances des glaciers fiers, rois blancs, frissons d'ombrelles;
I, pourpres, sang craché, rire des lèvres belles
Dans la colère ou les ivresses pénitentes;

U, cycles, vibrements divins des mers virides,
Paix des pâtis semés d'animaux, paix des rides
Que l'alchimie imprime aux grands fronts studieux;

O, suprême Clairon plein de strideurs étranges,
Silences traversés des Mondes et des Anges:
– O l'Oméga, rayon violet de Ses Yeux!

19 Edmund Wilson, *Axël's Castle* (New York: Charles Scribner's Sons, 1959), pp.
    294–295.
20 James Joyce, *Stephen Hero* (New York: New Directions, 1963), p. 32. See
    Claudine Hunting, 'La Voix de Rimbaud: Nouveau point de vue sur les "nais-
    sances latentes" des "Voyelles" ', *PMLA*, LXXXVIII (May 1973), pp.
    472–483. Apparently unaware that she was anticipated by Stephen, Hunting's
    point is that, more important than the configuration of the letters in 'Voyelles' is
    their function as 'cries for primitive emotions'.

21 All references to *A Portrait* are to the Viking Critical Edition (New York: The Viking Press, 1968), referred to in the text as *AP*.
22 References to *Ulysses* (*U* in text) are to the Modern Library Edition, New York, Random House, 1961.
23 Enid Starkie, *Arthur Rimbaud* (Norfolk, Ct.: New Directions, 1961), p. 17.
24 Henry Miller, *Time of the Assassins: A Study of Rimbaud* (Norfolk, Ct.: New Directions, 1956), p. 87.
25 James Joyce, *Finnegans Wake* (New York: The Viking Press, 1939). Cited as *FW* in the text.
26 For an example of ornament, see William York Tindall, *A Reader's Guide to Finnegans Wake* (New York: Farrar, Straus and Giroux, 1969), p. 277. Tindall cites 'Mithyphallic' (*FW*, 481.4) as 'a distortion of Rimbaud's 'Ithyphalliques' ("Le Cœur Volé")'. Some would disagree that Rimbaud was used in a way more ornamental than essential in *Finnegans Wake*. Both David Hayman and Adaline Glasheen see an important connection there between colours, rainbows (evoking Rimbaud's name), and 'Voyelles'.

JAMES JOYCE AND THE IRISH DRAMATIC MOVEMENT

ANN SADDLEMYER

His first public gesture was to stand alone, by denial taking action. There must have been other students of the Royal University who on 8 May 1899 refused to sign a letter of protest against Yeats's *The Countess Cathleen* – a protest foreshadowing both in its confused argument and mixed emotions the objections eight years later to Synge's *Playboy of the Western World* – but it was Joyce's abstention that was noticed.[1] He preferred to make his own statements. He delivered his first broadside, 'Drama and Life', eight months later before the university's Literary and Historical Society, in it raising drama from particularity to the universal and setting Wagner and Ibsen above the now exhausted theatres of the past. Standing above the snow line, these new archangels would draw for subject and sustenance on 'even the most commonplace, the deadest among the living' for the new world drama of the soul.[2] On that same day, 20 January 1900, Joyce received word that the prestigious English *Fortnightly Review* would consider a review of Ibsen's new play *When We Dead Awaken*. 'Ibsen's New Drama', published on 1 April, earned by way of William Archer the benediction of the Master himself.[3]

But although unfamiliar to most of his impressed classmates, the names of Wagner and Ibsen had already been much conjured with by Joyce's elders of the Irish Literary Theatre. Both Edward Martyn and his cousin George Moore had made their pilgrimage to Bayreuth, even before the publication of Shaw's *The Perfect Wagnerite*; one of Moore's closest friends was the editor of La Revue *wagnérienne*, Édouard Dujardin, whom Joyce would have cause to acknowledge later. Even the unmusical Yeats found much of value in the depth and breadth of structure, symbolism, emotional appeal and theory expressed in Wagner's work. For all the founders of the Irish dramatic movement – including Yeats's theosophist supporter Annie Horniman who would later provide a building for the elucidation of Yeats's dramatic theories – Wagner's Bayreuth had become a symbol for the revolutionary theatre they hoped to establish in Dublin.[4]

190

Ibsen, too, had already been acknowledged a force to reckon with. Moore had written enthusiastically of the impact of Ibsen on contemporary theatre before turning his attention to Irish concerns; his articles in 1890 on Antoine's production of *Ghosts* at the Théâtre Libre in Paris had helped initiate the founding of London's Independent Theatre and he was anxious to spread the gospel further. Here also he shared the platform with Martyn, whose play *The Heather Field*, closely modelled after Ibsen, had been performed with *The Countess Cathleen* in May 1899.[5] Moore's introduction to Martyn's play, published the previous February, spoke eloquently of the hero Carden Tyrrell's hopeless dreams of reclaiming the heather field as 'the eternal aspiration of man to the ideal', dreams in conflict with reality yet seductive in their attractiveness.[6] Martyn's own notes on Ibsen also suggest that in the conflict between Carden Tyrrell and his uncomprehending, unsympathetic wife he was attempting to emulate what he admired in *Little Eyolf:*

> When, out of the psychological subtleties of the characters of Alfred and Rita Allmers, the respective mental tragedies of husband and wife rise to a climax of conflict, there is brought home to an audience with tremendous impressiveness how greater far is the dramatic situation of psychology than that of the mere exteriority expressed only in bodily action.[7]

For the second season of the Irish Literary Theatre, in February 1900, Martyn's 'psychological drama' *Maeve* was followed by *The Bending of the Bough,* a revision by Moore, with some help from Yeats, of Martyn's *The Tale of a Town*. Although less politically biting and more generalized in characterization than Martyn's original, Moore's play still betrayed Ibsenite origins in its topicality and the satire of self-seeking, hypocritical place-hunters.[8] Moore's preface tells of art's flight from England, France, Germany and Russia; 'and when it leaves Norway it must find another small nation, one which has not yet achieved its destiny'. Ireland alone in the western world was art's likely refuge.[9] In April 1900 Yeats published a third and final issue of *Beltaine,* the organ of the Irish Literary Theatre, in which he proclaimed triumphantly, 'We have brought the "literary drama" to Ireland, and it has become a reality'.[19] But although almost every public comment by its founders had cited the example of Ibsen, unlike its sister movements in England and on the continent the Irish Literary Theatre did not offer any of his plays. Yeats, like Synge (who had read Ibsen in English, French and German translations), continued to believe that Ibsen's characters were imprisoned in their commonplace circumstances and everyday language.[11]

During the summer of 1900 Joyce wrote his first play. *A Brilliant Career* (which to William Archer's astonishment the author dedicated to his own soul) had a hero who like Moore's resembled Dr. Stockman in *An Enemy of the People*, and, like *The Heather Field*, told the story of an unwise marriage. Richard Ellmann tells us that about this time he also wrote a verse play called *Dream Stuff* and was writing poetry strongly influenced by Yeats. Neither play and little of the poetry survives, although we do have Archer's lengthy, puzzled response to the 'gigantic breadth of treatment' of the second and third acts of *A Brilliant Career*: 'If you had a symbolic purpose, I own it escapes me . . . [but] I am no great hand at reading hieroglyphics'.[12] Then in January 1901 Joyce himself went on stage, playing the stereotyped villain in an amateur production of his friend Margaret Sheehy's comedy, *Cupid's Confidante*; for years Joyce treasured the complimentary remarks concerning his performance, a 'revelation of amateur acting', by the drama critic for the *Evening Telegraph*.[13] (Possibly because of this encouragement, he later briefly contemplated a career as an actor, and chose as stage name George Brown, in tribute to his hero Giordano Bruno.[14])

By March of that year this self-styled defiant, hotheaded stripling had learned enough Dano-Norwegian to send birthday greetings on Ibsen's seventy-third birthday; but while kneeling in homage, Joyce was already looking past Ibsen to the future:

> Your work on earth draws to a close and you are near the silence. . . . You have only opened the way – though you have gone as far as you could upon it. . . . But I am sure that higher and holier enlightenment lies – onward.[15]

By 23 July 1901 he had completed the translation of *Vor Sonnenaufgang,* a harsh, naturalistic play by Gerhart Hauptmann; the manuscript of *Before Sunrise* clearly betrays an inadequate knowledge of German, but in the passages of country dialect there is a glimmer of linguistic flexibility and feeling for idiosyncratic dialogue. That same summer he translated a more recent play by Hauptmann, *Michael Kramer*; the manuscript has not survived, but in style and subject matter the play would doubtless have been more

192

congenial.[16] Clearly he had interpreted the challenge of the Irish Literary Theatre experiment in terms more sympathetic to Martyn and Moore than to Yeats: in an article published by the *Daily Express* in February 1899, Martyn had already suggested that in 'the modern drama of Germany' could be found Ibsen's successor, selecting Hauptmann's dream play, *Hannele,* as example.[17]

But in October 1901 Yeats announced in *Samhain* (the successor to *Beltaine*) plans for the third and final season of the Irish Literary Theatre – a play by Douglas Hyde in the Irish language, and a collaboration by Yeats and Moore based on the Irish legend of Diarmuid and Grania. Angered by what he interpreted as a deliberate rejection of Europeanization, Joyce responded with his second broadside, 'The Day of the Rabblement'. This was published privately in November 1901 together with Francis Skeffington's essay advocating equal status for women; both had been turned down by a new university magazine, *St. Stephen's*. Eighty-five copies were quickly distributed around Dublin, Joyce taking special care that George Moore (and doubtless Martyn, George Russell and Yeats) received one. The rabblement was, of course, the Irish version of Ibsen's trolls, 'the most belated race in Europe', 'the popular will'. *Beltaine*, Joyce complained, had spoken of producing European masterpieces but none had appeared; yet the presentation of Ibsen, Tolstoy or Hauptmann was essential to provide technical examples to a nation 'which never advanced so far as a miracle-play'. It was insufferable that, in a country which had no official censorship, the directors should yield to the 'placid and intensely moral' audience. Of the artists, Yeats (though a talented poet and prose writer) is an aesthete with 'a floating will' who had now obviously given in to his 'treacherous instinct of adaptability'; neither Martyn nor Moore could be considered an original writer and Martyn in particular lacked breadth and distinction despite his fleeting similarity to Strindberg; Moore, once a fine novelist, is now outdated. The future belongs to the true successors of the dying Ibsen: the author of *Michael Kramer* and an unnamed – but readily identifiable – further minister already knocked at the door.[18]

Too late, however, for the Irish Literary Theatre. Yeats returned to London, and we have no record of his reaction to 'The Day of the Rabblement'. Moore acknowledged that the essay was 'preposterously clever', but his influence – which was dependent on Martyn's – was waning; within a year he and Yeats would quarrel over the ownership of the plot to *Where There is Nothing*.[19] Martyn's *An*

Enchanted Sea, written in emulation of *The Lady from the Sea* and more powerful than his dream play *Maeve,* had been ignored; by 1903 he was sufficiently disillusioned to set up in opposition to the movement he had helped establish, hiring a professional company which, directed by Moore, performed *The Heather Field* and *A Doll's House* in June and, the following year, *An Enchanted Sea.* Martyn never referred publicly to Joyce, but a heavy-handed satire of Yeats, Lady Gregory, Moore and himself, which expresses charges similar to Joyce's, was published in 1907 – *Romulus and Remus, or The Makers of Delights.* In one of his later plays, *The Dream Physician,* Joyce himself appears, thinly disguised, in the sympathetic role of Otho Gerrard, a flamboyant idealistic poet longing for the unattainable Moon while comparing everyone else's foibles to his own 'magnificent' intellect; significantly, Martyn has written himself into the play also – as Otho Gerrard's father.[20] In 1919 Joyce unwittingly repaid the compliment by persuading the English Players of Zurich to produce *The Heather Field,* in his programme note writing approvingly of this 'accomplished musician and man of letters' who, as a follower of the school of Ibsen, occupied 'a unique position in Ireland'.[21]

Meanwhile, new energies were directing the theatre movement even further inward and away from Europe. George Russell (AE), until now only an interested observer, encouraged the Fay brothers who had produced Hyde's Irish play *The Twisting of the Rope*; he contributed a dramatization of yet another Irish saga. Lady Gregory, now back at Coole, was cautiously advising Yeats to throw his weight – and their recently completed play, based on Yeats's dream – behind this new indigenous activity. Maud Gonne offered to perform. And so on 2 April 1902, W.G. Fay's Irish National Dramatic Company clearly emerged as successor to the Irish Literary Theatre with the presentation, under the auspices of Inghinide na hEireann (The Daughters of Erin), of *Deirdre* by Russell and *Kathleen ni Houlihan* by Yeats and Lady Gregory. The forces of cosmopolitanism had been routed; new voices continued to swell from that very 'popular will' Joyce had warned against: 'your popular devil is more dangerous than your vulgar devil'.[22] One of the most effective voices belonged to Frank Fay, who in *The United Irishman* of 2 November 1901, had questioned Joyce's claim in 'The Day of the Rabblement' that neither the Irish Literary Theatre nor the Irish Language movement was popular. 'Mr. Joyce accuses the Irish Literary Theatre of not keeping its promise to produce European masterpieces. If he will read *Samhain* he will see that the Irish Literary Theatre still hopes to do that. That it has not done so, is mainly a matter of money.'[23] Time would disprove that promise also.

One night early in August 1902, Joyce selected George Russell's door to knock upon. After a lengthy discussion of mysticism, a dismissal of economics, a repetition of his complaints against Yeats – and by implication of AE's own surrender to the rabblement – he read some of his poems, and left. The generous but shrewdly cautious Russell wrote to a friend on August 15, 'I wouldn't be his Messiah for a thousand million pounds. He would be always criticizing the bad taste of his diety'. AE next wrote to Lady Gregory about his 'young genius': 'The first of a new race called on me a couple of days ago. He wanted to see whether I was he who was to come or was he to look for another. He is going to look for another, but he sat with me up to 4.00 a.m. telling me of the true inwardness of things from his point of view. . . . He is too superior for me. I belong to a lower order of thought than this spectre of fastidiousness.' And finally, to Yeats, who was also at Coole: 'He is an extremely clever boy who belongs to your clan more than to mine and more still to himself. But he has all the intellectual equipment, culture and education which all our other clever friends here lack. . . . I think you would find this youth of 21 with his assurance and self-confidence rather interesting.'[24] By October Yeats and Lady Gregory were both in Dublin for the productions of W.G. Fay's Irish National Dramatic Company, which included their new farce *The Pot of Broth,* revivals of *Deirdre* and *Kathleen ni Houlihan,* and, as added attraction, Florence Farr chanting to the psaltery accompanied by Yeats's explanations. It is uncertain whether Yeats or Lady Gregory met Joyce first, but certainly by the end of October Russell's role as avatar was over. The meeting between Yeats and Joyce has been revised in the telling many times, but it seems likely that the younger man did indeed suggest that it was too late for his influence to have any effect; it is equally plausible that the older poet was impressed both by Joyce's pretentiousness and his 'joyous vitality'.[25]

It was, however, Lady Gregory who most clearly understood Joyce's invitation. On 4 November she entertained him, W.B. Yeats and John Butler Yeats to dinner; on 15 November she noted in her diary,

> I have seen Joyce who came up to see me last night. His mind is quite made up for Paris. I think from any ordinary standpoint his action is wild, but with boys like Joyce there is always the over-shadowing powers to consider. I think he has genius of a kind and I like his pride and waywardness. . . . The more I know him the better I like him, and though I wish he could remain in Ireland still I would like to see him prosper somewhere. I am sure he will make a name somewhere.[26]

She wrote to John Synge on Aran, to Yeats in London,[27] to other friends in Paris and London, and recommended that he contact Ernest Longworth, editor of the *Daily Express*; she asked him to consider studying medicine at Trinity College instead, and advised him on selling his poems to magazines. Joyce was able to report on 1 December that he had seen Synge, and would be writing reviews for Longworth. Yeats wrote that he had duly entertained Joyce in London, taken him about to various editors in the hope of finding further commissions, and introduced him to Arthur Symons. Lady Gregory wrote to Joyce again with further advice and addresses, to which he replied, 'Paris amuses me very much, but I quite understand why there is no poetry in French literature; for to create poetry out of French life is impossible.'[28]

After spending Christmas in Dublin, he returned to Paris by way of London, where he saw Lady Gregory and more editors.

He returned her kindness with the same insouciant objectivity he accorded all other assistance: 'I sent in my review of Lady Gregory's book a week ago', he wrote to his mother on 20 March 1903. 'I do not know if Longworth put it in as I sent it: the review was very severe. I shall write to Lady Gregory one of these days.'[29] A week later the review appeared, over Joyce's initials, of Lady Gregory's *Poets and Dreamers*. The review damned with less than faint praise: 'wherever it treats of the "folk", [her book] sets forth in the fulness of its senility a class of mind which Mr. Yeats has set forth with such delicate scepticism in his happiest book, "The Celtic Twilight" '. Of her translations of four one-act plays by Douglas Hyde he is even more direct in his disapproval, 'The dwarf-drama (if one may use that term) is a form of art which is improper and ineffectual'.[30] Citing no evidence, Stanislaus Joyce reports that Lady Gregory was 'much annoyed' by the review, and in *Ulysses* Malachi Mulligan informs Stephen that Longworth is 'awfully sick' about it. But Longworth continued to provide Joyce with books for review, and

Lady Gregory in a letter to Synge enjoys the irony of Longworth's misplaced kindness in his selection of reviewer.[31] Twenty years later she in turn would ask a favour, and again Joyce would reply in form:

> While thanking you for the friendly remembrance . . . and for acts of kindness in the past I shall feel very much obliged if you will omit from your forthcoming book, which I understand is largely a history of the Irish literary movement, all letters of mine and all mention of me. In doing so you will be acting strictly in accordance with the spirit of that movement, inasmuch as since the date of my letter, twenty years ago, no mention of me or of my struggles or of my writings has been made publicly by any person connected with it.

Her memoir, which was not published, recalls merely, 'He was a handsome, petulant boy. I believed in his genius.'[32]

During the week of March 6 to 13, 1903, Synge was also in Paris; after a lengthy flirtation he had thrown his lot in with the Irish literary movement and was selling up the few belongings which had furnished his small apartment on the rue d'Assas. On his return to Dublin he also dutifully reported to Lady Gregory his impressions of Joyce:

> He seems to be pretty badly off, and is wandering about Paris rather unbrushed and rather indolent, spending his studious moments in the National Library reading Ben Jonson. French literature I understand is beneath him! Still he interested me a good deal and as he is being gradually won over by the charm of French life his time in Paris is not wasted. He talks of coming back to Dublin in the summer to live there on journalism while he does his serious work at his leisure. I cannot think that he will ever be a poet of importance, but his intellect is extraordinarily keen and if he keeps fairly sane he ought to do excellent essay-writing.[33]

Later Joyce would recall their meetings in *Ulysses*: 'Harsh gargoyle face that warred against me over our mess of hash of lights in rue Saint-André-des-Arts. In words of words for words, palabras.'[34] Joyce's portrayal is more accurate than Synge's deliberately offhand report to Lady Gregory. He and Joyce met frequently, and Stanislaus writes that the two 'had many quarrelsome discussions

197

. . . about language, style, poetry, the drama, and literature in general. . . . He was inclined to take the Irish language revival seriously, and when he was at a loss for an argument, was inclined to lose his temper, too. When that happened Synge's angry face and wagging beard used to send my brother into kinks of laughter that made Synge still angrier.'[35] Joyce later described Synge as 'a great lump of a man who could not be argued with. It is said that he was a silent man, but he was not.' They disagreed over how to spend their time together: when Joyce suggested picknicking in the Parc de St. Cloud, Synge objected to spending the holiday 'like any bourgeois'.[36] They argued over style, Synge dismissing Joyce's carefully culled solecisms.[37] Joyce told him of his aesthetic theories: Synge responded that he had a mind like Spinoza. Finally, Synge showed him *Riders to the Sea,* which Joyce had already heard praised by Yeats and Symons. 'I am glad to say that ever since I read it I have been riddling it mentally till it has not a sound spot', he wrote with anxious relief to Stanislaus, adding, 'thanks be to God Synge isn't an Aristotelian'.[38] He objected to the catastrophe being brought about by an animal rather than by the sea, and criticized it, as he had Hyde's plays, for being 'dwarf-drama'.[39] Synge, naturally, disagreed, but may well have had Joyce's Aristotelian strictures in mind when he defended *The Playboy* four years later with the argument, 'the story – in its *essence* – is probable given the psychic state of the locality'.[40] But Joyce was sufficiently impressed by *Riders to the Sea* to quote Maurya's speeches as examples of the musicality of language, and to translate the play into Italian, even visiting the Abbey Theatre in 1909 to gain the original music for the keen.[41] Nora Joyce performed the part of Maurya in the English Players production in Zurich in 1918, and Joyce's programme notes relented slightly with the admission, 'Whether a brief tragedy be possible or not (a point on which Aristotle had some doubts) the ear and the heart mislead one gravely if this brief scene from "poor Aran" be not the work of a tragic poet'.[42] Synge noted in his dairy an appointment with Joyce in Dublin in September 1903, but it was perhaps inevitable that the two never became friends.

By the time Joyce and Synge returned to Dublin in 1903, Synge to the comfort of his mother's orderly home in Kingstown, Joyce to his dying mother's bedside, the metamorphosis of Irish Literary Theatre into The Irish National Theatre Society was complete. The company had established a rehearsal hall in a back street next to a butcher's shop, which became the centre of literary activity for many poets and would-be playwrights. A visit to London in May 1903 under the auspices of the Irish Literary Society had reaped high praise for both plays and players from some of the most influential critics, including a lengthy rave review by A.B. Walkley in *The Times Literary Supplement*. In October 1903 Synge's one-act comedy *The Shadow of the Glen* was produced midst some notoriety; the following February saw the production at long last of *Riders to the Sea*. When the company made a second visit to London in March 1904, Synge's two plays earned even greater praise from Joyce's former adviser, William Archer. Despite his disdain for the 'mummers', Joyce and his new pal, the poet, wit and medical student Oliver St. John Gogarty, were frequent visitors at rehearsals and first readings, including that of Synge's next play, *The Well of the Saints*. It was at a rehearsal of one of Synge's plays that Joyce disgraced himself by arriving so drunk that he collapsed in front of the narrow entrance door and horrified some of the actresses. Even the discreet Synge recalled the incident in a history of the movement prepared for the *Manchester Guardian*, and this is obviously the basis for the exchange between Buck Mulligan and Stephen in *Ulysses*:

> – The tramper Synge is looking for you, he said, to murder you. He heard you pissed on his halldoor in Glasthule. He's out in pampooties to murder you.
> – Me! Stephen exclaimed. That was your contribution to literature.[43]

But Joyce was watching closer auxiliaries-in-rebellion succumb to the new dramatic movement. Stanislaus recorded in his diary of *The Shadow of the Glen,*

> The play is a very good comedy and, with another play also by Synge, is the best thing the Irish National Theatre Society has produced. . . . The position may be somewhat unusual, is unusual in as much as it is interesting, but the characters are Irish all of them – the woman, the young farmer, the old man, and the tramp; the humour is Irish and the treatment quite original.[44]

Even Gogarty was turning coat: he refused to sign George Moore's attack on the theatre productions in the new journal *Dana*, and had become so friendly with Yeats that at the older poet's suggestion some time later contemplated a translation of *Oedipus* for the company.[45] When another young journeyman poet-dramatist, Padraic Colum (whose early work Joyce had dismissed as 'rotten from the foundation up'), was selected for financial assistance by an American millionaire, Joyce walked to Celbridge and back offering himself and his schemes as worthy of patronage, but was rejected.[46] AE suggested he write stories for the *Irish Homestead,* thereby initiating the composition of *Dubliners* as well as providing some necessary funds, but did not include Joyce's poems in *New Songs,* an anthology of his Dublin protégés published in March 1904.[47] He had better luck with *Dana,* whose editors paid him the only fee they ever gave for a poem, but that good fortune, like the journal itself, was short-lived. Recalling Florence Farr's and Yeats's experiments with the psaltery, he even tried unsuccessfully to persuade Arnold Dolmetsch to make him a lute with which he would 'coast the south of England from Falmouth to Margate, singing old English songs'.[48] In each case Joyce's response was predictably aggrieved.

By 27 August 1904, even before Joyce's brief sojourn in the Martello tower at Sandycove, Gogarty wrote to a friend in Oxford, 'I have broken with Joyce, his want of generosity became to me inexcusable, he lampooned AE, Yeats, Colum and others to whom he was indebted in many ways'.[49] This was Joyce's third broadside, 'The Holy Office', which he had submitted to *St. Stephen's* magazine in response to the editor's request for something new. Combining his aesthetic argument and stance of the rebel angel with satirical thrusts which were Swiftian in their scatology, Joyce attacked not only the 'mumming company' but all the Camden Street hangers-on, including Gogarty. 'I am an enemy of the ignobleness and slavishness of people. ... We all wear masks', he declared to his new companion Nora Barnacle; in this last public thrust at his literary compatriots whose cowardice and squeamishness prevented them from open defiance of the trolls, he would perform the holy office of Katharsis.[50]

Lack of funds to release his poem from the printers prevented Joyce from distributing his attack until a year later, when he was in Trieste. But it is likely that even if he had, this would not have prevented him from turning to the mummers for assistance in his flight from Ireland. Lady Gregory telegraphed her good wishes and £5; he also appealed with some success to Colum, George Roberts, and Seumas O'Sullivan. Yeats repeated his offer of assistance in finding review work and publication of his poems, but did not offer any money. A graver rejection was his refusal to consider Joyce's translations of Hauptmann, criticizing their ineptness and pointing out that the theatre had no funds either. 'Later on of course we hope to be able to pay. Nor do I think it very likely we could attempt German work at present. We must get the ear of our public with Irish work.'[51] The implications rankled; two years later Joyce wrote to his brother, 'If it is not far-fetched to say that my action, and that of men like Ibsen &c, is a virtual intellectual strike I would call such people as Gogarty and Yeats and Colm the blacklegs of literature. Because they have tried to substitute us, to serve the old idols at a lower rate when we refused to do so for a higher.'[52] His relationship with Yeats would follow the same formal, arm's-length pattern until Yeats's death: Yeats refused to allow publication of the Italian translation Joyce and Nicolo Vidacovich made of *The Countess Cathleen* because Yeats preferred a later revision of his play, yet he was responsible for introducing Joyce's work to Ezra Pound and campaigned on Joyce's behalf for financial assistance from various public and not-so-public purses; Joyce accepted these gestures and, later, homage, but refused at least two invitations to Ireland and membership of the Irish Academy of Letters, all initiated by Yeats.[53]

Synge was the most difficult of the mummers to exorcise, despite his early death. From his remote perch on the continent, Joyce had anxiously observed the notoriety accompanying *The Playboy of the Western World* on its first production in January 1907. 'This whole affair has upset me,' he wrote to Stanislaus. 'I feel like a man in a house who hears a row in the street and voices he knows shouting but can't get up to see what the hell is going on. It has put me off the story I was going to write – to wit, *The Dead*.' Could it be that 'him who sober all the day/Mixes a naggin in his play' had in truth turned to stronger stuff, unnoticed and unpresaged? Synge had publicly defied the trolls, asserting his right as an artist to write about anything he chose. Perhaps, too, it needled that Yeats's critical judgment may have been more accurate than Joyce's own, in which case rejection of his own translations rankled further.

His first response was, by attacking, to deny. Based on a some-what garbled newspaper report which confused *Kathleen ni Houlihan* with *The Countess Cathleen* he condemned Yeats's defiance of the audience as the posturing of 'a tiresome idiot'; then, recalling his long critical attack on the catastrophe of *Riders to the Sea*, he grudgingly admitted, 'perhaps his later work has merit. If Synge really knows and understands the Irish peasant, the back-

201

bone of the nation, he might make a duodecimo Bjornsen.' It was hard to acknowledge any Ibsenite fury in the Dublin controversy. Retreating even further into fiction, he exulted, 'I suppose *Sinn Fein* and *The Leader* will find out all about Synge's life in Paris: which will be nice for Lady G and Miss H[orniman].'[54] Finally, condemning the Abbey as 'ruined', he bared a deeper concern: 'Synge is better at least he can set them by the ears. One writer speaks of Synge and his master Zola (!) so I suppose when *Dubliners* appears they will speak of me and my master Synge.'[55]

Had Synge snatched the golden ring first, after all? On 16 February he wrote again to Stanislaus, complaining of his failure to get *Dubliners* into print, 'Synge is a storm centre: but I have done nothing.' Finally, on 5 May he confided that Synge's art 'is more original than my own'.[56] It was no consolation when the publication of *Chamber Music* in May netted praise from Arthur Symons in *The Nation* as a book of pure poetry; the only substantial review from Dublin, by Thomas Kettle in the *Freeman's Journal*, heralded the 'clear, distinguished playing with harps, with wood birds, with Paul Verlaine', while leavening approval with the comment, 'There is no trace of the folklore, folk dialect, or even the national feeling that have coloured the work of practically every writer in contemporary Ireland.'[57] When *The Dead* was finally completed, small details reveal how strongly Synge's hovering spirit[58] affected him; and although Gabriel Conroy rejects Miss Ivors' challenge to go to Aran, Nora and James Joyce did go there in 1912.[59]

> Oisin with Patrick. Faunman he met in Clamart woods, brandishing a winebottle. *C'est vendredi saint!* Murthering Irish. His image, wandering he met. I mine. I met a fool i' the forest.[60]

It is not surprising that Synge should be marked for rivalry. Joyce had confidently predicted in 'Drama and Life' that the new drama would be 'at war with convention'.[61] As early as *The Shadow of the Glen* Synge had rustled the dovecotes, causing Maud Gonne and her nationalist followers to walk out of the theatre. *The Well of the Saints* had not caused open controversy, but it mocked not only the miraculous but the miracle-makers. *The Tinker's Wedding* was so anti-clerical it could not be performed in Ireland. Then with *The Playboy of the Western World* reality was transmuted into fantasy, fact into myth, folly made heroic; Christy Mahon's final words as he marches in to triumphant exile are as spirited as any of Joyce's early broadsides, and far more public:

> Ten thousand blessings upon all that's here, for you've turned
> me a likely gaffer in the end of all, the way I'll go romancing
> through a romping lifetime from this hour to the dawning of the
> judgment day.[62]

Synge's final play, *Deirdre of the Sorrows,* was even more pagan
still, drawing upon the legends published in Lady Gregory's
Cuchulain of Muirthemne and imbued with the nature-worship he
had substituted for his mother's strict evangelical faith. Even the
intensity of his musical training matched the younger man's, albeit
contrapuntal and progressive where Joyce's tended towards the
harmonic and Wagnerian. And Synge had even recorded in his
prose works those singular moments of vision which Joyce called
epiphanies.[63]

Yet even while the two met in Clamart woods to celebrate the
feast of St Euphrasia[64] Synge's days of wandering were over; not
until a year later would Joyce proclaim to Nora, 'I cannot enter the
social order except as a vagabond'.[65] Where Ireland was Europe's
afterthought for Joyce, it remained the westernmost part for Synge;
where Synge celebrated violence, 'murthering Irish', Joyce abhor-
red it; where Joyce wished to Europeanize Ireland, Synge deliberately courted the pagan romance of a pre-Christian world. Like
Oisin, 'the little faun', Synge had rejected Patrick, the 'man of many
croziers'; in Lady Gregory's words, 'My story is sorrowful. The
sound of your voice is not pleasant to me. I will cry my fill, but not
for God, but because Finn and the Fianna are not living.'[66] And
where Joyce called Ibsen master, Synge attacked him in company
with Zola for 'dealing with the reality of life in joyless and pallid
words'.[67] Yet for all this, he had returned to Ireland to reap critical
applause abroad: William Archer had singled him out for praise; his
plays were translated and performed in Berlin and Prague as early
as 1906. Despite Niamh's warning not to set foot on Irish soil 'Or
else at once thy strength shall go, / And thou shalt grow both blind
and old',[68] it appeared that Oisin-Synge, denying Patrick-Joyce's
book of rules, had triumphed.

Each had indeed found himself as wanderer. But parallel and
contrast go more deeply still. 'I met a fool i' the forest.'[69] Which was
Jaques, figure of fun for the Arden court with a melancholy of his
own, the loner given to moralizing; which, Touchstone, the ladies'

court jester fool, the merry mixer who descants so whimsically on time? Like Oisin and Patrick, the fools of Arden also parley, palaver, war by and worship with words, palabras. It is Jaques who casts 'a Greek invocation to call fools in a circle', Touchstone who wears the motley coat; Jaques who has been the libertine yet wishes to speak his mind and 'through and through

> Cleanse the foul body of th'infected world,
> If they will patiently receive my medicine'.

It is Touchstone who wins the maid, while praising foulness, horned beasts and husbands; Jaques who adopts the religious life, shunning social pastimes. A traveller by choice, Jaques' experience has made him sad. As for Touchstone, the journey makes him sanguine: 'Ay, now am I in Arden, the more fool I: when I was at home, I was in a better place; but travellers must be content'. In Paris Joyce teases Synge to anger, as the Duke does Jaques, coping 'him in these sullen fits/For then he's full of matter'. Jaques in turn comments on Touchstone's 'strange places cramm'd / With observation, the which he vents / In mangled forms', as Joyce will parody Synge's curious dramatic speech in *Ulysses*.[70] Yet despite his brief accusation about Synge's life in Paris, Joyce will acknowledge his own youthful sensuality in contrast to 'John Milicent Synge's' prudery. And to compound further, it is Joyce who marries, sings of adultery while remaining the solitary exile, while Synge, described (as the tinker Christopher Sly calls himself, 'paucas pallabris'[71]) as a man of few words, proves himself neither silent nor solitary. And while Joyce reads Ben Jonson in Paris, Synge returns to Dublin to emulate 'the Elizabethan dramatist [who] took his ink-horn and sat down to his work [using] many phrases that he had just heard, as he sat at dinner, from his mother or his children'.[72] It appears that, while meeting his own image, each also met the other's.

In August 1912, Joyce wrote to Nora in Galway, 'The *Abbey Theatre* will be open and they will give plays of Yeats and Synge. You have a right to be there because you are my bride: and I am one of the writers of this generation who are perhaps creating at last a conscience in the soul of this wretched race.'[73] In November 1916, writing to Harriet Shaw Weaver, he speaks of his first meeting with Yeats, 'He invited me to write a play for his theatre and I promised to do so in ten years'.[74] As early as 1902 he had informed George Russell that he was 'engaged in writing a comedy which he expects will occupy him five years or thereabouts', a statement Joyce repeated to his mother from Paris the following March after his encounter with Synge.[75] Quite clearly, Joyce considered himself a potential colleague and, later, successor to Synge in the Irish dramatic movement. When Martyn – and with him, the only voice speaking up for Ibsenite drama – left the Abbey Theatre it was clear that he would have to be replaced, if at all, by the purveyor of a newer drama still, of a 'noble and bare style appropriate to modern playwriting', as Joyce described it in his unfavourable review of Shaw's *The Shewing-up of Blanco Posnet* in 1909.[76] By the summer of 1912 the ten years he had promised Yeats were up, and shortly after his return with Nora to Trieste, his play *Exiles* was taking shape in his mind.

Described in his notes as 'three cat and mouse acts',[77] *Exiles* deals with estrangement and liberation, perversion and conversion, on the ethical, moral, aesthetic, and sexual planes – and hence, by implication, on the national plane also. The origins of plot are readily recognizable from Joyce's biography,[78] as is his determination to create a drama of Ibsenite clarity: 'either the perception of a great truth, or the opening up of a great question, or a great conflict which is almost independent of the conflicting actors'.[79] The conflict (and great question) is how to reconcile, while exploring, the opposite values of the soul and conscience, the fruitful and the sterile. The perception of truth, which Richard Rowan struggles toward and for which he must sacrifice all certainties, lies in what Joyce calls the 'virginity of the soul', 'a state of readiness'[80] which one must consciously strive for while acknowledging the hopelessness of recapturing it, once its initial energy is spent. There is no final end to such a conflict or perception, and so the play ends not in death, but spiritual, emotional, and physical stasis, a mood of lassitude tenuously balanced between physical longing and the wounding doubt of the soul.

Such an intricately patterned thematic structure required a matching rigidity of checks and counterchecks, comparisons and contrasts, in both plot and characterization. With Jonsonian precision Joyce presents the theme of putative cuckoldry through his 'humorous' characters: Richard Rowan, spiritual but not genetic heir to the Anglo-Irish patriot, 'an automystic', artist/author, warring within him the conflict of a previous generation in his generous, artistic father and an unforgiving, puritanical mother; Robert Hand, artisan/journalist, 'an automobile', sadist in his sensuality where Richard is masochistic in his self-denial, unwillingly-led betrayer to Richard's will towards betrayal; Richard's mistress-in-exile, Bertha, mother to his child, herself denied a patronym while Richard strives to free her soul and body from bondage to their love; Beatrice Justice, cousin and childhood sweetheart of Robert, spiritual mistress to Richard, while sickly in her own virginity; the inevitable folk mother Brigid; and Richard and Bertha's son Archie, herald of the future, combining the flexibility of his godfather Robert Hand with the lunar qualities of his mother and the openness to experience of his father.[81]

'When you are a recognized classic people will read it because you wrote it and be duly interested and duly instructed . . . but until then I'm hang'd if I see what's to be done with it.' With these words Ezra Pound gently turned away Joyce's eager gift of his only surviving play in September 1915. Joyce could not have been pleased by his insistent friend's further advice eleven months later that Edward Knoblock, who had collaborated successfully with Arnold Bennett, might 'see his way to a stage version . . . you could always have your original version used when the thing is printed'.[82] More important, however, was Yeats's cautious overture on 7 September 1915,

> I shall hope to see your play. My own players have had to go to the music halls with some of our one act pieces to live till the war is over. But for that I would have some hope of our theatre perhaps producing it in Dublin at any rate.[83]

After that, silence fell until 11 February 1917, when, flushed by the excitement of *A Portrait of the Artist*, Yeats wrote to Pound, 'If you have the play bring it tomorrow night. If at all possible the Abbey should face a riot for it.'[84] But it was not until August that Yeats formally rejected *Exiles* 'because it is a type of work we have never played well. It is too far from the folk drama; and just at present we do not play the folk drama very well.' Then, with a candour all the more painful for its bluntness, 'It is some time since I read your play and my memory is not very clear – I thought it sincere and interesting. . . . I do not think it at all so good as "A Portrait of the Artist" '.[85] On 8 November he wrote again, evidently in reply to a further request from Joyce,

> No I am afraid we cannot attempt your play. We have neither the players nor the audience. We are a folk theatre, and now that we

have no longer any subsidy as we had when Martyn's play was produced we have a hard struggle to live. . . . We can very seldom venture anything outside its range, and are chiefly experimental in one act pieces which can be buoyed up by old favourites. . . . If we could give you a really fine performance we might venture it. But it is not possible to face at the same moment the limitations of players and of audience.[86]

Exiles was not published until 1918.[87] Despite Shaw's support, the Stage Society of London rejected it in 1916,[88] recalled it in early 1917 when Joyce himself withdrew it, returned to it for consideration later that year, and after several further importunities, finally produced it in 1926; the director was W.G. Fay, himself an exile from the Abbey Theatre. In 1918 Joyce approached Carlo Linati, translator of Synge, with the suggestion that he translate *A Portrait of the Artist*; he translated *Exiles* instead, and the Italian version was published in 1920. A production of the play in German in Munich created 'a stormy evening' and the play was withdrawn.[89] After a year of flirtation, Lugné-Poë decided against producing a French translation at his theatre in Paris. In 1925 the play ran for forty-one performances at the Neighborhood Playhouse in New York.[90] Joyce continued to hope for a Dublin production, suggesting that his agent attempt to bypass Yeats and appeal directly to the Abbey Theatre manager, Lennox Robinson;[91] as late as 1937 a prospective production in Dublin was cancelled.[92] The play finally received its first Irish production in 1948, seven years after Joyce's death and thirty years after its publication. But by then the Irish stage had room for neither 'the naked drama' of Jonsonian Joyce, or the 'fiery and magnificent, and tender' Elizabethan richness of his fellow in folly, Synge.[93]

NOTES

1 Unless otherwise stated, all biographical information is taken from Richard Ellmann, *James Joyce,* New York, Oxford University Press, 1959.
2 *The Critical Writings of James Joyce*, ed. Ellsworth Mason and Richard Ellmann, London, Faber and Faber, 1959, pp. 39–46.
3 Archer wrote to Joyce on 23 April 1900 conveying Ibsen's thanks, *Selected Letters of James Joyce,* ed. Richard Ellmann, London, Faber and Faber, 1975, p. 6.
4 See, for example, Yeats's contributions to *Literary Ideals in Ireland* [ed. Edward

Martyn], London, T. Fisher Unwin, 1899 and *Letters from George Moore to Éd. Dujardin*, ed. John Eglinton, New York, Crosby Gaige, 1929, p. 38.

5   First produced 9 May 1899, but written as early as 1894.

6   Edward Martyn, *The Heather Field and Maeve*, London, Duckworth, 1899, pp. xxiv–xxv.

7   Quoted by Denis Gwynn, *Edward Martyn and the Irish Revival*, London, Jonathan Cape, 1930, p. 143; perhaps a description of the production at the Avenue Theatre, London, in November 1896.

8   William J. Feeney gives an excellent comparative study in his Introduction to George Moore, *The Bending of the Bough*, Chicago, De Paul University, 1969, pp. 1–21.

9   George Moore, *The Bending of the Bough*, London, T. Fisher Unwin, 1900, p. xi.

10   *Beltaine*, ed. W.B. Yeats, London, At the Sign of the Unicorn, April 1900, p. 4.

11   See Synge's preface to *The Playboy of the Western World* and Yeats in *Samhain*, 1904.

12   Ellmann, *James Joyce*, pp. 82–86.

13   According to Ellmann, *James Joyce*, p. 97, the play was first performed the previous March.

14   Richard Ellmann, *The Consciousness of Joyce*, Toronto, Oxford University Press, 1977, p. 11. Joyce began his essay, 'The Day of the Rabblement', with a reference to 'the Nolan' and reviewed a book on Bruno for the *Daily Express*, 30 October 1903.

15   *Selected Letters*, p. 7.

16   *The James Joyce Archive, vol. 2: Notes, Criticism, Translations & Miscellaneous Writings*, ed. Hans Walter Gabler and Michael Groden, New York, Garland, 1979, pp. 332–530.

17   Edward Martyn, 'The Modern Drama in Germany', *The Daily Express* (Dublin), 11 February 1899, p. 3.

18   *Critical Writings*, pp. 69–72.

19   *Where There is Nothing* was written in haste by Yeats with the help of Hyde and Lady Gregory, and published as a supplement to *The United Irishman*, 30 October 1902.

20   *An Enchanted Sea* was published with *The Tale of a Town* in 1902. *Romulus and Remus, or The Makers of Delights* was published in the Christmas Supplement to *Irish People*, 21 December 1907; Denis d'Oran, master hairdresser (Martyn) has two assistants; these are Romulus Malone (Moore) and Remus Delany (Yeats). Daisy Houlihan (Lady Gregory) is the shopwoman, while Mrs Cornucopia Moynihan (Miss Horniman) is a customer in search of a husband. *The Dream Physician* was published in 1914; Patricia McFate's Introduction to Seumas MacManus, *The Townland of Tamney* and Edward Martyn, *The Dream Physician*, Chicago, De Paul University, 1972, pp. 15–26, convincingly identifies the various characters.

21   *Critical Writings*, p. 70.

22   *Critical Writings*, p. 251. According to Stanislaus Joyce, *My Brother's Keeper*, ed. Richard Ellmann, London, Faber, 1958, p. 187, Joyce denounced Yeats for writing 'such political and dramatic claptrap'.

23   Fay's articles are reprinted in Frank J. Fay, *Towards a National Theatre*, ed. Robert Hogan, Dublin, Dolmen, 1970.

24   AE to Sarah Purser, 15 August 1902 and to Yeats, August 1902, in *Letters from*

AE, ed. Alan Denson, New York, Abelard-Schuman, 1961, pp. 42–43; AE to Lady Gregory, quoted in *Seventy Years, Being the Autobiography of Lady Gregory*, ed. Colin Smythe, Gerrards Cross, Colin Smythe, 1974, p. 425.

25 Russell, Yeats, Stanislaus Joyce, and, later, James Joyce agree on essential details; see Ellmann, *James Joyce*, pp. 104–107, *My Brother's Keeper*, p. 183, and Frank Budgen, *James Joyce and the Making of Ulysses*, London, Oxford University Press, 1972, p. 348.

26 *Seventy Years*, pp. 425–26.

27 'I wonder if Joyce has written to you? Poor boy, I am afraid he will knock his ribs against the earth, but he has grit and will succeed in the end. You should write and ask him to breakfast with you on the morning he arrives, if you can get up early enough, and feed him and take care of him and give him dinner at Victoria before he goes, and help him on his way. I am writing to various people who might possibly get him tuitions, and to Synge who could at least tell him of cheap lodgings.' Elizabeth Coxhead, *Lady Gregory*, London, Secker and Warburg, 1966, p. 124.

28 21 December 1902, *Selected Letters*, p. 11.

29 *Selected Letters*, p. 18.

30 *The Early Joyce: The Book Reviews, 1902–03*, ed. Stanislaus Joyce and Ellsworth Mason, Colorado Springs, Mamalujo Press, 1955, p. 21.

31 Lady Gregory wrote to Synge on 29 March, 'Poor Joyce! The funny thing is that Longworth of the Express whom I had asked for work for Joyce has sent him my *Poets & Dreamers* to review, as a kindness to us both! I wonder what the review will be like!' *Theatre Business*, ed. Ann Saddlemyer, Gerrards Cross, Colin Smythe, 1982, p. 38. Joyce published fourteen more reviews in the *Daily Express*.

32 8 August 1922, *Selected Letters*, p. 200; Coxhead, *Lady Gregory*, p. 124.

33 *Theatre Business*, p. 36. Cf. Stanislaus Joyce, Introduction to *The Early Joyce*, p. 1: 'He tried his hand . . . at dialogue in the style of Ben Jonson, not seriously but merely as an exercise'.

34 James Joyce, *Ulysses*, Harmondsworth, Penguin, 1968, p. 200; 'lights' = lungs of animals, usually food for cats and dogs.

35 *My Brother's Keeper*, p. 213. According to Herbert Gorman, *James Joyce*, London, Bodley Head, 1941, pp. 101–102, they met 'seven or eight times, lunching in the humble bistro-restaurant in the Rue Saint-André-des-Arts where a four- or five-course meal could be procured for one franc ten centimes'.

36 First quotation from Djuna Barnes, 'Vagaries Malicieux', *The Double-Dealer*, Ill. May 1922, p. 252; second from Arthur Power, 'Notes on a Friend', *The Irish Times*, 23 June 1964; Power's *Conversations with James Joyce*, London, Millington, 1974, pp. 33–34 has a slightly embellished version of the story. Among the Joyce papers at Cornell is Synge's student card, dated 4 April 1895, admitting him to membership in the Société Fraternelle d'Étudiants Protestants in Paris, where Synge made contacts with students wishing to have lessons in English.

37 Gorman, *James Joyce*, pp. 101–02.

38 James Joyce, *Letters*, vol. II, ed. Richard Ellmann, London, Faber, 1966, pp. 35 and 38. On 11 February 1907 *à propos* the *Playboy* riots, he reminded Stanislaus, 'When I told him what I thought of it [*Riders to the Sea*] and expounded a long critical attack on the catastrophe as he used it he did not pay the least attention to what I said. So perhaps his later work has merit', *Selected Letters*, p. 148.

39 Ellmann, *James Joyce,* p. 129.

40 'Synge to MacKenna', ed. Ann Saddlemyer, *Irish Renaissance,* eds. Robin Skelton and David R. Clark, Dublin, Dolmen, 1965, p. 75.

41 21 August and 2 September 1909, *Letters,* II, pp. 238 and 244. The translation was made by Joyce and Nicolo Vidacovich as early as 1908, and offered to the actor-manager of the Italian Grand Guignol company, Alfredo Sainati, but negotiations apparently ceased when Synge's executors demanded precise information concerning performance fees, letter from E. Synge 23/8/09 in Cornell University Library. Plans to produce a translation of Yeats's *The Countess Cathleen* also came to nothing, *Letters,* III, p. 195 and Ellmann, *James Joyce,* p. 276.

42 *Critical Writings,* p. 250. When he first visited her bookstore in 1920, Sylvia Beach recalls that he borrowed a copy of *Riders to the Sea* from her lending library, Ellmann, *James Joyce,* p. 503.

43 *Ulysses,* pp. 200 and 217. Ellmann, *James Joyce,* pp. 166–67, dates the incident 20 June 1904; Oliver St. John Gogarty, *Many Lines to Thee: Letters to G.K.A. Bell,* ed. James F. Carens, Dublin, Dolmen, 1971, pp. 11–12, 'The bard went to visit the "Mummers" – his name for Yeats's players'; 'J.M. Synge on the Irish Dramatic Movement: An Unpublished Article', ed. Ann Saddlemyer, *Modern Drama,* XXIV, 3 (September 1981), pp. 276–81. Joyce retaliated with a limerick, *James Joyce.* p. 167.

44 *The Dublin Diary of Stanislaus Joyce,* ed. George Harris Healey, London, Faber, 1962, pp. 74–75.

45 *Many Lines to Thee,* pp. 32–33 and 73. The translation of *Oedipus* was rejected the following year, but Moore's attack, signed 'Paul Ruttledge' (the hero of Yeats's play *Where There is Nothing*), was published in *Dana,* September 1904. Gogarty also defended Colum's play, *Broken Soil,* in *The United Irishman,* 19 December 1903.

46 Ellmann, *James Joyce,* pp. 140 and 146.

47 AE included eight of his 'singing birds', as Yeats contemptuously referred to them, Padraic Colum, Eva Gore-Booth, Thomas Keohler, Alice Milligan, Susan Mitchell, Seumas O'Sullivan, George Roberts, and Ella Young.

48 Ellmann, *James Joyce,* pp. 159–61.

49 *Many Lines to Thee,* p. 33. Padraic Colum and his wife later became close friends.

50 *Critical Writings,* pp. 149–52 and *Selected Letters,* 29 August, 1904, p. 26.

51 *Letters,* II, p. 58.

52 *Selected Letters,* p. 125.

53 *Letters,* II, 298, 321–22, 326–27, 349–57; III, 78–79, 100–101, etc.

54 Stanislaus more truthfully records that 'Synge was ribald only in his comedies, and occasionally in his language; his habits were puritanical', *My Brother's Keeper,* p. 213.

55 *Selected Letters,* pp. 143–49.

56 *Selected Letters,* p. 150; Ellmann, *James Joyce,* p. 276.

57 Ellmann, *James Joyce,* pp. 270–71.

58 Joyce cannot resist a final thrust in his fourth broadside, 'Gas from a Burner', written in 1912 after George Roberts (formerly a traveller in ladies' underwear, see Ellmann, *James Joyce,* pp. 179–80) reneges on Maunsel's contract to publish *Dubliners:*

'I printed the great John Milicent Synge
Who soars above on an angel's wing
In the playboy shift that he pinched as swag
From Maunsel's manager's travelling-bag' (*Critical Writings*, p. 244).

59   Joyce wrote two articles on his visit to the west for the *Piccolo della Sera; Critical Writings*, pp. 229–37.

60   *Ulysses*, p. 200.

61   *Critical Writings*, p. 41: 'Whatever form it takes must not be superimposed or conventional. . . . Drama will be for the future at war with convention, if it is to realize itself truly.'

62   J.M. Synge, *The Playboy of the Western World*, Act III, in *Plays*, ed. Ann Saddlemyer (London: Oxford University Press, 1969), p. 163.

63   See Ann Saddlemyer, 'Synge and the Doors of Perception', *Place, Personality and the Irish Writer*, ed. Andrew Carpenter (Gerrards Cross: Colin Smythe, 1977), pp. 97–120. In *Seventy Years*, pp. 507–08, Lady Gregory quotes a letter of 14 August 1920 from John Butler Yeats about 'that awful fiction written by Joyce'. 'I dislike it, yet have for him and it a profound respect. His portrait published in this month's *Little Review* reminds me of Synge. I wonder has he Synge's sweet and gentle temper. . . . Joyce's writing is a revelation of that obscenity, the mind of the Dublin "cad". . . . Now Joyce has dragged them into the light and it had to be done for they are powerful and making themselves felt. It was, of course, they that denounced the theatre and Synge.'

64   Synge met Joyce on Monday, March 9th, and several more times before he left for London on Friday 13th, so Joyce has altered the date of their picnic in Clamart for *Ulysses*. Saint Euphrasia (or Eupraxia, whose feast day is March 13th, 'saint vendredi'), was taken from Constantinople to Egypt by her mother, a wealthy widow. Refusing to marry into nobility, she became a nun, devoting her fortune to the poor and freeing her slaves. Noted for her asceticism and humility, she struggled against worldly temptations, once by removing a pile of stones from one place to another, and back again.

65   *Selected Letters*, p. 26.

66   Oisin's dialogue with St. Patrick, retold by Lady Gregory in *Gods and Fighting Men* (1904) Gerrards Cross: Colin Smythe, 1970, p. 351.

67   Preface to *The Playboy of the Western World*. According to Joseph Holloway, in 1909 Joyce complained that the last act of *The Playboy* was taken from *The Master Builder*, Ellmann, *James Joyce*, p. 129n.

68   Michael Comyn, 'Oisin in the Land of Youth', translated by Tomas O'Flann-ghaile, used as one of Yeats's sources for 'The Wanderings of Oisin'.

69   Shakespeare, *As You Like It*, II, vii; the following quotations are from: II, v; II, vii; II, iv; II, i; II, vii.

70   *Ulysses*, pp. 199–200 and 468.

71   The Induction to *The Taming of the Shrew*.

72   Preface to *The Playboy of the Western World*.

73   *Selected Letters*, p. 204.

74   *Selected Letters*, p. 223.

75   *Letters from AE*, p. 43; *Selected Letters*, p. 19.

76   *Critical Writings*, p. 208.

77   All quotations and references are to *Exiles* (London: Jonathan Cape, 1952), which includes Joyce's notes, pp. 163–75.

78   Ellmann, *James Joyce, passim;* see in particular among the many discussions of

autobiographical genesis, Robert M. Adams, 'Light on Joyce's *Exiles*. A New MS, a Curious Analogue, and Some Speculations', *Studies in Bibliography*, XVII (1964), pp. 83–105; John MacNicholas, *James Joyce's EXILES: A Textual Companion*, New York, Garland, 1979; Richard Ellmann, *The Consciousness of Joyce*, pp. 22, 49, 82–83.

79   *Critical Writings*, p. 63. Major works exploring the parallels with Ibsen are James T. Farrell, '*Exiles* and Ibsen', *James Joyce: Two Decades of Criticism*, ed. Seon Givens, New York, Vanguard, 1963, pp. 95–131; B.J. Tysdahl, *Joyce and Ibsen* (New York: Humanities Press, 1968).

80   See MacNicholas, *James Joyce's Exiles*, pp. 18–20, for an excellent summary of this philosophical argument.

81   Brigid is a thoroughly stage-Irish character of The Shavian and Abbey Theatre variety; Archie strongly resembles Kit, Carden Tyrell's son in Martyn's *The Heather Field*.

82   *Letters*, II, pp. 366 and 385.

83   *Letters*, II, p. 363.

84   *Letters*, II, p. 389.

85   *Letters*, II, p. 405.

86   *Theatre Business*, pp. 13–14.

87   On 1 April 1915 he had written to his agent James B. Pinker that he would 'prefer to hold it over till my novel *A Portrait of the Artist as a Young Man* has been published in book form', *Letters*, II, p. 338.

88   See William White, 'Irish Antitheses: Shaw and Joyce', *The Shavian*, II, 3 (February 1961), pp. 24–27, where Ellmann's description is corrected.

89   *Letters*, II, pp. 437, 451, and 457.

90   Ellmann, *James Joyce*, pp. 512 and 581.

91   *Letters*, II, p. 456.

92   *Letters*, III, pp. 398–400.

93   'Ibsen's New Drama', *Critical Writings*, p. 63; Preface to *The Playboy of the Western World*.

THE WANDERER

A poem in honour of the 100th anniversary of James Joyce, translated from the Arabic.

> 'I desire to press in my arms the loveliness which has not yet come into the world.'
>
> – James Joyce

I seek a shore
as a weather-beaten sailor
lost amid the seas of the world,
searching in the folds of the wind
for a haven and a refuge
compassionate and warm
to keep the woes of life at bay.

A Sinbad am I,
the oceans are my thoughts,
the seas my feelings,
carrying me
to you
on the winds of passion
across the vast expanses of the world.

I drift on the foam,
on the crest of every wave
washed against the coastal cliffs,
the rocks of separation
on which all my ships have foundered,
their sails utterly torn
to shrouds
for lost desires.

Where are you
amid the terrible storms?
pity me,
come forth,
make quiet approach,

carry your windblown sailor,
convey him safely ashore,
wash away his agony,
purge the wounds
of one who at your feet
bows down in meditative calm,
in sacred sanctuary.

Suheil Bushrui

JOYCE STUDIES IN THE NETHERLANDS

PAUL VAN CASPEL

On a November day in 1952, 36-year-old Peter Allt, who had been appointed Lecturer in English Literature in the University of Groningen, delivered his inaugural lecture, which dealt with the life and works of James Joyce. Having pointed out that *Ulysses* and *Finnegans Wake* had acquired, over the years, the status of compulsory reading in more than one American university, he continued as follows: 'And it is not unlikely that some American scholar or critic has even now started assembling materials for what will be the definitive study of Joyce and his works, when it finally reaches the book shops in perhaps twenty or thirty years time. I hope that somebody has, in fact, begun work upon such a study: *and if I am still alive when his book appears,* I hope that I shall be still sufficiently interested in Joyce, to buy it, and even perhaps to read it' (p. 3, italics mine). A tragic note is that Peter Allt was not granted the span of time he had visualized – he died in 1954. Had he lived, this English department in the northern region of the Netherlands might have blossomed out into a modest centre of Joycean studies. The mediocre level of these studies at the time may be gauged from the fact that a prominent journal of long standing, *Neophilologus,* saw fit to publish – in the very year of Peter Allt's death – a rather elementary paper on the role of the red carnation in *Ulysses* by Paul van Caspel.

In academic circles, in the thirties, one knew about *Ulysses*, of course. It had been signalled in reviews, and among those who were at all interested, Stuart Gilbert's well-known authoritative study (1930) was in great demand, counterbalanced, as it were, by such essays as 'Hoofdstukken over *Ulysses*' ('Some Chapters on *Ulysses*') by Simon Vestdijk, an outstanding novelist. In Vestdijk's essays, which appeared in a literary journal, *Forum*, for all the admiration he showed, more or less grudgingly, for Joyce as a literary genius, and for all the influence he must have undergone from him, there was an undercurrent of doubt and pessimism. This attitude, which proves that – at heart – Joyce just was not his cup of

215

tea, must have been reinforced after he had become acquainted with *Finnegans Wake*. In an essay written after Joyce's death in 1941, entitled 'Afscheid van Joyce' ('A Farewell to Joyce'), Vestdijk declared that in his view this book is not a dream, but pre-eminently, a *construction* imitating or feigning to reproduce the spontaneous nature of dreams, a product of 'erudition and malicious verbal fantasy' (p. 74).

On the whole, one got the impression, in those times, above all in the thirties, that *Ulysses* was more talked about than actually read.

After the war, interest was revived somehow. Jacques den Haan published a little study called *Joyce, Mythe van Erin* (1948), in a limited edition which was soon sold out. It appeared again in 1967, in a revised and augmented edition consisting mainly of more or less cursory notes on recent publications by various authors such as Herbert Gorman, Harry Levin, Richard M. Kain, James S. Atherton, Patricia Hutchins, Richard Ellmann, and some others whose studies had been published in the interval, roughly speaking, between 1940 and 1965.

The real break-through, however, came with the publication, in 1969, of the Dutch translation of *Ulysses* by John Vandenbergh (pseudonym of J.H.W. Schlamilch), who was awarded, subsequently, the 'Martin Nijhoff State Prize for Translation' in recognition of his admirable achievement. This translation made it possible to reach a wider public, and since then we have actually witnessed a growing interest in Joyce's work in the Netherlands, not only in Holland but also in the Dutch-speaking area of Belgium, a significant fact being that the Dutch *Ulysses* is already available in a seventh printing.

In Belgium, where Herman Servotte had already devoted a chapter to *Ulysses* in his study on the narrator in the English novel (1965), Vandenbergh's translation (which had taken him the best part of five years under difficult circumstances) was hailed by Joris Duytschaever of Antwerp University as a major event, a milestone in the history of the reception of Joyce's work. In an article in *De Vlaamse Gids* (1970), speaking of a 'masterly translation for an errand boy's wages', he stressed its importance for the cultural climate in the Netherlands and Flanders. In another paper, written in English and published in the *Revue des Langues Vivantes* (1971), Duytschaever dealt with a few technical aspects of the Dutch translation, such as the problems inherent in rendering – adequately and consistently – the mass of phrases constituting *leitmotifs* and *allusions*.

Levende Talen, the periodical of the Modern Language Association in the Netherlands, improved the occasion by bringing out a special issue (1970), intended, in particular, to celebrate the publication of *Ulysses* in Dutch and, in general, to give an impression of what was being done in the field of Joyce studies in Holland. In the same year, October 27, one of the Dutch networks brought an informative radio programme on *Ulysses*, and another network treated listeners, late at night, to a broadcast of 'Penelope', the final episode of *Ulysses* (in Vandenbergh's translation), which lasted three hours. In 1975, moreover, this same network broadcast a documentary on Joyce and Dublin (by Fred van Leeuwen) called 'Een stad in woorden' ('A City in Words'), featuring interviews with Noel Clery, Gerard O'Flaherty, Donagh McDonagh, Kevin Fitzgerald, and Roland Bourke Savage.

In the seventies there existed in Haarlem a Joyce Society, chairman G.H.J. de Leeuw, a local solicitor. Members met once a month for collective study of the Dutch *Ulysses* translation, drawing up lists of corrections suggested by them, which were then submitted to John Vandenbergh. The idea was, of course, that he might incorporate these in future reprints of the book. After Mr. De Leeuw's death the affair seems to have petered out. The long, detailed lists proved to be self-defeating, anyway. They probably discouraged the translation, or else the publisher may have baulked at the expense involved in bringing out a revised edition.

With a book of this size and this degree of complexity it would be simply inhuman to expect the translator to show a perfect command of each and every detail. Still, I think there are certain shortcomings in the Dutch translation which seem to be due to a general lack of feeling for the right Dutch idiom. It is quite possible that I, as a northerner, am more sensitive to non-idiomatic phrases than readers in Belgium, whose Dutch is often different from ours.

Here is an example: Molly, in her nocturnal monologue, remembers how, that afternoon, she 'fell asleep as sound as a top' (*U* 741.22 – references are to the Random House edition of *Ulysses*, New York, 1961). Now in Dutch, in connection with sleep, there is an idiomatic phrase, 'als een roos' ('like a rose'), as, e.g., in 'Het kind sliep als een roos' ('The child slept like a rose'), meaning that the child was enjoying a deep, healthy sleep. This phrase has a strictly static, by no means an inchoative connotation; in other words, we cannot say, 'The child fell asleep like a rose,' and that is just how Vandenbergh has translated Molly's words: 'ik viel in slaap als een roos' (p. 826). Such cases are relatively simple but there are enough that are rather more subtle.

Take this phrase, once more from Molly's soliloquy: 'if we had even a bath itself' (*U* 763.19). As I interpret it, this means something like, 'if we at least had a bath, actually', Molly's 'itself' being an Anglo-Irish feature, as far as I know, a kind of emphatic particle. In John Vandenbergh's translation the phrase runs: 'als we zelf maar een bad hadden' (p. 852), but that is not what Molly has in mind, for it means, 'if we ourselves had a bath at least', in which 'ourselves' is redundant, to say the least.

The trouble with Vandenbergh is, I believe, that he lacks imagination, and imagination or a certain power of empathy is needed in order to visualize scenes in which people perform concrete actions. I take a random sample from the 'Lestrygonians' episode: 'Tom Rochford *spilt* powder from a *twisted* paper into the water set before him' (*U* 179.1–2, italics mine), a simple scene in Davy Byrne's bar, featuring Tom Rochford, who is suffering from dyspepsia. As rendered by Vandenbergh, this sentence reads: 'Tom Rochford *gooide* poeder uit een *verkreukeld* papiertje in het water dat voor hem was neergezet' (p. 209, italics mine), but if we translate this Dutch sentence back into English, this is what we get: 'Tom Rochford *threw* powder from a *crumpled* paper into the water set before him'. The translator seems to believe that it is enough just to show the rough outlines of the action, neglecting the subtle shades Joyce weaves into the picture. After all, in taking their bicarbonate, people will not *throw* it into a glass of water but carefully allow it to run out from the paper, the latter having been either folded or *twisted* in a specific shape, and certainly not *crumpled* into a ball. It took Joyce seven years to write *Ulysses* – how could five years be enough to translate it?

A specific Dutch issue is the problem of the extent to which one of our greatest novelists, Simon Vestdijk (1898–1971), had been influenced by Joyce when conceiving one of his first novels, *Meneer Visser's hellevaart* ('Mr. Visser's Descent into Hell'), which he wrote in the first four months of 1934 and which was not published until 1936. The author alerted slow-witted critics by prefacing the book by a motto taken from the 'Hades' episode of *Ulysses*, alluding to suicide, the clue being that in the story Mr. Visser's father, just like Bloom's, is assumed to have killed himself.

As early as 1939, Jan Schepens, a Flemish critic, in a lengthy study on Vestdijk's novel, had stated as his opinion that one cannot

218

judge the style of this book without having read *Ulysses* first. The ins and outs of this question have been discussed most competently by Joris Duytschaever in *Dutch Studies* (1976) in a survey in which he points out a number of narrative techniques which Vestdijk may have borrowed from Joyce. He took up the subject again, covering a wider field this time, in a paper on Joyce's significance for modern literature in the Netherlands in general, published in a bimonthly Belgian cultural journal, *Ons Erfdeel* ('Our Heritage'), in 1977. A few years earlier, in 1972, Rob Delvigne had already drawn attention to a number of features which Vestdijk's novel and *Ulysses* have in common, both as to composition (structure) and to plot, in an article in *Spektator,* a journal for Dutch language and literature. This article drew a response from Paul van Caspel in a series of papers published in 1975 (see Bibliography).

Another author discussed by Duytshaever in his study on Joyce's influence on literature in the Netherlands is Martinus Nijhoff. In a talk on his own work (largely poetry), given in 1935, Nijhoff had mentioned – more or less in passing – his feelings of admiration for and, in a sense, envy of Joyce's major work, *Ulysses*, in which, as he saw it, the whole cosmos is contained in a single human being, a man walking through Dublin. Nijhoff was referring, specifically, to one of his longer poems, *Awater*, a 268-line epic which had appeared in 1934. It has been translated into English by James Holmes (1961). The hint given by Nijhoff himself was taken up by Karel Meeuwesse in 1967 in a series of essays in *De Nieuwe Taalgids* and *Ream*, in which he illustrated the underlying principle in Nijhoff's work, that of creative imitation. Some of his views were refuted subsequently by Paul van Caspel in a paper on *Awater* in *Spektator* (1976), in which he showed conclusively that Meeuwesse's statements were sometimes based on inaccurate readings of Joyce's text. Echoes of *Ulysses* in Nijhoff's *Awater* had also been signalled by M.H. Schenkeveld in the literary journal, *Raster* (1969). In particular, she pointed out some similarities between the so-called restaurant scene in *Awater* and the 'Sirens' episode in *Ulysses*.

Studies on other aspects of Joyce's writings published in Holland in the seventies included papers by Leo Knuth and Paul van Caspel (listed in the Bibliography), and the following books (full titles also in the Bibliography): *Notes on Joyce's Ulysses Part I* (1971) by Harry Vreeswijk, *The Wink of the Word* (1976) by Leo Knuth, and *Bloomers on the Liffey* (1980) by Paul van Caspel.

219

Bibliography or List of works referred to in the text

Peter Allt, *Some Aspects of the Life and Works of James Augustine Joyce,* Inaugural Lecture, Groningen: Wolters, 1952.
Rob Delvigne, *'Meneer Visser's hellevaart en Ulysses,'* Spektator, I (1971–1972), pp. 326–340.
Joris Duytschaever, 'Magistrale vertaling voor loopjongensloon: James Joyce in het Nederlands', *De Vlaamse Gids,* LIV (1970), No. 4, pp. 20–25.
—— 'James Joyce's *Ulysses* in Dutch', *Revue des Langues Vivantes/Tijdschrift voor Levende Talen,* XXXVII (1971), pp. 701–711.
—— 'James Joyce's Impact on Simon Vestdijk's Early Fiction', *Dutch Studies,* II, pp. 48–74, The Hague: Martinus Nijhoff, 1976.
—— 'De betekenis van James Joyce in de Nederlandse letteren,' *Ons Erfdeel,* XX (1977), pp. 95–108.
Stuart Gilbert, *James Joyce's Ulysses: A Study,* London: Faber & Faber, 1930. New ed., 1952.
Jacques den Haan, *James Joyce,* Amsterdam: De Bezige Bij, 1967.
'Joyce-nummer', *Levende Talen,* No. 269 (1970).
Leo Knuth, 'A Bathymetric Reading of Joyce's *Ulysses,* Chapter X', *Dutch Quarterly Review,* II (1972), pp. 49–64.
—— 'James Joyce', in: *Tijd en werkelijkheid in de moderne literatuur,* Wassenaar, Servire, 1974, pp. 35–65.
—— *The Wink of the Word: A Study of James Joyce's Phatic Communication,* Amsterdam; Rodopi, 1976.
Karel Meeuwesse, 'O Awater ik weet waarvan gij peinst', *Raam,* No. 34 (April 1967), pp. 43–65.
—— 'Aantekeningen bij *Awater*', *De Nieuwe Taalgids,* LX (1967), pp. 33–41; 171–176
Martinus Nijhoff, *Awater,* translated into English by James Holmes, *Delta,* IV (1961), No. 2, pp. 23–30.
M.H. Schenkeveld, 'De achtervolging voortgezet: Over Nijhoffs *Awater*', *Raster,* Jan. 1969, pp. 519–532.
Jan Schepens, 'Over *Meneer Visser's Hellevaart'*, *Werk,* I (1939), No. 6, pp. 36–62.
Herman Servotte, *De verteller in de Engelse roman: een studie over romantechniek,* Hasselt: Heideland, 1965.
Paul P.J. Van Caspel, 'The Theme of the Red Carnation in James Joyce's *Ulysses*', *Neophilologus,* XXXVIII (1954), pp. 189–198.

Paul P.J. Van Caspel, 'Nogmaals *Meneer Visser's hellevaart* en *Ulysses*', *Spektator*, V (1975–1976), 99–107.

—'Van Dublin naar Harlingen: Joyce en Vestdijk', in: *Gasten-boek voor Prof. Dr. G.A. van Es*, Groningen: 1975, pp. 177–187.

—— 'Vestdijk en Joyce: Visser en Bloom', *De Nieuwe Taalgids*, LXVIII (1975), pp. 481–485.

——'Er staat wel wat er staat', *Spektator*, VI (1976–1977), pp. 59–73.

—— 'A Plea for Intertranslation: Notes on the Cyclops Chapter of *Ulysses*', *Dutch Quarterly Review*, IX (1979), pp. 114–128.

—— 'Father and Son in the Lotus-eaters Episode of Joyce's *Ulysses*', *English Studies*, LX (1979), pp. 593–602.

—— *Bloomers on the Liffey: Eisegetical Readings of James Joyce's Ulysses Part* II, Groningen, 1980.

Simon Vestdijk, *Meneer Visser's hellevaart,* Den Haag: Nijgh & Van Ditmar, n.d. (1st ed. 1936).

——'Hoofdstukken over *Ulysses*', *Forum*, III (1934), pp. 196–211; 343–353. Also in: *Lier en Lancet,* Amsterdam: Polak & Van Gennep, 1976, pp. 219–246.

—— 'Afscheid van Joyce', in: *De Poolse Ruiter: Essays*, Den Haag: Bert Bakker/Daamen, 1958, pp. 65–75.

Harry Vreeswijk, *Notes on Joyce's Ulysses Part I (Chapters 1–3): A Very First Draft,* Amsterdam: Van Gennep, 1971.

Dutch translations

Allan M'Clelland, *Bloomsdag*, vertaling Gerardine Franken, Amsterdam: De Bezige Bij, 1965.

Hugh Leonard, *Stephen D.,* vertaling Gerardine Franken, Amsterdam: De Bezige Bij, 1968.

Dubliners, vertaald door Rein Bloem, Amsterdam; Polak & Van Gennep, 1968. Reprints 1971, 1978.

Ulysses, vertaling John Vandenbergh, Amsterdam: De Bezige Bij, 1969; 7th printing 1980.

Giacomo Joyce, vertaling Gerardine Franken, Amsterdam: De Bezige Bij, 1969.

Een portret van de kunstenaar als jongeman, vertaling Gerardine Franken en Leo Knuth, Amsterdam: De Bezige Bij, 1972. Reprint 1977.

Ballingen ('Exiles'), vertaling Gerardine Franken en Leo Knuth, Amsterdam: De Bezige Bij, 1974.

Brieven aan Nora, vertaling John Vandenbergh, Amsterdam: De Bezige Bij, 1976.

JOYCE IN GERMANY AND SWITZERLAND

PAUL F. BOTHEROYD AND SYLVIA BOTHEROYD

We do not know whether James Joyce was aware as he was working on *Finnegans Wake* in 1938 that a German translator, anthologist and reviewer of his work, Karl Arns, had included *Ulysses* in his *Index der anglo-jüdischen Literatur,* listing works which he warns teachers against dealing with in German schools and universities.[1] Joyce would have shown his characteristic indignation, but would not have been too surprised, one feels. Nor would he have been too astonished to have heard that on his death only one German newspaper, the *Frankfurter Zeitung,*[2] carried even a mention of his death and that, logically enough, a year after his death *Ulysses* was formally banned by Nazi Germany.[3,4]

Joyce once remarked to Padraic Colum about the Austro-Hungarian Empire, under whose rule he had lived for 11 years in Trieste before leaving for Zürich in 1915: 'They call it a ramshackle empire [. . .] I wish to God that there were more such empires'.[5] Germany, particularly in its Third Reich phase, was never 'ramshackle' enough for Joyce ever to spend considerable time in;[6] it was a country transited *en route* for somewhere else. In his early days of penury indeed transitting it had certain advantages: the German railways offered 4th class travel![7]

Joyce did of course admire certain Geman writers, Gerhart Hauptmann[8] for example, had great respect for individual Germans, academics like Professors Ernst Robert Curtius[9] and Heinrich Zimmer,[10] enjoyed cordial relations with his official German translator, Georg Goyert,[11] and had a considerable, although far from thorough, command of the German language.

Although he followed developments inside Germany and in Austria after *Anschluss*, and Hermann Broch[12] was not the only endangered person saved from Nazism through Joyce's good offices, Joyce went out of his way to transcend his own immediate feelings about Hitler, Nazism and anti-Semitism: Hitler embodied both personal and universal evil; the Nazi 'phenomenon' was a recurrent universal one.[13] It is as well that Joyce did not live to learn

222

the truth about the millions killed in concentration camps, which had nothing about them of the tennis-playing internment of Joyce's brother Stanislaus in Schloss Grossans[14] in the First World War.

Switzerland was not ramshackle, but not imperial either. It offered Joyce sanctuary twice (even if the second time rather reluctantly), in both World Wars, from the dangers of living as a British citizen (as he, and his family, remained) in Trieste and Vichy France. For Joyce Switzerland meant Zürich,[15] through its refugees even more polyglot, even more internationally minded than in peacetime. It was Joyce's home – in so far as any place ever deserved that title – from the end of June 1915 to October 1919 and again from mid-December 1940 until his death on January 13th, 1941. It was a place to be visited repeatedly in the inter-War years for eye-surgery.

Joyce was indebted to Switzerland for far more than motifs for *Finnegans Wake*,[16] the Zürich *Sechseläuten* festivities, river names, the Sihl and the Limmat at Zürich, the Rhine at Rheinfelden, complaining all night under his window in guttural Swiss-German,[17] and pressed into service to Anna Livia.

In 1938 a cashier at the Zürich hotel Carlton Elite refused a cheque of Joyce's: this brought down his curses on Zürich, faced, as was the rest of Switzerland at the time, with invasion: anyone is welcome to Zürich, 'he can hang all the staff of the Elite Hotel in comfortable sacks out of their own windows for all I care and meanwhile Heaven help the poor jews who fall into the hands of Mr Prager's [the hotel manager's] cashier'.[18] Joyce makes certain exceptions; this list, although uttered in a state of pique, does give some indication of what it was that Joyce appreciated about Zürich and Switzerland. The invaders are to respect the home of his cultivated, loyal, generous friends and patrons, the Giedion-Welckers; Othmar Schoeck, the composer whose settings of Gottfried Keller's *Lebendig Begraben*[19] so delighted Joyce (he might have extended this to cover the Zürich concert-hall, the *Tonhalle*); Professor Vogt's eye-clinic and Swiss medical expertise; the restaurant, the *Kronenhalle,* and Swiss culinary delights with presumably the Valais white wine Fendant figuring on any menu.

Switzerland did offer him, too, scurrilous eccentricities beneath its ordered surface: the manager of the Maggi soup factory, who was an ardent admirer of *Ulysses*, which according to Joyce 'apparently he reads between spoonfuls',[20] was one; the interminably slow-motion delights of the Dornach Anthroposophical Society's production of Goethe's *Faust* must have seemed to Joyce another. He complained to August Suter that nothing happened in the first hour, only to be reminded that nothing much happened in the first hour's reading of *Ulysses* either. Joyce persevered and was thrilled by the highly unorthodox acting and presentation.[21]

Not that Switzerland was free from Fascist 'phenomena' either: the wretched cashier at the Elite with all the makings of the Jew-baiter in Joyce's eyes, the unfortunate anti-Semite official in the Swiss 'Aliens' Police' who, perhaps confusing Joyce with Leopold Bloom, refused the Joyces' entry to Switzerland because of their alleged Jewishness[22] are two examples. The German military administration agreed readily enough in 1940 to allow Lucia Joyce to be transferred from a mental hospital in occupied France to one in Switzerland; it was Swiss officialdom which showed itself at its most inflexible and insatiable, subjecting Joyce to its full repertoire of chicanery for three months and so certainly hastening his death.

Through Daniel Brody's Rhein-Verlag, which published Joyce's *A Portrait of the Artist* in 1926, *Ulysses* in 1927 and *Dubliners* in 1928, all in Georg Goyert's translation, which it continued to reprint through the next 30 years, Switzerland was responsible for the distribution of Joyce in the German-speaking world. Switzerland provided, too, its share of early Joyce scholars, Bernhard Fehr,[23] Carola Giedion-Welcker,[24] the great psychologist Carl Gustav Jung[25] – for all his lack of understanding for *Ulysses*; without doubt one of the most important Joyce scholars working in the German-speaking world today is the Swiss Fritz Senn.[26]

The Federal Republic of Germany has made amends, too, for the treatment meted out to *Ulysses* by the Nazi regime, especially since the Frankfurt publisher Suhrkamp acquired the German translation rights for Joyce's works in 1967 and embarked upon a seven volume edition of completely new translations to replace, amongst others, the Georg Goyert translations. The controversy around the Goyert translations and the authenticity of the Joyce which they created came to a crisis in 1957 with a dispute carried on via the columns of the *Frankfurter Allgemeine Zeitung*[27] between the veteran translator Goyert and the German novelist, critic and translator Arno Schmidt. Highly perceptive critics like Kurt Tucholsky who had reviewed *Ulysses* for *Die Weltbühne* in 1927, had had their doubts from the very beginning.[28] The special translation number of *James Joyce Quarterly* of Spring 1967 carried the discussion of the Goyert translations into a more positive direction. Jack P. Dalton,[29] Breon

Mitchell[30] and Fritz Senn[31] were all more interested in the difficulties presented by the Joyce texts rather than in finding mistakes. Breon Mitchell has since presented us with a full length study of Goyert's translations of *Ulysses* and its influence on the three important German-language novelists, Hans Henny Jahn, Alfred Döblin and Hermann Broch.[32]

Publication of Joyce in the German Democratic Republic was inhibited for many years by literary-ideological problems,[33] but recently two of new Suhrkamp translations, those of *Dubliners* and *A Portrait of the Artist*, have appeared under licence.[34]

With the exception of that translator's nightmare, *Finnegans Wake*, of which however a multi-version of part, *Anna Livia Plurabelle*, has been published by Suhrkamp,[35] the Suhrkamp edition is now complete. The new German translations will no doubt be subject to scholarly scrutiny; beginnings have already been made.[36] With these virtuoso translations in front of us and with shelves full of Joyce literature at our disposal it is easy, but neither productive nor humane, to indulge in the rather dubious art of self-aggrandizing fault-finding which characterized Arno Schmidt's contributions, when we look back fifty years at the Goyert translations and their manipulation of the Joyce original.

Amongst other things the two sets of translations are products of two radically different commercial situations; they are products too of two totally different attitudes to Joyce and to translation. Goyert seems to have followed Goethe's first maxim on translation: 'the one requires that a foreign author be brought over to us in such a way that we can regard him as ours'; Suhrkamp's translators his second: 'the other demands from us that we should go over to the foreign and find our way into its conditions, its ways of speaking, its peculiarities'.[37] The German critic Helmut M. Braem has summed up the Germanization of Joyce's Dublin resulting from Goyert's method in the following words:

> His [Goyert's] Dublin was somewhere between Wernigerode and Celle [two central German towns] where the stout did not even taste exotic and the men at the bar spoke as if they were foreign workers who had a perfect command of German slang.[38]

Close examination of the Suhrkamp *Dubliners* has shown that the translator Dieter E. Zimmer has made a conscious effort to preserve the foreignness of the text;[39] along with Klaus Reichert and

Fritz Senn he has provided the reader with a volume of relevant documents,[40] notes, maps, photographs and bibliography to assist him/her.

The scholarly preoccupation with Joyce which has gradually developed in German-speaking countries, particularly in the Federal Republic of Germany, is surveyed up to 1967 by Rosemarie Franke (v.fn.4); Robert H. Deming's *A Bibliography of James Joyce Studies* (a number of the German-language entries are unfortunately marred by errors), Alan M. Cohn's on-going listings in *JJQ* and the annual German contribution to the 'IASAIL Bibliography' published annually in the Autumn number of *The Irish University Review* at least list, if they do not comment on, German-language Joyceana as they appear.

Apart from Klaus Reichert, the Swiss Fritz Senn, Hans Wollschläger and Dieter E. Zimmer, the most prominent members of the Suhrkamp team, a number of scholars have become important in the Federal Republic in the last few years, many of them initially through the publication of their doctoral theses on Joyce.

It should be mentioned that – for better or for worse – all German and Swiss dissertations are published in one form or another. The demands for stringent methodological direction, frequently for a high degree of abstraction and theoretical generalization, which shows little patience with Anglo-Saxon eclectic methodological dilettantism or even commonsensical positivism, often takes the reader to truly dizzying intellectual heights!

Many of these German Joyce scholars are represented in the collection of essays edited by Therese Fischer-Seidel on *Ulysses* in 1977.[41] Her own dissertation,[42] published in 1973, was an attempt to widen the frame of discussion of Joyce's narrative techniques into one of 'the presentation of consciousness'. In this discussion, which embraces both stylistic and narrative analyses, the treatment of 'personal' and 'impersonal segments', inner and outer representations of consciousness, plays an important role. Rosemarie Franke's historical treatment of the distribution, translation and criticism of Joyce in the German-speaking countries has been referred to previously; a revised version of her section on *Ulysses* in the German-speaking world appears here, as does that on *A Portrait* [43] in an earlier collection edited by another well-known German Joyce scholar, Wilhelm Füger; H.W. Gabler, well-known as a member of the international team working towards a definitive edition of Joyce's work, is represented here, as he is in Füger's collection. Fritz

Senn gives an overall view of the place of *Ulysses* within the Joyce canon. Eberhard Kreutzer, whose dissertation[44] on 'language and language-play' in Joyce's *Ulysses* appeared in book-form in 1969 here examines the function of punning, a subject on which Manfred Jahn wrote his dissertation[45] with reference to *Finnegans Wake* in 1975, using the linguistic method taken over from computer simulation 'analysis by synthesis'. Ulrich Schneider examines Biblical allusion in *Ulysses*; his dissertation[46] of 1970 is concerned more generally with the function of quotation in *Ulysses*. Viktor Link, whose recent paper on the Wollschläger *Ulysses* has been mentioned previously (fn.36), is here concerned with the 'Circe-episode' as he was in his 1970 dissertation.[47] Arno Esch, supervisor for Kreutzer's, Link's and Schneider's dissertations and himself the author of a *Ulysses* monograph,[48] explores the Homeric correspondences. One of the most important theorists on narrative technique writing today in German, F.K. Stanzel – his most recent book is *Theorie des Erzählens*[49] ('Theory of Narrating'), in which quite naturally *Ulysses* plays an important role – here both re-states his position on narrative situation in Joyce's novel and indicates something of the developments in the field of research into narrative problems which have occurred since the mid-1950s.

The contributors to Wilhelm Füger's collection on Joyce's *A Portrait* are not part of the Suhrkamp team, nor are some, for all their useful essays here, essentially Joyceans (Walter Höllerer on the epiphany; Fränzi Maierhöfer on the 'Bat-like Soul of Stephen Dedalus', L.W. Kahn on Stephen's role as a priest of art, Ortwin Kuhn on the significance of nationalism for particularly *A Portrait*, J. Drews, a short encyclopaedic article); Füger himself writes on door symbolism. Füger's most recent Joyce publication, apart from his on-going work on the elucidation of *Finnegans Wake*, has been a *Concordance to James Joyce's 'Dubliners'*.[50]

Both Fischer-Seidel's and Füger's collections are intended for the German general reader, as is another of Suhrkamp's volumes of materials, this, too, on *A Portrait*.[51] In all three cases the bibliographical material appended to the main body of text deserves international attention.

Amongst other German-language monographs devoted to Joyce which have appeared in the last few years have been the following: Hartmut Mietzner's,[52] in which the categories of immanence and transcendence are used to investigate the human consciousness and sub-consciousness as represented in *A Portrait* and in *Ulysses*, Uwe

Multhaup's[53] examination of the artistic consciousness in the same two novels, Norbert Schmuhl's examination of 'perspectivity and aperspectivity' in *Ulysses*,[54] and Sibylle Kisro-Völker's[55] confrontation of Joyce and Wittgenstein.

Perhaps the most remarkable Joyce monograph to have appeared in the last few years is, however, Eckhard Lobsien's[56] challenging ethnomethodological approach to *Ulysses*. Lobsien questions the validity of positivist, interpretive and communicative approaches to *Ulysses*, which threaten 'to routinize the book's charisma' (to modify slightly Brook Thomas's translation[57]); Lobsien pleads for the phenomenologically orientated branch of sociology founded by Harold Garfinkle, ethnomethodology, concerned as it is with the analysis of the everyday, as the adequate method of access to a book which in Hermann Broch's words captures the 'Welt-Alltag der Epoche', the 'universal quotidian of the epoch'.

This brief survey of literature written in German on Joyce is far from complete; there is a considerable body of critical and scholarly articles, e.g. on the fascinating problem of translating *Finnegans Wake*, whether at all, if so into what sort of German (Flann O'Brien has asked *from* what language), by what method and so on;[58] there is then the work that has been done on Joyce's poetry;[59] there is the study yet to be done, where Breon Mitchell left off, on the overall influence of Joyce (in the original or through translation) on German literature, an influence that has certainly not exhausted itself with Arno Schmidt's monster novel in the manner of *Finnegans Wake, Zettels Traum*;[60] who knows, the translator of *Ulysses*, Hans Wollschläger, may not be the only German or Swiss with a 400 page cross[61] between *Finnegans Wake* and *Zettels Traum* ready to be launched.

With all this varied activity going on around Joyce, Eckhard Lobsien's fears do not seem too well founded, but let us all the same conclude with a toast (to be drunk in some suitable Joycean beverage) to the centenary of James Joyce's birth: 'May the charisma of the man and the work continue to withstand routinization.'

NOTES

1 Bochum-Langendreer, 1941.
2 15.1.1941; Hans Hennecke published a short survey of Joyce's work and life, *Neue Rundschau*, (Berlin), Feb. 1941, pp. 120–122.

3   *Verzeichnis englischer und nordamerikanischer Schriftsteller,* Leipzig, 1942.
4   We are indebted to Rosemarie Franke's dissertation for the Free University of Berlin, *James Joyce und der deutsche Sprachbereich: Übersetzung, Verbreitung und Kritik in der Zeit von 1919–1967*, Bamberg, 1970, for the historical data of fns. 1–3.
5   'A Portrait of James Joyce', *New Republic*, 31.5.1931, p. 347, as quoted by Dominic Manganiello, *Joyce's Politics*, London, 1980, p. 149, Manganiello quotes a further passage from Joyce's comments on the Austro-Hungarian Empire which must have had great relevance for Joyce's feelings about both Germany and Switzerland: it 'tried to impose so little upon its own or upon other people. It was not war-like, it was not efficient, and its bureaucracy was not strict, it was the country for a peaceful man', ibid., p. 149.
6   The most useful work, Daniel von Recklinghausen, *James Joyce: Chronik von Leben und Werk,* Frankfurt/M., 1968, lists brief stays in Bonn (1938), Cologne (1938), Frankfurt/M. (1929), Hamburg (1936), Munich (1928) and Wiesbaden (1930).
7   As he recommends, too, to his brother Stanislaus for his journey from Dublin to Trieste in 1905, *Letters*, vol. II, ed. Richard Ellmann, London, 1966, pp. 120–121.
8   The Joyce-Hauptmann relationship is investigated by H.D. Tschörtner, 'Zu den Beziehungen zwischen Gerhart Hauptmann und James Joyce', *Zeitschrift für Anglistik und Amerikanistik,* XXVI (1978), 3, pp. 258–262.
9   Ernst Robert Curtius, professor at Bonn University, literary historian and critic, published the first book-length study of Joyce in German, *James Joyce und sein 'Ulysses'*, Zürich, 1929; he remained a firm supporter of Joyce although he became increasingly critical of the disintegration of language he saw in *Work in Progress*. He and Zimmer (v.fn.10) were according to Joyce the recipients of the only two review copies of the completed *Finnegans Wake* to be sent to Germany, *Letters*, vol. III, ed. Richard Ellmann, London, 1966, p. 452.
10   A famous Sanskrit scholar, professor at Heidelberg University, son of the Celtic professor of the same name, *Letters,* v.III, pp. 432–433.
11   Joyce's German voice from 1926 until the first volume in the new Suhrkamp edition of Joyce, Dieter E. Zimmer's translation of *Dubliners*, appeared in 1969.
12   The Austrian novelist, who published an essay devoted to *Ulysses*, *James Joyce und die Gegenwart,* Vienna, 1936.
13   Richard Ellmann, *James Joyce,* New York, 1959, p. 722; fuller in Carola Giedion-Welcker, 'Meeting with Joyce', in *Portraits of the Artist in Exile: Recollections of James Joyce by Europeans*, ed. Willard Potts, Portmarnock, 1979, pp. 270–271.
14   *Letters,* vol. I, ed. Stuart Gilbert, London, 1957, p. 85.
15   v. the relevant portions of Richard Ellmann, *James Joyce* and Fritz Senn, *James Joyce: Aufsätze,* Zürich, 1972.
16   In addition to Fritz Senn's essay v. Helmut Bonheim, *A Lexicon of the German in 'Finnegans Wake'*, Munich, 1967.
17   *Letters*, vol. I, p. 396.
18   Ibid., vol. III, p. 418.
19   Ibid., vol. III, p. 417.
20   Ibid., vol. I, p. 399.
21   *Portraits of the Artist in Exile,* p. 65.

22 *Letters,* vol.III, pp. 491–501; Joyce: 'je ne suis point juif de Judée mais aryen d'Erin', ibid., p. 500.

23 Professor of English at Zürich, he published amongst other publications on Joyce, a full-length essay on *Ulysses* in 1925; v. Franke, *James Joyce und der deutsch Sprachbereich*, pp. 198ff.

24 Art-historian and critic, friend and patron of Joyce, prolific writer on him and his works; Robert H. Deming, *A Bibliography of James Joyce Studies*, Boston, 1977, lists 24 items.

25 For the mutually unsatisfactory relations of Joyce and Jung in person and through their works v. Richard Ellmann, *James Joyce,* pp. 480–483 (Mrs McCormick cutting off financial aid to Joyce, allegedly under Jung's influence); pp. 641–642 (Jung's unsuitable introduction to the Rhein-Verlag's edition of *Ulysses*); p. 688 (Jung's unsuccessful treatment of Lucia Joyce). Jung published his introduction in the *Europäische Revue,* 8 (1932), pp. 132–189.

26 The author of over 100 publications on Joyce, v. Deming; Alan M. Cohn's on-going 'Current JJ Checklist' in *James Joyce Quarterly,* etc.

27 26.10.1957 (Schmidt); 6.12.1957 (Schmidt and Goyert); amongst others Goyert's publisher, Daniel Brody (5.11.1957), and Heinrich Straumann (16.11.1957), Professor of English at Zürich at the time of Joyce's death, took part, too, in the dispute.

28 *Gesammelte Werke,* vol.II, Hamburg, 1961, pp. 949–955. His comment on the German version: 'Here either a murder has happened or a corpse has been photographed', ibid., p. 951 (our translation) shows that he was not sure just where to put the blame for what he found, with Goyert or with Joyce.

29 *JJQ,* IV (1967), pp. 206–208.

30 Ibid., pp. 202–205 and p. 208.

31 Ibid., pp. 170–193.

32 *James Joyce and the German Novel, 1922–1933*, Athens/Ohio, 1976.

33 v. Sigfried Hoefort, 'James Joyce in East Germany', *James Joyce Quarterly,* V (1968), pp. 132–136.

34 v. Rüdiger Imhof, 'East and West', *Études Irlandaises,* V (1980), pp. 278–282.

35 Frankfurt/M., 1971. In addition to the original this edition contains German versions by Wolfgang Hildesheimer, Hans Wollschläger and Georg Goyert, a 'basic English' version by C.K. Ogden and a partial translation into French by Samuel Beckett, Philippe Soupault et al., together with a useful introductory essay by Klaus Reichert.

36 Amongst others: Sylvia Botheroyd-Muscheid's unpublished thesis for the University of Basle, 'A Comparative Study of the Two Translations of James Joyce's *Dubliners* by Georg Goyert (1928) and Dieter E. Zimmer (1969)', 1971; Rüdiger Imhof, 'East and West' (v.fn.33); Viktor Link's contribution to the Wuppertal IASAIL Symposium, July 1981. 'The new German translation of *Ulysses* by H. Wollschläger: A critical comparison with the French translation of A. Morel' (publication forthcoming).

37 *Rede auf Wieland,* 18.2.1813 as quoted by Fritz Güttinger, *Zielsprache und Technik des Übersetzens,* Zürich, 1963, p. 11 (our translation).

38 'Ein neuer James Joyce', *Süddeutsche Zeitung,* 4.12.1969 (our translation).

39 Sylvia Botheroyd-Muscheid, 'A Comparative Study', TS, p. 38.

40 Klaus Reichert, Fritz Senn and Dieter E. Zimmer (eds.), *Materialien zu 'Dubliner',* Frankfurt/M, 1969.

41 *James Joyces 'Ulysses': Neuere deutsche Aufsätze,* Frankfurt/M., 1977.
42 *Bewusstseinsdarstellung im Werk von James Joyce. Von 'Dubliners' zu 'Ulysses',* Frankfurt/M., 1973.
43 *James Joyces 'Portrait': 'Jugendbildnis' im Lichte neuerer deutscher Forschung,* Munich, 1972.
44 *Sprache und Spiel im 'Ulysses' von James Joyce,* Bonn, 1969.
45 *Sprachspielerische Wortbildungstechniken in James Joyces 'Finnegans Wake',* Cologne, 1975.
46 *Die Funktion der Zitate im 'Ulysses' von James Joyce,* Bonn, 1970.
47 *Bau und Funktion der Circe-Episode im 'Ulysses' von James Joyce,* Bonn, 1970.
48 *James Joyce und sein 'Ulysses',* Köln/Opladen, 1970.
49 Göttingen, 1979.
50 Hildesheim, 1980.
51 Klaus Reichert und Fritz Senn (eds.), *Materialien zu James Joyces 'Ein Porträt des Künstlers als junger Mann',* Frankfurt/M., 1975.
52 *Immanenz und Transzendenz in Joyces 'A Portrait of the Artist as a Young Man' und 'Ulysses',* Bern/Frankfurt am M./Las Vegas, 1978.
53 *Das künstlerische Bewusstsein und seine Gestaltung in James Joyces 'A Portrait of the Artist as a Young Man' und 'Ulysses',* Bern/Frankfurt/M., 1974.
54 *Erfahrungen des Aufbruchs. Zur Perspektivität und Aperspektivität in James Joyces Ulysses,* Bern/Frankfurt/M., 1976.
55 *Die unverantwortete Sprache: Esoterische Literatur und antitheoretische Philosophie als Grenzfälle medialer Selbstreflexion. Eine Konfrontation von James Joyces 'Finnegans Wake' und Wittgensteins 'Philosophische Untersuchungen',* Munich, 1978.
56 *Der Alltag des Ulysses. Die Vermittlung von ästhetischer und lebensweltlicher Erfahrung,* Stuttgart, 1978.
57 *James Joyce Quarterly,* XVII (1979), pp. 94–99.
58 e.g. the dispute around the translation of *Anna Livia Plurabelle* (v.fn.35) by Wolfgang Hildesheimer and Hans Wollschläger in 1972.
59 e.g. by Max Wildi, 'The Lyrical Poems of James Joyce', in *Language and Society,* Copenhagen, 1961, pp. 169–186; and Selwyn Jackson, *The Poems of James Joyce and the Use of Poems in his Novels,* Bern/Frankfurt/M., 1978.
60 Stuttgart, 1970.
61 To be called *Herzgewächse, oder der Fall Adams,* announced by Diogenes of Zürich for 1977 but still not published.

JOYCE IN THE ARAB WORLD

SUHEIL BADI BUSHRUI

I

Although a quarter of a century has elapsed since Joyce began to be translated, taught and written about in the Arab world, it is really only in the past decade that there has been widespread interest in his work among Arabs. That interest has yet to reach its peak, and this will surely come with the eventual translation into Arabic of the whole of *Ulysses* – a task of monumental proportions involving many problems that are virtually insurmountable.

James Joyce has an importance for the present-day Arab world that may not be immediately apparent to the outside observer. Arab critics, and most Arab novelists, have made the assumption that as the contemporary Arabic novel is almost entirely naturalistic, Joycean techniques in this respect provide an excellent innovative model – especially the 'stream-of-consciousness' style employed in *Ulysses* and *Finnegans Wake*. Such an assumption would be valid if the reference were to be exclusively related to *Dubliners*, which is still considered to be founded on naturalistic detail (as is *Ulysses* of course). But few contemporary critics would consider Joyce a naturalist at all – many critics would say with justification that the symbolic materials overshadow the naturalistic details. Nor would 'stream-of-consciousness' be considered a naturalistic technique, although there is considerable discussion on its merits as an aspect of psychological realism rather than a poetic technique. And *Finnegans Wake*, like the major portions of the latter half of *Ulysses*, is basically outside the 'stream-of-consciousness' narrative technique, although one would be at a loss to find a descriptive term that would satisfy most critics.

Notwithstanding the subtle distinctions that exist in the various narrative techniques employed by Joyce, Arab novelists have found *Dubliners* and *A Portrait of the Artist as a Young Man* more accessible examples of how to focus on various aspects of life, particularly the seedier aspect, in a personal, detailed and evocative manner. The influence of *Dubliners*, at least, is evident in such early short-story writing as ⌐*Rūsul al-Insāniyyāh* ¡*wa Qisas Ukhra** [*The Agents of Humanity and Other Stories*] by Abdul Malik Abdul-Latif Nuri, and more recently as¡*Nās min Rās* ¡*Beirut*** [*People from Beirut*] by Samir Sanbr.

No one who reads only *Dubliners* and *A Portrait of the Artist as a Young Man* among Joyce's works, however, can anticipate the enormous complexities of *Ulysses* and *Finnegans Wake*, although the mental attitude of these is already apparent in the earlier works. *Ulysses* has always made much more sense to those of its readers who are well versed in the European classical literature, and those who do not have such works as part of their heritage – the Arab reader, for instance – are at a great disadvantage in tackling it. For how is the Arab translator to assist his readers without a welter of cumbersome footnotes, more than doubling the size of an already vast volume?

However, as many writers on Joyce have observed before, the problems of *Ulysses* pale into relative insignificance when compared to those of *Finnegans Wake*. To translate this into Arabic one would quite simply have to invent an Arabic language of one's own and infuse it with a wealth of puns, mimicry and parody. The Arab has, in fact, two quite separate languages already at his disposal: classical, literary Arabic on the one hand, and colloquial Arabic on the other (the two are almost as different as, say, Latin and modern Italian). The less respected medium of the colloquial would seem quite appropriate for some aspects of Joyce's work, but then there is another problem: which colloquial? One can choose from Egyptian, Iraqi, Lebanese, Moroccan, Sudanese. . . . Granted these are all descended from the same mother tongue, but the variations between them are so great as to make it quite impossible for those of Joyce's works involved – primarily *Ulysses* and *Finnegans Wake* – to receive universal recognition in the Arab world.

Classical Arabic has, of course, only one standard, and that is the Qur'an, which is literally regarded by all Muslims, Arabs and non-Arabs alike, as the Word of God. It is difficult, however, for anyone who has not read the Qur'an in Arabic to appreciate it fully, or to understand the sanctity with which its followers regard it. The language which the Qur'an uses is, in fact, the *logos*; it is therefore sacred, and for anyone to destroy its conventions, as Joyce does in *Finnegans Wake* to the English language, would seem like sacrilege

* Baghgdad, Dar al-Amal, 1946.
** Beirut, Daṛ al-Nahar li al-Nashr, 1980

233

on a massive scale. Joyce appears to have demanded that we learn an entirely new language in order to read *Finnegans Wake*, for that purpose only, and the meanings we give each word are to apply only at the moment of reading and at no time afterwards. The question then is how is an Arab to invent a new language and still maintain absolute loyalty to that vehicle of expression which he regards as the absolute standard, and the integrity of whose style, structure, and rhetoric he is bound by faith to safeguard and preserve?

Another difficulty for Arabs is the psychological world represented in Joyce's works. Neither Freud nor his counterpart exists in Arab culture, and Arab novels are reticent on the subject of sex. Works such as the *Arabian Nights*, highly erotic though some of its tales undoubtedly are, are generally looked upon as part of the folk tradition – fictional tales with, in fact, a highly moral content – and therefore not considered distasteful.

Joyce himself would scarcely have found favour in the Arab world if he had chosen to go there, and the interest now being shown there in his work certainly has nothing to do with his own personality. In some ways, it is surprising that he should be appreciated at all, bearing in mind the spiritual, anti-nihilistic nature of the East, a very different ethos to that found in Joyce's work. Most Arab critics would probably condemn all that is false in Joyce – his sentimentality and arrogant ostentation in particular. But against these they would place many strengths, notably Joyce's ability to sum up the human predicament and depict, with impeccable sincerity, the crisis in the spiritual and material life of twentieth-century man.

Apart from 'Araby', the third tale in *Dubliners* – was Joyce comparing Arabia as he saw it to a bazaar? –, there is only one significant link between his work and the Arab world: the many references to the Qur'an, some more obvious than others, in *Finnegans Wake*. A list of these references and some elucidation of them may be found in an impeccably researched article by J.S. Atherton in *Comparative Literature* (VI, 3, Summer 1954, pp. 240–55)*, entitled 'Islam and the Koran in *Finnegans Wake*'. The author points out that not only had Joyce clearly studied the Qur'an in some detail, but there are signs that *Finnegans Wake* was an attempt to emulate it – in the sense that Joyce's book has so much in it that it defies exhaustive interpretation. He was certainly arrogant enough to have hoped that the work would be treated with as much

* Reprinted later in *The Books at the Wake* (Part III), London, Faber and Faber, 1959, pp. 201–217.

reverence as the Qur'an. Whatever else *Finnegans Wake* may be, however, it certainly cannot be said to be divinely inspired.

II

The earlist known Arabic translation of Joyce dates from 1950: the last part of Molly's monologue in *Ulysses* appeared in Louis 'Awad's critical essay on Joyce in *Fī al-Adab al-Inglīzī al-Hadith* [*On Modern English Literature*]. This was followed in 1956 by the first single work to be translated in its entirety: "The Boarding House" from *Dubliners* was included in a selection of short stories translated by Jamil al-Husni in *Mukhtārāt min al-Qisas al-Inglīzīyyah al-Qasīrah* [*Selections from English Short Stories*]. Soon afterwards critical works referring to Joyce began to be translated, one of the first of which was Leon Edel's *The Psychological Novel: 1900–1950*, a highly influential work which introduced an entirely new concept to Arab writers.

In the 1960s two further attempts at *Ulysses* were made by Taha Mahmoud Taha: a translation of Episode 4 ('Calypso'), followed a year later by 'The Wandering Rocks'. Taha, an Egyptian Professor of English at Kuwait University, has indeed made the most significant contribution yet to Joyce studies in the Arab World with his *Mawsu'at James Joyce: Hayatuh wa Fannuh wa Dirasat li A'malih* [*A James Joyce Encyclopaedia: His Life, Art and Works*], published in 1975. The *Mawsū'at*, a comprehensive survey of Joyce's output, includes a competent and lucid critical treatment of *Dubliners, The Portrait of the Artist as a Young Man, Exiles, Ulysses* and *Finnegans Wake*; a translation of two major short stories, "The Sisters" and "Ivy Day in the Committee Room"; translations of extensive key passages from *A Portrait of the Artist as a Young Man, Exiles, Stephen Hero* and *Ulysses* ('Calypso' and 'The Wandering Rocks' in their entirety). The author wisely refrains from translating passages from *Finnegans Wake*; he concentrates on explaining key words and phrases and relies heavily on *A Skeleton Key to 'Finnegans Wake'* by Joseph Campell and Henry Morton Robinson. In giving excellent and accurate biographical data, the author makes intelligent use of the extensive and voluminous Joyce criticism available in English, but somewhat restricts himself in his own critical approach. The *Mawsū'at* represents to date the most useful and comprehensive reference work in Arabic.

In many countries outside the English-speaking world Joyce has

ben read in French translation rather than the English original, and
this applies to some parts of the Arab world, notably Lebanon,
where French culture has been stronger than English. The Lebanese novelist and critic Suhayyel Idriss is an example of a writer
whose contact with Joyce came through French literature and
criticism. The Joyce influence that can be traced in Idriss's nevels
came from the French translation of *Ulysses* and of works by such
critics as R.M. Albérés, Michel Butor and Jean Ricardou.

Other translations of major works into Arabic –works that
include critical studies of Joyce and references to his achievement in
the field of the modern novel – include Georg Lukács's *Studies in
Realism* (translated in 1970), Robert Humphry's *Stream of Consciousness in the Modern Novel* (translated in 1975) and Edmund
Wilson's *Axel's Castle* (translated in 1976). These represent the
indirect influence of Joyce on the Arab writer, perhaps doing more
than any other works to help knowledge of Joyce's 'stream-of-consciousness' technique, method, style and structure to reach a wider
readership. Among aspiring Arab novelists in the early 1970s, the
distinguished Egyptian writer Gamal al-Ghitani found himself – as
he himself confessed to me last year – influenced more by works
such as these, especially Leon Edel's important work mentioned
above, than by Joyce's own writings. Most Arab writers have
learned about Joyce in this way, not having read his works. Al-
Ghitani's *al-Zayni Barakat* shows the influence of at least three
Joycean techniques: 'stream-of-consciousness', interior monologue,
and historical and mythical parody, in a way hitherto unpre-
cedented in the modern Arab novel.

Of Joyce's own work, the most frequently translated piece is his
play *Exiles* (1969, 1973 and 1980). *Dubliners* was translated (with
three omissions: 'Two Gallants', 'The Boarding House' and 'A
Painful Case') in the late 1960s, and seven of its stories have been
tackled individually, appearing in various Arabic publications ('The
Boarding House' has been translated on three separate occasions).
A Portrait of the Artist as a Young Man appeared in an Arabic
version in 1973, and *Ulysses* translations are so far limited to the
two excerpts mentioned above. There have also been two Arabic
translations of Hugh Leonard's play *Stephen D.,* which was based
on *A Portrait* and *Stephen Hero*: the first was published in 1970 and
the other, with *Exiles*, in 1973.

*   *   *

The following is an attempt at compiling the first list of works by or about Joyce available in Arabic. It is divided into three sections: translations of Joyce's own works, original Arabic writings on Joyce, and translations of critical studies dealing with Joyce and his influence on the twentieth century novel and short story. It is hoped that this checklist will lead, as interest in Joyce increases throughout the Arab world, to the publication of the first complete bibliography of Joyce in Arabic.

I. WORKS BY JAMES JOYCE

a) DUBLINERS

Nās min Dublin [*People from Dublin*]
Translated by Inayat 'Abdul 'Aziz
Revised by Mursi Sa'd al-Din
Cairo, Dār Sa'd Misr, n.d.
[1968?]
("The One Thousand Book" series
published by the Department of Public
Culture, Ministry of Education,
Southern Branch)

ناس من دبلن
ترجمة : عنايات عبد العزيز
مراجعة : مرسي سعد الدين
القاهرة ، دار سعد مصر ، بدون تاريخ ،
[١٩٦٨؟]
(«سلسلة الألف كتاب» ، نشر قسم الثقافة العامة
بوزارة المعارف ، المنطقة الجنوبية)

b) SINGLE STORIES FROM "DUBLINERS"

"al-Ukhtān ["The Sisters"]
in *Mawsū'at James Joyce:
Hayātuh wa Fannuh wa Dirāsāt li-
A'mālih* [*A James Joyce
Encyclopaedia: His Life, Art, and
Works*]
Translated by Taha M. Taha
Kuwait, Wikālat al-Maṭbū'āt,
1975
pp. 123 – 32

«الأختان»
في موسوعة جيمس جويس : حياته وفنّه
ودراسات لأعماله
ترجمة : طه محمود طه
الكويت ، وكالة المطبوعات ، ١٩٧٥
ص ١٢٣ – ١٣٢

"Eveline"
al-Tāli'ah al-Adabīyyah, Vol. IV,
No. 11
November 1978
Translated by Iman Muwaffaq
Musallam
pp. 37 – 39

«ايفيلين»
في الطليعة الأدبية ، ج ٤ ، عدد ١١
تشرين ثان – نوفمبر ١٩٧٨
ترجمة : إيمان موفق سليم
ص ٣٧ – ٣٩

238

"Eveline"
al-Ādāb al-Ajnabīyyah, No. 22
October 1979
Translated by Muhammad
Abu Khaddur
pp. 183 – 89

«ايڤلين»
في الآداب الأجنبية ، عدد ٢٢
تشرين أوّل – أكتوبر ١٩٧٩
ترجمة : محمّد أبو خضوّر
ص ١٨٣ – ١٨٩

"al-Nuzul" ["The Boarding
House"]
in *Mukhtārāt min al-Qiṣaṣ al-
Inglīzīyyah al-Qaṣīrah* [*Selections
from English Short Stories*]
Translated by Jamil al-Husni
Revised by Rashad Rushdi
Cairo, Maktabat Nahdat Misr,
1956
pp. 61 – 70

«النزل»
في مختارات من القصص الإنجليزيّة القصيرة
ترجمة : جميل الحسني
مراجعة : رشاد رشدي
القاهرة ، مكتبة نهضة مصر ، ١٩٥٦
ص ٦١ – ٧٠

"al-Nuzul" ["The Boarding
House"]
in *Qiṣaṣ ʿAlamīyyah* [*World
Stories*]
Translated by Ramzi Miftah
Revised by Muhammad Badran
Cairo, Dār al-Qalam, 1959
pp. 120 – 32

«النزل»
في قصص عالميّة
ترجمة : رمزي مفتاح
مراجعة : محمد بدران
القاهرة ، دار القلم ، ١٩٥٩
ص ١٢٠ – ١٣٢

"al-Nuzul" ["The Boarding
House"]
in *Min Rawāʾiʿ al-Adab al-ʿAlamī:
Qiṣaṣ Qaṣīrah* [*World
Masterpieces: Short Stories*]
Translated by Muʾnis al-Razaz
Beirut, al-Muʾassasah al-
Arabīyyah li al-Dirāsāt wa al-Nashr,
1980
pp. 133 – 42

«النزل»
في من روائع الأدب العالميّ : قصص قصيرة
ترجمة : مُونس الرزاز
بيروت ، المؤسّسة العربيّة للدراسات والنشر ،
١٩٨٠
ص ١٣٣ – ١٤٢

239

"Yawm al-Lablāb fī Qā'at al-
Ijtimā'āt" ["Ivy Day in the
Committee Room"]
in *Mawsū'at James Joyce:
Hayātuh wa Fannuh wa Dirāsāt li
A'mālih* [*A James Joyce
Encyclopaedia: His Life, Art, and
Works*]
Translated by Taha M. Taha
Kuwait, Wikālat al-Maṭbū'āt,
1975
pp. 139 – 56

«يوم اللبلاب في قاعة الاجتماعات»
في موسوعة جيمس جويس : حياته وفنّه
ودراسات لأعماله .
ترجمة : طه محمود طه
الكويت ، وكالة المطبوعات ، ١٩٧٥
ص ١٣٩ – ١٥٦

"al-Mawtā" ["The Dead"]
in *Sab'u Qiṣaṣ* [*Seven Stories*]
Translated by Amin Rufa'il
Revised by Yahya al-Hassab
Cairo, Maktabat al-Anglo al-
Miṣrīyyah, 1962
pp. 127 – 32

«الموتى»
في سبع قصص
ترجمة : أمين روفائيل
مراجعة : يحيىٰ الحسّاب
القاهرة ، مكتبة الأنجلو – المصريّة ، ١٩٦٢
ص ١٢٧ – ١٣٢

c) EXILES

"al-Manfiyyūn ["The Exiles"]
al-Masraḥ, No. 59
February 1969
Translated by Sami Khashabah
pp. 65 – 89

«المنفيّون»
في المسرح . عدد ٥٩
شباط – فبراير ١٩٦٩
ترجمة : سامي خشبة
ص ٦٥ – ٨٩

al-Manfiyyūn ["The Exiles"]
Translated by Sami Khashabah
Cairo, al-Hay'ah al-Miṣrīyyah al-
'Āmmah, 1980

المنفيّون
ترجمة : سامي خشبة
القاهرة ، الهيئة المصريّة العامّة ، ١٩٨٠

"Manfiyyūn" ["Exiles"]
in *Stephen D* (and) *Manfiyyūn*
Translated by Amin al-'Ayuti
Revised by Muhammad Ismail
al-Muwafi
Kuwait, Ministry of Information,
1973
pp. 135 – 355
("World Theatre" series No. 43,
published by the Ministry of
Information, Kuwait)

«منفيّون»
في ستيفن «د» [و] منفيّون
ترجمة : أمين العيّوطي
مراجعة : محمد إسماعيل الموافي
الكويت ، وزارة الإعلام ، ١٩٧٣
ص ١٥٣ – ٣٣٥
(في سلسلة شهرية «من المسرح العالمي» الصادرة عن
وزارة إعلام الكويت – الرقم ٤٣)

d) A PORTRAIT OF THE ARTIST AS A YOUNG MAN

*Ṣūrat al-Fannān fī Shabābih [A
Portrait of the Artist as a Young
Man]*
Translated by Maher Batuti
Beirut, Dār al-Ādāb, 1973

صورة الفنّان في شبابه
ترجمة : ماهر البطوطي
بيروت ، دار الآداب ، ١٩٧٣

e) ULYSSES

"Calypso" *
in *Mawsū'at James Joyce:
Hayātuh wa Fannuh wa Dirāsāt li
A'mālih [A James Joyce
Encyclopaedia: His Life, Art, and
Works]*
Translated by Taha M. Taha
Kuwait, Wikālat al-Maṭbū'āt,
1975
pp. 398 – 448

«كاليبسو»
في موسوعة جيمس جويس : حياته وفنّه
ودراسات لأعماله
ترجمة : طه محمود طه
الكويت ، وكالة المطبوعات ، ١٩٧٥
ص ٣٩٨ – ٤٤٨

---

* Originally translated under the title "45 Minutes of Blooms day: A Translation of Episode
4 ('Calypso')" with an introduction published in the Egyptian monthly *al-Kateb*, May 1964,
pp. 88 – 101 (a copy of this could not be examined by the editor).

"al-Matāhat al-Ṣughrā fī 'Olīs"
["The Lesser Labyrinth in
Ulysses:'The Wandering Rocks'"]
al-Majallah, No. 107
November 1965
Translated by Taha Mahmoud Taha
pp. 66 – 87

«المتاهة الصغرى في «عوليس ، [يوليسيس]»

في المجلّة ، عدد ١٠٧

تشرين ثان – نوفمبر ، ١٩٦٥

ترجمة : طه محمود طه

ص ٦٦ – ٨٧

"al-Ṣukhūr al-Ḍāllah" ["The
Wandering Rocks"]
in *Mawsū'at James Joyce:
Hayātuh wa Fannuh wa Dirāsāt li
A'mālih* [*A James Joyce
Encyclopaedia: His Life, Art, and
Works*]
Translated by Taha M. Taha
Kuwait, Wikālat al-Maṭbū'āt,
1975
pp. 297 – 314

«الصخور الضّالة»

في موسوعة جيمس جويس : حياته وفنّه
ودراسات لأعماله

ترجمة : طه محمود طه

الكويت ، وكالة المطبوعات ، ١٩٧٥

ص ٢٩٧ – ٣١٤

II. ORIGINAL ARABIC WRITING ON JAMES JOYCE DEALING WITH JOYCE'S WORKS IN WHOLE OR IN PART

'Awad, Louis
"James Joyce"
in *Fī al-Adab al-Inglīzī al-Ḥadīth*
[*On Modern English Literature*]
Cairo, Maktabat al-Anglo-
Miṣrīyyah, 1950
pp. 199 – 230

عوض ، لويس
«جيمس جويس»

في [دراسات] في الأدب الإنجليزيّ الحديث
القاهرة ، مكتبة الأنجلو – المصريّة ، ١٩٥٠

ص ١٩٩ – ٢٣٠

Habaisha, Huda
"James Joyce 'ala al-Masraḥ"
["James Joyce on the Stage"]
al-Majalla, No. 97
July 1963
pp. 95 – 96

حبيشه ، هدى
«جيمس جويس على المسرح»
في المجلّة ، عدد ٧٩
تمّوز – يوليه ١٩٦٣
ص ٩٥ – ٩٦

Haqqi, Badī'
"James Joyce: Rā'id al-Riwāyah
al-Ḥadīthah" ["James Joyce: The
Precursor of the Modern Novel"]
in *Qimam fī al-Adab al-'Ālamī:
Tolstoy, Joyce, Proust, Mallarmé,
Lorca* [*The Masters of World
Literature: Tolstoy, Joyce, Proust,
Mallarmé, Lorca*]
Damascus, Manshūrāt Ittiḥād al-
Kuttāb al-'Arab, 1973

حقّي ، بديع
«جيمس جويس : رائد الرواية الحديثة»
في قمم في الآداب العالمية : تولستوي ،
جويس ، يروست ، ماليرميه ، لوركا
دمشق ، منشورات اتحاد الكتّاب العرب ،
١٩٧٣

Ibrahim, 'Abdallah
'Awālim Joyce" ["The Worlds of
Joyce"]
al-Talī'ah al-Adabīyyah, Vol. VI,
No. 6
June 1980
pp. 26 – 31

إبراهيم ، عبد الله
«عوالم جويس»
في الطليعة الأدبيّة ، ج ٦ ، عدد ٦
حزيران – يونيه ١٩٨٠
ص ٢٦ – ٣١

Khashabah, Sami
"James Joyce: al-Hārib ām al-
Manfī" [James Joyce: Escapee or
Exile"]
al-Majallah, No. 157
January 1970
pp. 90 – 99

خشبة ، سامي
«جيمس جويس : الهارب أم المنفيّ»
في المجلّة ، عدد ١٥٧
كانون ثان – يناير ١٩٧٠
ص ٩٠ – ٩٩

243

al-Khatib, Hussam
*al-Adab al-Ūrubbī: Tāṭawwuruh
wa Nash'at Madhāhibih* [*European
Literature: Its Development and
the Origins of its Schools of
Thought*]
Damascus
[privately published?], 1972

الخطيب ، حُسام
الأدب الأوروبيّ : تطوره ونشأة مذاهبه
دمشق ، [نشر المؤلف] ، ١٩٧٢

Malhas, Ameen Faris
"James Joyce: Qimmat al-Qiṣṣah
al-Sīkolojīyyah al-Ḥadīthah"
["James Joyce: The Modern
Psychological Novel"]
Afkār, No. 21
November 1973
pp. 54 – 63

ملحس ، أمين فارس
«جيمس جويس : قمّة القصة السيكولوجيّة
الحديثة»
في أفكار ، عدد ٢١
تشرين ثان – نوفمبر ١٩٧٣
ص ٥٤ – ٦٣

al-Murani, Najiyyah
"Abṭāl min al-Madīnah al-
Mashlūlah" ["Heroes from the
Paralysed City"]
al-Aqlām, No. 12,
1976
pp. 40 – 50

الموراني ، نجيّة
«أبطال من المدينة المشلولة»
في الأقلام ، عدد ١٢
١٩٧٦
ص ٤٠ – ٥٠

al-Nahas, Hashim
"Bayn al-Binā' al-Riwā'ī wa al-
Binā' al-Filmī:al-Ḍa'i'Ulysses"
["Between the Novel Structure
and the Film Structure:Ulysses Lost"]
'Ālam al-Fikr
April/May/June 1975
pp. 256 – 57

النحّاس ، هاشم
«بين البناء الروائيّ والبناء الفيلميّ : الضائع
يوليسيس»
في عالم الفكر ،
نيسان – أبريل/ أيّار – مايو/ حزيران –
يونيه ، ١٩٧٥
ص ٢٥٦ – ٢٥٧

244

Sam'an, Angil Butrous
"James Joyce: Ṣūrat al-Fannān
shābban" ["James Joyce: A
Portrait of the Artist as a Young
Man"]
in *Bayn al-Riwā'ī wa al-Riwāyah:
Dirāsah Taṭbīqīyyah fī al-Riwāyah
al-Inglīzīyyah al-Ḥadīthah*
[*Between the Novelist and the
Novel: Studies in the Modern
English Novel*]
Cairo, Maktabat al-Anglo al-
Miṣrīyyah, 1972
pp. 235 – 76

سمعان ، انجيل بطرس
«جيمس جويس : صورة الفنان شابًا»
في بين الروائي والرواية : دراسة تطبيقية في
الرواية الانجليزية الحديثة
القاهرة ، مكتبة الانجلو – المصرية ، ١٩٧٢
ص ٢٣٥ – ٢٧٦

Taha, Taha Mahmoud
*Mawsū'at James Joyce: Hayātuh
wa Fannuh wa Dirāsāt li-A'mālih*
[*A James Joyce Encyclopaedia:
His Life, Art and Works*]
Kuwait, Wikālat al-Maṭbū'āt,
1975

طه ، طه محمود
موسوعة جيمس جويس : حياته وفنّه
ودراسات لأعماله
الكويت ، وكالة المطبوعات ، ١٩٧٥

Taha, Taha Mahmoud
*al-Qiṣṣa fī al-Adab al-inglīzī min
"Beowulf" ila "Finnegans Wake"*
[*The English Novel from "Beowulf"
to "Finnegans Wake"*],
Cairo, Hay'at al-Kitāb al-Miṣrī,
1966

طه ، طه محمود
القصّة في الأدب الأنجليزيّ من «بيولف» إلى
«فينيجانز ويك»
القاهرة ، هيئة الكتاب المصري ، ١٩٦٦

III. TRANSLATIONS OF CRITICAL WORKS DEALING WITH JAMES JOYCE IN WHOLE OR IN PART

Albérés, R.M.
[*Histoire du roman moderne*]
Translated as *Tārīkh al-Riwāyah
al-Ḥadīthah* by George Salem
Beirut, Manshūrāt 'Ouidāt, 1967

البيرس ، ر. م.
تاريخ الرواية الحديثة
ترجمة : جورج سالم
بيروت ، منشورات عويدات ، ١٩٦٧

Brennan, Joseph
[*Three Philosophical Novelists:
Joyce, Gide, Mann*]
Translated as *Thalāthah Ri-
wā'iyyīn Falsafiyyīn: Joyce, Gide,
Mann* by Hani al-Rahib
Damascus, Manshūrāt Wizārat al-
Thaqāfah, 1975

برنن ، جوزيف
ثلاثة روائيّين فلسفيّين : جويس ، جِيدْ ، مَان
ترجمة : هاني الراهب
دمشق ، منشورات وزارة الثقافة ، ١٩٧٥

Butor, Michel
[*Essais sur le roman*]
Translated as *Buhūth fī al-
Riwāyah al-Jadīdah* by Farid
Antonius
Beirut, Manshūrāt 'Ouidāt, 1971

بوتور ، ميشال
بحوث في الرواية الحديدة
ترجمة : فريد انطونيوس
بيروت ، منشورات عويدات ، ١٩٧١

Edel, Leon
[*The Psychological Novel: 1900 –
1950*]
Translated as *al-Qiṣṣah al-
Sīkolojīyyah: Dirāsah fī 'alāqat
'llm al-Nafs bi Fann al-Qiṣṣah* by
Mahmoud al-Samra
Beirut, al-Maṭba'ah al-Ahlīyyah
and Franklin (Beirut-New York),
1959

ايدال ، ليون
القصّة السيكولوجيّة : دراسة في علاقة علم
النفس بفنّ القصّة
ترجمة :. محمود السمرة
بيروت ، منشورات المكتبة الأهليّة بالاشتراك
مـع مؤسّسة فرنكلين للطبـاعـة والنشر
(بيروت – نيويورك) ، ١٩٥٩

Ellmann, Richard
"Ulysses"
Translated as *"Riwāyat Ulysses li
James Joyce"* by Faruq Hashem,
al-Ādāb al-Ajnabīyyah, No. 24
April 1979
pp. 204 – 35

إلمان ، ريتشارد
«رواية ' يوليسيس ' لجيمس جويس»
في الآداب الأجنبية ، عدد ٢٤
نيسان – أبريل ، ١٩٧٩
ترجمة : فاروق هاشم
ص ٢٠٤ – ٢٣٥

Gross, John
[*James Joyce*]
Translated as *James Joyce* by
Mujahid 'Abdul Mun'im
Beirut, al-Mu'assasah al-
'Arabīyyah li al- Dirāsāt wa al-
Nashr, 1975
("World Thinkers" series)

جروس ، جون
جيمس جويس
ترجمة : مجاهد عبد المنعم
بيروت ، المؤسّسة العربيّة للدراسات والنشر ،
١٩٧٥
(في سلسلة أعلام الفكر العالميّ)

Humphry, Robert
[*Stream of Consciousness in the
Modern Novel*]
Translated as *Tayyār al-Wa'y fī
al-Riwāyah al-Ḥadīthah*
by Mahmoud al-Rabi'i
Cairo, Dār al-Ma'āref, 1975

همفري ، روبرت
تيّار الوعي في الرواية الحديثة
ترجمة : محمود الربيعي
القاهرة ، دار المعارف ، ١٩٧٥

Kettle, Arnold
[*An Introduction to the English
Novel,* Vol. II]
Translated as *Madkhal ila al-
Riwāyah al-Inglīzīyyah* (al-
Mujallad al-Thānī) by Hani al-
Rahib
Damascus, Manshūrāt Wizārat al-
Thaqāfah, 1977

كيتل ، أرنولد
مدخل إلى الرواية الإنجليزيّة (المجلّد الثاني)
ترجمة : هاني الراهب
دمشق ، منشورات وزارة الثقافة ، ١٩٧٧

Levin, Harry
[*Refractions: Essays in
Comparative Literature*]
Translated as *Inkisārāt: Maqālah
fī al-Adab al-Muqāran* by 'Abdul
Karim Mahfouz
Damascus, Manshūrāt Wizārat al-
Thaqāfah, 1980

ليفن ، هاري
انكسارات : مقالة في الأدب المقارن
ترجمة : عبد الكريم محفوظ
دمشق ، منشورات وزارة الثقافة ، ١٩٧٠

Lukács, Georg
[*Studies in Realism*]
Translated as *Dirāsāt fī al-Wāqi'īyyah* by
Nayef Balluz
Damascus, Manshūrāt Wizārat al-Thaqāfah, 1970

لوكاش ، جورج
دراسات في الواقعية
ترجمة : نايف بلّوز
دمشق ، منشورات وزارة الثقافة ، ١٩٧٠

Lukács, Georg
[*The Meaning of Contemporary Realism*]
Translated as *Ma'nā al-Waqi'īyyah al-Mu'āṣirah* by Amin al-'Ayuti
Cairo, Dār al-Ma'āref, 1971
("Studies in Foreign Literatures" series)

لوكاش ، جورج
معنى الواقعيّة المعاصرة
ترجمة : أمين العيّوطي
القاهرة ، دار المعارف ، ١٩٧١
(في سلسلة «دراسات في الآداب الأجنبية»)

Meyerhoff, Hans [*Time in Literature*]
Translated as *al-Zamān fī al-Adab* by As'ad Razzouq
Revised by al-'Awadi al-Wakil
Cairo, Mu'assasat Sijill al-'Arab and Franklin (Cairo-New York), 1972

ميرهوف ، هانز
الزمن في الأدب
ترجمة : أسعد رزّوق
مراجعة : العوضي الوكيل
القاهرة ، مؤسّسة سجلّ العرب بالإشتراك مع مؤسّسة فرنكلين للطباعة والنشر (القاهرة – نيويورك) ، ١٩٨٢

Muir, Edwin
[*The Structure of the Novel*]
Translated as *Binā' al-Riwāyah* by Ibrahim al-Sayrafi
Revised by 'Abdul Qadir al-Qitt
Cairo, al-Mu'assasah al-Miṣrīyyah al-'Āmmah, 1965

ميُّور ، إدوين
بناء الرواية
ترجمة : ابراهيم الصيرفي
مراجعة : عبد القادر القطّ
القاهرة ، الموسوعة المصريّة العامّة ، ١٩٦٥

248

O'Connor, William Van
[*Forms of Modern Fiction*]
Translated as *Ashkāl al-Riwāyah
al-Ḥadīthah* by Najib al-Mani'
Baghdad, Wizārat al-I'lām wa al-
Thaqāfah, 1980

قان أكونور ، وليم
أشكال الرواية الحديثة : مجموعة مقالات
ترجمة : نجيب المانع
بغداد ، منشورات وزارة الإعلام والثقافة ،
١٩٨٠

Ricardou, Jean
[*Problèmes du nouveau roman*]
Translated as *Qāḍāyā al-Riwāyah
al-Ḥadīthah* by Sayyah al-
Juhayim
Damascus, Manshūrāt Wizārat al-
Thaqāfah, 1977

ريكاردو ، جين
قضايا الرواية الحديثة
ترجمة : صيّاح الجهيم
دمشق ، منشورات وزارة الثقافة ، ١٩٧٧

Robbe-Grillet, Alain
[*Pour un nouveau roman*]
Translated as *Nahwa Riwāyah
Jadīdah* by Mustafa Ibrahim
Mustafa
Cairo, Dār al-Ma'āref, n.d.

روب – غريليه ، ألان
نحو رواية جديدة
ترجمة : مصطفى ابراهيم مصطفى
القاهرة ، دار المعارف ، [بدون تاريخ]

Wilson, Edmund
[*Axel's Castle*]
Translated as *Qal'at Axel* by Jabra
Ibrahim Jabra
Baghdad, Manshūrāt Wizārat al-
I'lām wa al-Thaqāfah, 1976 (first
edition)
Beirut, al-Mu'assasah al-
'Arabīyyah li al-Dirāsāt wa al-
Nashr, 1979 (second edition)

ويلسون ، إدموند
قلعة أكسيل
ترجمة : جبرا ابراهيم جبرا
بغداد ، منشورات وزارة الإعلام والثقافة ،
١٩٧٦ (الطبعة الأولى)
بيروت ، المؤسّسة العربيّة للدراسات والنشر ،
١٩٧٩ (الطبعة الثانية)

Phototypesetting on pp. 238–49 by Graphic Arts Services, Hassib Derghan
and Sons – Phone 327870 – Beirut, Lebanon

FOLLOWING ARIADNE'S STRING: TRACING JOYCE SCHOLARSHIP INTO THE EIGHTIES

THOMAS F. STALEY

Writing in August of 1981, on the eve as it were of the centennial of Joyce's birth, I am attempting in this essay to discuss the most recent work in Joyce studies. This discussion is the second part of my essay on Joyce research published by the Modern Language Association of America in *Anglo-Irish Literature: A Review of Research* in 1976 which covered Joyce scholarship through 1974. This essay also incorporates my contribution to the supplement to that volume, but while it duplicates in part that supplement, it extends the coverage beyond it and eliminates, adds, and changes it, taking more liberties with imbalance to follow directions, trends, and wider issues.

During the later seventies and the first couple of years of the eighties, we can observe several important trends, the most important being the broadening of the critical outlook and theoretical approach in Joyce studies. Recent criticism has become more sensitive, for the most part, to the contemporary literary, and to the intellectual and historical context in which Joyce wrote. There are both good and bad examples of this development. Although it will be pointed out in this survey that the most important work published in Joyce studies since my last survey has been in the area of textual studies, lexicons, and other reference works, recent criticism has begun to reflect the central currents and conflicts in the theoretical study of literature. If those dozen or so years after the second World War deserve to be called the 'Age of Criticism', certainly this past decade is equally deserving of the title, 'The Age of Theory', or of some equally appropriate label. These developments, in spite of the constant reference to texts, have not generally drawn readers to particular or individual texts in the way that the New Criticism did, but the influence of these theoretical activities has been felt in recent Joyce criticism.

Before considering Joyce criticism, however, it is important to note that the major publishing event in Joyce studies is the completion of the publication of *The James Joyce Archive*. An introduction to this indispensable archive of Joyce's manuscripts is given in Michael Groden's *James Joyce's Manuscripts, An Index* (1980). Groden's volume provides a comprehensive index to the sixty-three-volume archive as well as the most complete check-list of all extant manuscripts, typescripts, and proofs. Groden also includes an index to the various library collections that hold Joyce manuscript material. The *Archive* itself, printed on acid-free paper, publishes in facsimile all extant and available notes, drafts, manuscripts, typescripts, and proofs – Joyce's entire 'workshop'. (Letters are not included.) Each *Archive* volume contains a preface by one of the editors, and collectively the *Archive* reproduces some 25,000 pages of original documents from all of the known Joyce collections. Michael Groden is general editor of the project and associate editors are Hans Walter Gabler, David Hayman, A. Walton Litz, and Danis Rose. The *Archive* is an invaluable aid to Joyce scholars, for it brings together in one place the widely and erratically dispersed pre-publication materials, but as the editor cautions in his 'General Introduction': 'It must be recognized . . . that these volumes are only reproductions, and a scholar would be irresponsible to rely exclusively on them.' And this caution is true enough for those engaged in textual studies, but for students, teachers, and critics the *Archive* can be an enormous aid. One minor disappointment is that the volumes are not numbered on the spine or anywhere else in each volume, but this is merely a small quibble with such an important contribution to Joyce studies. The *Archive* is a massive and unique enterprise; it makes available to scholars a body of material that will in the coming years have a profound effect on Joyce studies. It is far too early to assess all of the ramifications of this publication, but it is safe to predict its central importance to Joyce scholarship.

Much space was devoted in my earlier essay to the complex problem of Joyce's texts, and the past few years have seen important developments in this area of study, especially with regard to the most troublesome text, *Ulysses*. Hans Walter Gabler, with the help of the latest computer technology, is currently preparing a critical edition of *Ulysses* that promises to be definitive. The constituent parts of Gabler's edition will be: 'an authoritative reading text, and the critical apparatus as divided between a synopsis of the episodes (each of the eighteen), textual genesis (the synoptic text) and appended apparatus.' This quotation is from the preface of a 'Prototype of a critical edition in progress' (München, 1979). This prototype is a trial edition of the eighth episode of *Ulysses*, 'Lestrygonians'; this is not for sale and intended only for the use of Joyce scholars who might aid or comment upon the procedures. A thorough discussion of the textual problems with *Ulysses* and comment on Gabler's work appears in an essay by Hugh Kenner, 'The Computerized *Ulysses*', *Harper's* (April, 1980). Another essay on the subject by Michael Groden appears in *Scholarly Publishing* (1980). The edition will evidently offer interesting and innovative ways of presenting a corrected text which will at the same time be easily readable, along with the necessary apparatus. The specimen edition offers assurance that we will soon have a definitive one that will approximate what Joyce ideally intended.

An elaborate and expensive undertaking has been the publication in 1975 of the facsimile of the manuscript titled *James Joyce's Ulysses*, now reposited at the Rosenbach Foundation of Philadelphia. The entire enterprise consists of three boxed volumes, two of which are the faces of the manuscript and the third a reduced face of the first edition, 'marked to show the differences between it, the serial instalments as published in *The Little Review*, and the manuscript'. For further discussion of this text and other bibliographical questions see my essay in the *Supplement to Anglo-Irish Literature: A Review of the Research*.

Michael Groden's *'Ulysses' in Progress* (1977) is an excellent and detailed account of how *Ulysses* came to be *Ulysses*. Groden traces with impeccable care the process of composition, and examines in detail how Joyce wrote the book in three major stages rather than two. As Groden notes in his introduction, 'one major aspect of *Ulysses* that has remained obscure is its complicated and bizarre prepublication history'. Since Groden's study the manuscript history of *Ulysses* remains 'bizarre' but no longer 'obscure'. In some instances Groden had to work with as many as thirteen different stages of development. His study, with its intelligent if not definitively established speculation, is a clear and insightful account of an incredibly complex process.

Phillip Herring's important textual studies continue with the publication of *Joyce's Notes and Early Drafts for 'Ulysses': Selections from the Buffalo Collection* (1977). Herring's edition provides a reliable transcription of notebooks VIII.A.5 and V.A.2, and also the early manuscripts of 'Cyclops' and 'Circe'. The inclusion of the notebooks now gives scholars printed access to all the extant notes for *Ulysses*. Herring's work is scrupulous in the rendering of the text, his introductions are illuminating, and his editorial apparatus sound and consistent.

Gabler, Herring, and Groden have made and are making truly significant contributions to Joyce scholarship. Their work has at last shown us the shape and proportions of the genetive process of *Ulysses*, and the diligence and precision of their work is inspiring. Another contribution to textural scholarship is *James Joyce's The Index Manuscript 'Finnegans Wake' Holograph Workbook VI. B. 46*, (Colchester, 1978), transcribed, annotated, and with an introduction by Danis Rose. This workbook (now at Buffalo) was compiled by Joyce in 1938 as the 'work in progress' was nearing its conclusion. The complicated nature of this text and the way in which its parts were used and incorporated into *Finnegans Wake* are carefully elucidated by Rose. Rose demonstrates the importance of this notebook and others by showing that they act as textual witness to the first stage in the genetic process. More important, as Rose indicates, 'the method of their compilation and the manner in which they were used in the composition of the final text lead one to certain conclusions regarding the basic structure of *FW*.' From the evidence gleaned from Rose's study, he is able to draw several hypotheses related not only to the composition but the basic structure of *FW*.

The most sophisticated and extensive concordance ever done in Joyce studies in Wilhelm Füger's *Concordance to James Joyce's 'Dubliners'* (Hildesheim – New York, 1980). Füger's work includes a comprehensive concordance organized in the form of the key word within a context of 120 characters, keyed to the Viking Compass Edition with conversion tables to the Penguin and Cape edition. There is also a 'reverse index' in which the words are listed according to the alphabetical order that results from reading them backwards, a principle of arrangement used in traditional rhyming dictionaries. Such an arrangement facilitates the analysis of the microstructure of the text's vocabulary. A third part of this massive volume is a frequency list that comprises five columns per entry and gives additional data. For example, the word 'like' appears 131 times, holds the 60th rank of frequency, and has a relative frequency of 0.1939%. The user of this concordance will find even further refinements. Fuger's concordance offers an excellent example of how the computer can be brought to the service of literary studies. Once the text of *Ulysses* is established one can hope that Füger will do the concordance.

Two textual works on *Exiles* have been published by Garland. John MacNicholas's *James Joyce's 'Exiles': A Textual Companion* (1979) appraises the sources, text, and extant manuscripts of the play. MacNicholas's work fulfils his purpose in every way, which was 'to provide the reader with comprehensive information concerning the genesis, composition, and final authorial intent'. Besides establishing a critical text of *Exiles*, MacNicholas also devotes two chapters of his volume to the historical background of the play's genesis and its chronology of composition and publication. Of special interest is what MacNicholas's study of the manuscripts reveals of the evolution of Bertha from a meek to an enormously strong character in the final manuscript. This is a thorough and intelligent work, and the most important and comprehensive work to appear on *Exiles*. Ruth Bauerle's *A Word List to James Joyce's 'Exiles'* (1981) is based on the Penguin text of *Exiles*, the one most widely available. Joyce's important notes to the play have also been indexed. Departures from the Penguin text established by MacNicholas in his study have been incorporated, and alternate frequency counts are indicated where omissions or additions established by MacNicholas affect the count of a word.

The developments in Joyce criticism are perhaps more vividly reflected in essays in the scholarly journals than in the many books that have been published. And while I believe the books are more influential, they only tell part of the story. The specialized journals in Joyce studies remain indispensable.

The *James Joyce Quarterly* and *A Wake Newslitter*, the latter after a brief hiatus, continue to be the major periodical forums for Joyce studies. These are supplemented by the *James Joyce Foundation Newsletter*, which publishes news and announcements, and lists many current publications. Morris Beja and Fritz Senn have taken over the editorship from the founding editor, Bernard Benstock. The *Newsletter* is the official publication of the James Joyce Foundation, which is governed by an international board of Joyce scholars and sponsors biannual Joyce Symposia.

A new publication, *The James Joyce Broadsheet*, begun in 1979, is published from the James Joyce Centre, University College, London. Edited by Alison Armstrong, Pieter Bekker, and Richard Brown, a typical issue publishes one article, current book reviews and critical surveys, news of Joycean events, especially activities of the various European Joyce societies, and a notes and queries section. The first four issues are extremely promising. For example,

Number 2 (May 1980) features a review essay by Colin MacCabe, 'Joyce and Chomsky: The Body and Language'. The fourth number features an article by Giorgio Melchiori, 'The Language of Politics and the Politics of Language', and contains five reviews of current Joyce books, including a thorough review by Seamus Deane of Manganiello's *Joyce's Politics*. The layout of the issues thus far is very good and the writing lively and informed. Properly, the paper covers the European scene very well and is a welcome addition to Joyce publications.

A two-volume edition, one in French and one in English, *Joyce & Paris 1902 . . . 1920–1940 . . . 1975* (Paris, 1979), edited by Jacques Aubert and Maria Jolas, brings together selected papers from the Fifth International James Joyce Symposium held in Paris 16–20 June 1975, though many of the items are merely summaries of the papers that were delivered. The two volumes form an interesting contrast in approach as well as subject matter. The French volume, featuring the talks and remarks of Jacques Lacan, Michel Butor, Philippe Sollers, Nathalie Sarraute, and other French authors and critics, seems remote from the more traditional American concerns in the English volume. But that was 1975. By 1979, at the Zürich Symposium the critical approaches and theoretical concerns of the American and European participants had much more in common. This new balance reflects the shifting concerns in Joyce criticism mentioned earlier. This is not to say that Joyce studies have been taken over by the structuralist, post-structuralist, and deconstructionist camps, but Joyce criticism in the latter half of the seventies has obviously come under the influence of the theoretical developments in Europe, mainly France, for the past fifteen years; this is especially true in the work of a number of younger American critics. The work on Joyce by Umberto Eco, Hélène Cixous, Philippe Sollers and others, however, predates these more recent developments.

The Fall '78/Winter '79 issue of *JJQ* (a special 'Structuralist/ Reader Response Issue') provides further evidence of these developments in Joyce criticism. Featuring articles such as Jean Ricardou's 'Time of the Narration, Time of the Fiction', Jennifer Levine's survey of Joyce criticism in *Tel Quel,* Robert Scholes's 'Semiotic Approaches to a Fictional Text', and Herbert Schneidau's 'One Eye and Two Levels: On Joyce's "Cyclops" ', among a dozen articles, this issue gives a fairly broad example of shifting theoretical and critical concerns in Joyce studies.

A recent issue of *JJQ* (Spring '81) featured more explicitly contemporary interest in critical theory and practice, especially with reference to the nature of narrative. The issue published a summary of the MURGE project at Miami University, where a research group interested in Seymour Chatman's *Story and Discourse* applied many of his ideas and those of other contemporary theorists to 'Araby'. In the same issue James Sosnoski amplified the group's work and Gerald Prince, Jonathan Culler, and Seymour Chatman himself responded. As Chatman concludes in his detailed response, 'it is indeed rare that an author has an opportunity to meet a conscientious readership in so open and frank a discussion.' Such opportunities are indeed rare in scholarship and this fact is to our own impoverishment. What we have here is not some sycophantic, crypto-Franco-structuralist enterprise, but a serious engagement with narrative problems looked at from a fresh point of view. The former, however, is not absent from Joyce studies. The work in this entire issue, however, reflects the assimilation of many theoretical concerns into Joyce criticism as we move into the eighties.

While these trends are important and will be discussed further, they do not dominate Joyce studies, for the majority of the criticism continues to stem from more traditional scholarship and criticism. Psychoanalytic criticism, for example, is featured in a special issue of *JJQ* (1976), guest edited by Mark Shechner. The articles in this issue and in a later supplement (1977) represent refutations, revisions of former positions (see Darcy O'Brien's 'A Critique of Psychoanalytic Criticism'), and energetic new formulations. Shechner provides a selected check-list of psychoanalytic studies on Joyce, a useful starting point for further study on the subject.

A special two-number Joyce issue of *Modern British Literature* (1980) contains nine essays by such critics as Fritz Senn, Bernard Benstock, Thomas F. Staley, and Zack Bowen. It also includes essays by Joseph Kestner, 'Joyce, Wagner and Bizet: *Exiles*, Tannhauser, and Carmen'; by Michael Groden, 'James Joyce and the Classical, Romantic, and Modern Tempers'; and by Brook Thomas, 'Reading, Writing, and Joyce's Dublin'. This volume is also published in the *Modern British Literature* Monograph Series as Number Two under the title *James Joyce: New Glances* (1980) edited by Edward A. Kopper, Jr., the founding editor of *MBL*.

Phoebus (1980), a journal published by the Department of English of Chung-Ang University in Seoul, Korea, published a special Joyce number in English under the editorship of Chong-Keon Kim.

It includes essays by John P. Daly, S.J. and Thomas F. Staley, as well as three essays by Korean scholars, and an appendix offering a 'Korean' Version of *Pomes Penyeach*' by Chung-Ho Chung. Korean interest in Joyce continues to be lively.

Poétique 26 (1976) is a special issue on *Finnegans Wake*, edited by Hélène Cixous, and *Crane Bag* 2 (1978) has a large section on Joyce with essays by Vivian Mercier and Bernard Benstock, among others. The *Irish Renaissance Annual*, II (1981), edited by Zack Bowen, is an all-Joyce issue offering six more traditional essays on *Ulysses, Portrait*, and *Dubliners*.

There have been well over 600 essays of widely varying importance dealing with some aspect of Joyce's canon published over the past ten years. Space obviously does not permit even minimal discussion of any but a few of these; therefore, the remainder of this essay will concentrate on the critical books that have been published on Joyce from 1974 or 1975 to the present.

The most important general and comprehensive study of Joyce's work to be published in recent years is C.H. Peake's *James Joyce: The Citizen and the Artist* (1977). One could say that Peake's study looks backward rather than forward, that is assimilates rather than innovates, but such a view would be superficial; the book offers far more than its unpromising title suggests. Peake's commentaries on *Dubliners* and *A Portrait* are sound and frequently richly suggestive, but it is his work on *Ulysses* that is especially praiseworthy. His sections on 'Nestor', 'Proteus', 'Aeolus', and 'Cyclops' are of particular value for their close and revealing analyses of the text. Peake's emphasis on the political themes is illuminating in his treatment of 'Aeolus' and 'Cyclops', and especially informative and original regarding the function of the interpolations in 'Cyclops'. Peake is a careful reader who knows the previous scholarship very well and does not bore us with half a hundred details that are already known. For example, his treatment of the 'Aeolus' episode with its emphasis, not on the rhetorical forms but on the three specimens of oratory – those of Dan Dawson, Seymour Bushe, and John F. Taylor – alters the reading which previous criticism had stressed. These three speeches, 'epideictic, forensic, and deliberative respectively', are, according to Peake, what really underlie the rhetorical basis of the episode and not the rhetorical forms stressed by Stuart Gilbert. As Peake points out, all the forms which Gilbert stresses in 'Aeolus' can be found nearly as frequently in the other chapters. His discussion of Stephen's 'parable of the plums' is quite illuminating. He examines its nature and function, why it is called a 'Pisgah Sight of Palestine', and stresses the parable's relationship to the themes of the episode and the novel as a whole, especially in relation to Stephen's problems and ambition. Peake's entire book is filled with insights and carefully developed arguments that alter and expand one's understanding of many passages and even substantial themes in *Ulysses*. Peake's study is rare in that it serves both as a fine introduction for the general reader and a valuable book for the specialist as well. Dominic Manganiello's book, *Joyce's Politics* (1980), is much more directly concerned with Joyce's political thinking as it is reflected in his life and works. It is a thorough and interesting study that brings much new material to light, especially the political aspects of Joyce's work that were informed by continental sources and events. Manganiello's study, with its convincing concentration on political matters that surrounded and interested Joyce, blunts some of the easy assumptions in Joyce criticism that Joyce cared little for politics or political theory unless it was Irish. Manganiello is extremely well informed in political thought and the extent and ways in which Joyce absorbed these ideas, and he is convincing in his analyses of Joyce's eclectic assimilation and demonstration of political thought in his work.

This period has seen the publication of two books by Hugh Kenner, *Joyce's Voices* (1978), and *Ulysses* (1980); the latter will be treated with studies of *Ulysses*. Many regard Kenner's work as the most important criticism being written on Joyce today. His concerns from his first book, *Dublin's Joyce* (1956), have lain at the centre of Joyce studies, and most serious Joyce scholarship on *Ulysses* has had to come to terms with his work. *Joyce's Voices* (1978) is a study of a little over 100 pages and comes out of Kenner's four T.S. Eliot Memorial Lectures delivered in 1975 at the University of Kent. The first chapter is inspired in part by the setting of Kenner's lecture and the subject whom they memorialize. Drawing initially on Eliot's essay, '*Ulysses*, Order and Myth', Kenner focuses on objectivity and its effect on Joyce's language. In Joyce's work the fictional event is inseparable from its linguistic manifestation. Kenner uses the early story 'Grace' as an example of how Joyce worked with the resources of language. The second chapter coins a phrase that has already become a standard term in Joyce criticism: 'The Uncle Charles Principle'. This is a small instance of general truth about Joyce's method, that his fictions tend not to have a detached narrator though they seem to have. His words are in delicate equilibrium, like the components of a sensitive piece of apparatus, in that they detect the gravitational field of the nearest person. One reason the quiet little stories in *Dubliners* continue to fascinate is that the narrative point of view unobtrusively fluctuates. The illusion of dispassionate portrayal seems attended by an iridescence difficult to account for until we notice one person's sense of things inconspicuously giving place to another's. This is a developed principle, but it has some relation to what Ellmann once called 'the blurred margin technique'.

The two remaining chapters in *Joyce's Voices* also focus on Joyce's use of language and the varying voices that give energy and dimension to his texts. The growing interest in narratology in contemporary criticism brings increasing attention to Kenner's seminal studies, but this is only one reason for the central position of his work in Joyce studies. The originality of his insights, the thoroughness of his arguments, and his mastery of the entire modern period lie at the heart of his influence.

Two books on Joyce's Irish background are John Garvin's eccentric *James Joyce's Disunited Kingdom* (1976) and Bernard Benstock's thorough and reliable *James Joyce: The Undiscover'd Country* (1977). Garvin's contention is that *Ulysses* and *Finnegans Wake* are based on Irish history, folklore, and legend, and are deeply rooted in Irish culture generally, a view that has certainly not escaped earlier critics. From this position, however, Garvin makes many curious and sundry observations, some arcane and interesting, others unformulated, random, and remote. The book is unsystematic and frequently bizarre in its interpretations, but it is not without value. Garvin knows a great deal about Dublin, especially nineteenth-century bureaucracy, and can capture the milieu in which Joyce spent his youth. Benstock's study is very different. He is a thorough and knowledgeable guide through the intricate and complex political and social history that forms so much of the background of Joyce's work. Joyce used Ireland in nearly every way a writer can use his native country, and his fundamental love/hate relation is deeply, and, in a way, hopelessly complex. Benstock holds and convincingly argues that ultimately Joyce rejected Ireland, and made his commitment to the larger European literary tradition, but in arguing his position Benstock treats the full complex of Irish cultural and political thought that bears so heavily on Joyce's work. A work that may be of slight interest in this context is Leo Daly's *Titles* (Mullingar, Ireland, 1981) which features an essay, 'James Joyce in the Cloak of St. Patrick', with some Irish lore. Daly's earlier work, *James Joyce and the Mullinger Connection* (Dublin, 1973), is a handsome, illustrated volume published by the Dolmen Press and is of much more interest.

Leo Knuth's *The Wink of the Word* (Amsterdam, 1976) is a study of ingenuity and perception dealing with Joyce's phatic communication. Knuth's opening chapters present a close argument for linking Joyce the man and artist to his work; he concentrates on the formation of Joyce's thought, and stresses the necessity of more open models in reading Joyce's work, arguing against the restrictive and narrow generic model S.L. Goldberg used in *The Classical Temper*. His later chapters trace Joyce's movement from realist to multivalent writer. The value of Knuth's tracery lies particularly in his rigorous analysis of selective passages and sections, such as his treatment of 'Wandering Rocks'. This is a difficult book to summarize and several of Knuth's larger contentions elude me, but his commentary on motifs, words, and even letter arrangements is engrossing, and his analysis of Shem's riddle in *Finnegans Wake* is highly original.

Another European study is Carla Marengo Vaglio's *Invitio alla lettura di Joyce* (Milan, 1977), which is the best introductory study of Joyce to appear in Italy. It provides a full chronology of Joyce's life and work, discussions of all of the works and a good bibliography. Of less interest is Dolf Sorensen's *James Joyce's Aesthetic Theory* (Amsterdam, 1977), which proposes to treat the development and application of Joyce's aesthetic theories. Jacques Aubert's important book on the subject, *Introduction à l'esthétique de James Joyce* (1973), is not even mentioned in the bibliography, and that Joyce drew on Vico and Bruno is commonplace. Manto Aravantinou's *Ta Hellenika ou Tzaiems Tzoys (The Greek of James Joyce*, Athens, 1977) not only accounts for Joyce's use of Greek, but also notes Joyce's Greek friends and his interest in modern Greek generally. This work, meant for Greek readers, is remote from Joyce studies and is not carefully documented. See M. Byron Raizis's review in *JJQ* (1979).

Barbara Reich Gluck's *Beckett and Joyce: Friendship and Fiction* (1979) traces the complex relationship between Joyce and Beckett and the influence of the former on the latter. Kenner, Hayman, and Melvin Friedman have all written well on this subject, and Gluck has herself discovered some interesting parallels between Joyce and Beckett. She is especially informative in her treatment of Beckett's

Trilogy, where she is able to demonstrate how Beckett uses themes of circularity, recurrence, and time in ways similar to Joyce. We know more of Beckett's close contact with Joyce from 1928 to 1932 since Deirdre Bair's biography, whatever its limitations, but Gluck slights and even ignores some of the revelations in Bair's book. There is a great deal in Gluck's book, but there are many aspects of this complicated relationship, both literary and human, still to be unravelled.

Breon Mitchell's distinguished Oxford dissertation on Joyce's influence on the German novel was mentioned in the 1976 essay, and it has subsequently been published as *James Joyce and the German Novel, 1922–1933* (1976). Mitchell's volume is a careful and judicious comparative study that traces influence during an important period of development in the German novel.

Mary T. Reynold's long awaited *Joyce and Dante* (1981) fulfils the promise of her earlier essays on the subject. Her study reveals the presence of Dante in Joyce's work not only as a major influence, but, as her sub-title indicates, the central figure in the shaping of Joyce's imagination. She shows this not only in his life but in the way in which Dante's presence is manifest in all of Joyce's works, and 'influence' as a word is too weak to describe the force of Dante's work on Joyce. He was consumed by Dante, and Reynolds' fine study makes this fact reasonable and clear in a most thorough and precise way.

Another work that deals in large part with Joyce's Italian influences and affinities, especially D'Annunzio, is Jackson I. Cope's *Joyce's Cities* (1981). Cope clearly acknowledges Joyce as the supreme modernist, but he insists that he 'planted his fictions firmly in the novelistic traditions of his great predecessors.' Cope stresses throughout his study the metaphorical influences on Joyce that gave fire to his vision of Dublin as the modern metropolis of the dead. Cope is especially revealing in his discussion of D'Annunzio's influence on *A Portrait*, especially on its evolution from *Stephen Hero*, and in his suggestions of the influence of Jewish lore on *Ulysses* and the Egyptian *Book of the Dead* on *Finnegans Wake*.

Matthew Hodgart's *James Joyce, A Student's Guide* (1978) is a rather ample introduction, but it is idiosyncratic, occasionally inaccurate, and often arch. Kenneth Grose has also written an introductory study, *James Joyce* (1975), in the Evan Brothers Ltd. 'Literature in Perspective Series', and Peter Costello has written a brief biographical introduction, *James Joyce* (Dublin, 1980) in Gill and

Macmillan's 'Irish Lives' series. Costello has also completed another work on Joyce, *Leopold Bloom, A Biography*, which has been announced by the publisher for fall of 1981. There are four essays on Joyce in *Yeats, Joyce and Beckett* (1976), edited by Kathleen McGrory and John Unterecker, a volume dedicated to William York Tindall. Besides the essays, a selection of Tindall's fine photographs of the Joyce landscape is included. The essays by Raymond J. Porter on Joyce's Irishness and by Margaret Solomon and Nathan Halper are all quite strong. Bernard Benstock's essay, 'The James Joyce Industry: A Reassessment', is a thorough, informative and often witty discussion of recent Joyce criticism. There is also a valuable interview with Joyce's close friend from Zurich, the late Carola Giedion-Welker.

The interesting work of Robert M. Adams continues with his latest study, *AfterJoyce: Studies in Fiction After Ulysses* (1977). Among many other observations, Adams suggests a few of the contemporary reasons for the continued intense study of *Ulysses*:

> The book is infinitely more complex now than it was in 1922. Partly this is because the sort of questions we ask about it have been changed by our experience of other art-forms, other novelists – not excluding those whom Joyce himself influenced. The very shape and tempo of life as we experience it have changed, underlining some new patterns in the arabesque and erasing others. Out of this arrangement of emerging and retreating images, there is hardly any way to make a sequential history.

Adams curiously omits consideration of *Finnegans Wake* in his study; perhaps, curiously, he is convinced *Ulysses* had little influence on Joyce's last work.

Richard Ellmann's *The Consciousness of Joyce* (1977) is in part an outgrowth of his earlier *Ulysses on the Liffey*. In this work he tries 'to measure Joyce's response to his principal sources'. As noted earlier, Ellmann includes a listing of Joyce's Trieste library in 1920. Almost none of the books in this collection are annotated; there are a few markings, but they are not sufficient to gather any direct response from Joyce to the works that made up his working library during his years in Trieste. Ellmann is obviously at home with *Ulysses* and he ponders the way in which Joyce interwove and reacted to many of the works he valued, finally moving on to a chapter on Joyce and politics. There is little that is really conclusive in Ellmann's study, and it moves without the force that marked his earlier work.

An extremely valuable reference work published during this period is Shari and Bernard Benstock's *Who's He When He's at Home, A James Joyce Directory* (1980). The Directory includes over 3,000 personages who appear in Joyce's work, mythical, fictional, legendary, historical, and anonymous. All Joyce's work is included except *Finnegans Wake*, which is covered by Adaline Glasheen's *Third Census of Finnegans Wake* (1977), which will subsequently be discussed. Presented in a clear format with carefully prepared introductions, this reference work has many uses. So far I have not detected any omissions, even to the 'singing cake of soap' in 'Circe'. The introduction is also of great value, for the Benstocks discuss the use of names and particular problems associated with each work and episode by episode in *Ulysses*. They also provide appendices on 'The Joycean Method of Cataloguing' and on 'Molly's Masculine Pronouns'. This is a work of careful scholarship and great industry, and is of lasting value to Joyce studies.

As noted earlier, psychoanalytic interest in Joyce continues; evidence can be seen with the publication of Sheldon Brivic's thorough study, *Joyce Between Freud and Jung* (1980). Brivic investigates all of Joyce's work from the psychoanalytic point of view and attempts to trace Joyce's mental process through his works. The developments in psychoanalytic thought, such as the thinking of Klein, Lacan, and Winnicott, are recognized by Brivic, if not exploited. Brivic's study is not rigid and narrow, but expansive and flexible, his methodology eclectic, and he brings much psychological insight to the Joyce canon. Brivic examines A *Portrait* from a Freudian perspective, then goes on to connect the unconscious determinants of Joyce's personality to his sense of meaning and value (Brivic would say 'system'), and he concludes his study with an examination of Joyce's mythology. The prose in his work is frequently dense and a bit unrelieved, but it is a solid, knowledgeable, and well-informed work.

Joyce's texts are as self-conscious as any found in modern literature; the reader is constantly being made aware that he is in a language field wherever the text may point. Colin MacCabe's energetic and original study, *James Joyce and the Revolution of the Word* (1978), comes out of the context of structuralism, Freud, Marx, and Lacan, and gives new attention to Joyce's use of language and our practice of reading him. There are implications and exten-

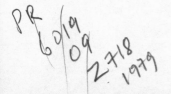

sions to MacCabe's thesis, especially political ones, that seem to push Joyce into political corners, but MacCabe's fresh examination of Joyce's work and the questions it raises about the relation between reader and text are critically important.

The enormous interest in narrative theory in recent years has brought a number of theoreticians to Joyce's text. Such critics as Wolfgang Iser in *The Implied Reader* (1974) and Dorrit Cohn in *Transparent Minds* (1978) have both dealt with *Ulysses* at length. Iser devotes two chapters of his book to *Ulysses*. Iser's concentration is reader-oriented, his orientation is phenomenological, and theoretically his work seems to fall between Stanley Fish and Norman Holland. Rather than adopt Holland's 'transactive' relationship or Fish's theory of interpretative strategies or 'affective stylistics', Iser sees an interaction between reader and text. Holland assumes an at least partially stable text, but for Iser the text is primarily indeterminate. This indeterminacy is reflected in his view of *Ulysses*:

> Herein lies the main difference between *Ulysses* and the tradition of the novel. Instead of providing an illusory coherence of the reality it presents, this novel offers only a potential presentation, the working out of which has to be done actively by the reader. He is not led into a ready-made world of meaning, but is made to search for this world.

Dorrit Cohn analyses the confessional scene in *A Portrait* and illustrates various narrative methods in *Ulysses*, concentrating on Molly's monologue. She is concerned with such methods as *style indirect libre* or *erlebte Rede*. This device is the presentation of characters' throughts in the third person and the past tense, a device usually used for present external actions and scenes in narrative. Cohn takes issue with Erwin Steinberg's study, *The Stream of Consciousness and Beyond in 'Ulysses'* (1973), among others. She is especially critical of Steinberg's view that Bloom's and Stephen's monologues are like prespeech speeches made of preverbal words. She notes that

> these contradictions pervade Erwin Steinberg's recent study of the 'stream-of-consciousness technique' in *Ulysses*. Since Steinberg conceives of this technique as a 'simulation' of pre- or non-verbal psychic phenomena, he understands the words of a

264

typical Bloomian monologue as 'symbolic printed analogues of Bloom's visceral sensations', rather than as direct quotations of Bloom's internal language. His non-verbal conception of the stream of consciousness, in other words, blinds him to Joyce's primary purpose in choosing the quoted-monologue technique over the other available techniques for depicting the inner life, namely to record his characters' *verbal* responses to their experience.

Cohn is primarily concerned with a theoretical framework; however, her observations on *Ulysses* are challenging, but one is uncertain just how specifically helpful they are with Joyce's texts. The issues to be raised with Cohn are in her theoretical models, which would require extensive argument. See John Paul Riquelme's review essay in *CLS* (1980), for one such argument.

It is interesting and even fruitful, if in the end perhaps too neat and too simple, to view the evaluation of the criticism of *Ulysses* as A. Walton Litz does, seeing it established by Pound and Eliot. Pound, Litz notes (*TLS* Dec. 12, 1980, and earlier and in more detail in *Ulysses: Fifty Years*, ed. Staley, 1974), saw *Ulysses* as the supreme achievement in English of the realist tradition that began with Flaubert. Eliot saw *Ulysses* in another light, looking upon it as the triumph of the mythic, symbolic, and ironic, a work, however, that even Eliot saw as ultimately a mimetic performance because it gave 'shape' and 'significance to the immense panorama of futility and anarchy' of the modern world. More recent *Ulysses* criticism is cast in much narrower terms, but yet it has begun to move outside these two poles which were of crucial importance to the modernist critic.

The question of Joyce's relation to Catholicism has been a persistent and important, if not a majory interest in Joyce scholarship. Robert Boyle's study, *James Joyce's Pauline Vision* (1978), is the best work on this subject to date. To see, as many have, Joyce's relationship with the Catholic Church as a great struggle for freedom from the oppressive Catholicism of his childhood and adolescence, and his work as a vindictive chronicle of his attempts to escape, is reductive and absurd, reduces Joyce's art to the level of personal animus, and ignores the depth and richness of Joyce's texts. Such a view has in the past also equated Stephen Dedalus's pronouncements with those of Joyce, failing to account for the transformation into language, to say nothing of the extra-textual evidence that separates Joyce from his creations. It is equally absurd to construct an elaborate apologetic view that Joyce never really escaped the Church's hold on him and longed to be at least spiritually reconciled. Joyce's mind and personality were such that no orthodoxy, no single world view could contain him. He saw truth in fragments and pieces of everything from Boehme, Vico, and the occult, to Aristotle, Aquinas, and Dante. Boyle has attempted to deal with Joyce's affinities with the various aspects of Catholicism by exploring its imaginative rather than rational force on Joyce. Boyle tells us in his foreword that he has grown increasingly suspicious of 'rational certitude', and this suspicion sets the foundation for the imaginative exploration which is his book. Those readers who have not read Boyle's earlier work on Hopkins and Joyce might well wonder what they are in for at this point, but they need not be uneasy, because few critics penetrate a text so deeply, so skilfully, so relentlessly the way Boyle does.

The texts of Shakespeare, St Paul, and Hopkins form important correlations for Boyle's study. He offers a brilliant analysis of Joyce's images to reveal the intricately interladen texture and development of Joyce's themes. The Trinitarian theme, for example, which assumes so much importance in *Ulysses*, is revealed by Boyle to be a vigorous and well thought-out aspect of Joyce's aesthetic theory. Boyle's treatment of *Finnegans Wake* in light of the Pauline vision is also deeply revealing. Difficult to summarize because of the nature of its development, this is a work of keen insight and fascinating exegesis even for those to whom much of what Boyle says may seen remote.

Interest in Joyce within the context of the Irish Revival is sustained by G.J. Watson in *Irish Identity and the Literary Revival* (1979), and Wayne E. Hall in *Shadowy Heroes: Irish Literature of the 1890s* (1980). Watson is careful from the outset in his treatment of Joyce not to draw the easy contrast between the Ascendancy ethos of Yeats and Synge and Joyce's discontent and desires to escape his native country. Joyce's art, as Watson points out, is far too complex for such contrast, especially in the attitude it reveals toward Ireland. Joyce is chronologically beyond Hall's study, but in his conclusion he correctly notes that Stephen in *A Portrait* 'maintains much of the conventional aestheticism of the 1890s', with his 'preferences for vision over experience, heroic failure over practical success, art over life'. Hall goes on to note, however, 'that Joyce's work completes the transformation of the 1890s hero into the humbled and suffering common man'. Hall's fine study has many virtues beyond the scope of this essay, but it offers an engaging and thorough background study for students of Joyce.

In spite of their dominant positions in modern literature, it is rare to find scholars with a deep professional interest in both D. H. Lawrence and Joyce. This lack of mutual interest in the two writers is evidenced by the lack of scholarship that treats both writers. Robert Kiely's book, *Beyond Egotism: The Fiction of James Joyce, Virginia Woolf, and D.H. Lawrence* (1980), is the first study to treat their literary relationship in any detailed and extended way. Kiely's work concentrates on the convergence of several themes, but particularly on the play of ego, especially in its relationship between author and reader, between character and author, and between the characters in a given work. It is from these relationships that Kiely explores their similarities. Although his angle seems at times confining, it yields some interesting common ground on which to view the three novelists.

There has been less attention paid to Joyce's earlier fiction in the past five years than during any comparable five-year period for the last fifteen years, at least in so far as extended studies are concerned. The flow of articles continues, but even this has abated.

Staley and Benstock have followed their *Approaches to Ulysses* (1970) with *Approaches to Joyce's Portrait: Ten Essays* (1976). The book includes, among others, Staley's essay on *Portrait* scholarship, Hans Walter Gabler's history of the text, Mitchell's on *Portrait*'s relation to the tradition of the *Bildungsroman*, James Naremore's quasi-Marxist approach, Chester Anderson's uncompromising Freudian reading, Kenner's well-known and updated essay, 'The Cubist *Portrait*', Benstock's essay on the symbolic structure, and Darcy O'Brien's 'In Ireland after *A Portrait*'. The volume provides a multiplicity of approaches to the novel and many of the essays pay particular attention ot the best previous scholarship on the different critical directions. The first issue of *Irish Renaissance Annual* (1980), edited by Zack Bowen, contains Maurice Beebe's extensive essay, 'The *Portrait* as Portrait: Joyce and Impressionism', a thorough historical and analytical study that carefully compares Joyce's techniques to those of the Impressionists.

Remo Ceserani's *Argilla* (Naples, 1975) provides the English text of 'Clay', an Italian translation, a chronological bibliography, and a long discussion of the story with an extensive review of the criticism. It is an introductory volume but fairly comprehensive. An extended study of the *Dubliners* stories is Marilyn French's long essay, 'Missing Pieces in Joyce's *Dubliners*' (*TCL* 1978). French sees the focus of *Dubliners* less on character than on an ethos, a Dublin way of thinking dominated by two sets of ideals, popular Catholicism and propriety. The two major devices French sees Joyce using to convey the Dublin mode of thinking are 'masking language' and 'gaps'. Masking language is euphemistic and cliché-ridden; gaps are ellipses in logic, language or information. Both of these devices French sees incorporated into the style of all the stories, and she demonstrates the way in which these modes of thinking and devices operate throughout the individual stories.

John Russell's *Style in Modern British Fiction* (1978) devotes a chapter to *Dubliners*. Although Russell reveals a rather limited notion of rhetoric, restricting his considerations to the 'expressive experience', in his analysis of Joyce's use of the colon, semi-colon (formal compounding), cadence and the like, he is, however, able to note several revealing stylistic patterns in the stories. An interesting essay on *A Portrait* appears in *Forms of British Fiction* (1975), edited by Alan Warren Friedman: Charles Rossman's 'Stephen Dedalus and the Spiritual-Heroic Refrigerating Apparatus: Art and Life in Joyce's *Portrait*' is a fully developed discussion of the relation between Stephen's aesthetic theory and the manner in which the aesthetics express Stephen's character and experience. Rossman contends that just as Stephen's discourse on Shakespeare in *Ulysses* reveals more about Stephen than *Hamlet*, so too does the aesthetic theory reveal more about Stephen's character than has previously been recognized. An argument similar to Rossman's but less amply developed appeared in Harold Kaplan's *The Passive Voice* (1966). Others, of course, have also written on this subject, but Rossman's discussion is lucid and detailed.

John B. Smith's *Imagery and the Mind of Stephen Dedalus* (1980), a computer-assisted study of *A Portrait*, extends Stephen's aesthetic theory that he poses to Lynch to a literary hypothesis and applies it. Smith traces the image clusters and patterns of association throughout *Portrait*. He notes how these images change and how they in turn reflect Stephen's development. Smith draws from Kenner and Tindall and shows in more detail how these patterns reveal the developing structure of Stephen's mind. There is much effort here, but one might sense an overridden horse at the end. It has been noted previously that the enormous contemporary interest in literary theory has been reflected in recent Joyce critic-

ism, and the *Dubliners* stories have been used as examples of
various approaches on several occasions. Seymour Chatman's
essay, previously cited, offers an extended narrative analysis of
'Eveline' in his test of Roland Barthes's and Tzvetan Todorov's
methods of analysis of narrative. Robert Scholes's 'Semiotic
Approaches to a Fictional Text: Joyce's "Eveline" ' (*JJQ*, 1979) is
as much a small-model demonstration of the critical resources in the
theories and methods of Todorov, Genette, and Barthes as it is a
reading of the story. Staley's 'A Beginning: Signification, Story and
Discourse in Joyce's "The Sisters" ' (*Genre*, 1979) is also as much a
demonstration of the possibility in the methods of the above, along
with glances at Maria Corti and Edward Said, as it is an analysis of
the beginning of 'The Sisters'. An example of how divergent
criticism of *Dubliners* remains can be seen by comparing Jackson I.
Cope's essay, 'Joyce's Waste Land', which immediately precedes
Staley's in the *Genre* volume. Cope argues that *Dubliners* is primarily a nineteenth-century text, planted firmly in that tradition, and his
argument is followed by Staley's which just as strongly argues for its
modernist affinities. Both of these essays are reprinted in *The
Genres of the Irish Literary Revival* (1980), edited by Ronald
Schleifer. In his *Modes of Modern Writing* (1977), David Lodge
discusses Joyce's early work, seeing it as a transition between
Roman Jakobson's metaphoric and metonymic poles, between the
realistic and modernist text. Lodge's work is especially interesting
in its application of a linguistic model to Joyce's texts since most
such studies of Joyce's work in the past have been devoted to *FW*.
Also of interest in this connection is Fred Miller Robinson's *The
Comedy of Language* (1980), which argues that comedies of language are the essential texts in the study of modern comedy. He
presents a theory of comedy that is especially revealing when
applied to modern works such as *Ulysses*. His theory is based on the
contradiction between the descriptive capacity of language and the
nature of reality as metaphysical flux. *Ulysses* is enforced by this
contradiction and he calls it, along with other modern works, a
comedy of language. Robinson's chapter on *Ulysses* supports his
theory as it reveals the way in which Joyce worked in this mode.

Hugh Kenner's latest book, *Ulysses* (1980), is published in the
Unwin Critical Library, a series 'addressed to serious students and
teachers of literature, and to knowledgeable non-academic readers'. The series also 'aims to provide a scholarly introduction and a
stimulus to critical thought and discussion'. Kenner's volume

succeeds admirably in these purposes, and in spite of the limited format suggested by the series, it is also an extension of the sustained
engagement Kenner has had with Joyce's work for more than
twenty-five years. This study brings the broad range of Kenner's
ideas from *Dublin's Joyce, The Counterfeiters, The Pound Era*, and
Joyce's Voices into perspective (see my 1976 essay for further
discussion). Just as Kenner applies the principle of parallax, an
organizing principle in *Ulysses*, and the second look, to Joyce's texts
with such illuminating results, so does he in his *Ulysses* frequently
give us a renewed and fresh look at some of his earlier observations
and judgments – a critical parallax. From *Dublin's Joyce* and his
discussion of 'Double Writing', Kenner has been concerned with
Joyce's rhetoric, its repetitions, its locutions, its interwoven system
of referents. In his *Ulysses* he notes: 'Virtually every scene in
Ulysses is narrated at least twice.' Narrative idiom that need not be
the narrator's, the 'Uncle Charles Principle' of *Joyce's Voices*, is
also prominent in this study; the mimetic is present, but it gives way
to the vast playfulness of the styles, the text itself. Kenner also
re-examines the Homeric parallel and its primarily ironic function
in the earlier chapters to its 'coercive' role in the last eight. Technique binds the episodes; the complex narrative voices, 'the
Arranger', he calls 'the aesthetics of delay', further revelations
that refocus the reader's previous thoughts. This 'aesthetics of
delay' engages the reader as active participant. Such a technique
'restores a governing rhythm of the book, whereby impression in
the first half is modified by knowledge in the second, though only
after resolute rereading has extracted the knowledge from a stylistic
that tends to render it inconspicuous.' Kenner's study is not a
complete and systematic one that covers each episode; rather the
study becomes an opportunity to look again at those aspects of
Ulysses that continue to engage him and that he judges by inclusion
are the central concerns of the text. This is a work by a major critic
that modifies, reasserts, refocuses and renews his reading and
interpretation of a text, and the results are important and enduring.

Kenner's study affirms the thematic and structural ties between
Ulysses and Homer which have, since Stuart Gilbert's early study,
long been the frequent subject of critical investigation. Michael
Seidel's *Epic Geography: James Joyce's 'Ulysses'* (1976) argues
cunningly that Joyce recreates the epic geography of the *Odyssey* in
Ulysses and does so according to the Homeric action as cartog-
raphed by Victor Bérard in his *Les Phéniciens et l'Odyssée*. Bérard's

influence has long been acknowledged but it has never been so comprehensibly accounted for, not its implications so thoroughly discussed. Some of the elaborate charting and epic movement and placement seem inflated, even remote to the action, but Seidel's study is especially interesting for its discussion of mythology, philosophy, and epic poetry generally, in light of Bérardian parallels. His discoveries lead Seidel to conclusions which account for major patterns within *Ulysses*. For example, we are given an Homeric reason for Bloom's drifting too far east at the beginning of 'Lotus-Eaters'. *Epic Geography*. is an intriguing source study.

James H. Maddox, Jr.'s *Joyce's 'Ulysses' and the Assault upon Character* (1978) emerges out of the critical environment of S.L. Goldberg's *The Classical Temper* with its emphasis on character and moral enactment. His study of character develops from the treatment Goldberg gave to Joyce's aesthetic theories. He proposes that Joyce's characterization is predicated upon the coexistence of opposites, and, furthermore, his stylistic variations are the corollary of Stephen's axiom: 'Proteus thought the world can be known only through refracted signatures'. Goldberg was unable to see redeeming features in the stylistic narrative and extravagance of the last part of *Ulysses*, but Maddox does through these 'refracted signatures', and Joyce's profound faith in the individual. Proceeding from these propositions, Maddox's *Ulysses* becomes an integrated work, but not a schematized one. Maddox is a careful reader and his book reflects a struggle for openness and precision.

Stanley Sultan's brief study, *'Ulysses', 'The Waste Land', and Modernism* (1977), sees these two works in relation to each other and rather than dwell on what has now become a critical commonplace, the influence of *Ulysses* on *The Waste Land*, Sultan looks at the two works together and sees them as the richest expression of Modernism.

Three later and more specialized studies of *Ulysses* are Elliot B. Gose, Jr.'s *The | Transformation Process in Joyce's 'Ulysses'* (Toronto, 1980), Craig Wallace Barrow's *Montage in James Joyce's 'Ulysses'* (Madrid, 1980; distributed in the U.S.A. by Studio Humanitos), and Constantin-George Sandulescu's *The Joycean Monologue, a Study of 'Ulysses'* (Colchester, 1979). All three studies are uneven, but may have some interest for the specialist. Gose emphasizes Bergson's influence and contends that his ideas helped Joyce develop his own about life or a process of transformation along with other ideas. This is not a convincing thesis. Sandulescu's study is needlessly rigid and at the same time discursive; it attempts to set Joyce's monologues and character development against the modern literary tradition. But his treatment of Dorothy Richardson, for example, is far less than adequate for the conclusions he draws, and his contentions regarding Joyce's influence on Svevo are hardly convincing. Barrow's work is slightly better informed.

It has been generally agreed, although perhaps less firmly held of late, that Anglo-American literary criticism insists on a less speculative, more practical orientation than its European counterpart. For example, phenomenological criticism in spite of Georges Poulet and others has never taken a firm hold on the American scene, so when an American critic such as Suzette Henke proposes a study of *Ulysses* from a phenomenological and existential orientation in her *Joyce's Moraculous Sindbook* (1978), it promises something both unusual and original. The results, however, are disappointing in the extreme. Not to dwell on a disappointing study, but the work is not an informed example of phenomenology and its method, and its effusive prose becomes a mishmash of pretension, cliché, and fantasy. Waxing on the ending of *Ulysses*, the author writes: 'By inflating the content of our own experience, by exalting joy and compensation for pain, we become artists of the imagination. . . .' The foregoing was merely an example. To the unitiated such readings as this, and they run throughout the book, must made the phenomenological method seem like an exercise in free association, substituting euphoria for rigour. Such a study does nothing for Joyce criticism and probably retards international understanding. Other critics see danger in a study such as this; I am more sanguine – surely its faults and pretentions are self-evident, even to students. The damage lies, however, not in its extravagantly banal commentary on Joyce, but in its potential for turning student readers away in despair at ever coming to terms with important European intellectual currents.

Roy K. Gottfried's *The Art of Joyce's Syntax in 'Ulysses'* (1980) takes us far away from such loose and impressionistic criticism; his is a thorough and informative study of the diverse sentence patterns in *Ulysses* and the stylistic variations that Joyce's syntactical arrangements create. Gottfried's work is especially valuable for the close attention it gives to the way in which Joyce used various sentence patterns to form the varying styles from episode to episode in *Ulysses*, and the way in which these styles reflect the tension in the novel between freedom and order. Gottfried's study is careful, thorough and informative. Roger Moss's essay, 'Difficult Language: The Justification of Joyce's Syntax in *Ulysses*', that appears in *The Modern English Novel, the Reader, the Writer, and the Work* (1976), offers further discussion on this subject.

Four books published in Europe that deal with *Ulysses* are: Hartmut Mietzner's *Immanenz und Transzendenz in Joyce's 'A Portrait' . . . und 'Ulysses'* (Frankfurt am Main, 1978); a collection of essays edited by Therese Fischer-Seidel, *James Joyces 'Ulysses'*; Paul P.J. Van Caspel, *Bloomers on the Liffey* (Groningen, 1980); and Eckard Lobsien, *Der Alltag der 'Ulysses'* (Stuttgart, 1978), a sound phenomenologically-oriented study that perhaps argues too strenuously with positivistic-oriented criticism. Fischer-Seidel's collection contains contributions of Fritz Senn, Hans Gabler, Arno Esch, Franz K. Stanzel, and Viktor Link, as well as an excellent bibliography of *Ulysses* studies. Paul van Caspel's study is both curious and enjoyable. He examines a number of introductions and guide books for errors, and the results of his study are amazing; the misquotations, the factual errors in all of these books are incredibly numerous. Translations are in an equally bad state, as this interesting study reveals. The present error-filled text of *Ulysses* seems reliable by comparison.

Many who teach *Ulysses* frequently have over the years drawn up modest chronologies of the lives of Leopold and Molly Bloom, but now these can be replaced by John Henry Raleigh's *The Chronicle of Leopold and Molly Bloom* (1977), which also includes lists of Bloom's addresses and jobs, and more than a half dozen maps and diagrams of such things as the floor plan of 7 Eccles Street. Raleigh sub-titles his work '*Ulysses* as Narrative', because his book, with its year-by-year chronicle, highlights, "as no other method could, the immense and detailed naturalistic base upon which *Ulysses* is constructed". Raleigh's task was not an easy one, because the naturalistic base itself has as many conflicting facts as one finds in the life it reflects. Bloom and Molly often disagree on what he or she did when. Raleigh, rather than speculate on who's right in the absence of further evidence, presents the conflicting facts. There are even more difficult problems present in *Ulysses* that Raleigh must encounter, not the least of which is the fundamental question of what the precise nature of evidence is in *Ulysses*. Are we to accept anything that appears in 'Circe', for example? The Benstocks in their *Directory*, for instance, accept 'absolutely nothing' in

'Circe' as reality unless it is corroborated in one of the succeeding chapters; Raleigh is less restrictive. Or how does one distinguish between the many actual events recorded in *Ulysses* that occurred on June 16, 1904, and, for example, Bloom's attendance at Paddy Dignam's funeral? There is a distinction here between fictional and historical reality that the chronology does not distinguish. Raleigh's book, however, is virtually complete, and he puts the facts of the Blooms' life in order, and in so doing, gives the reader yet another, if partial, view of the controlled universe Joyce created in *Ulysses*. Hart and Knuth's valuable *A Topographical Guide to James Joyce's 'Ulysses'* (Colchester, 1976) has come out in a second edition with corrections, and will remain a valuable tool for the study of *Ulysses* for the specialist and student as well.

Adaline Glasheen's *Third Census of 'Finnegans Wake'* (1977), initiates what has been an active and productive period in *Wake* scholarship. The *Third Census* greatly amplifies the list of personal names and the other litter of the 'divine and human comedy', and, although the author modestly claims that even this *Third Census* is an interim report, it is of enormous value to the student of the *Wake*. Glasheen's revised synopsis is more detailed, and her chart 'Who is Who When Everybody is Somebody Else' is extremely helpful in putting the almost hopelessly variegated connections in some kind of order; to use her own words in a different context, Glasheen is the archaeologist and augur who reads the signs of the *Wake* as well as anyone.

Louis Mink's *A 'Finnegans Wake' Gazetteer* (1978), Brendan O Hehir and John Dillon's *A Classical Lexicon for 'Finnegans Wake'* (1977), and Roland McHugh's *Annotations to 'Finnegans Wake'* (1980) provide strong evidence of the sustained scholarly work that the text evokes. O Hehir and Dillon's work gives a glossary of the Greek and Latin in all of Joyce's work, as well as *Finnegans Wake*, and the appendices in this lengthy volume provide more detailed explanation of Joyce's use of classical language. Louis Mink's study belongs beside Atherton's (see 1976 essay) and Glasheen's work. He gives 2,800 topographical identifications from the *Wake*, and 'topographical' refers not only to geographical allusions, but also words and phrases that have literary, biographical, and historical overtones; this latter is especially valuable for the Dublin references. We learn, too, that many places are not places as we had assumed, but things that might have been named after places. The book is divided into two parts, a 'Linear Guide' and the

'Alphabetical Gazetteer', this second part arranged to the 'plain-text' rubric in Part I; and it also includes a complete inventory of the same identifications numerically listed by page. Part II includes four well detailed maps. Mink also prefaces this work of impeccable scholarship with a number of short introductions that discuss the patterns of topographical allusion in *Finnegans Wake*. This book is indispensable to the serious study of *Finnegans Wake*. McHugh's study, as he readily notes in his preface, is the outgrowth of many years of exegetical study by Hart, Knuth, Senn, and many others; it 'attempts to cope with the formidable secondary task of identifying the components of the text, by applying the cream of all available exegesis in as condensed and accessible a form as possible'. The form of McHugh's volume is a masterstroke, providing as it does a single numbered page for every numbered page of the *Wake*, and the annotations are placed on the corresponding lines and place as the text of the *Wake*. The value of this volume will be tested after extensive use of it is made by knowledgeable readers.

Patrick A. McCarthy's *The Riddle of Finnegans Wake* (1980) gives thorough attention to the riddles of the *Wake* and in so doing demonstrates that the riddle is a model for the work itself. He carefully discusses the riddles, and from such discussion he poses much larger questions about the entire structure of the *Wake*. McCarthy's work is interesting and convincing.

Critical studies of the *Wake* continue to appear with frequency. Margot Norris's *The Decentred Universe of 'Finnegans Wake': A Structuralist Analysis* (1976) is one of the first books on the *Wake* to make extensive use of the structuralist method, and the author is also indebted to psychoanalytic approaches to literature. For Norris the dislocated dream meanings produce a decentered universe in the *Wake*. The method in this study is more revealing than the author's interpretation of the *Wake*. Roland McHugh's *The Sigla of 'Finnegans Wake'* (1976) is primarily exegetical, but his 'sigla' approach substitutes ciphers for established terminology. Both Norris's and McHugh's work reflect a later critical context. Hart in his earlier study of the *Wake* (see 1976 essay), for example, speaks of assembled structures and motifs, but Norris admits to no such patterning; she sees Hart's work as too rigid and confining. Michael H. Begnal and Grace Eckley's *Narrator and Character in 'Finnegans Wake'* (1975) is more traditional in approach. Begnal analyses the ironies of the *Wake* in his study of narration and point of view, which is actually a careful isolation of the separate speakers in the *Wake* to determine who is speaking. He contends that the book is not quite as complicated as previous critics have made out once the reader is able to isolate the various characters and determine the point of view. Eckley analyses the 'Anna Livia Plurabelle' chapter and sees it at the centre of the book. Of little note is Reinhard Motz's *Time as Joyce Tells It* (n.d., 1977), a bizarre book that among other diversions comments on what he concludes are "time" passages in the *Wake*.

Originally an issue of *TriQuarterly, In the Wake of the 'Wake'* (1978) is a collection of essays edited by David Hayman and Elliott Anderson that offers a variety of responses or pieces written in the spirit of the *Wake*. It would be simplistic and therefore rash to categorize the contributors to this volume, but all of them reflect a post-modern orientation either in their criticism or creative work, such as Samuel Beckett, John Cage, Raymond Federman, and William Gass, or their criticism emerges from a variety of fairly recent European theoretical concerns as in the contributions by Philippe Sollers, Michael Finney, and Hélène Cixous. The editors' introduction sets an excellent context both for the *Wake* and the contributions that follow. Finney's essay provides interesting commentary and context for 'Work in Progress' as it appeared in Eugene Jolas's *transition*, especially in light of Jolas's manifesto, 'Revolution of the World', and other pronouncements which were running concurrently in *transition* with 'Work in Progress'. As Finney points out, Joyce surely only tolerated these views because Jolas was the editor and was publishing parts of the *Wake* in each issue. A thorough history of *transition*, which includes a great deal on Joyce's relation with the magazine and the Jolases is Dougald McMillan's *'transition': The History of a Literary Era 1927–1938* (1975). It is a bit awkward at times and confusing in its organization, but it gives important information. One is far too often led to plead for historical and intellectual context in studies of the *Wake*, and Finney and McMillan give us that.

Besides his contribution to the Hayman and Anderson volume, John Cage has also written *Writing Through 'Finnegans Wake'* (1978), which was published as a special supplement to Volume 15 of *JJQ*. This curious work grew out of his piece for Elliott Anderson, in *TriQuarterly*. Cage has rewritten the *Wake* in 'mesostics' always spelling 'James Joyce' vertically. Using a fine line structure, he attempts to show the relation of Joyce's text to his name. Jacob Drachler's *Id-Grids and Ego-Graphs* (1979) is a suite of 44 black and white mixed media graphics and is described as 'a confabulation with *FW*'.

Alchemy and 'Finnegans Wake' (1980) by Barbara DiBernard, as its title acknowledges, is a detailed study of alchemy and its various uses in the *Wake*. That Joyce was interested in the subject fairly early in his literary career has been discussed before. Eliphas Levi's theories of magic were known to Joyce and Stuart Gilbert, and magic, spiritualism, mysticism, and Freemasonry were also of interest to Joyce. DiBernard's study concentrates on the uses of alchemy in the *Wake*, and sees Joyce using it as a metaphor for change and the artistic process, especially the idea of transmutation. This is a clear and well-developed discussion on a difficult and elusive subject.

The purpose of this essay has been to look backward rather than forward, but the recent past in Joyce criticism expresses a vitality and strength of mind that bodes well for the immediate future of Joyce studies. This is not to say that much that is written is inadequate at best, for there is frequently an absence of critical rigour in Joyce scholarship, but the best is equal to the best in modern scholarship generally.

CHRONOLOGY

SUHEIL BADI BUSHRUI

1882   James Joyce was born at 41 Brighton Square West, Rathgar, a suburb in the south of Dublin, on February 2, the first child of John Stanislaus Joyce, a tax-collector, and of Mary Jane Murray Joyce

1884   Stanislaus Joyce was born. Of the ten Joyce children he was most intimate with James

1888   Joyce's family moved to Bray, a coastal suburb south of Dublin, and in September James was enrolled in a Jesuit Boarding School, Clongowes Wood College, about twenty miles west of Dublin, where he remained a pupil until June 1891

1891   Joyce was forced to leave Clongowes because of his father's financial difficulties. The death of Parnell on October 6 affected the nine-year-old Joyce so deeply that he composed a poem, 'Et tu, Healy', denouncing Parnell's 'Betrayer', Tim Healy. Joyce's father was so impressed that he had the poem printed, but unfortunately no copy has survived

1892   The Joyce household moved to Blackrock, about half-way between Bray and Dublin

1893   As their fortunes rapidly declined the family moved to Dublin, where Joyce entered the Jesuit Belvedere College. The young Joyce proved to be an outstanding student, winning prizes in national competitions and serving two terms as prefect of the Sodality of the Blessed Virgin Mary

1894   In February Joyce visited Cork with his father to sell the last of the family properties. In the spring he won the first of his exhibitions (cash prizes for scholarship awarded in national competitions)

278

1898   Joyce graduated from Belvedere and entered University College, Dublin, a Jesuit institution founded by Cardinal Newman. It was here that Joyce began his revolt against Catholicism and Provincial Patriotism

1899   In opposition to his fellow students Joyce refused to sign a protest letter attacking the 'heresy' of Yeats's *Countess Cathleen*

1900   In January of a year marked by literary activity Joyce read a paper on 'Drama and Life' before the College Literary and Historical Society. In April his article on 'Ibsen's New Drama' was published in the prestigious *Fortnightly Review*. He also wrote a play that has not survived, dedicated to 'His Own Soul', called *A Brilliant Career*

1901   Towards the end of the year Joyce attacked the provincialism of the 'Irish Literary Theatre' in 'The Day of the Rabblement', an essay that appeared in a pamphlet that also included an article by F.J.C. Skeffington. Joyce's essay had been intended for a college magazine but was rejected by the Jesuit adviser

1902   Joyce's paper 'James Clarence Mangan', which asserted that the Irish poet had been the victim of narrow nationalism, appeared in the University College magazine, *St. Stephen's*. In October Joyce, who by now had a fair knowledge of Italian, French, German, literary Norwegian, and Latin, graduated from the University with a degree in modern languages. He then left Dublin to study medicine in Paris, but stopped briefly in London, where through the good offices of W.B. Yeats and Lady Gregory he met some London editors and had two book reviews published for the Dublin *Daily Express*

1903   Having arrived in Paris, Joyce soon lost interest in his medical studies and turned to book-reviewing, publishing twenty-one reviews in the *Daily Express*. On April 10 he received the following telegram: 'Mother dying come home Father', whereupon he immediately returned to Dublin, although his mother did not, in fact, die until August 13

1904　On January 7 Joyce wrote an essay-story called *A Portrait of the Artist* which he was later to expand into *Stephen Hero*, and finally into *A Portrait of the Artist as a Young Man*. He also published poems in *The Speaker, Saturday Review, Dana*, and *The Venture*, and wrote stories ('The Sisters', 'Eveline', and 'After The Race') for *The Irish Homestead*, edited by George Russell ('A.E.'). As the situation of the Joyce family deteriorated following the death of Mary Joyce, James Joyce gradually withdrew from the family and in March left to become a teacher at the Clifton School, Dalkey and to live in the Martello Tower, Sandycove, with Oliver St. John Gogarty (the Mulligan of *Ulysses*). He also won a bronze medal for his singing in the Feis Ceoil. On June 10 he met Nora Barnacle, with whom he soon fell in love. Disapproving of marriage and being unable to live with Nora in Dublin, Joyce decided that they should leave for Europe, and on October 8 they started out from Dublin, travelling *via* London, Paris, Zürich, and Trieste to Pola (Now called Pulj in Yugoslavia), where Joyce began teaching English at the Berlitz School

1905　In March Joyce and Nora moved to Trieste, where he also taught at the Berlitz School. On July 27 their son, Giorgio, was born; later in the year Joyce's brother, Stanislaus, joined them in Trieste. Joyce submitted *Chamber Music* and *Dubliners* (save for 'Two Gallants', 'A Little Cloud', and 'The Dead', yet to be written) to Grant Richards

1906　Joyce and his family moved to Rome, where he worked as the Foreign Correspondent of a bank. He wrote 'Two Gallants' and 'A Little Cloud'

1907　Joyce left the bank in March and returned to Trieste, where he gave private English lessons. In May the London publisher, Elkin Mathews, brought out *Chamber Music*. Joyce began to write articles in Italian for the Trieste newspaper *Il Piccolo Della Sera*. A daughter, Lucia Anna, was born on July 26. He wrote 'The Dead', and in September began to rewrite the twenty-six completed chapters of the unfinished *Stephen Hero* in five long chapters as *A Portrait of the Artist as a Young Man*.

1908 ¹Joyce completed three chapters of *A Portrait of the Artist as a Young Man*, after which he abandoned the manuscript

1909 On August 1 Joyce travelled to Ireland where he signed a contract with Maunsel & Co. for the publication of *Dubliners*. The following month he returned to Trieste with his sister Eva, but after receiving financial support he went to Dublin again to organize the Cinematograph Volta. He also published two articles and two poems

1910 In January Joyce returned to Trieste and the cinema venture soon failed. Maunsel & Co. postponed the publication of *Dubliners*. Joyce's first visit to Dublin was the occasion of an emotional crisis that he afterwards used as the substance of his play, *Exiles*

1911 Publication of *Dubliners* was postponed yet again after quarrels over content. After another move of house, Joyce announced his intention of leaving Trieste for good.

1912 In July Joyce returned to Ireland with his family for a final visit, staying at Galway and Dublin. He published four newspaper articles but was unable to arrange for the publication of *Dubliners*, the printer destroying the edition. Joyce reacted with great bitterness and while on the journey back to Trieste wrote a savage counter-attack, *Gas From a Burner*

1913 Joyce published one poem, and Yeats persuaded Ezra Pound to write to Joyce for manuscripts

1914 Joyce's luck finally turned. *A Portrait of the Artist as a Young Man* was published in serial form by Dora Marsden, and later by Harriet Shaw Weaver, in *The Egoist* (London), beginning in February and ending in September of the following year, with two gaps caused by Joyce's inability to complete chapter five on schedule. *Dubliners* was finally published by Grant Richards in June, while in March Joyce began work on *Ulysses*, which he soon gave up to concentrate on *Exiles*

1915   After giving a pledge of neutrality to the Austrians, Joyce managed to move himself and his family to Zürich in neutral Switzerland. In the spring he finished *Exiles*. At the instigation of Yeats, Ezra Pound, and Edmund Gosse, Joyce was given money by the British Royal Literary Fund

1916   The British Treasury Fund awarded Joyce a grant and on December 29 *A Portrait of the Artist as a Young Man* was published in book form by B.W. Huebsch (now the Viking Press) in New York

1917   Joyce received the first of his gifts from Miss Weaver, who was to give him thousand of pounds, and published eight poems in *Poetry* (Chicago). By the end of the year he had completed the draft of the first three episodes of *Ulysses*. Joyce underwent the first of his eye operations and spent three months in Locarno

1918   Joyce received a monthly allowance from Mrs. Harold McCormick and with Claud W. Sykes organized the English Players. *Ulysses* was serialized in *The Little Review* from March 1918 until December 1920 and *Exiles* was published by Grant Richards in London and B.W. Huebsch in New York

1919   Mrs. McCormick stopped Joyce's monthly allowance and in October he returned to Trieste to teach English again. He published one poem and continued to work on the serialization of *Ulysses*, five instalments of which were published in *The Egoist*

1920   Joyce met Pound at Sirmione and at his insistence moved with his family to Paris in early July. In October the *Little Review* was forced to stop publishing *Ulysses* following a complaint by the Society for the Prevention of Vice that it was pornographic

1921   Joyce spent the year revising *Ulysses* and completing the last episodes. He was helped in his career by Pound, Sylvia Beach, Adrienne Monnier, Valéry Larbaud, and others, and he agreed to have Sylvia Beach publish *Ulysses* in Paris

1922   Miss Beach's Shakespeare and Company published *Ulysses* on February 2, Joyce's fortieth birthday. Nora and the children visited Galway, where their train was fired on by Civil War troops

1923   On March 10 Joyce wrote the first few pages of *Finnegans Wake*, a work he had been planning for some time and which before its publication in 1939 was known as 'Work in Progress'. He and his family spent the summer in England

1924   The first fragment of 'Work in Progress' appeared in the April issue of the *Transatlantic Review* (Paris). Joyce was afflicted with severe eye trouble. He visited Brittany and London. B.W. Huebsch published Herbert Gorman's Biography of Joyce

1925   Several more fragments of 'Work in Progress' were published and Joyce visited Fécamp and Arcachon

1926   Joyce published more fragments of 'Work in Progress'. Most of *Ulysses* was pirated and serialized by *Two Worlds Monthly* (New York)

1927   Many authors and others protested at the pirating of *Ulysses* in New York. Joyce spent three months in London, The Hague, and Amsterdam. *Pomes Penyeach* was published by Shakespeare and Company. Eugene Jolas published seventeen instalments of 'Work in Progress' in *transition* (Paris) between 1927 and 1938

1928   Parts of 'Work in Progress' were published in book form in New York to safeguard the copyright. Joyce visited Dieppe, Rouen, Toulon, and Salzburg

1929   *Ulysse*, the French translation of *Ulysses*, appeared and Shakespeare and Company published *Our Exagmination Round his Factification for Incamination of Work in Progress*. Joyce visited London, Torquay and Bristol

1930   Stuart Gilbert's *James Joyce's 'Ulysses'* was published and Joyce embarked on his four-year promotion of the Irish tenor, John Sullivan. Joyce underwent more eye surgery and visited England and Wales

1931   The Joyce family moved to London in May and on July 4 Joyce and Nora were married at a registry office 'for testamentary reasons'. They returned to Paris in September; Joyce's father died on December 29. More fragments of 'Work in Progress' were published

1932   On February 15 Joyce's grandson, Stephen James Joyce, was born to Giorgio and Helen Joyce and on that day Joyce composed the poem 'Ecce Puer', which was published in the *New Republic* and reprinted in three other magazines. In March Joyce's daughter, Lucia, suffered her first nervous breakdown as a result of Schizophrenia. The Joyce family spent the summer in Zürich, Austria, and Nice. Paul Leon was engaged as Joyce's secretary

1933   Lucia was confined to a hospital near Zürich and the rest of the family spent the summer on Lake Geneva to be near her. In New York Judge John M. Woolsey ruled that *Ulysses* was not pornographic

1934   Joyce and Nora spent most the year in Switzerland so that they could be near Lucia and also the Swiss doctor who had cared for Joyce's eyes since 1930. They also visited Grenoble and Monte Carlo. Frank Bugden's *James Joyce and the Making of 'Ulysses'* was published. Giorgio and his family moved to New York, where they remained for a year and a half

1935   Although Lucia spent ten months with relatives in Ireland and with Miss Weaver in London, her condition became worse. Joyce and Nora visited Fontainebleau

1936   Joyce's *Collected Poems* was published in New York and *A Chaucer A.B.C.*, with initial letters illuminated by Lucia Joyce, was published in Paris

1937   *Storiella as she is Syung*, the last 'Work in Progress' fragment to be published separately, appeared in London. The Joyces visited Zürich and Dieppe.

1938   The Joyces made frequent trips from their Paris home to other parts of France and to Switzerland and Denmark. Joyce finally completed 'Work in Progress'

1939   *Finnegans Wake* was published on May 4 by Faber and Faber in London and the Viking Press in New York (Joyce received a copy in time for his fifty-seventh birthday). The Joyces visited Etretat, Berne, and Zürich, but returned to France when war was declared, staying at La Baule and then St. Gérand-Le-Puy, near Vichy, to be close to Lucia, who was still in hospital

1940   A revised edition of Gorman's biography of Joyce was published in New York. The Joyces managed to escape to Zürich after the fall of France

1941   James Joyce died on January 13 in Zürich after an abdominal operation. He was buried in the Fluntern Cemetery, Zürich.

NOTES ON CONTRIBUTORS

BERNARD BENSTOCK is Professor of English and Comparative Literature at the University of Illinois, and Director of the Program in Comparative Literature. He has written two books on Joyce, *Joyce-again's Wake* (1965) and *James Joyce: The Undiscover'd Country* (1977), and co-authored *Who's He When He's at Home: A James Joyce Directory* (1980). For the 1982 Joyce Centenary he is serving as Coordinator for the 8th International James Joyce Symposium in Dublin in June 1982, has edited *The Seventh of Joyce: Panel Papers from the James Joyce Symposium in Zurich 1979*, as well as a "Joyce and His Contemporaries" issue of *Comparative Literature Studies*, and selected a volume of *Pomes for James Joyce* (Malton Press, 1982).

PAUL F. BOTHEROYD and SYLVIA BOTHEROYD have been teaching English at the Ruhr-University Bochum, Federal Republic of Germany, for the last ten years; the main emphasis of their teaching and research has been on Irish Literature in English and Irish culture. Sylvia Botheroyd holds a lic.phil.degree from the University of Basle; Paul F. Botheroyd holds a Ph.D. from the University of Birmingham (UK). They have published in Ireland, the Netherlands, France, Nigeria and the Federal Republic of Germany; the next book-length publications are an Art and Travel Guide to Ireland and a socio-cultural approach to J.M. Synge's prose. They are both active members of the International Association for the Study of Anglo-Irish Literature (IASAIL).

SUZANNE BROWN received her undergraduate education at Mount Holyoke College in Massachusetts. She has a Diploma in Anglo-Irish Literature from the University of Dublin, and holds her Ph.D. from the same university. She is the author of a critical guide to Dickens's *Oliver Twist* and of a forthcoming critical guide to Hawthorne's *The Scarlet Letter*. She has published poetry in various periodicals and essays on educational matters.

TERENCE BROWN is Director of Studies in Modern English in Trinity College, Dublin. He is also a Fellow of the College. Among his publications are *Louis MacNeice: Sceptical Vision; Northern Voices: Poets from Ulster*, and *Ireland: A Social and Cultural History 1922–79*. He is currently at work on a book on Victorian Ireland. He was Secretary of the International Association for the Study of Anglo-Irish Literature 1976–79.

SUHEIL BADI BUSHRUI is Professor of English and Anglo-Irish Literature at the American University of Beirut, Lebanon, and a Ph.D. of Southampton University (UK), where he was a British Council Scholar and Research Fellow from 1959 to 1962. He has taught at the Universities of Oxford (UK), Ibadan (Nigeria), Calgary and York (Canada), and has lectured in many other countries. In 1963 he was awarded the Una Ellis-Fermor Prize for his work on W.B. Yeats, on whom he has written four books, including the first full-length critical study in Arabic of the poet. He has also written on English, Arabic and African literatures. He is an authority on Kahlil Gibran the Lebanese poet, has published two volumes of his own Arabic poetry, and is a regular broadcaster in the Arab world. He holds the Presidency of the Association of University Teachers of English in the Arab World, and is the Collector for the English Association's 1982 volume of *Essays and Studies*.

DOMINIC DANIEL, whose real name is Browne, or Le Brun, traces his family back to the Lords of the Marches, the Normans who came to Ireland with Strongbow. He was educated in England and Scotland, and his family property was in Mayo. He went to Trinity College, Dublin, and since marrying he has lived in London, Majorca and Co. Donegal, with his wife and daughter. He has written a collection of verse, some short stories, articles and plays, some of which have been published in Ireland, England and America. He has had plays performed in Belfast and Cork, and is developing an interest in scriptwriting for films.

RICHARD ELLMANN is Goldsmiths' Professor of English Literature at Oxford University. Apart from his biography of Joyce (1959), he has edited volumes 2 and 3 of the *Letters* (1966), and written many books and articles on Joyce, as well as editing a number of his works. He has also written extensively on Yeats and Wilde.

288

PHILLIP F. HERRING is Professor of English at the University of Wisconsin-Madison, is Visiting Professor at the University of New Mexico (1981–82), and was Visiting Fellow, Clare Hall, Cambridge (1975–6) and Andrew Mellon Fellow, University of Pittsburgh (1969–70). He is author of *Joyce's* Ulysses *Notesheets in the British Museum* (1972), *Joyce's Notes and Drafts for* Ulysses: *Selections from the Buffalo Collection* (1977), "The Lotus Eaters" in Clive Hart and David Hayman (eds.) *James Joyce's* Ulysses: *Critical Essays* (1974), "Toward an Historical Molly Bloom" in *ELH* (1978), "Caliban in Nottingham: D.H. Lawrence's *The Lost Girl*" in *MOSAIC* (1979), "Zur Textgenese des *Ulysses*: James Notizen und seine Arbeitsmethode", in Therese Fischer-Seidel (ed.) *James Joyces* Ulysses: *Neuere deutsche Aufsätze* (1977) and many more articles.

DECLAN KIBERD is a graduate of Dublin University (T.C.D.) who went on to take his doctorate at Oxford University. He has held lecturing posts at Trinity College, Dublin, the University of Kent at Canterbury, and is now Lecturer in Anglo-Irish Literature at University College, Dublin. He is the author of *Synge and the Irish Language* (1979) and a commentary on *The Merchant of Venice* (1980).

AUGUSTINE MARTIN was born in Co. Leitrim in 1935 and educated at the Cistercian College, Roscrea, and University College, Dublin, where he took the degrees of M.A. and Ph.D. and where he has been teaching since 1965. He was elected by the graduates of the National University to the Irish Senate in 1973 and 1977. He was Visiting Professor to Hofstra University (1974), and Scholar in Residence at Miami, Ohio (1980), and has been Professor of Anglo-Irish Literature and Drama at University College, Dublin, since 1979. He was Associate Director of the Yeats Summer School in 1977, and Director since 1978. Among his publications are *James Stephens, A Critical Study* (1977), *Anglo-Irish Literature, A History* (1980), an edition of *Winter's Tales from Ireland* (1971) of *The Charwoman's Daughter* (1972), and articles on Yeats, Joyce, Synge, Behan, Mary Lavin, and Sean O'Casey. He is engaged on a history of the Irish Short Story and a book on the politics of W.B. Yeats.

VIVIAN MERCIER has contributed to three earlier symposia on

Joyce: *James Joyce: Two Decades of Criticism*, ed. Seon Givens (1948); *A James Joyce Miscellany*, 3rd ser., ed. Marvin Magalaner (1962), and *Twelve and a Tilly*, eds Jack P. Dalton and Clive Hart (1966). He included a chapter on Joyce and parody in *The Irish Comic Tradition* (1962 and devoted nearly half the introduction of *A Reader's Guide to the New Novel* (1971) to claiming Joyce as "the greatest precursor" of the *nouveau roman*: both books are in print as paperbacks. Born in Dublin, like Joyce, he hopes also to die there. Meanwhile he survives as a Professor of English at the University of California, Santa Barbara.

JOHN MONTAGUE is one of Ireland's leading poets. His *Selected Poems* will appear in 1983, the selection being made from six previous volumes. His stories, *Death of a Chieftain* are being reissued, and a *Selected Essays* is in progress, as well as a new long poem.

DAVID NORRIS was educated at St. Andrew's College, the High School, Dublin, the Reade Pianoforte School, and Trinity College Dublin, where he is now a lecturer. He has been awarded, during his career, a Council of Europe Travelling Scholarship, the Walter Wormser Harris Prize, First Foundation Scholarship in English Language and Literature, the Gold and Silver medals of the Dublin University Philosophical Society. He is Chairman of, among others, the International James Joyce Symposium, the Campaign for Homosexual Law Reform; and organizer of the Centenary Celebrations in Dublin, as well as being a trustee of the James Joyce Foundation (representing Ireland).

GEARÓID Ó CLÉRIGH was born in Dublin, and educated at Clongowes Wood College and at Emo near Portarlington, before going to University College Cork, where he gained his B.A. in Ancient Classics in 1952 and then went to University College, Dublin, and King's Inns to read law. He gained his LL.B. and B.L. in 1956. He entered Ireland's Foreign Service in 1955. His postings have been to Chicago (Vice-Consul 1959–63), Boston (Consul General 1963–69), The Hague (Embassy Secretary 1971–75), New York (Consul General 1975–80), and to Beirut (Ambassador since 1980). He is married, with two children. His verse collection *Ál Fiaich* was published in 1975.

JOHN PAUL RIQUELME is Associate Professor of English at Southern Methodist University in Dallas, Texas. He has published reviews and essays on Marx, T.S. Eliot, Joyce and contemporary literary theory in *CLO*, *Comparative Literary Studies*, *The Denver Quarterly*, *Diacritics*, *History and Theory*, and *The James Joyce Quarterly*. The essay in this volume is an excerpt from his forthcoming study *Teller and Tale in Joyce's Fiction: A Study of Narration*.

CHARLES ROSSMAN is an Associate Professor of English at the University of Texas. He has also taught at the University of Southern California, U.C.L.A., the National Autonomous University of Mexico, and Paul Valéry University in France. His essays and reviews on modern writers, chiefly D.H. Lawrence and James Joyce, have appeared in a wide variety of journals and books in the United States and Europe. He has co-ordinated two collections of essays on Latin American writers, the Mexican Carlos Fuentes, and the Peruvian Mario Vargas Llosa, and is presently completing a book-length study on the latter. He is on the editorial boards of *The D.H. Lawrence Review, Studies in the Novel* and *Texas Studies in Literature and Language*.

ANN SADDLEMYER is Professor of English and Drama and formerly Director of the Graduate Centre for the Study of Drama at the University of Toronto. She is the author of books and articles on Yeats, Synge and Lady Gregory, the letters of Synge to Molly Allgood, *Letters to Molly* (1971), *Theatre Business, the Correspondence of the first Abbey Theatre Directors, W.B. Yeats, Lady Gregory and J.M. Synge* (1982), and is currently completing a two-volume edition of the collected letters of Synge. A Fellow of the Royal Society of Canada and twice Guggenheim Fellow, Dr. Saddlemyer has held the Berg Chair at New York University and been Chairman of the International Association for the Study of Anglo-Irish Literature. She has lectured in Ireland, France and the U.S.A., and one of her recent projects is the establishment of a new journal, *Theatre History in Canada*, of which she is co-editor.

THOMAS F. STALEY is Trustees Professor of Modern Literature and Dean of the College of Arts and Sciences at the University of Tulsa, where he also edits *The James Joyce Quarterly*. He has written widely on Joyce and other modern literary figures. His most recent book is *Jean Rhys: A Critical Study* and he has edited a forthcoming volume of essays *Contemporary British Women Novelists*. He and Hugh Kenner have edited a centennial volume on Joyce for the University of California Press.

PAUL P.J. VAN CASPEL was born in Amsterdam in 1912. He took degrees in Dutch (Amsterdam) and Sanskrit (Groningen), taught in colleges and in Groningen University, wrote a study on Dutch post-war poetry, *Experimenten op Experimentelen* (1955), and published articles on Joyce, as well as on Kafka, in various journals. His Ph.D. thesis was *Bloomers on the Liffey: Eisegetical Readings of James Joyce's* Ulysses, *Part II*, Groningen, 1980.

FRANCIS WARNER was educated at Christ's Hospital, the London College of Music, and at St. Catharine's College, Cambridge, where he also taught 1959–65. Since then he has been the Fellow and Tutor in English Literature at St. Peter's College, Oxford. He was Assistant Director of the Yeats International Summer School in Sligo 1961–67. In 1967 he was a director of the first James Joyce Symposium in Dublin, and founded the Samuel Beckett Theatre in Oxford. He was for some time a director of the James Joyce Foundation, Tulsa, Oklahoma. He was awarded the Messing International Award for distinguished contributions to literature on the publication of his collected *Poetry of Francis Warner* in 1972. His ninth play, *Moving Reflections*, has been commissioned for performance in St. Giles Cathedral during the 1982 Edinburgh Festival.

INDEX

See also pp. 238–249. Notes to essays are not normally included in this index.

Index

Fay, William G., 194, 195, 207
Federman, Raymond, 276
Fehr, Bernhard, 224
Finneran, Richard (ed.), *Anglo-Irish Literature, A Review of Research*, 250
Finney, Michael, 276
Fischer-Seidel, Therese, 226, 227, 273
Fish, Stanley, 264
Fitzgerald, Kevin, 217
Flanagan, Thomas, 11
Flaubert, Gustave, 68, 265
Forster, E.M., 135
Fortnightly Review, 190, 279
Forum, 215
Fowlie, Wallace, 175
Franke, Rosemarie, 226
Frankfurter Allgemeine Zeitung, 222, 224
Freeman, W., *Everyman's Dictionary of Fictional Characters*, 46
Freeman's Journal, 202
French, Marilyn, 53, 54, 55, 56, 268; *The Book as World*, 52–53
Freud, Sigmund, 263
Friedman, Alan Warren, 268
Friedman, Melvin, 260
Füger, Wilhelm, 226, 227; *Concordance to James Joyce's 'Dubliners'*, 227, 253

Gabler, Hans Walter, 173, 226, 251, 253, 267
Garfinkle, Harold, 228
Garvin, John, *James Joyce's Disunited Kingdom*, 259
Gass, William, 276
Gautier, Théophile, 175
General Post Office, Dublin, 13
Ghent, Dorothy Van, 148
Giedion, Siegfried, 223
Giedion-Welcker, Carola (Mrs. Siegfried Giedion), 223, 224
Gifford, Don, *Notes for Joyce*, 64
Gilbert, Stuart, 168, 215, 257, 270, 277; *James Joyce's 'Ulysses'*, 283
Gill, André, 173
Glasheen, Adaline, 263, 274
Gluck, B.R., *Beckett and Joyce*, 260
Goethe, Johann Wolfgang von, xi, xii, 225; *Faust*, 224

Gogarty, Oliver St. John, 39–40, 122, 170, 171, 181, 185, 186, 199, 200, 201, 280
Goldberg, S.L., *The Classical Temper*, 260, 271
Gonne, Maud, *see* Maud Gonne MacBride
Gordon, Caroline, 34–35
Gore-Booth, Eva, 76, 210
Gorman, Herbert, 216, 283, 285
Gose, Elliott B., 271
Gosse, Sir Edmund, 282
Gottfried, Roy K., 272–73
Goyert, Georg, 222, 224, 225
Gregory, Isabella Augusta, Lady, 65, 116, 157, 159, 163, 194, 195, 197, 200, 201, 280; *Cuchulain of Muirthemne*, 157–58, 163, 164, 203; *Kathleen ni Houlihan* (with Yeats), 194, 195, 201; *Poets and Dreamers*, 196
Greville, Sir Fulke, 118
Grierson, Sir Herbert, 116, 118
Griffith, Arthur, 51
Groden, Michael, 251, 252, 253, 256; *The James Joyce Archive* (ed.), 250, 251; *James Joyce's Manuscripts, An Index*, 251, *'Ulysses' in Progress*, 252
Grose, Kenneth, 261
Gross, John, 248
Gutenberg, Johann, 98, 99, 101, 103, 109

Haan, Jacques den, *Joyce, Mythe van Erin*, 216
Habaisha, Huda, 243
Hall, Wayne E., 266
Halper, Nathan, 262
Harper's Magazine, 252
Harris, Frank, 66
Hart, Clive, 95, 274, 275
Hathaway, Ann, 73, 75
Hauptmann, Gerhart, 187, 193, 200, 222; *Michael Kramer*, 192, 193; *Vor Sonnenaufgang (Before Sunrise)*, 192
Hayman, David, 48, 251, 260, 276
Healy, Tim, 278
Hemingway, Ernest, 137; *Farewell to Arms*, 156
Henke, Suzette, 272

Index

Index